The *Faith* I LIVE By

*Her Only Book Devoted Exclusively
to the Study of Bible Doctrines*

*Inspirational and Doctrinal Bible Texts
With an Inspired
Commentary by*

ELLEN G. WHITE

REVIEW AND HERALD® PUBLISHING ASSOCIATION
Since 1861 | www.reviewandherald.com

Cover designed by Gerald Lee Monks
Cover design resources from iStockphoto.com

Copyright © 1958, 1973, 2000 by The Ellen G. White® Estate, Inc.

Printed by Pacific Press® Publishing Association.

Printed in the United States of America
All rights reserved.

Additional copies of this book can be obtained by calling toll-free 1-800-765-6955
or by visiting http://www.adventistbookcenter.com.

ISBN 978-0-8280-1505-9

June 2016

DAILY DEVOTIONAL BOOKS
FROM THE WRITINGS OF ELLEN G. WHITE

Christ Triumphant
Conflict and Courage
The Faith I Live By
God's Amazing Grace
In Heavenly Places
Lift Him Up
Maranatha—The Lord Is Coming
My Life Today
Our High Calling
Reflecting Christ
Sons and Daughters of God
That I May Know Him
This Day With God
The Upward Look
Ye Shall Receive Power

A WORD TO THE READER

With the publication of this devotional volume, a demand, often expressed, for a select group of Ellen G. White comments upon the central truths of Christianity will be realized. The principal doctrines of the Christian faith, supported by carefully chosen texts of Scripture and Spirit of prophecy statements, are here presented, not as theological pronouncements, but as spiritual truths relating to the work of redemption wrought out for us by Jesus Christ, our Lord and Saviour.

This volume, it should be noted, provides vastly more than *inspiration*. Here is vital *information* for our youth and the readers of this book. A faith that we do not know and comprehend cannot be shared. Sharing is dependent upon knowing.

In this E. G. White devotional book the Scripture texts are presented as the basic authority. The Bible speaks out on behalf of the foundation truths. The author's comments enlarge upon and exalt Scripture truth, making it personal and bringing home the lesson to the heart. In this volume we hear the Scripture speaking, and in this volume we hear the Spirit of prophecy speaking. The two are in their right relationship, the Bible making the doctrinal statement, the Spirit of prophecy providing the commentary.

In finding appropriate Ellen G. White statements dealing with Bible doctrine, the compilers have consulted the published works by the author in which representative statements from her pen appear. Keep in mind, however, that in addition to well-known comments, others less known but not less forceful are here presented. Ellen G. White Supplementary Material used in the *Seventh-day Adventist Bible Commentary,* portions of articles from *The Youth's Instructor, Signs of the Times, The Review and Herald,* and a number of previously unpublished statements are included.

Because each daily reading is limited to just one printed page, much valuable material on related subjects could not be used, and at times omissions had to be made within the statements quoted. Omissions are recognized in the usual way. Frequently as many as five or six sources are quoted on one page. In some places where a statement is only a sentence or two in length, the compilers have faithfully observed the thoughts expressed in the context, and so presented the sequence as to accurately represent the ideas communicated to Mrs. Ellen G. White by the Holy Spirit.

The Faith I Live By was compiled under the direction of the Board of Trustees of the Ellen G. White Publications, who carry the responsibility of the care and publication of the E. G. White writings. The work has been done in harmony with Mrs. White's instruction to the trustees providing for the printing of compilations from her writings.

That the brief day-by-day messages concerning the inspiring truths of the Christian faith may serve as a daily guide and an encouragement to every reader is the sincere prayer and wish of the publishers and

THE TRUSTEES OF THE ELLEN G. WHITE ESTATE

MONTHLY TOPICS

January
The Word and Works of God

February
The Three Dignitaries of Heaven

March
Satan and the Great Rebellion

April
God's Remedy for Sin

May
Conversion and the New Life

June
Here and Hereafter

July
The Sanctuary of God

August
Walking as Christ Walked

September
The Christ-centered Home

October
The Last Church of Christ

November
Facing the Final Test

December
The Triumph of the Gospel

January

THE WORD AND WORKS OF GOD

A LIGHT FOR MY PATH

Thy word is a lamp unto my feet, and a light unto my path.
_Ps. 119:105._

We all need a guide through the many strait places in life as much
as the sailor needs a pilot over the sandy bar or up the rocky river,
and where is this guide to be found? We point you . . . to the Bible.[1]

God has given us His Word as a lamp to our feet and a light to
our path. Its teachings have a vital bearing on our prosperity in all
the relations of life. . . .

The Bible is the great standard of right and wrong, clearly defin-
ing sin and holiness. Its living principles, running through our lives
like threads of gold, are our only safeguard in trial and temptation.
The Bible is a chart, showing us the waymarks of truth. Those who
are acquainted with this chart will be enabled to tread with certainty
in the path of duty, wherever they may be called to go.[2]

When faith in God's Word is lost, the soul has no guide, no safeguard. The youth are drawn into paths which lead away from God
and from everlasting life.

To this cause may in great degree be attributed the widespread
iniquity in our world today. When the Word of God is set aside, its
power to restrain the evil passions of the natural heart is rejected.[3]

When God's Word is made the man of our counsel, when we
search the Scriptures for light, heavenly angels come near to impress
the mind and to enlighten the understanding, so that it can be truly
said, "The entrance of thy words giveth light. . . ." Ps. 119:130.[4]

The Word of God is light and truth. . . . It is able to guide every
step of the way to the city of God.[5]

MY DEFENSE IN TEMPTATION

Thy word have I hid in mine heart, that I might not sin against thee. Ps. 119:11.

If we would not be misled by error and falsehood, the heart must be preoccupied with the truth. The Word of God will furnish the mind with weapons of divine power, to vanquish the enemy. Happy is the man, who, when tempted, finds his soul rich in the knowledge of the Scriptures, who finds shelter beneath the promises of God. "Thy word," said the psalmist, "have I hid in mine heart, that I might not sin against thee."[6]

This Word is ever to be in our hearts and on our lips. "It is written" is to be our anchor. Those who make God's Word their counselor realize the weakness of the human heart and the power of the grace of God to subdue every unsanctified, unholy impulse. Their hearts are ever prayerful, and they have the guardianship of holy angels. When the enemy comes in like a flood, the Spirit of God lifts up for them a standard against him. There is harmony in the heart, for the precious, powerful influences of truth bear sway.[7]

The Word of God is a channel of communication with the living God. He who feeds upon the Word will become fruitful in all good works. He . . . will be the discoverer of rich mines of truth which he must work to find the hidden treasure. When [he is] surrounded with temptations, the Holy Spirit will bring to his mind the very words with which to meet the temptation at the very moment when they are most needed, and he can use them effectually.[8]

We must be better acquainted with our Bibles. We might close the door to many temptations, if we would commit to memory passages of Scripture. Let us hedge up the way to Satan's temptations with "It is written." We shall meet with conflicts to test our faith and courage, but they will make us strong if we conquer through the grace Jesus is willing to give. But we must believe; we must grasp the promises without a doubt.[9]

ITS PROMISES ARE MINE

For all the Promises of God in him are yea, and in him Amen, unto the glory of God by us. 2 Cor. 1:20.

The precious Bible is the garden of God, and His promises are the lilies, and the roses, and the pinks.[10]

How I wish that we might all believe in the promises of God. . . . We are not to look into our hearts for a joyful emotion as an evidence of our acceptance with Heaven, but we are to take God's promises and say, "They are mine. The Lord is letting His Holy Spirit rest upon me. I am receiving the light; for the promise is, 'Believe that ye receive the things ye ask for, and ye shall have them.' By faith I reach within the veil and lay hold of Christ, my strength. I thank God that I have a Saviour."[11]

The Scriptures are to be received as God's word to us, not written merely, but spoken. When the afflicted ones came to Christ, He beheld not only those who asked for help, but all who throughout the ages should come to Him in like need and with like faith. When He said to the paralytic, "Son, be of good cheer; thy sins be forgiven thee"; when He said to the woman of Capernaum, "Daughter, be of good comfort: thy faith hath made thee whole; go in peace," He spoke to other afflicted, sin-burdened ones who should seek His help.

So with all the promises of God's Word. In them He is speaking to us individually, speaking as directly as if we could listen to His voice. It is in these promises that Christ communicates to us His grace and power. They are leaves from that tree which is "for the healing of the nations." Received, assimilated, they are to be the strength of the character, the inspiration and sustenance of the life.[12]

Let youth grasp the hand of infinite power. Faith grows by exercise. Feed upon the promises; be content to rely on the simple promise of God's Word.[13]

Hang in memory's hall the precious words of Christ. They are to be valued far above silver or gold.[14]

LESSON BOOK FOR ALL HUMANITY

For the prophecy, came not in old time by the will of man; but holy men of God spake as they were moved by the Holy Ghost. 2 Peter 1:21.

God committed the preparation of His divinely inspired Word to finite man. This Word, arranged into books, the Old and New Testaments is the guidebook to the inhabitants of a fallen world, bequeathed to them that by studying and obeying the directions, not one soul would lose its way to heaven.[15]

The Bible points to God as its author; yet it was written by human hands; and in the varied style of its different books it presents the characteristics of the several writers. The truths revealed are all "given by inspiration of God" (2 Tim. 3:16); yet they are expressed in the words of men. The Infinite One by His Holy Spirit has shed light into the minds and hearts of His servants. He has given dreams and visions, symbols and figures; and those to whom the truth was thus revealed, have themselves embodied the thought in human language.[16]

The Lord speaks to human beings in imperfect speech, in order that the degenerate senses, the dull, earthly perception, of earthly beings may comprehend His words. Thus is shown God's condescension. He meets fallen human beings where they are. The Bible, perfect as it is in its simplicity, does not answer to the great ideas of God; for infinite ideas cannot be perfectly embodied in finite vehicles of thought. Instead of the expressions of the Bible being exaggerated, as many people suppose, the strong expressions break down before the magnificence of the thought, though the penman selected the most expressive language through which to convey the truths of higher education.[17]

God designed the Bible to be a lesson-book to all mankind, in childhood, youth, and manhood, and to be studied through all time. He gave His Word to men as a revelation of Himself. . . . It is the medium of communication between God and man.[18]

THE BIBLE FROM HEAVEN

But we have this treasure in earthen vessels, that the excellency of the power may be of God, and not of us. 2 Cor. 4:7.

God has been pleased to communicate His truth to the world by human agencies, and He Himself, by His Holy Spirit, qualified men and enabled them to do this work. He guided the mind in the selection of what to speak and what to write. The treasure was intrusted to earthen vessels, yet it is, none the less, from Heaven. . . . The obedient, believing child of God beholds in it [the testimony of God] the glory of a divine power, full of grace and truth.[19]

The writers of the Bible had to express their ideas in human language. It was written by human men. These men were inspired of the Holy Spirit. Because of the imperfections of human understanding of language, or the perversity of the human mind, ingenious in evading truth, many read and understand the Bible to please themselves. It is not that the difficulty is in the Bible. . . .

The Scriptures were given to men, not in a continuous chain of unbroken utterances, but piece by piece through successive generations, as God in His providence saw a fitting opportunity to impress man at sundry times and divers places. Men wrote as they were moved upon by the Holy Ghost. . . .

There is not always perfect order or apparent unity in the Scriptures. . . . The truths of the Bible are as pearls hidden. They must be searched, dug out by painstaking effort. Those who take only a surface view of the Scriptures will, with their superficial knowledge, which they think is very deep, talk of the contradictions of the Bible, and question the authority of the Scriptures. But those whose hearts are in harmony with truth and duty will search the Scriptures with a heart prepared to receive divine impressions. The illuminated soul sees a spiritual unity, one grand golden thread running through the whole, but it requires patience, thought, and prayer to trace out the precious golden thread.[20]

ALL THE BIBLE INSPIRED

All scripture is given by inspiration of God, and is profitable for doctrine, for reproof, for correction, for instruction in righteousness. 2 Tim. 3:16.

The Word of God includes the Scriptures of the Old Testament as well as of the New. One is not complete without the other.[21]

The Old Testament, no less than the New, should receive attention. As we study the Old Testament, we shall find living springs bubbling up where the careless reader discerns only a desert.[22]

There is no discord between the Old Testament and the New. In the Old Testament we find the gospel of a coming Saviour; in the New Testament we have the gospel of a Saviour revealed as the prophecies had foretold. While the Old Testament is constantly pointing forward to the true offering, the New Testament shows that the Saviour prefigured by the typical offerings has come. The dim glory of the Jewish age has been succeeded by the brighter, clearer glory of the Christian age.[23]

Christ as manifested to the, patriarchs, as symbolized in the sacrificial service, as portrayed in the law, and as revealed by the prophets, is the riches of the Old Testament. Christ in His life, His death, and His resurrection, Christ as He is manifested by the Holy Spirit, is the treasure of the New Testament. Our Saviour, the outshining of the Father's glory, is both the Old and the New. . . . The Old Testament sheds light upon the New, and the New upon the Old. Each is a revelation of the glory of God in Christ. Both present truths that will continually reveal new depths of meaning to the earnest seeker.[24]

Jesus said of the Old Testament Scriptures—and how much more it is true of the New—"They are they which testify of me" (John 5:39). . . . Yes, the whole Bible tells of Christ. From the first record of creation, for "without him was not any thing made that was made" (John 1:3), to the closing promise, "Behold, I come quickly" (Rev. 22:12), we are reading of His works and listening to His voice. If you would become acquainted with the Saviour, study the Holy Scriptures.[25]

10

AN INFALLIBLE REVELATION

The words of the Lord are pure words: as silver tried in a furnace of earth, purified seven times. Ps. 12:6.

In His Word, God has committed to men the knowledge necessary for salvation. The Holy Scriptures are to be accepted as an authoritative, infallible revelation of His will. They are the standard of character, the revealer of doctrines, and the test of experience.[26]

Spiritual darkness has covered the earth and gross darkness the people. . . . Many, very many, are questioning the verity and truth of the Scriptures. Human reasoning and the imaginings of the human heart are undermining the inspiration of the Word of God, and that which should be received as granted, is surrounded with a cloud of mysticism. Nothing stands out in clear and distinct lines, upon rock bottom. This is one of the marked signs of the last days. . . .

There are men who strive to be original, who are wise above what is written; therefore, their wisdom is foolishness. . . . In seeking to make plain or to unravel mysteries hid from ages from mortal man, they are like a man floundering about in the mud, unable to extricate himself and yet telling others how to get out of the muddy sea they themselves are in. This is a fit representation of the men who set themselves to correct the errors of the Bible. No man can improve the Bible by suggesting what the Lord meant to say or ought to have said. . . .

I take the Bible just as it is, as the Inspired Word. I believe its utterances in an entire Bible.[27]

This Holy Book has withstood the assaults of Satan, who has united with evil men to make everything of divine character shrouded in clouds and darkness. But the Lord has preserved this Holy Book by His own miraculous power in its present shape—a chart or guidebook to the human family to show them the way to heaven. . . .

We thank God that the Bible is prepared for the poor man as well as for the learned man. It is fitted for all ages and all classes.[28]

MYSTERIES WE CANNOT FATHOM

O the depth of the riches both of the wisdom and knowledge of God! how unsearchable are his judgments, and his ways past finding out! Rom. 11:33.

The Word of God, like the character of its divine Author, presents mysteries that can never be fully comprehended by finite beings. . . .

If it were possible for created beings to attain to a full understanding of God and His works, then, having reached this point, there would be for them no further discovery of truth, no growth in knowledge, no further development of mind or heart. God would no longer be supreme; and men, having reached the limit of knowledge and attainment, would cease to advance. Let us thank God that it is not so. God is infinite; in Him are "all the treasures of wisdom and knowledge." Col. 2:3. And to all eternity men may be ever searching, ever learning, and yet they can never exhaust the treasures of His wisdom, His goodness, and His power.[29]

In the natural world we are constantly surrounded with mysteries that we cannot fathom. . . . Should we then be surprised to find that in the spiritual world also there are mysteries that we cannot fathom?[30]

The mysteries of the Bible . . . are among the strongest evidences of its divine inspiration. If it contained no account of God but that which we could comprehend; if His greatness and majesty could be grasped by finite minds, then the Bible would not, as now, bear the unmistakable evidences of divinity. . . . The more we search the Bible, the deeper is our conviction that it is the word of the living God, and human reason bows before the majesty of divine revelation.[31]

Christ will lead the redeemed ones beside the river of life, and will open to them that which while on this earth they could not understand.[32]

In the light that shines from the throne, mysteries will disappear, and the soul will be filled with astonishment at the simplicity of the things that were never before comprehended.[33]

THE BOOK THAT ENDURES

Heaven and earth shall pass away, but my words shall not pass away. Matt. 24:35.

He [Christ] pointed to the Scriptures as of unquestionable authority, and we should do the same. The Bible is to be presented as the word of the infinite God, as the end of all controversy and the foundation of all faith.[34]

The infidel Voltaire once boastingly said: "I am weary of hearing people repeat that twelve men established the Christian religion. I will prove that one man may suffice to overthrow it." . . . Millions have joined in the war upon the Bible. But it is so far from being destroyed, that where there were a hundred in Voltaire's time, there are now ten thousand, yes, a hundred thousand copies of the Book of God. In the words of an early Reformer concerning the Christian church, "The Bible is an anvil that has worn out many hammers." Saith the Lord, "No weapon that is formed against thee shall prosper; and every tongue that shall rise against thee in judgment thou shalt condemn." Isa. 54:17.[35]

At this time, before the great final crisis, as before the world's first destruction, men are absorbed in the pleasures and the pursuits of sense. Engrossed with the seen and transitory, they have lost sight of the unseen and eternal. For the things that perish with the using, they are sacrificing imperishable riches. . . . From the rise and fall of nations as made plain in the pages of Holy Writ, they need to learn how worthless is mere outward and worldly glory.[36]

The Word of God is the only steadfast thing our world knows. It is the sure foundation. "Heaven and earth shall pass away," said Jesus. "but my words shall not pass away."[37]

"The word of God shall stand for ever." "All his commandments are sure. They stand fast for ever and ever, and are done in truth and uprightness." Isa. 40:8; Ps. 111:7, 8. Whatever is built upon the authority of man will be overthrown; but that which is founded upon the rock of God's immutable Word shall stand forever.[38]

THE EVIDENCE OF EXPERIENCE

O taste and see that the Lord is good: blessed is the man that trusteth in him. Ps. 34:8.

There is an evidence that is open to all—the most highly educated, and the most illiterate—the evidence of experience. God invites us to prove for ourselves the reality of His Word, the truth of His promises. He bids us "taste and see that the Lord is good." Instead of depending upon the word of another, we are to taste for ourselves. . . . And as we draw near to Jesus, and rejoice in the fullness of His love, our doubt and darkness will disappear in the light of His presence.[39]

The Christian knows in whom he has believed. He does not only read the Bible; he experiences the power of its teaching. He has not only heard of Christ's righteousness; he has opened the windows of the soul to the light of the Sun of Righteousness.[40]

Every one who has passed from death unto life is able to "set to his seal that God is true." John 3:33. He can testify, "I needed help, and I found it in Jesus. Every want was supplied, the hunger of my soul was satisfied; and now the Bible is to me the revelation of Jesus Christ. Do you ask why I believe in Jesus?—Because He is to me a divine Saviour. Why do I believe the Bible?—Because I have found it to be the voice of God to my soul." We may have the witness in ourselves that the Bible is true, that Christ is the Son of God. We know that we are not following cunningly devised fables.[41]

Let the youth make the Word of God the food of mind and soul. . . . Thus through faith they will come to know God by an experimental knowledge. They have proved for themselves the reality of His Word, the truth of His promises. They have tasted, and they know that the Lord is good. . . . It is our privilege to reach higher and still higher for clearer revealings of the character of God. . . . In His light shall we see light, until mind and heart and soul are transformed into the image of His holiness.[42]

CHRIST THE LIVING WORD

And the Word was made flesh, and dwelt among us, (and we beheld his glory, the glory as of the only begotten of the Father,) full of grace and truth. John 1:14.

Jesus is called the Word of God. He accepted His Father's law, wrought out its principles in His life, manifested its spirit, and showed its beneficent power in the heart. Says John: "The Word was made flesh, and dwelt among us, (and we beheld his glory, the glory as of the only begotten of the Father,) full of grace and truth."[43]

All that man needs to know or can know of God has been revealed in the life and character of His Son. . . .

Taking humanity upon Him, Christ came to be one with humanity and at the same time to reveal our heavenly Father to sinful human beings. He was in all things made like unto His brethren. He became flesh, even as we are. He was hungry and thirsty and weary. He was sustained by food and refreshed by sleep. He shared the lot of men, and yet He was the blameless Son of God. . . .

Tender, compassionate, sympathetic, ever considerate of others, He represented the character of God, and was constantly engaged in service for God and man.[44]

The followers of Christ must be partakers of His experience. They must assimilate the Word of God. They must be changed into its likeness by the power of Christ and reflect the divine attributes. . . . The spirit and work of Christ must become the spirit and work of His disciples.[45]

In the study of the Bible the converted soul eats the flesh and drinks the blood of the Son of God, which He Himself interprets as the receiving and doing of His words, that are spirit and life. The Word is made flesh, and dwells among us, in those who receive the holy precepts of the Word of God. The Saviour of the world has left a holy, pure example for all men. It illuminates, uplifts, and brings immortality to all who obey the divine requirements.[46]

THE SECRET OF POWER

Wherewithal shall a young man cleanse his way? by taking heed thereto according to thy word. Ps. 119:9.

It is one thing to treat the Bible as a book of good moral instruction, to be heeded so far as is consistent with the spirit of the times and our position in the world; it is another thing to regard it as it really is—the Word of the living God, the Word that is our life, the Word that is to mold our actions, our words, and our thoughts. To hold God's Word as anything less than this is to reject it.[47]

The Word of God is a character-detector, a motive-tester. We are to read this Word with heart and mind open to receive the impressions that God will give. We must not think that the reading of the Word can accomplish that which only He whom the Word reveals, who stands behind the Word, can accomplish. Some are in danger of hastening to the conclusion that because they hold firmly to the doctrines of the truth, they are actually in possession of the blessings which these doctrines declare shall come to the receiver of truth. Many keep the truth in the outer court. Its sacred principles have not a controlling influence over the words, the thoughts, the actions.[48]

In this perilous day of evil, when allurements to vice and corruption are on every hand, let the earnest, heartfelt cry of the young be raised to heaven: "Wherewithal shall a young man cleanse his way?" And may his ears be open and his heart inclined to obey the instruction given in the answer: "By taking heed thereto according to thy word." The only safety for the youth in this age of pollution is to make God their trust. Without divine help they will be unable to control human passions and appetites. In Christ is the very help needed.[49]

Truth must reach down to the deepest recesses of the soul, and cleanse away everything unlike the spirit of Christ, and the vacuum be supplied by the attributes of His character who was pure and holy and undefiled, that all the springs of the heart may be as flowers, fragrant with perfume, a sweet smelling savor, a savor of life unto life.[50]

BORN OF THE WORD

Being born again, not of corruptible seed, but of incorruptible, by the word of God, which liveth and abideth for ever. 1 Peter 1:23.

The change of heart by which we become children of God is in the Bible spoken of as birth. Again, it is compared to the germination of the good seed sown by the husbandman. . . . So from natural life, illustrations are drawn, to help us better to understand the mysterious truths of spiritual life. Not all the wisdom and skill of man can produce life in the smallest object in nature. It is only through the life which God Himself has imparted, that either plant or animal can live. So it is only through the life from God that spiritual life is begotten in the hearts of men.[51]

When truth becomes an abiding principle in the life, the soul is "born again, not of corruptible seed, but of incorruptible, by the word of God, which liveth and abideth for ever." This new birth is the result of receiving Christ as the word of God. Then by the Holy Spirit divine truths are impressed upon the heart, new conceptions are awakened, and the energies hitherto dormant are aroused to co-operate with God. . . . Christ was the revealer of truth to the world. By Him the incorruptible seed—the Word of God—was sown in the hearts of men.[52]

The Word destroys the natural, earthly nature, and imparts a new life in Christ Jesus. The Holy Spirit comes to the soul as a Comforter. By the transforming agency of His grace, the image of God is reproduced in the disciple; he becomes a new creature. Love takes the place of hatred, and the heart receives the divine similitude.[53]

Henceforth you are not your own; you are bought with a price. "Ye were not redeemed with corruptible things, as silver and gold, . . . but with the precious blood of Christ. . . ." 1 Peter 1:18, 19. Through this simple act of believing God, the Holy Spirit has begotten a new life in your heart. You are as a child born into the family of God, and He loves you as He loves His son.[54]

FOOD FOR MY SOUL

*And Jesus answered him, saying, It is written, That man shall not
live by bread alone, but by every word of God. Luke 4:4.*

The Word of God is to be our spiritual food.[55]

The life of Christ that gives life to the world is in His word. It
was by His word that Jesus healed disease and cast out demons; by
His word He stilled the sea, and raised the dead. . . .

As our physical life is sustained by food, so our spiritual life is
sustained by the Word of God. And every soul is to receive life from
God's Word for himself. As we must eat for ourselves in order to receive nourishment, so we must receive the Word for ourselves. . . .

In His promises and warnings, Jesus means me. . . . The experiences related in God's Word are to be *my* experiences. Prayer and
promise, precept and warning, are mine.[56]

The creative energy that called the worlds into existence is in the
word of God. This word imparts power; it begets life. Every command is a promise; accepted by the will, received into the soul, it
brings with it the life of the Infinite One. . . .

The life thus imparted is in like manner sustained. "By every
word that proceedeth out of the mouth of God" (Matt. 4:4) shall man
live. The mind, the soul, is built up by that upon which it feeds; and
it rests with us to determine upon what it shall be fed. It is within
the power of every one to choose the topics that shall occupy the
thoughts and shape the character.[57]

Youth, in the name of Jesus I appeal to you whom I shall soon
meet around the throne of God, Study your Bible. It will prove to
you not only the pillar of cloud by day but the pillar of fire by night.
It opens before you a path leading up and still upward, bidding you
go forward. The Bible—you do not know its worth! It is a book for
the mind, for the heart, for the conscience, the will, and the life. It
is the message of God to you, in such simple style that it meets the
comprehension of a little child. The Bible—precious Book![58]

LIFE IN GOD'S WORD

It is the spirit that quickeneth; the flesh profiteth nothing: the words that I speak unto you, they are spirit, and they are life. John 6:63.

Every seed has in itself a germinating principle. In it the life of the plant is enfolded. So there is life in God's Word. Christ says, "The words that I speak unto you, they are spirit, and they are life." . . . In every command and in every promise of the Word of God is the power, the very life of God, by which the command may be fulfilled and the promise realized. He who by faith receives the Word is receiving the very life and character of God.[59]

By partaking of this Word our spiritual strength is increased; we grow in grace and in a knowledge of the truth. Habits of self-control are formed and strengthened. The infirmities of childhood—fretfulness, willfulness, selfishness, hasty words, passionate acts—disappear, and in their place are developed the graces of Christian manhood and womanhood.[60]

In its power, men and women have broken the chains of sinful habit. They have renounced selfishness. The profane have become reverent, the drunken sober, the profligate pure. Souls that have borne the likeness of Satan have been transformed into the image of God.[61]

Would you become assimilated to the divine image? . . . Would you drink of the water which Christ shall give you, which shall be in you a well of water springing up into everlasting life? Would you bear fruit to the glory of God? Would you refresh others? Then with heart hungering for the bread of life, the Word of God, search the Scriptures, and live by every word that proceedeth out of the mouth of God. Your soul's sanctification and righteousness will result from faith in the Word of God, which leads to obedience of its commands. Let the Word of God be to you as the voice of God instructing you, and saying, "This is the way, walk ye in it." Isa. 30:21. Christ prayed, "Sanctify them through thy truth: thy word is truth." John 17:17.[62]

A TABLE SET BEFORE ME

Whoso eateth my flesh, and drinketh my blood, hath eternal life; and I will raise him up at the last day. For my flesh is meat indeed, and my blood is drink indeed. John 6:54, 55.

Eternal life is the receiving of the living elements in the Scriptures, the doing of the will of God. This is what is meant by eating the flesh and drinking the blood of the Son of God. It is the privilege of all to partake of the bread of heaven by studying the Word, and thus gain spiritual sinew and muscle.[63]

Each one must appropriate the blessing to his own soul, or he will not be fed. . . . You know you would not be nourished by seeing a well-spread table, and by others eating. We would starve if we did not partake of physical nourishment, and we shall lose our spiritual strength and vitality if we do not feed on spiritual bread. . . .

The table has been spread, and Christ invites you to the feast. Shall we stand back, refusing His bounties, and declaring, "He does not mean this for me"? We used to sing a hymn that described a feast where a happy household gathered to partake of the bounties of the board at a kind father's invitation. While the happy children gathered at the table, there stood a hungry beggar child at the threshold. She was invited to come in; but sadly she turned away, exclaiming, "I have no father there." Will you take this position as Jesus invites you in? Oh! if you have a Father in the courts above, I entreat you to reveal the fact. He wants to make you a partaker of His rich bounties and blessings. All who come with the confiding love of a little child will find a Father there.[64]

Come to the water of life, and drink. Do not stay away and complain of thirst. The water of life is free to all.[65]

Those who eat and digest this Word, making it a part of every action and of every attribute of character, grow strong in the strength of God. It gives immortal vigor to the soul, perfecting the experience, and bringing joys that will abide forever.[66]

LINKED TO THE DIVINE

Whereby are given unto us exceeding great and precious promises: that by these ye might be partakers of the divine nature, having escaped the corruption that is in the world through lust. 2 Peter 1:4.

The Saviour took upon Himself the infirmities of humanity, and lived a sinless life, that men might have no fear that because of the weakness of human nature they could not overcome.[67]

"The prince of this world cometh," said Jesus, "and hath nothing in me." John 14:30. There was in Him nothing that responded to Satan's sophistry. He did not consent to sin. Not even by a thought did He yield to temptation. So it may be with us. Christ's humanity was united with divinity; He was fitted for the conflict by the indwelling of the Holy Spirit. And He came to make us partakers of the divine nature. So long as we are united to Him by faith, sin has no more dominion over us.[68]

We need not retain one sinful propensity. . . . As we partake of the divine nature, hereditary and cultivated tendencies to wrong are cut away from the character, and we are made a living power for good. Ever learning of the divine Teacher, daily partaking of His nature, we cooperate with God in overcoming Satan's temptations.[69]

How this is accomplished, Christ has shown us. By what means did He overcome in the conflict with Satan? By the Word of God. Only by the Word could He resist temptation. "It is written," He said. And unto us are given "exceeding great and precious promises: that by these ye might be partakers of the divine nature. . . ." Every promise in God's Word is ours. . . . When assailed by temptation, look not to circumstances or to the weakness of self, but to the power of the Word. All its strength is yours.[70]

Grasp His promises as leaves from the tree of life: "Him that cometh to me I will in no wise cast out." John 6:37. As you come to Him, believe that He accepts you, because He has promised. You can never perish while you do this—never.[71]

ORIGIN BY CREATION

Through faith we understand that the worlds were framed by the word of God, so that things which are seen were not made of things which do appear. Heb. 11:3.

It is the Word of God alone that gives to us an authentic account of the creation of our world.[72]

The theory that God did not create matter when He brought the world into existence is without foundation. In the formation of our world, God was not indebted to pre-existing matter. On the contrary, all things, material or spiritual, stood up before the Lord Jehovah at His voice and were created for His own purpose. The heavens and all the host of them, the earth and all things therein, are not only the work of His hand; they came into existence by the breath of His mouth.[73]

While there is an individuality and variety in nature, there is a oneness in their diversity; for all things receive their usefulness and beauty from the same source. The great Master Artist writes His name on all His created works, from the loftiest cedar of Lebanon to the hyssop upon the wall. They all declare His handiwork, from the lofty mountain and the grand ocean to the tiniest shell upon the seashore.[74]

He made the night, marshaling the shining stars in the firmament. He calls them all by name. The heavens declare the glory of God, and the firmament showeth his handiwork, showing man that this little world is but a jot in God's creation.[75]

The deepest students of science are constrained to recognize in nature the working of infinite power. But to man's unaided reason, nature's teaching cannot but be contradictory and disappointing. Only in the light of revelation can it be read aright. "Through faith we understand."

"In the beginning God." Gen. 1:1. Here alone can the mind in its eager questioning, fleeing as the dove to the ark, find rest. Above, beneath, beyond, abides Infinite Love, working out all things to accomplish "the good pleasure of his goodness." 2 Thess. 1:11.[76]

NATURE SPEAKS OF GOD

Consider the lilies how they grow: they toil not, they spin not, and yet I say unto you, that Solomon in all his glory was not arrayed like one of these. Luke 12:27.

In their original perfection all created things were an expression of the thought of God. To Adam and Eve in their Eden home nature was full of the knowledge of God, teeming with divine instruction. Wisdom spoke to the eye and was received into the heart; for they communed with God in His created works. . . . The earth is now marred and defiled by sin. Yet even in its blighted state much that is beautiful remains.[77]

Why did not our heavenly Father carpet the earth with brown or gray? He chose the color that was most restful, the most acceptable to the senses. How it cheers the heart and refreshes the weary spirit to look upon the earth, clad in its garments of living green! . . . Every spire of grass, every opening bud and blooming flower, is a token of God's love, and should teach us a lesson of faith and trust in Him.[78]

The beauties of nature have a tongue that speaks to us without ceasing. The open heart can be impressed with the love and glory of God, as seen in the works of His hand. The listening ear can hear and understand the communications of God through the things of nature. There is a lesson in the sunbeam, and in the various objects of nature that God has presented to our view. The green fields, the lofty trees, the buds and flowers, the passing cloud, the falling rain, the babbling brook, the sun, moon, and stars in the heavens—all invite our attention and meditation.[79]

You who are sighing for the artificial splendor which wealth alone can purchase, for costly paintings, furniture, and dress, listen to the voice of the divine Teacher. He points you to the flower of the field, the simple design of which cannot be equaled by human skill.[80]

He is a lover of the beautiful, and above all that is outwardly attractive He loves beauty of character; He would have us cultivate purity and simplicity, the quiet graces of the flowers.[81]

THE HEAVENS ARE TELLING

Lift up your eyes on high, and behold who hath created these things, that bringeth out their host by number: he calleth them all by names by the greatness of his might, for that he is strong in power; not one faileth. Isa. 40:26.

God's great book of nature is open for us to study, and from it we are to gain more exalted ideas of His greatness and unexcelled love and glory. He . . . would have His children appreciate His works, and delight in the simple, quiet beauty with which He has adorned their earthly home.[82]

God calls upon His creatures to turn their attention from the confusion and perplexity around them, and admire His handiwork. The heavenly bodies are worthy of contemplation. God has made them for the benefit of man, and as we study His works, angels of God will be by our side to enlighten our minds, and guard them from satanic deception.[83]

Go out, dear young man, at night, and behold the glories of the firmament. Look up to the gems of light which like precious gold stud the heavens. There is a wealth of glory there, but millions of minds are so obtuse they cannot appreciate this treasure. It is a little bit of heaven hung out before our senses to testify of the surpassing glories within.[84]

We are not merely to gaze upon the heavens; we are to consider the works of God. He would have us study the works of infinity, and from this study, learn to love and reverence and obey Him.[85]

Every shining star which God has placed in the heavens obeys His mandate, and gives its distinctive measure of light to make beautiful the heavens at night; so let every converted soul show the measure of light committed to him; and as it shines forth the light will increase and grow brighter. Give out your light, . . . pour forth your beams mirrored from heaven. O daughter of Zion, "Arise, shine; for thy light is come, and the glory of the Lord is risen upon thee." Isa. 60:1.[86]

CREATION NOT EVOLUTION

By the word of The Lord were the heavens made; and all the host of them by the breath of his mouth. Ps. 33:6.

Since the book of nature and the book of revelation bear the impress of the same master mind, they cannot but speak in harmony. . . .

Inferences erroneously drawn from facts observed in nature have, however, led to supposed conflict between science and revelation. . . . Millions of years, it is claimed, were required for the evolution of the earth from chaos; and in order to accommodate the Bible to this supposed revelation of science, the days of creation are assumed to have been vast, indefinite periods. . . . Such a conclusion is wholly uncalled for.[87]

Of each successive day of creation, the Sacred Record declares that it consisted of the evening and the morning, like all other days that have followed.[88]

In regard to the work of creation itself the divine testimony is, "He spake, and it was done; he commanded, and it stood fast." Ps. 33:9. With Him who could thus call into existence unnumbered worlds, how long a time would be required for the evolution of the earth from chaos? . . .

It is true that remains found in the earth testify to the existence of men, animals, and plants much larger than any now known. . . . But concerning these things Bible history furnishes ample explanation. Before the Flood, the development of vegetable and animal life was immeasurably superior to that which has since been known. At the Flood the surface of the earth was broken up, marked changes took place, and in the re-formation of the earth's crust were preserved many evidences of the life previously existing. . . . These things . . . are so many witnesses mutely testifying to the truth of the Word of God.[89]

Just how God accomplished the work of creation He has never revealed to men; human science cannot search out the secrets of the Most High. His creative power is as incomprehensible as His existence.[90]

ALL NATURE UPHELD BY GOD

And he is before all things, and by him all things consist. Col. 1:17.

As regards this earth, Scripture declares the work of creation to have been completed. "The works were finished from the foundation of the world." Heb. 4:3. But the power of God is still exercised in upholding the objects of His creation. . . . Every breath, every pulsation of the heart, is an evidence of the care of Him in whom we live and move and have our being.[91]

Not by its own inherent energy does the earth produce its bounties, and year by year continue its motion around the sun. An unseen hand guides the planets in their circuit of the heavens.[92]

The God of heaven is constantly at work. It is by His power that vegetation is caused to flourish, that every leaf appears and every flower blooms. Every drop of rain or flake of snow, every spire of grass, every leaf and flower and shrub, testifies of God. These little things so common around us teach the lesson that nothing is beneath the notice of the infinite God, nothing is too small for His attention.[93]

Many teach that matter possesses vital power. . . . and that the operations of nature are conducted in harmony with fixed laws, with which God Himself cannot interfere. This is false science, and is not sustained by the Word of God. Nature is the servant of her Creator. God does not annul His laws, or work contrary to them; but He is continually using them as His instruments.[94]

God's handiwork in nature is not God Himself in nature. . . . While nature is an expression of God's thought, it is not nature but the God of nature that is to be exalted.[95]

There is in nature the continual working of the Father and the Son. Christ says, "My Father worketh hitherto, and I work." John 5:17.[96]

The hand that sustains the worlds in space, the hand that holds in their orderly arrangement and tireless activity all things throughout the universe of God, is the hand that was nailed to the cross for us.[97]

THE CROWNING ACT OF CREATION

So God created man in his own image, in the image of God created he him. Gen. 1:27.

Here is clearly set forth the origin of the human race; and the divine record is so plainly stated that there is no occasion for erroneous conclusions.[98]

After the earth, with its teeming animal and vegetable life, had been called into existence, man, the crowning work of the Creator, and the one for whom the beautiful earth had been fitted up, was brought upon the stage of action. . . .

As man came forth from the hand of his Creator, he was of lofty stature and perfect symmetry. His countenance bore the ruddy tint of health, and glowed with the light of life and joy. Adam's height was much greater than that of men who now inhabit the earth. Eve was somewhat less in stature; yet her form was noble, and full of beauty.[99]

There is no ground for the supposition that man was evolved, by slow degrees of development, from the lower forms of animal or vegetable life. . . . He who set the starry worlds on high, and tinted with delicate skill the flowers of the field, who filled the earth and the heavens with the wonders of His power, when He came to crown His glorious work, to place one in the midst to stand as ruler of the fair earth, did not fail to create a being worthy of the hand that gave him life. The genealogy of our race, as given by inspiration, traces back its origin, not to a line of developing germs, mollusks, and quadrupeds, but to the great Creator. Though formed from the dust, Adam was "the son of God."[100]

Next to the angelic beings, the human family, formed in "the image of God," are the noblest of His created works.[101]

When Adam came from the Creator's hand, he bore, in his physical, mental, and spiritual nature, a likeness to his Maker. . . . It was His purpose that the longer man lived the more fully he should reveal this image—the more fully reflect the glory of the Creator.[102]

WHAT IS YOUR LIFE?

The life is more than meat, and the body is more than raiment.
Luke 12:23.

Our life was given us of God, and is dependent upon Him, as the leaf is dependent upon the bough for sustenance.[103]

Life is a manifestation of God's love. It is a talent which God has committed to our care, and it is a very costly talent, as viewed in the light of the sacrifice of God's Son. It is an expression of the owner-ship of God. We are His by creation, and doubly His by redemption. We derive our life from Him. He is the Creator and the Source of all life. He is the Author of the higher life which He desires the beings formed in His image to have.[104]

Every one should consider the solemn question, What is my life toward God and my fellow men? No man liveth unto himself. No life is simply neutral in its results. . . .

Every soul is under obligation to live a Christian life. Our indi-viduality, our talents, our time, our influence, our abilities, all given to us of God, are to be rendered back to Him in willing service. The aim and object of life is not to secure temporal advantages, but to make sure of the eternal advantages. God claims your soul, your body, your capabilities; for He has bought them by His own pre-cious blood, and they all belong to Him. It is robbery to withhold yourself from God. . . . The question of importance to us is, Is our life interwoven with that of Jesus?[105]

What is Christian life? It is a life rescued, a life taken out of a world of sin, and attached to the life of Christ.[106]

If our life is hid with Christ in God, we shall, when Christ shall appear, also appear with Him in glory. And while in this world we will give to God, in sanctified service, all the capabilities He has given us.[107]

What is your life? You must meet and answer that question sometime.[108]

INSTITUTED AT CREATION

And on the seventh day God ended his work which he had made; and he rested on the seventh day from all his work which he had made. And God blessed the seventh day, and sanctified it: because that in it he had rested from all his work which God created and made. Gen. 2:2, 3.

The great Jehovah had laid the foundations of the earth; He had dressed the whole world in the garb of beauty, and had filled it with things useful to man; He had created all the wonders of the land and of the sea. In six days the great work of creation had been accomplished. And God "rested on the seventh day from all his work which he had made. . . ." God looked with satisfaction upon the work of His hands. All was perfect, worthy of its divine Author, and He rested, not as one weary, but as well pleased with the fruits of His wisdom and goodness and the manifestations of His glory.

After resting upon the seventh day, God sanctified it, or set it apart, as a day of rest for man. Following the example of the Creator, man was to rest upon this sacred day, that as he should look upon the heavens and the earth, he might reflect upon God's great work of creation; and that as he should behold the evidences of God's wisdom and goodness, his heart might be filled with love and reverence for his Maker. . . .

God saw that a Sabbath was essential for man, even in Paradise. He needed to lay aside his own interests and pursuits for one day of the seven, that he might more fully contemplate the works of God, and meditate upon His power and goodness. He needed a Sabbath, to remind him more vividly of God, and to awaken gratitude because all that he enjoyed and possessed came from the beneficent hand of the Creator.[109]

When the foundations of the earth were laid, . . . then was laid the foundation of the Sabbath. Well may this institution demand our reverence: it was ordained by no human authority, and rests upon no human traditions; it was established by the Ancient of days, and commanded by His eternal word.[110]

A HOLY MEMORIAL

He hath made his wonderful works to be remembered: the Lord is gracious and full of compassion. Ps. 111:4.

In Eden, God set up the memorial of His work of creation, in placing His blessing upon the seventh day. The Sabbath was committed to Adam, the father and representative of the whole human family. Its observance was to be an act of grateful acknowledgment, on the part of all who should dwell upon the earth, that God was their creator and their rightful sovereign; that they were the work of His hands, and the subjects of His authority. Thus the institution was wholly commemorative, and given to all mankind. There was nothing in it shadowy, or of restricted application to any people.[111]

All things were created by the Son of God. "In the beginning was the Word, and the Word was with God. . . . All things were made by him; and without him was not any thing made that was made." John 1:1-3. And since the Sabbath is a memorial of the work of creation, it is a token of the love and power of Christ.

The Sabbath calls our thoughts to nature, and brings us into communion with the Creator. In the song of the bird, the sighing of the trees, and the music of the sea, we still may hear His voice who talked with Adam in Eden in the cool of the day. And as we behold His power in nature we find comfort, for the word that created all things is that which speaks life to the soul.[112]

God . . . has given man six days in which to labor. But He sanctified the day of His rest, and gave it to man to be kept, free from all secular labor. By thus setting apart the Sabbath, God gave the world a memorial. He did not set apart one day and any day in seven, but one particular day, the seventh day. And by observing the Sabbath, we show that we recognize God as the living God, the Creator of the heaven and the earth.[113]

Had the Sabbath always been sacredly observed, there could never have been an atheist or an idolater.[114]

A SPECIAL SIGN

Moreover also I gave them my sabbaths, to be a sign between me and them, that they might know that I am the Lord that sanctify them. Eze. 20:12.

As the Sabbath was the sign that distinguished Israel when they came out of Egypt to enter the earthly Canaan, so it is the sign that now distinguishes God's people as they come out from the world to enter the heavenly rest.[115]

The observance of the Sabbath is the means ordained by God of preserving a knowledge of Himself and of distinguishing between His loyal subjects and the transgressors of His law.[116]

It [the Sabbath] belongs to Christ. . . . Since He made all things, He made the Sabbath. By Him it was set apart as a memorial of the work of creation. It points to Him as both the Creator and the Sanctifier. It declares that He who created all things in heaven and in earth, and by whom all things hold together, is the head of the church, and that by His power we are reconciled to God. For, speaking of Israel, He said, "I gave them my sabbaths, to be a sign between me and them, that they might know that I am the Lord that sanctify them"—make them holy. Then the Sabbath is a sign of Christ's power to make us holy. And it is given to all whom Christ makes holy. As a sign of His sanctifying power, the Sabbath is given to all who through Christ become a part of the Israel of God. . . .

To all who receive the Sabbath as a sign of Christ's creative and redeeming power, it will be a delight. Seeing Christ in it, they delight themselves in Him. The Sabbath points them to the works of creation as an evidence of His mighty power in redemption. While it calls to mind the lost peace of Eden, it tells of peace restored through the Saviour. And every object in nature repeats His invitation, "Come unto me, all ye that labour and are heavy laden, and I will give you rest." Matt. 11:28.[117]

The Sabbath is a golden clasp that unites God and His people.[118]

PREPARING FOR THE HOLY DAY

Remember the sabbath day, to keep it holy. Ex. 20:8.

At the very beginning of the fourth commandment the Lord said, "Remember." He knew that amid the multitude of cares and perplexities man would be tempted to excuse himself from meeting the full requirement of the law, or would forget its sacred importance. Therefore He said: "Remember the sabbath day, to keep it holy."

All through the week we are to have the Sabbath in mind and be making preparation to keep it according to the commandment. . . .

When the Sabbath is thus remembered, the temporal will not be allowed to encroach upon the spiritual. No duty pertaining to the six working days will be left for the Sabbath. During the week our energies will not be so exhausted in temporal labor that on the day when the Lord rested and was refreshed we shall be too weary to engage in His service. . . .

On Friday let the preparation for the Sabbath be completed. See that all the clothing is in readiness and that all the cooking is done. . . . The Sabbath is not to be given to the repairing of garments, to the cooking of food, to pleasure seeking, or to any other worldly employment. Before the setting of the sun let all secular work be laid aside and all secular papers be put out of sight. Parents, explain your work and its purpose to your children, and let them share in your preparation to keep the Sabbath according to the commandment.[119]

There is another work that should receive attention on the preparation day. On this day all differences between brethren, whether in the family or in the church, should be put away. Let all bitterness and wrath and malice be expelled from the soul. In a humble spirit, "confess your faults one to another, and pray one for another."

Before the setting of the sun let the members of the family assemble to read God's Word, to sing and pray.[120]

We should jealously guard the edges of the Sabbath. Remember that every moment is consecrated, holy time.[121]

SANCTIFIED FOR WORSHIP

I was glad when they said unto me, Let us go into the house of the Lord. Ps. 122:1.

God has given us the whole of six days in which to do our work, and has reserved only one to Himself. This should be a day of blessing to us—a day when we should lay aside all our secular matters and center our thoughts upon God and heaven.[122]

All heaven is keeping the Sabbath, but not in a listless, do-nothing way. On this day every energy of the soul should be awake, for are we not to meet with God and with Christ our Saviour? We may behold Him by faith. He is longing to refresh and bless every soul.[123]

On Sabbath morning the family should be astir early. If they rise late, there is confusion and bustle in preparing for breakfast and Sabbath school. There is hurrying, jostling, and impatience. Thus unholy feelings come into the home. The Sabbath, thus desecrated, becomes a weariness, and its coming is dreaded rather than loved.[124]

The Sabbath is God's time. He sanctified and hallowed the seventh day. He set it apart for man to keep as a day of worship.[125]

We need to cherish and cultivate a spirit of true worship, a spirit of devotion upon the Lord's holy, sanctified day. We should assemble together believing that we shall receive comfort and hope, light and peace from Jesus Christ.[126]

All heaven was represented to me as beholding and watching upon the Sabbath those who acknowledge the claims of the fourth commandment and are observing the Sabbath. Angels were marking their interest in, and high regard for, this divine institution. Those who sanctified the Lord God in their hearts by a strictly devotional frame of mind, and who sought to improve the sacred hours in keeping the Sabbath to the best of their ability, and to honor God by calling the Sabbath a delight—these the angels were specially blessing with light and health, and special strength was given them.[127]

HAPPIEST DAY OF THE WEEK

If thou turn away thy foot from the sabbath, from doing thy pleasure on my holy day; and call the sabbath a delight, the holy of the Lord, honourable; and shall honour him, not doing thine own ways, nor finding thine own pleasure, nor speaking thine own words: then shalt thou delight thyself in the Lord. Isa. 58:13, 14.

God's love has set a limit to the demands of toil. Over the Sabbath He places His merciful hand. In His own day He preserves for the family opportunity for communion with Him, with nature, and with one another.[128]

The Sabbath and the family were alike instituted in Eden, and in God's purpose they are indissolubly linked together. On this day more than on any other, it is possible for us to live the life of Eden. It was God's plan for the members of the family to be associated in work and study, in worship and recreation.[129]

God's holy rest day was made for man, and acts of mercy are in perfect harmony with its intent.[130]

To relieve the afflicted, to comfort the sorrowing, is a labor of love that does honor to God's holy day.[131]

Since the Sabbath is the memorial of creative power, it is the day above all others when we should acquaint ourselves with God through His works.[132]

During a portion of the day, all should have an opportunity to be out of doors. How can children receive a more correct knowledge of God . . . than in spending a portion of their time out of doors, not in play, but in company with their parents? Let their young minds be associated with God in the beautiful scenery of nature. . . . As they view the beautiful things which He has created for the happiness of man, they will be led to regard Him as a tender, loving Father. . . . As the character of God puts on the aspect of love, benevolence, beauty, and attraction, they are drawn to love Him.[133]

The Sabbath—oh!—make it the sweetest, the most blessed day of the whole week.[134]

TO BE KEPT IN ETERNITY

And it shall come to pass, that from one new moon to another, and from one sabbath to another, shall all flesh come to worship before me, saith the Lord. Isa. 66:23.

How beautiful the earth was when it came from the Creator's hand! God presented before the universe a world in which even His all-seeing eye could find no spot or stain. Each part of the creation occupied the part assigned to it, and answered the purpose for which it was created. Peace and holy joy filled the earth. There was no confusion, no clashing. There was no disease to afflict man or beast, and the vegetable kingdom was without taint or corruption. God looked upon the work of His hands, wrought out by Christ, and pronounced it "very good." [135]

The Sabbath was hallowed at the creation. As ordained for man, it had its origin when "the morning stars sang together, and all the sons of God shouted for joy." Job 38:7. . . .

The Sabbath was not for Israel merely, but for the world. It had been made known to man in Eden, and, like the other precepts of the Decalogue, it is of imperishable obligation. Of that law of which the fourth commandment forms a part, Christ declares, "Till heaven and earth pass, one jot or one tittle shall in no wise pass from the law." Matt. 5:18. So long as the heavens and the earth endure, the Sabbath will continue as a sign of the Creator's power. And when Eden shall bloom on earth again, God's holy rest day will be honored by all beneath the sun. "From one sabbath to another" the inhabitants of the glorified new earth shall . . . "worship before me, saith the Lord." [136]

God teaches that we should assemble in His house to cultivate the attributes of perfect love. This will fit the dwellers of earth for the mansions that Christ has gone to prepare for all who love Him. There they will assemble in the sanctuary from Sabbath to Sabbath, from one new moon to another, to unite in loftiest strains of song, in praise and thanksgiving to Him who sits upon the throne, and to the Lamb forever and ever. [137]

THE THREE DIGNITARIES OF HEAVEN

The Wonderful Father   *February 1*

OUR LOVING HEAVENLY FATHER

To us there is but one God, the Father, of whom are all things, and we in him; and one Lord Jesus Christ, by whom are all things, and we by him. 1 Cor. 8:6.

God is our tender, pitiful Father, and every believing child is the object of His special care.[1]

He [Jesus] pointed . . . to the Ruler of the universe, under the new name, "Our Father."[2]

This name, spoken to Him and of Him, is a sign of our love and trust toward Him, and a pledge of His regard and relationship to us. Spoken when asking His favor or blessing, it is as music in His ears. . . .

He invites us to trust in Him with a trust deeper and stronger than that of a child in his earthly father. Parents love their children, but the love of God is larger, broader, deeper, than human love can possibly be. It is immeasurable.[3]

Such a conception of God was never given to the world by any religion but that of the Bible. Heathenism teaches men to look upon the Supreme Being as an object of fear rather than of love—a malign deity to be appeased by sacrifices, rather than a Father pouring upon His children the gift of His love. . . .

It is not earthly rank, nor birth, nor nationality, nor religious privilege, which proves that we are members of the family of God; it is love, a love that embraces all humanity. . . . To be kind to the unthankful and to the evil, to do good hoping for nothing again, is the insignia of the royalty of heaven, the sure token by which the children of the Highest reveal their high estate.[4]

HIS MAJESTY AND GREATNESS

Thine, O Lord, is the greatness, and the power, and the glory, and the victory, and the majesty: for all that is in the heaven and in the earth is thine; thine is the kingdom, O Lord, and thou art exalted as head above all. 1 Chron. 29:11.

God is our Father, who loves and cares for us as His children; He is also the great King of the universe.[5]

God cannot be compared with the things His hands have made. These are mere earthly things, suffering under the curse of God because of the sins of man. The Father cannot be described by the things of earth. The Father is all the fullness of the Godhead bodily, and is invisible to mortal sight.[6]

We must not attempt to lift with presumptuous hand the curtain behind which He veils His majesty. The apostle exclaims: "How unsearchable are his judgments, and his ways past finding out!" Rom. 11:33. It is a proof of His mercy that there is the hiding of His power, that He is enshrouded in the awful clouds of mystery and obscurity; for to lift the curtain that conceals the divine presence is death. No mortal mind can penetrate the secrecy in which the Mighty One dwells and works. We can comprehend no more of His dealings with us and the motives that actuate Him than He sees fit to reveal. He orders everything in righteousness, and we are not to be dissatisfied and distrustful, but to bow in reverent submission. He will reveal to us as much of His purposes as it is for our good to know; and beyond that we must trust the hand that is omnipotent, the heart that is full of love.[7]

Jehovah is the fountain of all wisdom, of all truth, of all knowledge. . . . Man can now only linger upon the borders of that vast expanse, and let imagination take its flight. Finite man cannot fathom the deep things of God.[8]

True reverence for God is inspired by a sense of His infinite greatness and a realization of His presence. With this sense of the Unseen, every heart should be deeply impressed.[9]

A PERSONAL GOD

God . . . hath in these last days spoken unto us by his Son who being the brightness of his glory, and the express image of his person, and upholding all things by the word of his power, when he had by himself purged our sins, sat down on the right hand of the Majesty on high. Heb. 1:1-3.

God is a Spirit; yet He is a personal being; for so He has revealed Himself.[10]

As a personal being, God has revealed Himself in His Son. The outshining of the Father's glory, "and the express image of his person," Jesus, as a personal Saviour, came to the world. As a personal Saviour He ascended on high. As a personal Saviour He intercedes in the heavenly courts.[11]

I saw a throne, and on it sat the Father and the Son. I gazed on Jesus' countenance and admired His lovely person. The Father's person I could not behold, for a cloud of glorious light covered Him. I asked Jesus if His Father had a form like Himself. He said He had, but I could not behold it, for said He, "If you should once behold the glory of His person, you would cease to exist."[12]

The theory that God is an essence pervading all nature is received by many who profess to believe the Scriptures; but, however beautifully clothed, this theory is a most dangerous deception. . . . If God is an essence pervading all nature, then He dwells in all men; and in order to attain holiness, man has only to develop the power within him. These theories [pantheism, etc.], followed to their logical conclusion, . . . do away with the necessity for the atonement and make man his own savior. . . . Those who accept them are in great danger of being led finally to look upon the whole Bible as a fiction. . . .

The revelation of Himself that God has given in His Word is for our study. This we may seek to understand. But beyond this we are not to penetrate. . . . None are to indulge in speculation regarding His nature. Here silence is eloquence. The Omniscient One is above discussion.[13]

HOLY AND REVEREND IS HIS NAME

He sent redemption unto his people: he hath commanded his covenant for ever: holy and reverend is his name. Ps. 111:9.

We are never in any manner to treat lightly the titles or appellations of the Deity. . . . The angels veil their faces in His presence. The cherubim and the bright and holy seraphim approach His throne with solemn reverence. How much more should we finite, sinful beings, come in a reverent manner before the Lord, our Maker![14]

I saw that God's holy name should be used with reverence and awe.[15]

Some think it a mark of humility to pray to God in a common manner. . . . They profane His name by needlessly and irreverently mingling with their prayers the words, "God Almighty"—awful, sacred words, which should never pass the lips except in subdued tones and with a feeling of awe.[16]

Those who realize the greatness and majesty of God, will take His name on their lips with holy awe. He dwelleth in light unapproachable; no man can see Him and live.[17]

If Christ were on earth today, surrounded by those who bear the title of "Reverend" or "Right Reverend," would He not repeat His saying, "Neither be ye called masters: for one is your Master, even Christ"? Matt. 23:10. The Scripture declares of God, "Holy and reverend is his name." To what human being is such a title befitting? How little does man reveal of the wisdom and righteousness it indicates! How many of those who assume this title are misrepresenting the name and character of God! Alas, how often have worldly ambition, despotism, and the basest sins been hidden under the broidered garments of a high and holy office![18]

"The name of the Lord" is "merciful and gracious, longsuffering, and abundant in goodness and truth, . . . forgiving iniquity and transgression and sin." Ex. 34:5-7. Of the church of Christ it is written "This is the name wherewith she shall be called, The Lord our righteousness." Jer. 33:16. This name is put upon every follower of Christ.[19]

FAITHFUL AND TRUE

For I am the Lord, I change not; therefore ye sons of Jacob are not consumed. Mal. 3:6.

In regard to the personality and prerogatives of God, where He is, and what He is, this is a subject which we are not to dare to touch. . . . The one who in the daily life holds closest communion with God, and who has the deepest knowledge of Him, realizes most keenly the utter inability of human beings to explain the Creator. . . .

God always has been. He is the great I AM. The psalmist declares, "Before the mountains were brought forth, or ever thou hadst formed the earth and the world, even from everlasting to everlasting thou art God." Ps. 90:2. He is the high and lofty One that inhabiteth eternity. "I am the Lord, I change not," He declares. With Him there is no variableness, neither shadow of turning. He is "the same yesterday, and to day and for ever." Heb. 13:8. He is infinite and omnipresent. No words of ours can describe His greatness and majesty.[20]

Above the distractions of the earth He sits enthroned; all things are open to His divine survey; and from His great and calm eternity He orders that which His providence sees best.[21]

God does not propose to be called to account for His ways and works. It is for His glory to conceal His purposes now; but by and by they will be revealed in their true importance. But He has not concealed His great love, which lies at the foundation of all His dealings with His children.[22]

The rainbow about the throne is an assurance that God is true. . . . We have sinned against Him and are undeserving of His favor; yet He Himself has put into our lips that most wonderful of pleas: "Do not abhor us, for thy name's sake, do not disgrace the throne of thy glory: remember, break not thy covenant with us." Jer. 14:21. He has pledged Himself to give heed to our cry when we come to Him confessing our unworthiness and sin. The honor of His throne is staked for the fulfillment of His Word to us.[23]

HIS WONDERFUL LOVE EXPRESSED

Behold, what manner of love the Father hath bestowed upon as, that we should be called the sons of God: therefore the world knoweth us not, because it knew him not. 1 John 3:1.

Love is the principle that underlies God's government in heaven and on earth, and this love must be interwoven in the life of the Christian. . . . The heart that is influenced by this holy principle will be carried above everything of a selfish nature.[24]

When we seek for appropriate language in which to describe the love of God, we find words too tame, too weak, too far beneath the theme, and we lay down our pen and say, "No, it cannot be described." We can only do as did the beloved disciple, and say, "Behold, what manner of love the Father hath bestowed upon us, that we should be called the sons of God." 1 John 3:1. In attempting any description of this love, we feel that we are as infants lisping their first words. Silently we may adore; for silence in this matter is the only eloquence. This love is past all language to describe.[25]

All the paternal love which has come down from generation to generation through the channel of human hearts, all the springs of tenderness which have opened in the souls of men, are but as a tiny rill to the boundless ocean when compared with the infinite, exhaustless love of God. Tongue cannot utter it; pen cannot portray it. You may meditate upon it every day of your life; you may search the Scriptures diligently in order to understand it; you may summon every power and capability that God has given you, in the endeavor to comprehend the love and compassion of the heavenly Father; and yet there is an infinity beyond. You may study that love for ages; yet you can never fully comprehend the length and the breadth, the depth and the height, of the love of God in giving His Son to die for the world. Eternity itself can never fully reveal it. Yet as we study the Bible and meditate upon the life of Christ and the plan of redemption, these great themes will open to our understanding more and more.[26]

PERFECT IN ALL HIS WAYS

Be ye therefore perfect, even as your Father which is in heaven is perfect. Matt. 5:48.

God's work is perfect as a whole because it is perfect in every part, however minute. He fashions the tiny spear of grass with as much care as He would exercise in making a world. If we desire to be perfect, even as our Father in heaven is perfect, we must be faithful in doing little things. That which is worth doing at all is worth doing well.[27]

God's ideal for His children is higher than the highest human thought can reach. . . . The plan of redemption contemplates our complete recovery from the power of Satan. Christ always separates the contrite soul from sin. He came to destroy the works of the devil, and He has made provision that the Holy Spirit shall be imparted to every repentant soul, to keep him from sinning.

The tempter's agency is not to be accounted an excuse for one wrong act. Satan is jubilant when he hears the professed followers of Christ making excuses for their deformity of character. It is these excuses that lead to sin. There is no excuse for sinning. A holy temper, a Christlike life, is accessible to every repenting, believing child of God.

The ideal of Christian character is Christlikeness. As the Son of man was perfect in His life, so His followers are to be perfect in their life. . . . He bids us by faith in Him attain to the glory of the character of God.[28]

A well-balanced character is formed by single acts well performed. One defect, cultivated instead of being overcome, makes the man imperfect, and closes against him the gate of the Holy City. . . . In all the redeemed host not one defect will be seen. . . .

Whatever your work may be, do it faithfully. . . . As you work in this way, God will place His approval on you, and Christ will one day say to you. "Well done, thou good and faithful servant." Matt. 25:21.[29]

GOD'S GIFT TO THE HUMAN RACE

For God so loved the world, that he gave his only begotten Son, that whosoever believeth in him should not perish, but have everlasting life. John 3:16.

The heart of God yearns over His earthly children with a love stronger than death. In giving up His Son, He has poured out to us all heaven in one gift.[30]

Through that gift there comes to us day by day the unfailing flow of Jehovah's goodness. Every flower, with its delicate tints and sweet fragrance, is given for our enjoyment through that one Gift. The sun and moon were made by Him; there is not a star that beautifies the heavens which He did not make. There is not an article of food upon our tables that He has not provided for our sustenance. The superscription of Christ is upon it all. Everything is supplied to man through the one unspeakable Gift, the only-begotten Son of God. He was nailed to the cross that all these bounties might flow to God's workmanship.[31]

In taking our nature, the Saviour has bound Himself to humanity by a tie that is never to be broken. Through the eternal ages He is linked with us. "God so loved the world, that he gave his only begotten Son." He gave Him not only to bear our sins, and to die as our sacrifice; He gave Him to the fallen race. To assure us of His immutable counsel of peace, God gave His only-begotten Son to become one of the human family, forever to retain His human nature. This is the pledge that God will fulfill His word. "Unto *us* a child is born, unto *us* a son is given: and the government shall be upon his shoulder." Isa. 9:6. God has adopted human nature in the person of His Son, and has carried the same into the highest heaven. . . . Heaven is enshrined in humanity, and humanity is enfolded in the bosom of Infinite Love.[32]

Christ bowed down in unparalleled humility, that in His exaltation to the throne of God, He might also exalt those who believe in Him, to a seat with Him upon His throne.[33]

HIS ETERNAL PREEXISTENCE

And now, O Father, glorify thou me with thine own self with the glory which I had with thee before the world was. John 17:5.

Christ was one with the Father before the foundation of the world was laid. This is the light shining in a dark place, making it resplendent with divine, original glory.[34]

Christ is the pre-existent, self-existent Son of God. . . . In speaking of His pre-existence, Christ carries the mind back through dateless ages. He assures us that there never was a time when He was not in close fellowship with the eternal God. . . .

His divine life could not be reckoned by human computation. The existence of Christ before His incarnation is not measured by figures.[35]

Christ was God essentially, and in the highest sense. He was with God from all eternity, God over all, blessed forevermore. The Lord Jesus Christ, the divine Son of God, existed from eternity, a distinct person, yet one with the Father. He was the surpassing glory of heaven. He was the commander of the heavenly intelligences, and the adoring homage of the angels was received by Him as His right.[36]

He was equal with God, infinite and omnipotent.[37]

But He humbled Himself, and took mortality upon Him. As a member of the human family, He was mortal; but as a God, He was the fountain of life to the world. He could, in His divine person, ever have withstood the advances of death, and refused to come under its dominion; but He voluntarily laid down His life, that in so doing He might give life and bring immortality to light. He bore the sins of the world, and endured the penalty, which rolled like a mountain upon His divine soul. He yielded up His life a sacrifice, that man should not eternally die. He died, not through being compelled to die, but by His own free will.[38]

And this wonderful mystery, the incarnation of Christ and the atonement that He made, must be declared to every son and daughter of Adam.[39]

THE GREAT "I AM"

And God said unto Moses, I AM THAT I AM: and he said, Thus shalt thou say unto the children of Israel, I AM hath sent me unto you. Ex. 3:14.

In Christ is life, original, unborrowed, underived. "He that hath the Son hath life." 1 John 5:12. The divinity of Christ is the believer's assurance of eternal life.[40]

All the communion between heaven and the fallen race has been through Christ. It was the Son of God that gave to our first parents the promise of redemption. It was He who revealed Himself to the patriarchs. Adam . . . understood the gospel. . . .

Jesus was the light of His people—the light of the world—before He came to earth in the form of humanity. The first gleam of light that pierced the gloom in which sin had wrapped the world, came from Christ. And from Him has come every ray of heaven's brightness that has fallen upon the inhabitants of the earth. In the plan of redemption, Christ is the Alpha and the Omega—the First and the Last.[41]

It was Christ who from the bush on Mount Horeb spoke to Moses saying, "I AM THAT I AM: . . . Thus shalt thou say unto the children of Israel, I AM hath sent me unto you." This was the pledge of Israel's deliverance. So when He came "in the likeness of men," He declared Himself the I AM. The Child of Bethlehem, the meek and lowly Saviour, is God "manifest in the flesh." 1 Tim. 3:16.[42]

This unconscious babe was the promised seed, to whom the first altar at the gate of Eden pointed. This was Shiloh, the peace giver. . . . This was He whom seers had long foretold. He was the Desire of all nations, the Root and the Offspring of David, and the Bright and Morning Star.[43]

And to us He says: "I AM the good shepherd. . . . I AM the living bread." "I AM the way, the truth, and the life.". . . I AM the assurance of every promise. I AM; be not afraid. "God with us" is the surety of our deliverance from sin.[44]

THE CREATOR INCARNATE

And without controversy great is the mystery of godliness: God was manifest in the flesh, justified in the Spirit, seen of angels, preached unto the Gentiles, believed on in the world, received up into glory. 1 Tim. 3:16.

The incarnation of Christ is the mystery of all mysteries.[45]

Christ was one with the Father, yet . . . He was willing to step down from the exaltation of one who was equal with God.[46]

That He might accomplish His purpose of love for the fallen race, He became bone of our bone and flesh of our flesh.[47]

How wide is the contrast between the divinity of Christ and the helpless infant in Bethlehem's manger! How can we span the distance between the mighty God and a helpless child? And yet the Creator of worlds, He in whom was the fullness of the Godhead bodily, was manifest in the helpless babe in the manger. Far higher than any of the angels, equal with the Father in dignity and glory, and yet wearing the garb of humanity! Divinity and humanity were mysteriously combined, and man and God became one.[48]

It would have been an almost infinite humiliation for the Son of God to take man's nature, even when Adam stood in his innocence in Eden. But Jesus accepted humanity when the race had been weakened by four thousand years of sin. Like every child of Adam He accepted the results of the working of the great law of heredity. What these results were is shown in the history of His earthly ancestors. He came with such a heredity to share our sorrows and temptations, and to give us the example of a sinless life.[49]

Those who claim that it was not possible for Christ to sin, cannot believe that He really took upon Himself human nature. But was not Christ actually tempted, not only by Satan in the wilderness, but all through His life, from childhood to manhood?[50]

Our Saviour took humanity, with all its liabilities. He took the nature of man, with the possibility of yielding to temptation. We have nothing to bear which He has not endured.[51]

HIS BLAMELESS LIFE

Hereafter I will not talk much with you: for the prince of this world cometh, and hath nothing in me. John 14:30.

We should have no misgivings in regard to the perfect sinlessness of the human nature of Christ.[52]

He is a brother in our infirmities, but not in possessing like passions. As the sinless One, His nature recoiled from evil. He endured struggles and torture of soul in a world of sin. His humanity made prayer a necessity and privilege.[53]

He could have sinned; He could have fallen, but not for one moment was there in Him an evil propensity.[54]

In taking upon Himself man's nature in its fallen condition, Christ did not in the least participate in its sin. He was subject to the infirmities and weaknesses by which man is encompassed. . . . He was touched with the feeling of our infirmities, and was in all points tempted like as we are. And yet He "knew no sin." He was the lamb "without blemish and without spot." Could Satan in the least particular have tempted Christ to sin, he would have bruised the Saviour's head. As it was, he could only touch His heel. Had the head of Christ been touched, the hope of the human race would have perished. Divine wrath would have come upon Christ as it came upon Adam. Christ and the church would have been without hope.[55]

Not even by a thought could Christ be brought to yield to the power of temptation. . . . Christ declared of Himself, "The prince of this world cometh, and hath nothing in me."[56]

Jesus did not allow the enemy to pull Him into the mire of unbelief, or crowd Him into the mire of despondency and despair.[57]

Christ's humanity was united with divinity, and in this strength He would bear all the temptations that Satan could bring against Him, and yet keep His soul untainted by sin. And this power to overcome He would give to every son and daughter of Adam who would accept by faith the righteous attributes of His character.[58]

HE DIED FOR US

But God commendeth his love toward us, in that, while we were yet sinners, Christ died for us. Rom. 5:8.

There is one great central truth to be kept ever before the mind in the searching of the Scriptures—Christ and Him crucified. Every other truth is invested with influence and power corresponding to its relation to this theme. . . . The soul palsied by sin can be endowed with life only through the work wrought out upon the cross by the Author of our salvation.[59]

When Christ bowed His head and died, He bore the pillars of Satan's kingdom with Him to the earth. He vanquished Satan.[60]

Christ submitted to crucifixion, although the heavenly host could have delivered Him. The angels suffered with Christ. God Himself was crucified with Christ; for Christ was one with the Father. Those who reject Christ, those who will not have this man to rule over them, choose to place themselves under the rule of Satan, to do his work as his bondslaves. Yet for them Christ yielded up His life on Calvary.[61]

He who died for the sins of the world was to remain in the tomb the allotted time. He was in that stony prison house as a prisoner of divine justice. He was responsible to the judge of the universe. He was bearing the sins of the world, and His Father only could release Him.[62]

He identified Himself with our interests, bared His breast for the stroke of death, took man's guilt and its penalty, and offered in man's behalf a complete sacrifice to God. By virtue of this atonement, He has power to offer to man perfect righteousness and full salvation. Whosoever shall believe on Him as a personal Saviour shall not perish, but have everlasting life.[63]

The price of man's redemption has been paid, and all he has and is should be sprinkled with the blood of Christ, dedicated to God; for it belongs to Him.[64]

JESUS' RESURRECTION AND THE NEW LIFE

The thief cometh not, but for to steal, and to kill, and to destroy: I am come that they might have life, and that they might have it more abundantly. John 10:10.

The resurrection of Jesus was a type of the final resurrection of all who sleep in Him.[65]

He who had said, "I lay down my life, that I might take it again," came forth from the grave to life that was in Himself. Humanity died: divinity did not die. In His divinity, Christ possessed the power to break the bonds of death. He declares that He has life in Himself to quicken whom He will. . . .

He is the spring, the fountain, of life. Only He who alone hath immortality, dwelling in light and life, could say, "I have power to lay down my life, and I have power to take it again." . . .

Christ was invested with the right to give immortality. The life which He had laid down in humanity, He again took up and gave to humanity. "I am come," He says, "that they might have life, and that they might have it more abundantly."[66]

Christ is life itself. He who passed through death to destroy him that had the power of death is the Source of all vitality. There is balm in Gilead, and a Physician there. Christ endured an agonizing death under the most humiliating circumstances that we might have life. He gave up His precious life that He might vanquish death. But He rose from the tomb, and the myriads of angels who came to behold Him take up the life He had laid down heard His words of triumphant joy as He stood above Joseph's rent sepulcher proclaiming: "I am the resurrection, and the life."[67]

The resurrection and ascension of our Lord is a sure evidence of the triumph of the saints of God over death and the grave, and a pledge that heaven is open to those who wash their robes of character and make them white in the blood of the Lamb. Jesus ascended to the Father as a representative of the human race, and God will bring those who reflect His image to behold and share with Him His glory.[68]

THIRD PERSON OF THE GODHEAD

The grace of the Lord Jesus Christ, and the love of God, and the communion of the Holy Ghost, be with you all. Amen. 2 Cor. 13:14.

We need to realize that the Holy Spirit . . . is as much a person as God is a person. . . .

The Holy Spirit has a personality, else He could not bear our spirits and with our spirits that we are the children of God. He must also be a divine person, else He could not search out the secrets which lie hidden in the mind of God.[69]

The Holy Spirit is a free, working, independent agency. The God of heaven uses His Spirit as it pleases Him; and human minds, human judgment, and human methods can no more set boundaries to its working, or prescribe the channel through which it shall operate, than they can say to the wind, "I bid you to blow in a certain direction, and to conduct yourself in such and such a manner."[70]

From the beginning God has been working by His Holy Spirit through human instrumentalities for the accomplishment of His purpose in behalf of the fallen race. . . . The same power that sustained the patriarchs, that gave Caleb and Joshua faith and courage, and that made the work of the apostolic church effective, has upheld God's faithful children in every succeeding age.[71]

The Holy Spirit was the highest of all gifts that He [Jesus] could solicit from His Father for the exaltation of His people. The Spirit was to be given as a regenerating agent, and without this the sacrifice of Christ would have been of no avail. The power of evil had been strengthening for centuries, and the submission of men to this satanic captivity was amazing. Sin could be resisted and overcome only through the mighty agency of the third person of the Godhead, who would come with no modified energy, but in the fullness of divine power.[72]

The Holy Spirit is an effective helper in restoring the image of God in the human soul.[73]

THE GIFT OF GOD TO YOU

Then Peter said unto them, Repent, and be baptized every one of you in the name of Jesus Christ for the remission of sins, and ye shall receive the gift of the Holy Ghost. Acts 2:38.

Christ has promised the gift of the Holy Spirit to His church, and the promise belongs to us as much as to the first disciples.[74]

We should pray as earnestly for the descent of the Holy Spirit as the disciples prayed on the day of Pentecost. If they needed it at that time, we need it more today.[75]

The measure of the Holy Spirit we receive will be proportioned to the measure of our desire and the faith exercised for it, and the use we shall make of the light and knowledge that shall be given to us.[76]

There are many who believe and profess to claim the Lord's promise; they talk *about* Christ and *about* the Holy Spirit, yet receive no benefit. They do not surrender the soul to be guided and con trolled by the divine agencies. We cannot use the Holy Spirit. The Spirit is to use us. Through the Spirit God works in His people "to will and to do of his good pleasure." Phil. 2:13. But many will not submit to this. They want to manage themselves. This is why they do not receive the heavenly gift. Only to those who wait humbly upon God, who watch for His guidance and grace, is the Spirit given. The power of God awaits their demand and reception. This promised blessing, claimed by faith, brings all other blessings in its train. It is given according to the riches of the grace of Christ, and He is ready to supply every soul according to the capacity to receive.[77]

When the Holy Spirit is abiding in the heart, it will lead the human agent to see his own defects of character, to pity the weakness of others, to forgive as he wishes to be forgiven. He will be pitiful, courteous, Christlike.[78]

The Holy Spirit imparts love, joy, peace, strength, and consolation; it is as a well of water springing up unto everlasting life. The blessing is free to all.[79]

A MYSTERIOUS AND TENDER PRESENCE

The wind bloweth where it listeth, and thou hearest the sound thereof, but canst not tell whence it cometh, and whither it goeth: so is every one that is born of the Spirit. John 3:8.

The greatness of God is to us incomprehensible. "The Lord's throne is in heaven" (Ps. 11:4); yet by His Spirit He is everywhere present. He has an intimate knowledge of, and a personal interest in, all the works of His hand. . . .

It was the Maker of all things . . . who created the human soul, with its capacity for knowing and for loving. And He is not in Himself such as to leave the demands of the soul unsatisfied. No intangible principle, no impersonal essence or mere abstraction, can satisfy the needs and longings of human beings in this life of struggle with sin and sorrow and pain. It is not enough to believe in law and force, in things that have no pity, and never hear the cry for help. We need to know of an almighty arm that will hold us up, of an infinite Friend that pities us. We need to clasp a hand that is warm, to trust in a heart full of tenderness. And even so God has in His Word revealed Himself.[80]

Spiritual things are spiritually discerned. The carnal mind cannot comprehend these mysteries. . . . The worldly-wise have attempted to explain upon scientific principles the influence of the Spirit of God upon the heart. The least advance in this direction will lead the soul into the mazes of skepticism. The religion of the Bible is simply the mystery of godliness; no human mind can fully understand it, and it is utterly incomprehensible to the unregenerate heart.[81]

The nature of the Holy Spirit is a mystery. Men cannot explain it, because the Lord has not revealed it to them. Men having fanciful views may bring together passages of Scripture and put a human construction on them; but the acceptance of these views will not strengthen the church. Regarding such mysteries, which are too deep for human understanding, silence is golden.[82]

AGENT IN REDEMPTION

And hope maketh not ashamed; because the love of God is shed abroad in our hearts by the Holy Ghost which is given unto us. Rom. 5:5.

By nature the heart is evil, and "who can bring a clean thing out of an unclean? not one." Job 14:4. No human invention can find a remedy for the sinning soul. . . . The fountain of the heart must be purified before the streams can become pure. He who is trying to reach heaven by his own works in keeping the law is attempting an impossibility. There is no safety for one who has merely a legal religion, a form of godliness. The Christian's life is not a modification or improvement of the old, but a transformation of nature. There is a death to self and sin, and a new life altogether. This change can be brought about only by the effectual working of the Holy Spirit.[83]

It is the Spirit that makes effectual what has been wrought out by the world's Redeemer. It is by the Spirit that the heart is made pure. Through the Spirit the believer becomes a partaker of the divine nature. Christ has given His Spirit as a divine power to overcome all hereditary and cultivated tendencies to evil, and to impress His own character upon His church.[84]

Like the wind, which is invisible, yet the effects of which are plainly seen and felt, is the Spirit of God in its work upon the human heart. That regenerating power, which no human eye can see, begets a new life in the soul; it creates a new being in the image of God.[85]

The thoughtless and wayward become serious. The hardened repent of their sins, and the faithless believe. The gambler, the drunkard, the licentious, become steady, sober, and pure. The rebellious and obstinate become meek and Christlike. When we see these changes in the character, we may be assured that the converting power of God has transformed the entire man.[86]

He who looks to Christ in simple, childlike faith is made a partaker of the divine nature through the agency of the Holy Spirit.[87]

COMFORTER AND TEACHER

But the Comforter, which is the Holy Ghost, whom the Father will send in my name, he shall teach you all things, and bring all things to your remembrance, whatsoever I have said unto you. John 14:26.

The Holy Spirit is Christ's representative, but divested of the personality of humanity, and independent thereof. Cumbered with humanity, Christ could not be in every place personally. Therefore it was for their [the disciples'] interest that He should go to the Father, and send the Spirit to be His successor on earth. No one could then have any advantage because of his location or his personal contact with Christ. By the Spirit the Saviour would be accessible to all. . . .

At all times and in all places, in all sorrows and in all afflictions, when the outlook seems dark and the future perplexing, and we feel helpless and alone, the Comforter will be sent in answer to the prayer of faith. Circumstances may separate us from every earthly friend; but no circumstance, no distance, can separate us from the heavenly Comforter. Wherever we are, wherever we may go, He is always at our right hand to support, sustain, uphold, and cheer. . . .

The Comforter is called "the Spirit of truth." His work is to define and maintain the truth. He first dwells in the heart as the Spirit of truth, and thus He becomes the Comforter. There is comfort and peace in the truth, but no real peace or comfort can be found in falsehood. . . . Through the Scriptures the Holy Spirit speaks to the mind, and impresses truth upon the heart.[88]

Those who are under the influence of the Spirit of God will not be fanatical but calm and steadfast, free from extravagance in thought, word, or deed. Amid the confusion of delusive doctrines, the Spirit of God will be a guide and a shield to those who have not resisted the evidences of truth.[89]

Every man, woman, and child that is not under the control of the Spirit of God is under the influence of Satan's sorcery, and by his words and example he will lead others away from the path of truth.[90]

THE INDWELLING SPIRIT

And he that keepeth his commandments dwelleth in him, and he in him. And hereby we know that he abideth in us, by the Spirit which he hath given us. 1 John 3:24.

The Holy Spirit is the breath of spiritual life in the soul. The impartation of the Spirit is the impartation of the life of Christ. It imbues the receiver with the attributes of Christ.[91]

The Holy Spirit will enter the heart that can boast of nothing. The love of Jesus will fill the vacuum that is made by the emptying out of self.[92]

Those who see Christ in His true character, and receive Him into the heart, have everlasting life. It is through the Spirit that Christ dwells in us; and the Spirit of God, received into the heart by faith, is the beginning of the life eternal.[93]

We do not see Christ and speak to Him, but His Holy Spirit is just as near us in one place as in another. It works in and through every one who receives Christ. Those who know the indwelling of the Spirit reveal the fruits of the Spirit—love, joy, peace, long-suffering, gentleness, goodness, faith.[94]

The Holy Spirit is to be continually present with the believer. We have need more carefully to consider the fact that the Comforter is to abide with us. If we individually comprehended this truth, we should never feel alone. When assailed by the enemy, when overwhelmed by temptation, we are to repose our faith in God; for we have His pledged word that we are never to be left to battle alone. Every soul, pardoned of sin, is precious in His sight—more precious than the whole world. It has been purchased at infinite cost, and Christ will never abandon the soul for whom He has died.[95]

Christ is represented by the Holy Spirit; and when this Spirit is appreciated, when those controlled by the Spirit communicate to others the energy with which they are imbued, an invisible chord is touched which electrifies the whole. Would that we could all understand how boundless are the divine resources.[96]

GRIEVE NOT THE SPIRIT

And grieve not the holy Spirit of God, whereby ye are sealed unto the day of redemption. Eph. 4:30.

Conscience is the voice of God, heard amid the conflict of human passions; when it is resisted, the Spirit of God is grieved.[97]

Men have the power to quench the Spirit of God; the power of choosing is left with them. They are allowed freedom of action. They may be obedient through the name and grace of our Redeemer, or they may be disobedient, and realize the consequences.[98]

The sin of blasphemy against the Holy Spirit does not lie in any sudden word or deed; it is the firm, determined resistance of truth and evidence.[99]

It is not that God sends out a decree that man shall not be saved. He does not throw a darkness before the eyes which cannot be penetrated. But man at first resists a motion of the Spirit of God, and, having once resisted, it is less difficult to do so the second time, less the third, and far less the fourth. Then comes the harvest to be reaped from the seed of unbelief and resistance. Oh what a harvest of sinful indulgences is preparing for the sickle! . . .

On the other hand, every ray of light cherished will yield a harvest of light. Temptation once resisted will give power to more firmly resist the second time; every new victory gained over self will smooth the way for higher and nobler triumphs. Every victory is a seed sown to eternal life.[100]

God destroys no one. The sinner destroys himself by his own impenitence.[101]

No one need look upon the sin against the Holy Ghost as something mysterious and indefinable. The sin against the Holy Ghost is the sin of persistent refusal to respond to the invitation to repent.[102]

There is no . . . hope of the higher life, but through the submission of the soul to Christ.[103]

GOD IS LOVE

He that loveth not knoweth not God, for God is love. 1 John 4:8.

"God is love." His nature, His law, is love. It ever has been; it ever will be. . . .

Every manifestation of creative power is an expression of infinite love.[104]

It is through His power that summer and winter, seedtime and harvest, day and night, follow each other in their regular succession. It is by His word that vegetation flourishes, that leaves appear, and the flowers bloom. Every good thing we have, each ray of sunshine and shower of rain, every morsel of food, every moment of life, is a gift of love.[105]

The history of the great conflict between good and evil, from the time it first began in heaven to the final overthrow of rebellion and the total eradication of sin, is also a demonstration of God's unchanging love.[106]

The gift of Christ reveals the Father's heart.[107]

God made to our world the wonderful gift of His only-begotten Son. In the light of this act, it could never be said by the inhabitants of other worlds that God could have done more than He did to show His love for the children of men. He made a sacrifice that defies all computation.[108]

Thousands have a false conception of God and His attributes. They are as verily serving a false god as were the servants of Baal. Are we worshiping the true God as He is revealed in His Word, in Christ, in nature, or are we adoring some philosophical idol enshrined in His place? God is a God of truth. Justice and mercy are the attributes of His throne. He is a God of love, of pity and tender compassion. Thus He is represented in His Son, our Saviour. He is a God of patience and long-suffering. If such is the being whom we adore and to whose character we are seeking to assimilate, we are worshiping the true God.[109]

NO RESPECTER OF PERSONS

Then Peter opened his mouth, and said, Of a truth I perceive that God is no respecter of persons: but in every nation he that feareth him, and worketh righteousness, is accepted with him. Acts 10:34, 35.

God is no respecter of persons. . . . Those who have the light and do not follow it, but disregard the requirements of God, will find that their blessings will be changed into curses and their mercies into judgments.[110]

God does not regard all sins as of equal magnitude; there are degrees of guilt in His estimation, as well as in that of man; but however trifling this or that wrong act may seem in the eyes of men, no sin is small in the sight of God. Man's judgment is partial, imperfect; but God estimates all things as they really are. The drunkard is despised, and is told that his sin will exclude him from heaven; while pride, selfishness, and covetousness too often go unrebuked. But these are sins that are especially offensive to God; for they are contrary to the benevolence of His character, to that unselfish love which is the very atmosphere of the unfallen universe.[111]

The exceeding sinfulness of sin can be estimated only in the light of the cross. When men urge that God is too good to cast off the sinner, let them look to Calvary. It was because there was no other way in which man could be saved, because without this sacrifice it was impossible for the human race to escape from the defiling power of sin, and be restored to communion with holy beings—impossible for them again to become partakers of spiritual life—it was because of this that Christ took upon Himself the guilt of the disobedient, and suffered in the sinner's stead. The love and suffering and death of the Son of God all testify to the terrible enormity of sin, and declare that there is no escape from its power, no hope of the higher life, but through the submission of the soul to Christ.[112]

Let the soul be uplifted from the lowlands of sin to contemplate the God of all goodness, mercy, and love, but who will in no wise clear the guilty.[113]

INFINITELY WISE AND GOOD

The Lord is good, a strong hold in the day of trouble; and he knoweth them that trust in him. Nahum 1:7.

God is the source of all wisdom. He is infinitely wise and just and good. Apart from Christ, the wisest men that ever lived cannot comprehend Him. . . . If men could see for a moment beyond the range of finite vision, if they could catch a glimpse of the Eternal, every mouth would be stopped in its boasting. Men living in this little atom of a world are finite; God has unnumbered worlds that are obedient to His laws, and are conducted with reference to His glory.[114]

Nothing can happen in any part of the universe without the knowledge of Him who is omnipresent. Not a single event of human life is unknown to our Maker. While Satan is constantly devising evil, the Lord our God overrules all, so that it will not harm His obedient, trusting children. The same power that controls the boisterous waves of the ocean can hold in check all the power of rebellion and of crime. God says to one as to the other, "Thus far shalt thou go, and no farther."

What lessons of humility and faith may we not learn as we trace the dealings of God with His creatures. The Lord can do but little for the children of men, because they are so full of pride and vain glory. They exalt self, magnifying their own strength, learning, and wisdom. It is necessary for God to disappoint their hopes and frustrate their plans, that they may learn to trust in Him alone. All our powers are from God; we can do nothing independent of the strength which He has given us. Where is the man or woman or child that God does not sustain? Where is the desolate place which God does not fill? Where is the want that any but God can supply?[115]

We are as ignorant of God as little children, but as little children we may love and obey Him. Instead of speculating in regard to His nature or His prerogatives, let us give heed to the word He has spoken: "Be still, and know that I am God." Ps. 46:10.[116]

THE DIVINE PRESENCE WITH US ALWAYS

Whither shall I go from thy Spirit? or whither shall I flee from thy presence? If I ascend up into heaven, thou art there: if I make my bed in hell, behold, thou art there. Ps. 139:7, 8.

The psalmist represents the presence of the Infinite One as pervading the universe. "If I ascend up into heaven, thou art there: if I make my bed in hell, behold, thou art there." We can never find a solitude where God is not.[117]

The Lord God omnipotent, who reigneth in the heavens, declares, "I am with you." He assures His people that those who are obedient are in a position where He can bless them, to the glory of His name. . . . He will be a present help to all who serve Him in preference to serving self.[118]

Although God dwells not in temples made with hands, yet He honors with His presence the assemblies of His people. He has promised that when they come together to seek Him, to acknowledge their sins, and to pray for one another, He will meet with them by His Spirit.[119]

When Christ ascended to heaven, the sense of His presence was still with His followers. It was a personal presence, full of love and light. . . .

Henceforth through the Spirit, Christ was to abide continually in the hearts of the children. Their union with Him was closer than when He was personally with them. The light, and love, and power of the indwelling Christ shone out through them, so that men, beholding, "marvelled; and they took knowledge of them, that they had been with Jesus." Acts 4:13. All that Christ was to the disciples, He desires to be to His children today.[120]

We may be strong in the Lord and in the power of His might. Receiving Christ, we are clothed with power. An indwelling Saviour makes His power our property. . . . Christ's presence in the heart is a vitalizing power, strengthening the entire being.[121]

Never feel that Christ is far away. He is always near. His loving presence surrounds you.[122]

HIS GENTLE, LOVING CARE

Casting all your care upon him, for he careth for you. 1 Peter 5:7.

The Lord's care is over all His creatures. He loves them all and makes no difference, except that He has the most tender pity for those who are called to bear life's heaviest burdens. God's children must meet trials and difficulties. But they should accept their lot with a cheerful spirit, remembering that for all that the world neglects to bestow, God Himself will make up to them in the best of favors.

It is when we come into difficult places that He reveals His power and wisdom in answer to humble prayer. Have confidence in Him as a prayer-hearing, prayer-answering God. He will reveal Himself to you as One who can help in every emergency. He who created man, who gave him his wonderful physical, mental, and spiritual faculties, will not withhold that which is necessary to sustain the life He has given. He who has given us His Word—the leaves of the tree of life—will not withhold from us a knowledge of how to provide food for His needy children.[123]

Some are always anticipating evil, or magnifying the difficulties that really exist, so that their eyes are blinded to the many blessings which demand their gratitude. The obstacles they encounter, instead of leading them to seek help from God, the only source of strength, separate them from Him, because they awaken unrest and repining.

Do we well to be thus unbelieving? Why should we be ungrateful and distrustful? Jesus is our friend; all heaven is interested in our welfare; and our anxiety and fear grieve the Holy Spirit of God. We should not indulge in a solicitude that only frets and wears us, but does not help us to bear trials. . . . He invites the weary and care-laden, "Come unto me, all ye that labour and are heavy laden, and I will give you rest." Lay off the yoke of anxiety and worldly care that you have placed on your own neck, and "take my yoke upon you, and learn of me; for I am meek and lowly in heart: and ye shall find rest unto your souls." Matt. 11:28, 29. We may find rest and peace in God.[124]

THE SAVING PROVIDENCES OF GOD

And we know that all things work together for good to them that love God, to them who are the called according to his purpose. Rom. 8:28.

The fact that we are called upon to endure trial shows that the Lord Jesus sees in us something precious which He desires to develop. If He saw in us nothing whereby He might glorify His name, He would not spend time in refining us. He does not cast worthless stones into His furnace. It is valuable ore that He refines.[125]

God never leads His children otherwise than they would choose to be led, if they could see the end from the beginning and discern the glory of the purpose which they are fulfilling as co-workers with Him.[126]

All that has perplexed us in the providences of God will in the world to come be made plain. The things hard to be understood will then find explanation. The mysteries of grace will unfold before us. Where our finite minds discovered only confusion and broken promises, we shall see the most perfect and beautiful harmony. We shall know that infinite love ordered the experiences that seemed most trying.[127]

He who is imbued with the Spirit of Christ abides in Christ. The blow that is aimed at him falls upon the Saviour, who surrounds him with His presence. Whatever comes to him comes from Christ. He has no need to resist evil, for Christ is his defense. Nothing can touch him except by our Lord's permission, and "all things" that are permitted "work together for good to them that love God."[128]

Our heavenly Father has a thousand ways to provide for us of which we know nothing. Those who accept the one principle of making the service of God supreme, will find perplexities vanish and a plain path before their feet.[129]

As a little child, trust to the guidance of Him who will "keep the feet of his saints." 1 Sam. 2:9.[130]

As we commit our ways to Him, He will direct our steps.[131]

LOVER OF ALL MEN

For this cause I bow my knees unto the Father of our Lord Jesus Christ, of whom the whole family in heaven and earth is named. Eph. 3:14, 15.

The perception of God's love works the renunciation of selfishness. In calling God our Father, we recognize all His children as our brethren. We are all a part of the great web of humanity, all members of one family.[132]

No distinction on account of nationality, race, or caste, is recognized by God. He is the Maker of all mankind. All men are of one family by creation, and all are one through redemption. Christ came to demolish every wall of partition, to throw open every compartment of the temple courts, that every soul may have free access to God.[133]

He came to show that His gift of mercy and love is as unconfined as the air, the light, or the showers of rain that refresh the earth.[134]

His love is so broad, so deep, so full, that it penetrates everywhere. It lifts out of Satan's influence those who have been deluded by his deceptions, and places them within reach of the throne of God, the throne encircled by the rainbow of promise.[135]

God is our Father and Governor. . . . The principles which rule in heaven should rule upon earth, the same love that animates the angels, the same purity and holiness that reign in heaven, should, as far as possible, be reproduced upon earth.[136]

If you call God your Father, you acknowledge yourselves His children, to be guided by His wisdom and to be obedient in all things, knowing that His love is changeless. You will accept His plan for your life. As children of God, you will hold His honor, His character, His family, His work, as the objects of your highest interest. It will be your joy to recognize and honor your relation to your Father and to every member of His family. You will rejoice to do any act, however humble, that will tend to His glory or to the well-being of your kindred.[137]

SATAN AND THE GREAT REBELLION

Sin and the First Rebel   *March 1*

THE UPRISING OF REBELLION

But your iniquities have separated between you and your God, and your sins have hid his face from you, that he will not hear. Isa. 59:2.

Evil originated with Lucifer, who rebelled against the government of God. Before his fall he was a covering cherub, distinguished by his excellence. God made him good and beautiful, as near as possible like Himself.[1]

Nothing is more plainly taught in Scripture than that God was in no wise responsible for the entrance of sin; that there was no arbitrary withdrawal of divine grace, no deficiency in the divine government, that gave occasion for the uprising of rebellion. Sin is an intruder, for whose presence no reason can be given. It is mysterious, unaccountable; to excuse it, is to defend it. Could excuse for it be found, or cause shown for its existence, it would cease to be sin.[2]

The first sinner was one whom God had greatly exalted. He is represented under the figure of the prince of Tyrus flourishing in might and magnificence. Little by little Satan came to indulge the desire for self-exaltation. . . . Though all his glory was from God, this mighty angel came to regard it as pertaining to himself. Not content with his position, though honored above the heavenly host, he ventured to covet homage due alone to the Creator. Instead of seeking to make God supreme in the affections and allegiance of all created beings, it was his endeavor to secure their service and loyalty to himself. . . .

Is he [Satan] not the first great apostate from God?[3]

It is at Lucifer's throne that every evil work finds its starting point, and obtains its support.[4]

AMBITION BRINGS SORROW

The blessing of the Lord, it maketh rich, and he addeth no sorrow with it. Prov. 10:22.

Lucifer . . . , before his rebellion, was a high and exalted angel, next in honor to God's dear Son. His countenance, like those of the other angels, was mild and expressive of happiness. His forehead was high and broad, showing a powerful intellect. His form was perfect; his bearing noble and majestic. A special light beamed in his countenance and shone around him brighter and more beautiful than around the other angels; yet Christ, God's dear Son, had the pre-eminence over all the angelic host. He was one with the Father before the angels were created. . . .

Lucifer was envious and jealous of Jesus Christ. Yet when all the angels bowed to Jesus to acknowledge His supremacy and high authority and rightful rule, he bowed with them; but his heart was filled with envy and hatred. Why should Christ thus be honored before himself?[5]

Lucifer in heaven desired to be first in power and authority; he wanted to be God, to have the rulership of heaven; and to this end he won many of the angels to his side. When with his rebel host he was cast out from the courts of God, the work of rebellion and self-seeking was continued on earth. Through the temptation to self-indulgence and ambition Satan accomplished the fall of our first parents; and from that time to the present the gratification of human ambition and the indulgence of selfish hopes and desires have proved the ruin of mankind.[6]

He who makes self-glorification his aim will find himself destitute of the grace of God, through whose efficiency the truest riches and the most satisfying joys are won. But he who gives all and does all for Christ will know the fulfillment of the promise, "The blessing of the Lord, it maketh rich, and he addeth no sorrow with it."[7]

PRIDE COMES BEFORE A FALL

Pride goeth before destruction, and an haughty spirit before a fall. Prov. 16:18.

Satan fell because of his ambition to be equal with God. He desired to enter into the divine counsels and purposes, from which he was excluded by his own inability, as a created being, to comprehend the wisdom of the Infinite One. It was this ambitious pride that led to his rebellion, and by the same means he seeks to cause the ruin of man.[8]

Sin originated in self-seeking. Lucifer, the covering cherub, desired to be first in heaven. He sought to gain control of heavenly beings, to draw them away from their Creator, and to win their homage to himself. Therefore he misrepresented God, attributing to Him the desire for self-exaltation. With his own evil characteristics he sought to invest the loving Creator.[9]

Had Lucifer really desired to be like the Most High, he would never have deserted his appointed place in heaven; for the spirit of the Most High is manifested in unselfish ministry. Lucifer desired God's power, but not His character. He sought for himself the highest place, and every being who is actuated by his spirit will do the same.[10]

Whenever pride and ambition are indulged, the life is marred; for pride, feeling no need, closes the heart against the infinite blessings of Heaven.[11]

Pride of heart is a fearful trait of character. "Pride goeth before destruction." This is true in the family, the church, and the nation.[12]

God's people should be subject one to another. They should counsel with each other, that the lack of one be supplied by the sufficiency of the other.[13]

God hates pride, and . . . all the proud and all that do wickedly shall be stubble, and the day that cometh shall burn them up.[14]

"Learn of me," said Christ; "for I am meek and lowly in heart: and ye shall find rest unto your souls." Matt. 11:29.[15]

GUARD AGAINST UNTRUTHFULNESS!

Stand therefore, having your loins girt about with truth. Eph. 6:14.

God permitted Satan to carry forward his work until the spirit of disaffection ripened into active revolt. It was necessary for his plans to be fully developed, that their true nature and tendency might be seen by all. . . . His power to deceive was very great. By disguising himself in a cloak of falsehood, he had gained an advantage. All his acts were so clothed with mystery, that it was difficult to disclose to the angels the true nature of his work. . . . It was his policy to perplex with subtle arguments concerning the purposes of God. Everything that was simple he shrouded in mystery, and by artful perversion cast doubt upon the plainest statements of Jehovah.[16]

The underworking was so subtle that it could not be made to appear before the heavenly host as the thing that it really was; and so there was war in heaven, and Satan was expelled with all who would not stand on the side of loyalty to God's government.[17]

I am bidden to warn all who make untruthful statements that they are serving him who has been a liar from the beginning. Let us be on our guard against untruthfulness, which grows upon him who practices it. I say to all, Make truth your girdle. . . . Put away all prevarication and exaggeration; never make a false statement.[18]

An intention to deceive is what constitutes falsehood. By a glance of the eye, a motion of the hand, an expression of the countenance, a falsehood may be told as effectually as by words. All intentional overstatement, every hint or insinuation calculated to convey an erroneous or exaggerated impression, even the statement of facts in such a manner as to mislead, is falsehood.[19]

There should be a continual effort to imitate the society we expect soon to join; namely, angels of God who have never fallen by sin. The character should be holy, the manners comely, the words without guile, and thus should we follow on step by step until we are fitted for translation.[20]

SIN—EXCEEDINGLY SINFUL

That sin by the commandment might become exceeding sinful.
Rom. 7:13.

In great mercy, according to His divine character, God bore long with Lucifer. The spirit of discontent and disaffection had never before been known in heaven. It was a new element, strange, mysterious, unaccountable.

Lucifer himself had not at first been acquainted with the real nature of his feelings; for a time he had feared to express the working and imaginings of his mind; yet he did not dismiss them. He did not see whither he was drifting. But such efforts as infinite love and wisdom only could devise, were made to convince him of his error. His disaffection was proved to be without cause, and he was made to see what would be the result of persisting in revolt. Lucifer was convinced that he was in the wrong. He saw that "the Lord is righteous in all his ways, and holy in all his works" (Ps. 145:17); that the divine statutes are just, and that he ought to acknowledge them as such before all heaven. . . . He nearly reached the decision to return; but pride forbade him. . . . He persistently defended his own course, and fully committed himself to the great controversy against his Maker. . . .

Satan's rebellion was to be a lesson to the universe through all coming ages—a perpetual testimony to the nature of sin and its terrible results. The working out of Satan's rule, its effects upon both men and angels, would show what must be the fruit of setting aside the divine authority. It would testify that with the existence of God's government is bound up the well-being of all the creatures He has made. Thus the history of this terrible experiment of rebellion was to be a perpetual safeguard to all holy beings, to prevent them from being deceived as to the nature of transgression, to save them from committing sin, and suffering its penalty.[21]

The infinite value of the sacrifice required for our redemption reveals the fact that sin is a tremendous evil.[22]

LIFE OR DEATH?

For the wages of sin is death: but the gift of God is eternal life through Jesus Christ our Lord. Rom. 6:23.

God, the One infinite and all-wise, sees the end from the beginning, and in dealing with evil His plans were far reaching and comprehensive. It was His purpose, not merely to put down the rebellion, but to demonstrate to all the universe the nature of rebellion. . . . It will be seen that all who have forsaken the divine precepts have placed themselves on the side of Satan, in warfare against Christ. When the prince of this world shall be judged, and all who have united with him shall share his fate, the whole universe as witnesses to the sentence will declare, "Just and true are thy ways, thou King of saints." Rev. 15:3.[23]

In the final execution of the judgment it will be seen that no cause for sin exists. When the judge of all the earth shall demand of Satan, "Why hast thou rebelled against Me, and robbed Me of the subjects of My kingdom?" the originator of evil can render no excuse. Every mouth will be stopped, and all the hosts of rebellion will be speechless. . . . The whole universe will have become witnesses to the nature and results of sin. And its utter extermination, which in the beginning would have brought fear to angels and dishonor to God, will now vindicate His love and establish His honor before the universe. . . . Never will evil again be manifest. Says the Word of God, "Affliction shall not rise up the second time." Nahum 1:9. . . . A tested and proved creation will never again be turned from allegiance to Him whose character has been fully manifested before them.[24]

He who chooses a course of disobedience to God's law is deciding his future destiny; he is sowing to the flesh, earning the wages of sin, even eternal destruction, the opposite of life eternal. Submission to God and obedience to His holy law bring the sure result. "This is life eternal, that they might know thee the only true God, and Jesus Christ, whom thou hast sent." John 17:3.[25]

REBELLION WILL BE PUT DOWN

And the God of peace shall bruise Satan under your feet shortly. The grace of our Lord Jesus Christ be with you. Amen. Rom. 16:20.

Ever since Adam yielded his mind to Satan's device, the conflict has raged between right and wrong, between God and Satan. Connected with the doing of right there is a power that Satan cannot overcome. Righteousness has a vitality that is divine. Truth will triumph at last over falsehood, and God will vanquish the enemy.[26]

Christ conquered Satan in our behalf. . . . He is mightier than Satan, and He will shortly bruise him under our feet.[27]

In mercy to the universe . . . God will finally destroy the rejecters of His grace.[28]

"Upon the wicked he shall rain quick burning coals, fire and brimstone, and an horrible tempest: this shall be the portion of their cup." Ps. 11:6 (margin).[29]

While life is the inheritance of the righteous, death is the portion of the wicked. Moses declared to Israel, "I have set before thee this day life and good, and death and evil." Deut. 30:15. The death referred to in these scriptures is not that pronounced upon Adam, for all mankind suffer the penalty of his transgression. It is the "second death" that is placed in contrast with everlasting life.[30]

In the cleansing flames the wicked are at last destroyed, root and branch—Satan the root, his followers the branches. The full penalty of the law has been visited; the demands of justice have been met; and heaven and earth, beholding, declare the righteousness of Jehovah.

Satan's work of ruin is forever ended. For six thousand years he has wrought his will, filling the earth with woe, and causing grief throughout the universe. The whole creation has groaned and travailed together in pain. Now God's creatures are forever delivered from his presence and temptations.[31]

It should be the aim of your life to fit yourself for association with the redeemed, with holy angels, and with Jesus, the world's Redeemer.[32]

WAYWARDNESS OF HUMANITY

O that there were such an heart in them, that they would fear me, and keep all my commandments always, that it might be well with them, and with their children for ever! Deut. 5:29.

After Satan was shut out of heaven, with those who fell with him, he realized that he had lost all the purity and glory of heaven forever. . . .

He consulted with his angels, and a plan was laid to still work against God's government. When Adam and Eve were placed in the beautiful garden, Satan was laying plans to destroy them. . . .

Satan commenced his work with Eve, to cause her to disobey. She first erred in wandering from her husband, next, in lingering around the forbidden tree, and next in listening to the voice of the tempter, and even daring to doubt what God had said—In the day that thou eatest thereof thou shalt surely die. She thought, Perhaps it does not mean just as the Lord said. She ventured to disobey. She put forth her hand, took of the fruit, and ate. . . . She offered the fruit to her husband, thereby tempting him. . . .

I saw a sadness come over Adam's countenance. He appeared afraid and astonished. A struggle appeared to be going on in his mind. He felt . . . that his wife must die. They must be separated. His love for Eve was strong. And in utter discouragement he resolved to share her fate. He seized the fruit, and quickly ate it. Then Satan exulted. . . .

Adam, through his love for Eve, disobeyed the command of God, and fell with her.[33]

Notwithstanding the sophistry of Satan to the contrary, it is always disastrous to disobey God. We must set our hearts to know what is truth. All the lessons which God has caused to be placed on record in His Word are for our warning and instruction. They are given to save us from deception. Their neglect will result in ruin to ourselves. Whatever contradicts God's Word, we may be sure proceeds from Satan.[34]

THE WAY OF TRANSGRESSORS

Good understanding giveth favour: but the way of transgressors is hard. Prov. 13:15.

The news of man's fall spread through heaven. Every harp was hushed. The angels cast their crowns from their heads in sorrow. All heaven was in agitation. A counsel was held to decide what must be done with the guilty pair. The angels feared that they would put forth the hand, and eat of the tree of life, and be immortal sinners. But God said that He would drive the transgressors from the garden. Angels were commissioned immediately to guard the way of the tree of life. It had been Satan's studied plan that Adam and Eve should disobey God, receive His frown, and then be led on to partake of the tree of life, that they might live forever in sin and disobedience, and thus sin be immortalized. But holy angels were sent to drive them out of the garden, while another company of angels were commissioned to guard the way to the tree of life. . . .

Satan triumphed. Others he had made to suffer by his fall. He had been shut out of heaven, they out of Paradise.[35]

By transgression Adam lost Eden. By the transgression of God's commandments man will lose heaven, and an eternity of bliss. These are no idle tales, but truth. . . . I ask, On which side are you standing?[36]

It is true that Satan's path is made to appear attractive, but it is all a deception; in the way of evil there are bitter remorse and cankering care. . . . In the downward road the gateway may be bright with flowers, but thorns are in the path. . . .

"The way of transgressors is hard," but wisdom's "ways are ways of pleasantness, and all her paths are peace." Prov. 13:15; 3:17. Every act of obedience to Christ, every act of self-denial for His sake, every trial well endured, every victory gained over temptation, is a step in the march to the glory of final victory. If we take Christ for our guide, He will lead us safely.[37]

FIRST PROMISE OF REDEMPTION

And I will put enmity between thee and the woman, and between thy seed and her seed; it shall bruise thy head, and thou shalt bruise his heel. Gen. 3:15.

To man the first intimation of redemption was communicated in the sentence pronounced upon Satan in the garden. The Lord declared, "I will put enmity between thee and the woman, and between thy seed and her seed; it shall bruise thy head, and thou shalt bruise his heel." This sentence, uttered in the hearing of our first parents, was to them a promise. While it foretold war between man and Satan, it declared that the power of the great adversary would finally be broken. . . . Adam and his companion were assured that notwithstanding their great sin, they were not to be abandoned to the control of Satan. The Son of God had offered to atone, with His own life, for their transgression. A period of probation would be granted them, and through repentance, and faith in Christ, they might again become the children of God.[38]

The instant man accepted the temptations of Satan, and did the very things God had said he should not do, Christ, the Son of God, stood between the living and the dead, saying, "Let the punishment fall on Me. I will stand in man's place. He shall have another chance."[39]

As soon as there was sin, there was a Saviour. Christ knew that He would have to suffer, yet He became man's substitute. As soon as Adam sinned, the Son of God presented Himself as surety for the human race, with just as much power to avert the doom pronounced upon the guilty as when He died upon the cross of Calvary.[40]

Although gloom and darkness hung, like the pall of death, over the future, yet in the promise of the Redeemer, the Star of hope lighted up the dark future. The gospel was first preached to Adam by Christ. Adam and Eve felt sincere sorrow and repentance for their guilt. They believed the precious promise of God, and were saved from utter ruin.[41]

A SAVIOUR FROM ETERNITY

Blessed be the God and Father of our Lord Jesus Christ, who hath blessed us with all spiritual blessings in heavenly places in Christ: according as he hath chosen us in him before the foundation of the world, that we should be holy and without blame before him in love. Eph. 1:3, 4.

Since the Fall the Lord has wrought out His will in the plan of redemption, a plan by which He is seeking to restore man to his original perfection. Christ's death on the cross has made it possible for God to receive and pardon every repentant soul.[42]

As the divine Sufferer hung upon the cross, angels gathered about Him, and as they looked upon Him, and heard His cry, they asked, with intense emotion, "Will not the Lord Jehovah save Him?" . . . Then were the words spoken: "The Lord hath sworn, and He will not repent. Father and Son are pledged to fulfill the terms of the everlasting covenant. God so loved the world, that He gave His only-begotten Son, that whosoever believeth in Him should not perish, but have everlasting life." Christ was not alone in making His great sacrifice. It was the fulfillment of the covenant made between Him and His Father before the foundation of the world was laid. With clasped hands they had entered into the solemn pledge that Christ would become the surety for the human race if they were overcome by Satan's sophistry.[43]

The salvation of the human race has ever been the object of the councils of heaven. The covenant of mercy was made before the foundation of the world. It has existed from all eternity, and is called the everlasting covenant. So surely as there never was a time when God was not, so surely there never was a moment when it was not the delight of the eternal mind to manifest His grace to humanity.[44]

The more we consider this subject, the greater depths we find, and yet there are depths that we do not reach as we study the Redeemer's glory. It is the glory of the Prince of life, and the mightiest powers of man cannot reach it. The angels themselves desire to look into this mysterious and wonderful theme, the redemption of the human race.[45]

GOD'S PLAN TO RANSOM HUMANITY

And I will establish my covenant between me and thee and thy seed after thee in their generations for an everlasting covenant, to be a God unto thee, and to thy seed after thee. Gen. 17:7.

As the Bible presents two laws, one changeless and eternal, the other provisional and temporary, so there are two covenants. The covenant of grace was first made with man in Eden, when after the Fall, there was given a divine promise that the seed of the woman should bruise the serpent's head. To all men this covenant offered pardon, and the assisting grace of God for future obedience through faith in Christ. It also promised them eternal life on condition of fidelity to God's law. Thus the patriarchs received the hope of salvation.

This same covenant was renewed to Abraham in the promise, "In thy seed shall all the nations of the earth be blessed." Gen. 22:18. This promise pointed to Christ. So Abraham understood it, and he trusted in Christ for the forgiveness of sins. It was this faith that was accounted unto him for righteousness. The covenant with Abraham also maintained the authority of God's law. The Lord appeared unto Abraham, and said, "I am the Almighty God; walk before me, and be thou perfect." The testimony of God concerning His faithful servant was, "Abraham obeyed my voice, and kept my charge, my commandments, my statutes, and my laws." Gen. 17:1; 26:5. . . .

The Abrahamic covenant was ratified by the blood of Christ, and it is called the "second," or "new," covenant, because the blood by which it was sealed was shed after the blood of the first covenant.[46]

The covenant of grace is not a new truth, for it existed in the mind of God from all eternity. This is why it is called the everlasting covenant.[47]

There is hope for us only as we come under the Abrahamic covenant, which is the covenant of grace by faith in Christ Jesus. The gospel preached to Abraham, through which he had hope, was the same gospel that is preached to us today. . . . Abraham looked unto Jesus, who is also the author and the finisher of our faith.[48]

HUMANITY'S INABILITY TO SAVE ITSELF

Knowing that a man is not justified by the works of the law, but by the faith of Jesus Christ, even we have believed in Jesus Christ, that we might be justified by the faith of Christ, and not by the works of the law: for by the works of the law shall no flesh be justified. Gal. 2:16.

Another compact—called in Scripture the "old" covenant—was formed between God and Israel at Sinai, and was then ratified by the blood of a sacrifice. . . .

God . . . gave them [Israel] His law, with the promise of great blessings on condition of obedience: "If ye will obey my voice indeed, and keep my covenant, then . . . ye shall be unto me a kingdom of priests, and an holy nation." Ex. 19:5, 6. The people did not realize the sinfulness of their own hearts, and that without Christ it was impossible for them to keep God's law; and they readily entered into covenant with God. Feeling that they were able to establish their own righteousness, they declared, "All that the Lord hath said will we do, and be obedient." Ex. 24:7. They had witnessed the proclamation of the law in awful majesty, and had trembled with terror before the mount; and yet only a few weeks passed before they broke their covenant with God, and bowed down to worship a graven image. They could not hope for the favor of God through a covenant which they had broken; and now, seeing their sinfulness and their need of pardon, they were brought to feel their need of the Saviour revealed in the Abrahamic covenant, and shadowed forth in the sacrificial offerings. . . .

The terms of the "old covenant" were, Obey and live: "If a man do, he shall even live in them;" but "cursed be he that confirmeth not all the words of this law to do them." Eze. 20:11; Lev. 18:5; Deut. 27:26. The "new covenant" was established upon "better promises"—the promise of forgiveness of sins, and of the grace of God to renew the heart, and bring it into harmony with the principles of God's law.[49]

The only means of salvation is provided under the Abrahamic covenant.[50]

OUR ANGEL FRIENDS AND GUARDIANS

Are they not all ministering spirits, sent forth to minister for them who shall be heirs of salvation? Heb. 1:14.

The plan by which alone man's salvation could be secured, involved all heaven in its infinite sacrifice. The angels could not rejoice as Christ opened before them the plan of redemption; for they saw that man's salvation must cost their loved Commander unutterable woe. In grief and wonder they listened to His words as He told them how He must descend from heaven's purity and peace. . . . and come in contact with the degradation of earth, to endure its sorrow, shame, and death. . . .

The angels . . . offered to become a sacrifice for man. But an angel's life could not pay the debt; only He who created man had power to redeem him. Yet the angels were to have a part to act in the plan of redemption. Christ was to be made "a little lower than the angels for the suffering of death." Heb. 2:9. As He should take human nature upon Him, His strength would not be equal to theirs, and they were to minister to Him, to strengthen and soothe Him under His sufferings. They were also to be ministering spirits, sent forth to minister for them who should be heirs of salvation. They would guard the subjects of grace from the power of evil angels, and from the darkness constantly thrown around them by Satan.[51]

Angels are ever present where they are most needed, with those who have the hardest battles with self to fight, and whose surroundings are the most discouraging. Weak and trembling souls who have many objectionable traits of character are their special charge. That which selfish hearts would regard as humiliating service, ministering to those who are wretched and in every way inferior in character, is the work of the pure, sinless beings from the courts above.[52]

All the angels of heaven are united in the work of bringing to man the infinite treasures of the better world.[53]

God and Christ and the heavenly angels are fighting with you. . . . In the strength of the Redeemer, you can be more than conquerors.[54]

GOD'S COMMANDMENTS ARE SURE

The works of his hands are verity and judgment; all his commandments are sure. They stand fast for ever and ever, and are done in truth and uprightness. Ps. 111:7, 8.

The law of God existed before the creation of man or else Adam could not have sinned. After the transgression of Adam the principles of the law were not changed, but were definitely arranged and expressed to meet man in his fallen condition.[55]

The angels were governed by it [the law]. Satan fell because he transgressed the principles of God's government. After Adam and Eve were created, God made known to them His law. It was not then written, but was rehearsed to them by Jehovah.[56]

In love, with a desire to elevate and ennoble us, God provided for us a standard of obedience. In awful majesty, amid thundering and lightning, He proclaimed from Mount Sinai His ten holy precepts. This law reveals the whole duty of the human family; the first four precepts define our duty to God, and the last six our duty to man.[57]

The law of God, being a revelation of His will, a transcript of His character, must forever endure, "as a faithful witness in heaven." Not one command has been annulled; not a jot or tittle has been changed. Says the psalmist: "For ever, O Lord, thy word is settled in heaven." Ps. 119:89.[58]

From the first, the great controversy had been upon the law of God. Satan had sought to prove that God was unjust, that His law was faulty, and that the good of the universe required it to be changed. In attacking the law, he aimed to overthrow the authority of its Author.[59]

Through Satan's temptations the whole human race have become transgressors of God's law; but by the sacrifice of His Son a way is opened whereby they may return to God. Through the grace of Christ they may be enabled to render obedience to the Father's law.[60]

When we trust God fully, when we rely upon the merits of Jesus as a sin-pardoning Saviour, we shall receive all the help that we can desire.[61]

TAMPERING WITH THE COMMANDMENTS

And he shall speak great words against the most High, and shall wear out the saints of the most High, and think to change times and laws. Dan. 7:25.

Satan could not hinder the plan of salvation. Jesus was crucified, and arose again the third day. He [Satan] told his angels that he would make even the crucifixion and resurrection tell to his advantage. He was willing that those who professed faith in Jesus should believe that the laws regulating the Jewish sacrifices and offerings ceased at the death of Christ, if he could push them further, and make them believe that the law of ten commandments died also with Christ. . . .

He [Satan] told his angels . . . that the Ten Commandments were so plain that many would believe that they were still binding; therefore he must seek to corrupt the fourth commandment, which brings to view the living God. He led on his representatives to attempt to change the Sabbath, and alter the only commandment of the ten which brings to view the true God, the maker of the heavens and the earth. Satan presented before them the glorious resurrection of Jesus, and told them that by His rising on the first day of the week, He changed the Sabbath from the seventh to the first day of the week. Thus Satan used the resurrection to serve his purpose. He and his angels rejoiced that the errors they had prepared took so well with the professed friends of Christ.[62]

Satan, working through unconsecrated leaders of the church, tampered with the fourth commandment . . . and essayed to set aside the ancient Sabbath, the day which God had blessed and sanctified (Gen. 2:2, 3), and in its stead to exalt the festival observed by the heathen as "the venerable day of the sun."[63]

The Lord has clearly defined the road to the city of God; but the great apostate has changed the signpost, setting up a false one—a spurious sabbath. . . . The enemy of all good has turned the signpost round, so that it points to the path of disobedience as the path of happiness. . . . He has thought to change times and laws.[64]

MAN A FREE MORAL AGENT

If any man will do his will, he shall know of the doctrine, whether it be of God, or whether I speak of myself. John 7:17.

Man was created a free moral agent. Like the inhabitants of all other worlds, he must be subjected to the test of obedience; but he is never brought into such a position that yielding to evil becomes a matter of necessity. No temptation or trial is permitted to come to him which he is unable to resist. God made such ample provision that man need never have been defeated in the conflict with Satan.[65]

Satan is the great originator of sin; yet this does not excuse any man for sinning; for he cannot force men to do evil. He tempts them to it, and makes sin look enticing and pleasant; but he has to leave it to their own wills whether they will do it or not. . . . Man is a free moral agent to accept or refuse.

Conversion is a work that most do not appreciate. It is not a small matter to transform an earthly, sin-loving mind and bring it to understand the unspeakable love of Christ, the charms of His grace, and the excellency of God, so that the soul shall be imbued with divine love.[66]

Every provision has been made; everything in God's plan has been arranged so that man should not be left to his own impulses, to his own finite powers, to carry on the warfare against the powers of darkness in his own finite strength; because he would certainly fail if he were thus left to himself.[67]

As a redeemed, free moral agent, ransomed by an infinite price, God calls upon you to assert your liberty, and employ your God-given powers as a free subject of the kingdom of heaven. . . . You are to refuse to be in subjection to the power of evil.[68]

Let a solemn, unalterable purpose take possession of you, and resolve in the strength and grace of God, that henceforth you will live for Him, and that no earthly consideration shall persuade you to disown the divine law of ten commandments.[69]

IN HARMONY WITH HEAVEN

Great peace have they which love thy law: and nothing shall offend them. Ps. 119:165.

Adam taught his descendants the law of God, and it was handed down from father to son through successive generations. But . . . there were few who accepted it and rendered obedience. By transgression the world became so vile that it was necessary to cleanse it by the Flood from its corruption. The law was preserved by Noah and his family, and Noah taught his descendants the Ten Commandments. As men again departed from God, the Lord chose Abraham, of whom He declared, "Abraham obeyed my voice, and kept my charge, my commandments, my statutes, and my laws." Gen. 26:5. . . .

Concerning the law proclaimed from Sinai, Nehemiah says, "Thou camest down also upon mount Sinai, and spakest with them from heaven, and gavest them *right judgments, and true laws, good statutes and commandments.*" Neh. 9:13. And Paul . . . declares, "The law is holy, and the commandment holy, and just, and good." Rom. 7:12.[70]

The whole world will be judged by the moral law according to their opportunity of becoming acquainted with it, whether by reason, or tradition, or the written Word.[71]

We behold in it the goodness of God, who by revealing to men the immutable principles of righteousness seeks to shield them from the evils that result from transgression. . . .

The law is an expression of God's idea. When we receive it in Christ, it becomes our idea. It lifts us above the power of natural desires and tendencies, above temptations that lead to sin. "Great peace have they which love thy law; and nothing shall offend them"—cause them to stumble. There is no peace in unrighteousness; the wicked are at war with God. But he who receives the righteousness of the law in Christ is in harmony with heaven.[72]

As received in Christ, it [God's law] works in us the purity of character that will bring joy to us through eternal ages.[73]

WONDROUS THINGS IN GOD'S LAW

Open thou mine eyes, that I may behold wondrous things out of thy law. Ps. 119:18.

Jesus Christ is the glory of the law. The bright beams of the Sun of Righteousness are to be reflected from His messengers upon the minds of sinners, in order that they may be led to say, with one of old, "Open thou mine eyes, that I may behold wondrous things out of thy law." Many . . . do not discern the wondrous things that are to be seen in God's law. They have not beheld that which was revealed to Moses when he prayed, "I beseech thee, shew me thy glory." Ex. 33:18. To Moses was revealed God's character.[74]

In the law every specification is the character of the infinite God.[75]

Heaven's law is always merciful, kind, tender, helpful, uplifting to others.[76]

The downtrodden law of God is to be exalted before the people; as soon as they turn with earnestness and reverence to the Holy Scriptures, light from heaven will reveal to them wondrous things out of God's law. . . . Truths which have proved an overmatch for giant intellects are understood by babes in Christ.[77]

The law of ten commandments is not to be looked upon as much from the prohibitory side as from the mercy side. Its prohibitions are the sure guarantee of happiness in obedience. . . .

We are not to regard God as waiting to punish the sinner for his sin. The sinner brings punishment upon himself. His own actions start a train of circumstances that bring the sure result. Every act of transgression reacts upon the sinner, works in him a change of character, and makes it more easy for him to transgress again. By choosing to sin, men separate themselves from God, cut themselves off from the channel of blessing, and the sure result is ruin and death.[78]

By obedience to this law the intellect is strengthened, and the conscience is enlightened and made sensitive. The youth need to gain a clear understanding of God's law.[79]

JESUS' EXAMPLE IN LAW KEEPING

If ye keep my commandments, ye shall abide in my love; even as I have kept my Father's commandments, and abide in his love. John 15:10.

The law of God is the only true standard of moral perfection. That law was practically exemplified in the life of Christ. He says of Himself, "I have kept my Father's commandments."[80]

The law is an expression of the thought of God; when received in Christ, it becomes our thought. . . . God desires us to be happy, and He gave us the precepts of the law that in obeying them we might have joy. When at Jesus' birth the angels sang—

"Glory to God in the highest,

And on earth peace, good will toward men" (Luke 2:14),

they were declaring the principles of the law which He had come to magnify and make honorable. . . .

"Till heaven and earth pass," said Jesus, "one jot or one tittle shall in no wise pass from the law, till all be fulfilled." Matt. 5:18. The sun shining in the heavens, the solid earth upon which you dwell, are God's witnesses that His law is changeless and eternal. Though they may pass away, the divine precepts shall endure. "It is easier for heaven and earth to pass, than one tittle of the law to fail." Luke 16:17. . . .

Since "the law of the Lord is perfect," every variation from it must be evil. Those who disobey the commandments of God, and teach others to do so, are condemned by Christ. The Saviour's life of obedience maintained the claims of the law, it proved that the law could be kept in humanity, and showed the excellence of character that obedience would develop. All who obey as He did are likewise declaring that the law is "holy, and just, and good." Rom. 7:12.[81]

When, through faith in Jesus Christ, man does according to the very best of his ability, and seeks to keep the way of the Lord by obedience to the Ten Commandments, the perfection of Christ is imputed to cover the transgression of the repentant and obedient soul.[82]

THE GREAT PRINCIPLE OF THE LAW

If ye love me, keep my commandments. John 14:15.

The law was not spoken . . . exclusively for the benefit of the Hebrews. God honored them by making them the guardians and keepers of His law, but it was to be held as a sacred trust for the whole world. The precepts of the Decalogue are adapted to all mankind, and they were given for the instruction and government of all. Ten precepts, brief, comprehensive, and authoritative, cover the duty of man to God and to his fellow man; and all based upon the great fundamental principle of love. "Thou shalt love the Lord thy God with all thy heart, and with all thy soul, and with all thy strength, and with all thy mind; and thy neighbour as thyself." Luke 10:27.[83]

God's law is not a new thing. It is not holiness created, but holiness made known. It is a code of principles expressing mercy, goodness, and love. It presents to fallen humanity the character of God, and states plainly the whole duty of man.[84]

In the precepts of His holy law, God has given a perfect rule of life; and He has declared that until the close of time this law, unchanged in a single jot or tittle, is to maintain its claim upon human beings. Christ came to magnify the law and make it honorable. . . . In His own life He gave an example of obedience to the law of God. In the sermon on the mount He showed how its requirements extend beyond the outward acts, and take cognizance of the thoughts and intents of the heart.[85]

Today God gives men opportunity to show whether they love their neighbor. He who truly loves God and his fellow man is he who shows mercy to the destitute, the suffering, the wounded, those who are ready to die. God calls upon every man to take up his neglected work, to seek to restore the moral image of the Creator in humanity.[86]

The Ten Commandments, Thou shalt, and Thou shalt not, are ten promises, assured to us if we render obedience to the law governing the universe. "If ye love me, keep my commandments." John 14:15.[87]

OUR HELPLESS CONDITION IN SIN

And ye shall seek me, and find me, when ye shall search for me with all your heart. And I will be found of you, saith the Lord. Jer. 29:13, 14.

By sin we have been severed from the life of God. Our souls are palsied. . . . The sense of sin has poisoned the springs of life.[88]

By nature we are alienated from God. The Holy Spirit describes our condition in such words as these: "Dead in trespasses and sins;" "the whole head is sick, and the whole heart faint"; "no soundness in it." We are held fast in the snare of Satan; "taken captive by him at his will." Eph. 2:1; Isa. 1:5, 6; 2 Tim. 2:26. God desires to heal us, to set us free. But since this requires an entire transformation, a renewing of our whole nature, we must yield ourselves wholly to Him.

The warfare against self is the greatest battle that was ever fought. The yielding of self, surrendering all to the will of God, requires a struggle; but the soul must submit to God before it can be renewed in holiness.[89]

Many realize their helplessness; they are longing for that spiritual life which will bring them into harmony with God, and are striving to obtain it. But in vain. . . . Let those desponding, struggling ones look up. . . .

When sin struggles for the mastery . . . look to the Saviour. His grace is sufficient to subdue sin. Let your grateful heart, trembling with uncertainty, turn to Him. Lay hold on the hope set before you. . . . His strength will help your weakness; He will lead you step by step. Place your hand in His, and let Him guide you.[90]

He will set free the captive that is held by weakness and misfortune and the chains of sin. . . .

He is always near. His loving presence surrounds you. Seek Him as One who desires to be found of you.[91]

God's promise is, "Ye shall seek me, and find me, when ye shall search for me with all your heart."[92]

THE GOSPEL FOR BOTH DISPENSATIONS

Every good gift and every perfect gift is from above, and cometh down from the Father of lights, with whom is no variableness, neither shadow of turning. James 1:17.

Since the fall of Adam, it has been the fashion of the world to sin, and it is for our interest to know what sin is. John declares: "Whosoever committeth sin transgresseth also the law: for sin is the transgression of the law." 1 John 3:4.[93]

God's purpose is . . . to save from sin. . . . The soul, corrupted and deformed, is to be purified, transformed.[94]

Through the gospel, souls that are degraded and enslaved by Satan are to be redeemed to share the glorious liberty of the sons of God.[95]

The gospel is the power and wisdom of God.[96]

Christ had been sent to earth to represent God in character. . . . He Himself was the gospel.[97]

Many who claim to believe and to teach the gospel . . . set aside the Old Testament Scriptures, of which Christ declared, "They are they which testify of me." John 5:39. In rejecting the Old, they virtually reject the New; for both are parts of an inseparable whole. No man can rightly present the law of God without the gospel, or the gospel without the law. The law is the gospel embodied, and the gospel is the law unfolded. The law is the root, the gospel is the fragrant blossom and fruit which it bears.[98]

He who proclaimed the law from Sinai, and delivered to Moses the precepts of the ritual law, is the same that spoke the sermon on the mount. . . . The teacher is the same in both dispensations. God's claims are the same. The principles of His government are the same. For all proceed from Him "with whom is no variableness, neither shadow of turning."[99]

The gospel of the New Testament is not the Old Testament standard lowered to meet the sinner and save him in his sins. God requires of all His subjects obedience, entire obedience to all His commandments.[100]

ABUNDANT GRACE FOR OBEDIENCE

For sin shall not have dominion over you: for ye are not under the law, but under grace. Rom. 6:14.

It is the sophistry of Satan that the death of Christ brought in grace to take the place of the law. The death of Jesus did not change, or annul, or lessen in the slightest degree, the law of ten commandments. That precious grace offered to men through a Saviour's blood, establishes the law of God. Since the fall of man, God's moral government and His grace are inseparable. They go hand in hand through all dispensations. "Mercy and truth are met together; righteousness and peace have kissed each other." Ps. 85:10.[101]

Each law of God is an enactment of mercy, love, and saving power. These laws, obeyed, are our life, our salvation, our happiness, our peace.[102]

Obedience to His statutes and laws is the life and prosperity of His people.[103]

The influence of a gospel hope will not lead the sinner to look upon the salvation of Christ as a matter of free grace, while he continues to live in transgression of the law of God. . . . He will reform his ways, become loyal to God through the strength obtained from his Saviour, and lead a new and purer life.[104]

As the sacrifice in our behalf was complete, so our restoration from the defilement of sin is to be complete. No act of wickedness will the law of God excuse; no unrighteousness can escape its condemnation. The ethics of the gospel acknowledge no standard but the perfection of the divine character. The life of Christ was a perfect fulfillment of every precept of the law. He said, "I have kept my Father's commandments." John 15:10. His life is our example of obedience and service. God alone can renew the heart. "It is God which worketh in you both to will and to do of his good pleasure." But we are bidden, "Work out your own salvation." Phil. 2:13, 12.[105]

To the obedient child of God, the commandments are a delight.[106]

THE FAITH THAT WORKS

But without faith it is impossible to please him: for he that cometh to God must believe that he is, and that he is a rewarder of them that diligently seek him. Heb. 11:6.

Faith is not certainty of knowledge, it is the substance of things hoped for, the evidence of things not seen.[107]

Faith is trusting in God—believing that He loves us, and knows what is for our best good. Thus, instead of our own way, it leads us to choose His way. In place of our ignorance, it accepts His wisdom; in place of our weakness, His strength; in place of our sinfulness, His righteousness. Our lives, ourselves, are already His; faith acknowledges His ownership, and accepts its blessing. Truth, uprightness, purity, are pointed out as secrets of life's success. It is faith that puts us in possession of these. Every good impulse or aspiration is the gift of God; faith receives from God the life that alone can produce true growth and efficiency.[108]

When we speak of faith, there is a distinction that should be borne in mind. There is a kind of belief that is wholly distinct from faith. The existence and power of God, the truth of His Word, are facts that even Satan and his hosts cannot at heart deny. The Bible says that "the devils also believe, and tremble"; but this is not faith. Where there is not only a belief in God's Word, but a submission of the will to Him; where the heart is yielded to Him, the affections fixed upon Him, there is faith—faith that works by love and purifies the soul. Through this faith the heart is renewed in the image of God. And the heart that in its unrenewed state is not subject to the law of God, neither indeed can be, now delights in its holy precepts, exclaiming with the psalmist, "O how love I thy law! it is my meditation all the day." Ps. 119:97. And the righteousness of the law is fulfilled in us, "who walk not after the flesh, but after the Spirit." Rom. 8:1.[109]

Faith earns nothing for us; it is the gift of God, which we may receive and cherish by making Christ our personal Saviour.[110]

HOW FAITH IS MADE PERFECT

Even so faith, if it hath not works, is dead, being alone. James 2:17.

The expulsion of sin is the act of the soul itself. In its great need the soul cries out for a power out of and above itself; and through the operation of the Holy Spirit the nobler powers of the mind are imbued with strength to break away from the bondage of sin.

When man surrenders to Christ, the mind is brought under the control of the law, but it is the royal law, which proclaims liberty to every captive. Only by becoming one with Christ can men be made free. Subjection to the will of Christ means restoration to perfect manhood. Sin can triumph only by . . . destroying soul.

Do you realize your sinfulness? Do you despise sin? Then remember that the righteousness of Christ is yours if you will grasp it. Can you not see what a strong foundation is placed beneath your feet when you accept Christ? God has accepted the offering of His Son as a complete atonement for the sins of the world.[111]

True faith, which relies wholly upon Christ, will be manifested by obedience to all the requirements of God. . . . In all ages there have been those who claimed a right to the favor of God even while they were disregarding some of His commands. But the Scriptures declare that by works is "faith made perfect"; and that, without the works of obedience, faith "is dead."[112]

Satan believes and trembles. He works. He knows his time is short, and he has come down in great power to do his evil works according to his faith. But God's professed people do not support their faith by their works. They believe in the shortness of time, yet grasp just as eagerly after this world's goods as though the world were to stand a thousand years as it now is.[113]

Do you believe that the end of all things is at hand, that the scenes of this earth's history are fast closing? If so, show your faith by your works. A man will show all the faith he has.[114]

DO WE CONTRADICT OUR PROFESSION?

Thou that makest thy boast of the law, through breaking the law dishonourest thou God? For the name of God is blasphemed among the Gentiles through you, as it is written. Rom. 2:23, 24.

All who join themselves to the church but not to the Lord will in time develop their true character. "Ye shall know them by their fruits." Matt. 7:16. The precious fruit of godliness, temperance, patience, kindness, love, and charity, does not appear in their lives. They bear only thorns and briers. God is dishonored before the world by all such professors. . . . They are, Satan knows, his best working agents while they are unchanged in heart and life, and their works are in such marked contrast to their profession that they are a stumbling block to unbelievers and a great trial to believers. . . .

What an account will those have to give in the day of final reckoning, who profess to be keeping the commandments of God, while their lives contradict their profession, for they bear no precious fruit.[115]

Many who would shrink with horror from some great transgression are led to look upon sin in little matters as of trifling consequence. But these little sins eat out the life of godliness in the soul. The feet which enter upon a path diverging from the right way are tending toward the broad road that ends in death. When once a retrograde movement begins, no one can tell where it may end.[116]

A true disciple of Christ will seek to imitate the Pattern. His love will lead to perfect obedience. He will study to do the will of God on earth, as it is done in heaven. He whose heart is still defiled with sin cannot be zealous of good works, and is not careful to abstain from evil. . . . is not jealous over his unruly tongue; he is not careful to deny self and lift the cross of Christ. . . .

The fruits of the Spirit, ruling in the heart and controlling the life, are love, joy, peace, long-suffering, gentleness, bowels of mercies, and humbleness of mind. True believers walk after the Spirit, and the Spirit of God dwells in them.[117]

DOES FAITH CANCEL OBEDIENCE?

Do we then make void the law through faith? God forbid: yea, we establish the law. Rom. 3:31.

Faith is not an opiate, but a stimulant. Looking to Calvary will not quiet your soul into nonperformance of duty, but will create faith that will work, purifying the soul from all selfishness.[118]

The faith in Christ which saves the soul is not what it is represented to be by many. "Believe, believe," is their cry; "only believe in Christ, and you will be saved. It is all you have to do." While true faith trusts wholly in Christ for salvation, it will lead to perfect conformity to the law of God.[119]

There are two errors against which the children of God—particularly those who have just come to trust in His grace—especially need to guard. The first . . . is that of looking to their own works, trusting to anything they can do, to bring themselves into harmony with God. He who is trying to become holy by his own works in keeping the law, is attempting an impossibility. . . . It is the grace of Christ alone, through faith, that can make us holy.

The opposite and no less dangerous error is that belief in Christ releases men from keeping the law of God; that since by faith alone we become partakers of the grace of Christ, our works have nothing to do with our redemption.

But notice here that obedience is not a mere outward compliance, but the service of love. The law of God is an expression of His very nature; it is an embodiment of the great principle of love, and hence is the foundation of His government in heaven and earth. . . . Instead of releasing man from obedience, it is faith, and faith only, that makes us partakers of the grace of Christ, which enables us to render obedience.[120]

As Jesus was in human nature, so God means His followers to be. In His strength we are to live the life of purity and nobility which the Saviour lived.[121]

THE GREAT ELEMENT OF SAVING POWER

For by grace are ye saved through faith; and that not of yourselves: it is the gift of God: not of works, lest any man should boast. Eph. 2:8, 9.

Grace is an attribute of God exercised toward undeserving human beings. We did not seek for it, but it was sent in search of us.[122]

Divine grace is the great element of saving power; without it all human effort is unavailing.[123]

Are you in Christ? Not if you do not acknowledge yourselves erring, helpless, condemned sinners. Not if you are exalting and glorifying self. If there is any good in you, it is wholly attributable to the mercy of a compassionate Saviour. Your birth, your reputation, your wealth, your talents, your virtues, your piety, your philanthropy, or anything else in you or connected with you, will not form a bond of union between your soul and Christ. Your connection with the church, the manner in which your brethren regard you, will be of no avail unless you believe in Christ. It is not enough to believe about Him; you must believe in Him. You must rely wholly upon His saving grace.[124]

Would that you could conceive of the rich supplies of grace and power awaiting your demand.[125]

In the matchless gift of His Son, God has encircled the whole world with an atmosphere of grace as real as the air which circulates around the globe. All who choose to breathe this life-giving atmosphere will live, and grow up to the stature of men and women in Christ Jesus.[126]

Christ . . . died for us. He does not treat us according to our desert. Although our sins have merited condemnation, He does not condemn us. Year after year He has borne with our weakness and ignorance, with our ingratitude and waywardness. Notwithstanding our wanderings, . . . His hand is stretched out still.[127]

Through the grace of Christ we may accomplish everything that God requires.[128]

PRAYING FOR A LARGER EXPERIENCE

I will run the way of thy commandments, when thou shalt enlarge my heart. Ps. 119:32.

The ten holy precepts spoken by Christ upon Sinai's mount made known to the world the fact that He had jurisdiction over the whole human heritage. That law of ten precepts of the greatest love that can be presented to man is the voice of God from heaven speaking to the soul in promise, "This do, and you will not come under the dominion and control of Satan." There is not a negative in that law, although it may appear thus. It is DO, and Live.[129]

The God of heaven has placed a benediction upon them that keep the commandments of God. Shall we stand as a peculiar people of God, or shall we trample upon the law of God and say it is not binding? God might just as well have abolished Himself.[130]

His law is the echo of His own voice, giving to all the invitation, "Come up higher. Be holy, holier still." Every day we may advance in perfection of Christian character.[131]

As the stars tell us that there is a great light in heaven with whose glory they are made bright, so Christians are to make it manifest that there is a God on the throne of the universe whose character is worthy of praise and imitation.[132]

The bright beams of heaven's light are shining upon your pathway, dear youth, and I pray that you may make the most of your opportunities. Receive and cherish every heaven-sent ray, and your path will grow brighter and brighter unto the perfect day.[133]

We gain . . . strength by walking in the light, that we may have energy to run in the way of God's commandments. We may gain an increase of strength at every step we advance heavenward."[134]

We need constantly a fresh revelation of Christ, a daily experience that harmonizes with His teachings. High and holy attainments are within our reach. Continual progress in knowledge and virtue is God's purpose for us.[135]

THE SAVING POWER OF JESUS

And he said unto me, My grace is sufficient for thee: for my strength is made perfect in weakness. Most gladly therefore will I rather glory in my infirmities, that the power of Christ may rest upon me. 2 Cor. 12:9.

Our precious Saviour has invited us to join ourselves to Him and unite our weakness with His strength, our ignorance with His wisdom, our unworthiness with His merit.[136]

Rigid precision in obeying the law would entitle no man to enter the kingdom of heaven.

There must be a new birth, a new mind through the operation of the Spirit of God, which purifies the life and ennobles the character. This connection with God fits man for the glorious kingdom of heaven. No human invention can ever find a remedy for the sinning soul.[137]

There must be a power working from within, a new life from above, before men can be changed from sin to holiness. That power is Christ, His grace alone can quicken the lifeless faculties of the soul, and attract it to God, to holiness. . . . The idea that it is necessary only to develop the good that exists in man by nature, is a fatal deception. "The natural man receiveth not the things of the Spirit of God: for they are foolishness unto him: neither can he know them, because they are spiritually discerned." 1 Cor. 2:14. . . . Of Christ it is written, "In him was life; and the life was the light of men"—the only "name under heaven given among men, whereby we must be saved." John 1:4; Acts 4:12. . . .

Paul the apostle . . . longed for the purity, the righteousness, to which in himself he was powerless to attain, and he cried out, "O wretched man that I am! who shall deliver me from this body of death?" Rom. 7:24, margin. Such is the cry that has gone up from burdened hearts in all lands and in all ages. To all, there is but one answer, "Behold the Lamb of God, which taketh away the sin of the world." John 1:29.[138]

April

GOD'S REMEDY FOR SIN

THE SAVIOUR OF HUMANITY

But he was wounded for our transgressions, he was bruised for our iniquities: the chastisement of our peace was upon him; and with his stripes we are healed. Isa. 53:5.

The blood of Christ is the eternal antidote for sin.[1]

Christ's death on the cross was one of willing obedience, else in it there would have been no merit; for justice would not punish in the place of the sinner an innocent being who was unwilling to bear the penalty.[2]

Jesus . . . became a "Man of sorrows," that we might be made partakers of everlasting joy. God permitted His beloved Son, full of grace and truth, to come from a world of indescribable glory, to a world marred and blighted with sin, darkened with the shadow of death and the curse. He permitted Him to leave the bosom of His love, the adoration of the angels, to suffer shame . . . and death.[3]

Behold the cross, and the Victim uplifted upon it. . . . Christ bore our sins in His own body. That suffering, that agony, is the price of your redemption.[4]

The bitter cup was apportioned to us to drink. Our sins mingled it. But our dear Saviour took the cup from our lips and drank it Himself, and in its stead He presents to us a cup of . . . salvation.[5]

We cannot measure how much deeper our afflictions would have been, how much greater our woes, had not Jesus encircled us with His human arm of sympathy and love, and lifted us up.

We may rejoice in hope. . . . Through His [our Advocate's] merits we have pardon and peace. He died that He might wash away our sins, clothe us with His righteousness, and fit us for the society of heaven, where we may dwell in light forever.[6]

THE SINNER'S FRIEND

A man that hath friends must shew himself friendly: and there is a friend that sticketh closer than a brother. Prov. 18:24.

Jesus is the sinner's friend, His heart is ever open, ever touched with human woe; He has all power, both in heaven and upon earth.[7]

In the person of Christ we behold the eternal God engaged in an enterprise of boundless mercy toward fallen man.[8]

Christ came to this world to show that by receiving power from on high, man can live an unsullied life. . . .

He could say to whom He pleased, "Follow Me," and the one addressed arose and followed Him. The spell of the world's enchantment was broken. At the sound of His voice the spirit of greed and ambition fled from the heart, and men arose, emancipated, to follow the Saviour. . . .

He passed by no human being as worthless, but sought to apply the healing remedy to every soul. . . . He sought to inspire with hope the roughest and most unpromising, setting before them the assurance that they might become blameless and harmless, attaining such a character as would make them manifest as the children of God.

Often He met those who had drifted under Satan's control, and who had no power to break from his snare. To such a one, discouraged, sick, tempted, fallen, Jesus would speak words of tenderest pity, words that were needed and could be understood. Others He met who were fighting a hand-to-hand battle with the adversary of souls. These He encouraged to persevere, assuring them that they would win; for angels of God were on their side and would give them the victory.[9]

The Sinless One pities the weakness of the sinner. . . .

Men hate the sinner, while they love the sin. Christ hates the sin, but loves the sinner. This will be the spirit of all who follow Him. Christian love is slow to censure, quick to discern penitence, ready to forgive, to encourage, to set the wanderer in the path of holiness, and to stay his feet therein.[10]

A WELLSPRING OF LIFE

But whosoever drinketh of the water that I shall give him shall never thirst; but the water that I shall give him shall be in him a well of water springing up into everlasting life. John 4:14.

Many are suffering from maladies of the soul far more than from diseases of the body, and they will find no relief until they come to Christ, the wellspring of life. . . . Christ is the mighty Healer of the sin-sick soul.[11]

If we let go of Jesus we have nothing to hold on to. . . . Perpetual grace in ever-flowing streams is blessing those who will, if athirst, come unto Him and drink.[12]

He who seeks to quench his thirst at the fountains of this world will drink only to thirst again. Everywhere men are unsatisfied. They long for something to supply the need of the soul. Only One can meet that want. The need of the world, "the desire of all nations," is Christ. The divine grace which He alone can impart, is as living water, purifying, refreshing, and invigorating the soul. . . .

He who tastes of the love of Christ will continually long for more; but he seeks for nothing else. The riches, honors, and pleasures of the world do not attract him. The constant cry of his heart is, More of Thee. And He who reveals to the soul its necessity is waiting to satisfy its hunger and thirst. Every human resource and dependence will fail. The cisterns will be emptied, the pools become dry; but our Redeemer is an inexhaustible fountain. We may drink, and drink again, and ever find a fresh supply. He in whom Christ dwells has within himself the fountain of blessing—"a well of water springing up into everlasting life." From this source he may draw strength and grace sufficient for all his needs.[13]

He who drinks of the living water becomes a fountain of life. The receiver becomes a giver. The grace of Christ in the soul is like a spring in the desert, welling up to refresh all, and making those who are ready to perish eager to drink of the water of life.[14]

MY GUIDE AND PILOT

I will instruct thee and teach thee in the way which thou shalt go: I will guide thee with mine eye. Ps. 32:8.

Often the Christian life is beset with dangers, and duty seems hard to perform. The imagination pictures impending ruin before, and bondage and death behind. Yet the voice of God speaks clearly, Go forward. . . . Faith looks beyond the difficulties, and lays hold of the unseen, even Omnipotence, therefore it cannot be baffled. Faith is the clasping of the hand of Christ in every emergency.[15]

Every ship sailing the sea of life needs to have the divine Pilot on board; but when storms arise, when tempests threaten, many persons push their Pilot overboard, and commit their bark into the hand of finite man, or try to steer it themselves. Then disaster and wreckage generally follow, and the Pilot is blamed for running them into such dangerous waters. Do not commit yourselves into the keeping of men, but say, "The Lord is my helper"; I will seek His counsel; I will be a doer of His will. . . . It is as impossible for us to receive qualification from man, without the divine enlightenment, as it was for the gods of Egypt to deliver those who trusted in them. . . . Do not trust yourself to men. Act under the divine Guide.

You have been chosen by Christ. You have been redeemed by the precious blood of the Lamb. Plead before God the efficacy of that blood. Say unto Him: "I am Thine by creation; I am Thine by redemption. I respect human authority, and the advice of my brethren; but I cannot depend wholly upon these. I want Thee, O God, to teach me. I have covenanted with Thee to adopt the divine standard of character, and make Thee my counselor and guide—a party to every plan of my life; therefore teach me." Let the glory of the Lord be your first consideration. . . . Let every act of your life be sanctified by a holy endeavor to do the Lord's will, that your influence may not lead others into forbidden paths.[16]

THE SACRIFICIAL BLOOD OF CHRIST

Forasmuch as ye know that ye were not redeemed with corruptible things, as silver and gold, from your vain conversation received by tradition from your fathers; but with the precious blood of Christ, as of a lamb without blemish and without spot. 1 Peter 1:18, 19.

Upon Christ as our substitute and surety was laid the iniquity of us all. He was counted a transgressor, that He might redeem us from the condemnation of the law.[17]

Hating sin with a perfect hatred, He yet gathered to His soul the sins of the whole world. Guiltless, He bore the punishment of the guilty. Innocent, yet offering Himself as a substitute for the transgressor. The guilt of every sin pressed its weight upon the divine soul of the world's Redeemer. The evil thoughts, the evil words, the evil deeds of every son and daughter of Adam, called for retribution upon Himself; for He had become man's substitute.[18]

Behold Him in the wilderness, in Gethsemane, upon the cross! The spotless Son of God took upon Himself the burden of sin. He who had been one with God, felt in His soul the awful separation that sin makes between God and man. This wrung from His lips the anguished cry, "My God, my God, why hast thou forsaken me?" Matt. 27:46. It was the burden of sin, the sense of its terrible enormity, of its separation of the soul from God—it was this that broke the heart of the Son of God.[19]

"Ye know," says Peter, "that ye were not redeemed with corruptible things, as silver and gold." 1 Peter 1:18. Oh, had these been sufficient to purchase the salvation of man, how easily it might have been accomplished by Him who says, "The silver is mine, and the gold is mine"! Haggai 2:8. But the sinner could be redeemed only by the precious blood of the Son of God.[20]

By pouring the whole treasury of heaven into this world, by giving us in Christ all heaven, God has purchased the will, the affections, the mind, the soul, of every human being.[21]

JUSTIFIED BY HIS BLOOD

Much more then, being now justified by his blood, we shall be saved from wrath through him. Rom. 5:9.

God calls for faith in Christ as our atoning sacrifice. His blood is the only remedy for sin.[22]

It is not God's will that you should be distrustful, and torture your soul with the fear that God will not accept you because you are sinful and unworthy. . . . You can say: "I know I am a sinner, and that is the reason I need a Saviour. . . . I have no merit or goodness whereby I may claim salvation, but I present before God the all-atoning blood of the spotless Lamb of God, which taketh away the sin of the world. This is my only plea."[23]

God is approached through Jesus Christ, the Mediator, the only way through which He forgives sins. God cannot forgive sins at the expense of His justice, His holiness, and His truth. But He does forgive sins and that fully. There are no sins He will not forgive in and through the Lord Jesus Christ. This is the sinner's only hope, and if he rests here in sincere faith, he is sure of pardon and that full and free. There is only one channel and that is accessible to all, and through that channel a rich and abundant forgiveness awaits the penitent, contrite soul and the darkest sins are forgiven. These lessons were taught to the chosen people of God thousands of years ago, and repeated in various symbols and figures, that the work of truth might be riveted in every heart, that without the shedding of blood there is no remission of sins. . . . Justice demanded the sufferings of man; but Christ rendered the sufferings of a God. He needed no atonement of suffering for Himself; all His sufferings were for us; all His merits and holiness were open to fallen man, presented as a gift.[24]

Christ calls upon us to lay our sins upon Him, the Sin-Bearer. . . . But if we refuse to let them go, taking the responsibility ourselves, we will be lost. We may fall upon Christ, the living stone, and be broken, but if that Stone falls upon us, it will grind us to powder.[25]

PEACE THROUGH THE CROSS

There is therefore now no condemnation to them which are in Christ Jesus, who walk not after the flesh, but after the Spirit. Rom. 8:1.

If sinners can be led to give one earnest look at the cross, if they can obtain a full view of the crucified Saviour, they will realize the depth of God's compassion and the sinfulness of sin.[26]

As your conscience has been quickened by the Holy Spirit, you have seen something of the evil of sin, of its power, its guilt, its woe; and you look upon it with abhorrence. . . . You long to be forgiven, to be cleansed, to be set free. Harmony with God, likeness to Him—what can you do to obtain it?

It is peace that you need—Heaven's forgiveness and peace and love in the soul. Money cannot buy it, intellect cannot procure it, wisdom cannot attain to it; you can never hope, by your own efforts, to secure it. But God offers it to you as a gift, "without money and without price." Isa. 55:1. . . .

Go to Him, and ask that He will wash away your sins, and give you a new heart. Then believe that He does this *because He has promised.* . . . It is our privilege to go to Jesus and be cleansed, and to stand before the law without shame or remorse.[27]

When at the foot of the cross the sinner looks up to the One who died to save him, he may rejoice with fullness of joy; for his sins are pardoned. Kneeling in faith at the cross, he has reached the highest place to which man can attain.[28]

Thank God for the gift of His dear Son, and pray that He may not have died for you in vain. The Spirit invites you today. Come with your whole heart to Jesus, and you may claim His blessing.

As you read the promises, remember they are the expression of unutterable love and pity. . . . Yes, only believe that God is your helper. He wants to restore His moral image in man. As you draw near to Him with confession and repentance, He will draw near to you with mercy and forgiveness.[29]

A GLORIOUS SUBSTITUTION

Christ hath redeemed us from the curse of the law, being made a curse for us: for it is written, Cursed is every one that hangeth on a tree. Gal. 3:13.

It is the province of the law to condemn, but there is in it no power to pardon or to redeem.[30]

Without Christ the law of itself was only condemnation and death to the transgressor. It has no saving quality—no power to shield the transgressor from its penalty. . . .

The transgression of God's law made the death of Christ essential to save man and yet maintain the dignity and honor of the law. Christ took upon Himself the condemnation of sin. He opened His bosom to the woes of man. He who knew no sin became sin for us.[31]

As man's substitute and surety, the iniquity of men was laid upon Christ; He was counted a transgressor that He might redeem them from the curse of the law. . . . He, the Sin-Bearer, endures judicial punishment for iniquity and becomes sin itself for man.[32]

Sin, so hateful to His sight, was heaped upon Him till He groaned beneath its weight. The despairing agony of the Son of God was so much greater than His physical pain, that the latter was hardly felt by Him.[33]

God permits His Son to be delivered up for our offenses. He Himself assumes toward the Sin-Bearer the character of a judge, divesting Himself of the endearing qualities of a father.

Herein His love commends itself in the most marvelous manner to the rebellious race.[34]

The sin of the whole world was laid upon Jesus, and divinity gave its highest value to the suffering of humanity in Jesus, that the whole world might be pardoned through faith in the Substitute. The most guilty need have no fear that God will not pardon, for because of the efficacy of the divine sacrifice the penalty of the law will be remitted. Through Christ the sinner may return to allegiance to God.[35]

A PERFECT ATONEMENT

And not only so, but we also joy in God through our Lord Jesus Christ, by whom we have now received the atonement. Rom. 5:11.

The infinite sufficiency of Christ is demonstrated by His bearing the sins of the whole world. He occupies the double position of offerer and of offering, of priest and of victim.[36]

In the atonement made for him the believer sees such breadth, and length, and height, and depth of efficiency—sees such completeness of salvation, purchased at such infinite cost, that his soul is filled with praise and thanksgiving. He sees as in a glass the glory of the Lord, and is changed into the same image as by the Spirit of the Lord.[37]

The great High Priest has made the only sacrifice that will be of any value. The incense that is offered now by men, the masses that are said for the deliverance of souls from purgatory, are not of the least avail with God. All the altars and sacrifices, the traditions and inventions whereby men hope to earn salvation, are fallacies. . . . Christ is the only sin-bearer, the only sin-offering. . . .

Priests and rulers have no right to interpose between Christ and the souls for whom He has died, as though invested with the Saviour's attributes, and able to pardon transgression and sin. They themselves are sinners. They are only human.[38]

Prayer and confession are to be offered only to Him who has entered once for all into the holy place. Christ has declared, "If any man sin, we have an advocate with the Father, Jesus Christ the righteous." 1 John 2:1. He will save to the uttermost all who come to Him in faith.[39]

The Elder Brother of our race is by the eternal throne. He looks upon every soul who is turning his face toward Him as the Saviour.[40]

The heaviest burden that we bear is the burden of sin. . . . He will take the load from our weary shoulders. He will give us rest. The burden of care and sorrow also He will bear. He invites us to cast all our care upon Him; for He carries us upon His heart.[41]

TYPE MEETS ANTITYPE

But now in Christ Jesus ye who sometimes were far off are made nigh by the blood of Christ. Eph. 2:13.

God's people, whom He calls His peculiar treasure, were privileged with a twofold system of law; the moral and the ceremonial. . . .

From the creation the moral law was an essential part of God's divine plan, and was as unchangeable as Himself. The ceremonial law was to answer a particular purpose in Christ's plan for the salvation of the race. The typical system of sacrifices and offerings was established that through these services the sinner might discern the great offering, Christ. . . . The ceremonial law was glorious; it was the provision made by Jesus Christ in counsel with His Father, to aid in the salvation of the race. The whole arrangement of the typical system was founded on Christ. Adam saw Christ prefigured in the innocent beast suffering the penalty of his transgression of Jehovah's law.[42]

The need for the service of sacrifices and offerings ceased when type met antitype in the death of Christ. In Him the shadow reached the substance. . . . The law of God will maintain its exalted character as long as the throne of Jehovah endures. This law is the expression of God's character. . . . Types and shadows, offerings and sacrifices, had no virtue after Christ's death on the cross; but God's law was not crucified with Christ. . . . Today he [Satan] is deceiving human beings in regard to the law of God.[43]

The law of the ten commandments lives and will live through the eternal ages. . . .

God did not make the infinite sacrifice of giving His only-begotten Son to our world, to secure for man the privilege of breaking the commandments of God in this life and in the future eternal life.[44]

He [Jesus] gave His precious, innocent life to save guilty human beings from eternal ruin, that through faith in Him they might stand guiltless before the throne of God.[45]

REDEMPTION AND FORGIVENESS

In whom we have redemption through his blood, the forgiveness of sins, according to the riches of his grace. Eph. 1:7.

The grace of Christ is freely to justify the sinner without merit or claim on his part. Justification is a full, complete pardon of sin. The moment a sinner accepts Christ by faith, that moment he is pardoned. The righteousness of Christ is imputed to him, and he is no more to doubt God's forgiving grace.

There is nothing in faith that makes it our saviour. Faith cannot remove our guilt. Christ is the power of God unto salvation to all them that believe. The justification comes through the merits of Jesus Christ. He has paid the price for the sinner's redemption. Yet it is only through faith in His blood that Jesus can justify the believer.

The sinner cannot depend upon his own good works as a means of justification. He must come to the point where he will renounce all his sin, and embrace one degree of light after another as it shines upon his pathway. He simply grasps by faith the free and ample provision made in the blood of Christ. He believes the promises of God, which through Christ are made unto him sanctification and righteousness and redemption. And if he follows Jesus, he will walk humbly in the light, rejoicing in the light and diffusing that light to others.[46]

Let the repenting sinner fix his eyes upon "the Lamb of God, which taketh away the sin of the world." . . . When we see Jesus, a Man of Sorrows and acquainted with grief, working to save the lost, slighted, scorned, derided, driven from city to city till His mission was accomplished; when we behold Him in Gethsemane, sweating great drops of blood, and on the cross dying in agony—when we see this, self will no longer clamor to be recognized. Looking unto Jesus, we shall be ashamed of our coldness, our lethargy, our self-seeking. We shall be willing to be anything or nothing, so that we may do heart service for the Master. We shall rejoice to bear the cross after Jesus, to endure trial, shame, or persecution for His dear sake.[47]

SELF-RIGHTEOUSNESS INSUFFICIENT

For I say unto you, That except your righteousness shall exceed the righteousness of the scribes and Pharisees, ye shall in no case enter into the kingdom of heaven. Matt. 5:20.

The greatest deception of the human mind in Christ's day was that a mere assent to the truth constitutes righteousness. In all human experience a theoretical knowledge of the truth has been proved to be insufficient for the saving of the soul. It does not bring forth the fruits of righteousness. . . . The Pharisees claimed to be children of Abraham, and boasted of their possession of the oracles of God; yet these advantages did not preserve them from selfishness, malignity, greed for gain, and the basest hypocrisy. . . .

The same danger still exists. Many take it for granted that they are Christians, simply because they subscribe to certain theological tenets. But they have not brought the truth into practical life. They have not believed and loved it, therefore they have not received the power and grace that come through sanctification of the truth. Men may profess faith in the truth; but if it does not make them sincere, kind, patient, forbearing, heavenly-minded, it is a curse to its possessors, and through their influence it is a curse to the world.

The righteousness which Christ taught is conformity of heart and life to the revealed will of God. Sinful men can become righteous only as they have faith in God and maintain a vital connection with Him. Then true godliness will elevate the thoughts and ennoble the life. Then the external forms of religion accord with the Christian's internal purity. Then the ceremonies required in the service of God are not meaningless rites, like those of the hypocritical Pharisees.[48]

Salvation is God's free gift to the believer, given to him for Christ's sake alone. The troubled soul may find peace through faith in Christ, and his peace will be in proportion to his faith and trust. He cannot present his good works as a plea for the salvation of his soul.[49]

FILLED WITH HIS RIGHTEOUSNESS

Blessed are they which do hunger and thirst after righteousness: for they shall be filled. Matt. 5:6.

Righteousness is holiness, likeness to God, and "God is love." 1 John 4:16. It is conformity to the law of God, for "all thy commandments are righteousness" (Ps. 119:172), and "love is the fulfilling of the law" (Rom. 13:10). Righteousness is love, and love is the light and the life of God. The righteousness of God is embodied in Christ. We receive righteousness by receiving Him.

Not by painful struggles or wearisome toil, not by gift or sacrifice, is righteousness obtained; but it is freely given to every soul who hungers and thirsts to receive it. "Ho, every one that thirsteth, come ye to the waters, and he that hath no money; come ye, buy, and eat; . . . without money and without price." Isa. 55:1. "Their righteousness is of me, saith the Lord," and, "This is his name whereby he shall be called, The Lord our righteousness." Isa. 54:17; Jer. 23:6.

No human agent can supply that which will satisfy the hunger and thirst of the soul. But Jesus says, . . . "I am the bread of life: he that cometh to me shall never hunger; and he that believeth on me shall never thirst." John 6:35. . . .

The more we know of God, the higher will be our ideal of character and the more earnest our longing to reflect His likeness. A divine element combines with the human when the soul reaches out after God and the longing heart can say, "My soul, wait thou only upon God; for my expectation is from him." Ps. 62:5. . . .

The continual cry of the heart is, "More of Thee," and ever the Spirit's answer is, "Much more." Rom. 5:9, 10. . . . It was the good pleasure of the Father that in Christ should "all the fulness dwell," and "in him ye are made full." Col. 1:19, RV; 2:10, RV[50]

Christ is the great depository of justifying righteousness and sanctifying grace.

All may come to Him, and receive of His fullness.[51]

THE FIRST STEPS IN JUSTIFICATION

Him hath God exalted with his right hand to be a Prince and a Saviour, for to give repentance to Israel, and forgiveness of sins. Acts 5:31.

Many are confused as to what constitutes the first steps in the work of salvation. Repentance is thought to be a work the sinner must do for himself in order that he may come to Christ. They think that the sinner must procure for himself a fitness in order to obtain the blessing of God's grace. But while it is true that repentance must precede forgiveness, for it is only the broken and contrite heart that is acceptable to God, yet the sinner cannot bring himself to repentance, or prepare himself to come to Christ. . . . The very first step to Christ is taken through the drawing of the Spirit of God; as man responds to this drawing, he advances toward Christ in order that he may repent. . . .

When before the high priests and Sadducees, Peter clearly presented the fact that repentance is the gift of God. Speaking of Christ, he said, "Him hath God exalted with his right hand to be a Prince and a Saviour, for to give repentance to Israel, and forgiveness of sins." Repentance is no less the gift of God than are pardon and justification, and it cannot be experienced except as it is given to the soul by Christ. If we are drawn to Christ, it is through His power and virtue. The grace of contrition comes through Him, and from Him comes justification.[52]

Who is desirous of becoming truly repentant? What must he do? He must come to Jesus, just as he is, without delay. He must believe that the word of Christ is true, and, believing the promise, ask, that he may receive. When sincere desire prompts men to pray, they will not pray in vain. The Lord will fulfill His word, and will give the Holy Spirit to lead to repentance. . . . With prayer he [the repentant sinner] will mingle faith, and not only believe in but obey the precepts of the law. . . . He will renounce all habits and associations that tend to draw the heart from God.[53]

108

THE RIGHTEOUSNESS OF CHRIST SUFFICIENT

But now the righteousness of God without the law is manifested, being witnessed by the law and the prophets; even the righteousness of God which is by faith of Jesus Christ unto all and upon all them that believe: for there is no difference. Rom. 3:21, 22.

What is justification by faith? It is the work of God in laying the glory of man in the dust, and doing for man that which it is not in his power to do for himself. When men see their own nothingness, they are prepared to be clothed with the righteousness of Christ.[54]

Those whom heaven recognizes as holy ones are the last to parade their own goodness. The apostle Peter became a faithful minister of Christ, and he was greatly honored with divine light and power; he had an active part in the upbuilding of Christ's church; but Peter never forgot the fearful experience of his humiliation; his sin was forgiven; yet well he knew that for the weakness of character which had caused his fall only the grace of Christ could avail. He found in himself nothing in which to glory.

None of the apostles or prophets ever claimed to be without sin. Men who have lived nearest to God, men who would sacrifice life itself rather than knowingly commit a wrong act, men whom God had honored with divine light and power, have confessed the sinfulness of their own nature. They have put no confidence in the flesh, have claimed no righteousness of their own, but have trusted wholly in the righteousness of Christ. So will it be with all who behold Christ.[55]

The righteousness of Christ, as a pure white pearl, has no defect, no stain, no guilt. This righteousness may be ours. Salvation, with its blood-bought, inestimable treasures, is the pearl of great price.[56]

The thought that the righteousness of Christ is imputed to us, not because of any merit on our part, but as a free gift from God, is a precious thought. The enemy of God and man is not willing that this truth should be clearly presented; for he knows that if the people receive it fully, his power will be broken.[57]

HIS RIGHTEOUSNESS OBTAINED BY FAITH

But to him that worketh not, but believeth on him that justifieth the ungodly, his faith is counted for righteousness. Rom. 4:5.

The faith that is unto salvation is not a casual faith, it is not the mere consent of the intellect, it is belief rooted in the heart, that embraces Christ as a personal Saviour, assured that He can save unto the uttermost all that come unto God by Him. . . .

The perishing sinner may say: "I am a lost sinner; but Christ came to seek and to save that which was lost. He says, 'I came not to call the righteous, but sinners to repentance.' I am a sinner, and He died upon Calvary's cross to save me. I need not remain a moment longer unsaved. He died and rose again for my justification, and He will save me now. I accept the forgiveness He has promised." . . .

The great work that is wrought for the sinner who is spotted and stained by evil is the work of justification. By Him who speaketh truth he is declared righteous. The Lord imputes unto the believer the righteousness of Christ and pronounces him righteous before the universe. He transfers his sins to Jesus, the sinner's representative, substitute, and surety. Upon Christ He lays the iniquity of every soul that believeth. "He hath made him to be sin for us, who knew no sin; that we might be made the righteousness of God in him." 2 Cor. 5:21. . . .

Through repentance and faith we are rid of sin, and look unto the Lord our righteousness. Jesus suffered, the just for the unjust. . . .

Having made us righteous through the imputed righteousness of Christ, God pronounces us just, and treats us as just. He looks upon us as His dear children. Christ works against the power of sin, and where sin abounded, grace much more abounds. "Therefore being justified by faith, we have peace with God through our Lord Jesus Christ: by whom also we have access by faith into this grace wherein we stand, and rejoice in hope of the glory of God." Rom. 5:1, 2.[58]

God has made ample provision that we may stand perfect in His grace, wanting in nothing, waiting for the appearing of our Lord.[59]

CLOTHED IN HIS RIGHTEOUSNESS

I will greatly rejoice in the Lord, my soul shall be joyful in my God; for he hath clothed me with the garments of salvation, he hath covered me with the robe of righteousness, as a bridegroom decketh himself with ornaments, and as a bride adorneth herself with her jewels. Isa. 61:10.

Only the covering which Christ Himself has provided can make us meet to appear in God's presence. This covering, the robe of His own righteousness, Christ will put upon every repenting, believing soul. "I counsel thee," He says, "to buy of me . . . white raiment, that thou mayest be clothed. . . ." Rev. 3:18.

This robe, woven in the loom of heaven, has in it not one thread of human devising. Christ in His humanity wrought out a perfect character, and this character He offers to impart to us. "All our righteousnesses are as filthy rags." Isa. 64:6. Everything that we of ourselves can do is defiled by sin. But the Son of God "was manifested to take away our sins; and in him is no sin." Sin is defined to be "the transgression of the law." 1 John 3:5, 4. But Christ was obedient to every requirement of the law. . . .

By His perfect obedience He has made it possible for every human being to obey God's commandments. When we submit ourselves to Christ, the heart is united with His heart, the will is merged in His will, the mind becomes one with His mind, the thoughts are brought into captivity to Him; we live His life. This is what it means to be clothed with the garment of His righteousness. Then as the Lord looks upon us He sees, not the fig-leaf garment, not the nakedness and deformity of sin, but His own robe of righteousness, which is perfect obedience to the law of Jehovah.[60]

Those who . . . accept of Christ are looked upon by God, not as they are in Adam, but as they are in Jesus Christ, as the sons and daughters of God.[61]

We are not to be anxious about what Christ and God think of us, but about what God thinks of Christ, our Substitute.[62]

PROVING THE WILL OF GOD

And be not conformed to this world: but be ye transformed by the renewing of your mind, that ye may prove what is that good, and acceptable, and perfect, will of God. Rom. 12:2.

Christ came to the world to counteract Satan's falsehood that God had made a law which men could not keep. Taking humanity upon Himself, He came to this earth, and by a life of obedience showed that God has not made a law that man cannot keep. He showed that it is possible for man perfectly to obey the law. Those who accept Christ as their Saviour, becoming partakers of His divine nature, are enabled to follow His example, living in obedience to every precept of the law. Through the merits of Christ, man is to show by his obedience that he could be trusted in heaven, that he would not rebel.[63]

In all His Godlike deeds, the world's Redeemer declares, "I can of mine own self do nothing." "This commandment have I received of my Father." John 5:30; 10:18. All I do is in fulfillment of the counsel and will of My heavenly Father. The history of the daily earthly life of Jesus is the exact record of the fulfillment of the purposes of God toward man. His life and character were the unfolding or representation of the perfection of the character that man may attain by becoming a partaker of the divine nature, and overcoming the world through daily conflicts.[64]

The youth need to keep ever before them the course that Christ followed. . . . In the study of His life we shall learn how much God through Him will do for His children. And we shall learn that, however great our trials may be, they cannot exceed what Christ endured.[65]

Those who walk even as Christ walked, who are patient, gentle, kind, meek and lowly in heart, those who yoke up with Christ and lift His burdens, who yearn for souls as He yearned for them—these will enter into the joy of their Lord. They will see with Christ the travail of His soul, and be satisfied. Heaven will triumph, for the vacancies made in heaven by the fall of Satan and his angels will be filled by the redeemed of the Lord.[66]

FAITH DEMONSTRATED BY WORKS

Yea, a man may say, Thou hast faith, and I have works: shew me thy faith without thy works, and I will shew thee my faith by my works. James 2:18.

The part man has to act in the salvation of the soul is to believe on Jesus Christ as a perfect Redeemer, not for some other man, but for his own self.[67]

Christ imputes His perfection and righteousness to the believing sinner when he does not continue in sin, but turns from transgression to obedience of the commandments.[68]

While God can be just, and yet justify the sinner through the merits of Christ, no man can cover his soul with the garments of Christ's righteousness while practicing known sins, or neglecting known duties.[69]

The apostle James saw that dangers would arise in presenting the subject of justification by faith, and he labored to show that genuine faith cannot exist without corresponding works. The experience of Abraham is presented. "Seest thou," he says, "how faith wrought with his works, and by works was faith made perfect?" James 2:22. Thus genuine faith does a genuine work in the believer. Faith and obedience bring a solid, valuable experience.[70]

Faith and works are two oars which we must use equally if we [would] press our way up the stream against the current of unbelief.[71]

The so-called faith that does not work by love and purify the soul will not justify any man. "Ye see," says the apostle, "how that by works a man is justified, and not by faith only." James 2:24. Abraham believed God. How do we know that he believed? His works testified to the character of his faith, and his faith was accounted to him for righteousness. We need the faith of Abraham in our day, to lighten the darkness that gathers around us, shutting out the sweet sunlight of God's love, and dwarfing spiritual growth. Our faith should be prolific of good works; for faith without works is dead.[72]

SANCTIFICATION THE WORK OF A LIFETIME

And for their sakes I sanctify myself, that they also might be sanctified through the truth. John 17:19.

The righteousness by which we are justified is imputed; the righteousness by which we are sanctified is imparted. The first is our title to heaven, the second is our fitness for heaven.[73]

Many commit the error of trying to define minutely the fine points of distinction between justification and sanctification. Into the definitions of these two terms they often bring their own ideas and speculations. Why try to be more minute than is Inspiration on the vital question of righteousness by faith?[74]

As the penitent sinner, contrite before God, discerns Christ's atonement in his behalf, and accepts this atonement as his only hope in this life and the future life, his sins are pardoned. This is justification by faith.[75]

Sanctification is not the work of a moment, an hour, a day, but of a lifetime. It is not gained by a happy flight of feeling, but is the result of constantly dying to sin, and constantly living for Christ. Wrongs cannot be righted nor reformations wrought in the character by feeble, intermittent efforts. It is only by long, persevering effort, sore discipline, and stern conflict, that we shall overcome.[76]

It [sanctification] is not merely a theory, an emotion, or a form of words, but a living, active principle, entering into the everyday life. It requires that our habits of eating, drinking, and dressing be such as to secure the preservation of physical, mental, and moral health, that we may present to the Lord our bodies—not an offering corrupted by wrong habits but—"a living sacrifice, holy, acceptable unto God."[77]

The Scriptures are the great agency in the transformation of character. . . . If studied and obeyed, the Word of God works in the heart, subduing every unholy attribute.[78]

There is no such thing as instantaneous sanctification. True sanctification is a daily work, continuing as long as life shall last.[79]

A HATRED OF SIN

Thou hast loved righteousness, and hated iniquity; therefore God, even thy God, hath anointed thee with the oil of gladness above thy fellows. Heb. 1:9.

When in conversion the sinner finds peace with God through the blood of the atonement, the Christian life has but just begun.[80]

The grace that Christ implants in the soul . . . creates in man enmity against Satan. Without this converting grace and renewing power, man would continue the captive of Satan, a servant ever ready to do his bidding. But the new principle in the soul creates conflict where hitherto had been peace. The power which Christ imparts, enables man to resist the tyrant and usurper. Whoever is seen to abhor sin instead of loving it, whoever resists and conquers those passions that have held sway within, displays the operation of a principle wholly from above.[81]

Conformity to the world and harmony with Christ cannot be maintained. Worldly maxims and worldly practices sap spirituality from heart and life. Conformity to the world means resemblance to the world in meeting the world's standard. . . . No man can serve the world and Jesus Christ at the same time. There is an irreconcilable antagonism between Christ and the world.[82]

How few can say: "I am dead to the world; the life I now live is by faith in the Son of God!" . . . While those around us may be vain and engaged in pleasure-seeking and folly, our conversation is in heaven, whence we look for the Saviour; the soul is reaching out after God for pardon and peace, for righteousness and true holiness. Converse with God and contemplation of things above transform the soul into the likeness of Christ.[83]

Let your heart be softened and melted under the divine influence of the Spirit of God. You should not talk so much about yourself, for this will strengthen no one. Talk of Jesus, and let self go; let it be submerged in Christ.[84]

"IF ANY MAN SIN"

If any man sin, we have an advocate with the Father, Jesus Christ the righteous. 1 John 2:1.

When we are clothed with the righteousness of Christ, we shall have no relish for sin; for Christ will be working with us. We may make mistakes, but we will hate the sin that caused the suffering of the Son of God.[85]

If one who daily communes with God errs from the path, if he turns a moment from looking steadfastly unto Jesus, it is not because he sins willfully; for when he sees his mistake, he turns again, and fastens his eyes upon Jesus, and the fact that he has erred does not make him less dear to the heart of God. He knows that he has communion with the Saviour; and when reproved for his mistake in some matter of judgment, he does not walk sullenly, and complain of God, but turns the mistake into a victory.[86]

There are those who have known the pardoning love of Christ, and who really desire to be children of God, yet they realize that their character is imperfect, their life faulty, and they are ready to doubt whether their hearts have been renewed by the Holy Spirit. To such I would say, Do not draw back in despair. We shall often have to bow down and weep at the feet of Jesus because of our shortcomings and mistakes; but we are not to be discouraged. Even if we are overcome by the enemy, we are not cast off, not forsaken and rejected of God. No; Christ is at the right hand of God, who also maketh intercession for us. Said the beloved John, "These things write I unto you, that ye sin not. And if any man sin, we have an advocate with the Father, Jesus Christ the righteous." And do not forget the words of Christ, "The Father himself loveth you." John 16:27. He desires to restore you to Himself, to see His own purity and holiness reflected in you. And if you will but yield yourself to Him, He that hath begun a good work in you will carry it forward to the day of Jesus Christ.[87]

All sin . . . may be overcome by the Holy Spirit's power.[88]

THE TEST OF CHARACTER

And he shall sit as a refiner and purifier of silver: and he shall purify the sons of Levi, and purge them as gold and silver, that they may offer unto the Lord an offering in righteousness. Mal. 3:3.

Many who profess sanctification are entirely ignorant of the work of grace upon the heart. . . . They lay aside reason and judgment, and depend wholly upon their feelings, basing their claims to sanctification upon emotions which they have at some time experienced. . . .

Bible sanctification does not consist in strong emotion. Here is where many are led into error. They make feelings their criterion. When they feel elated or happy, they claim that they are sanctified. Happy feelings or the absence of joy is no evidence that a person is or is not sanctified. . . . Those who are battling with daily temptations, overcoming their own sinful tendencies, and seeking for holiness of heart and life, make no boastful claims of holiness. They are hungering and thirsting for righteousness. Sin appears to them exceedingly sinful.[89]

In summer, as we look upon the trees of the distant forest, all clothed with a beautiful mantle of green, we may not be able to distinguish between the evergreens and the other trees. But as winter approaches, and the frost king encloses them in his icy embrace, stripping the other trees of their beautiful foliage, the evergreens are readily discerned. Thus it will be with all who are walking in humility, distrustful of self, but clinging tremblingly to the hand of Christ. While those who are self-confident, and trust in their own perfection of character, lose their false robe of righteousness when subjected to the storms of trial, the truly righteous, who sincerely love and fear God, wear the robe of Christ's righteousness in prosperity and adversity alike.[90]

It requires the testing time to reveal the pure gold of love and faith in the character. When trials and perplexities come upon the church, then the steadfast zeal and warm affections of Christ's true followers are developed.[91]

THE LADDER TO PERFECTION

According as his divine power hath given unto us all things that pertain unto life and godliness, through the knowledge of him that hath called us to glory and virtue. 2 Peter 1:3.

Jesus is the ladder to heaven, . . . and God calls upon us to mount this ladder. But we cannot do this while we load ourselves down with earthly treasures. We wrong ourselves when we place our convenience and personal advantages before the things of God. There is no salvation in earthly possessions or surroundings. A man is not exalted in God's sight, or accredited by Him as possessing goodness, because he has earthly riches. If we gain a genuine experience in climbing, . . . we must leave every hindrance behind. Those who mount must place their feet firmly on *every* round of the ladder.[92]

We are saved by climbing round after round of the ladder, looking to Christ, clinging to Christ, mounting step by step to the height of Christ, so that He is made unto us wisdom and righteousness and sanctification and redemption. Faith, virtue, knowledge, temperance, patience, godliness, brotherly kindness, and charity are the rounds of this ladder.[93]

Courage, fortitude, faith, and implicit trust in God's power to save are needed. These heavenly graces do not come in a moment; they are acquired by the experience of years. But every sincere and earnest seeker will become a partaker of the divine nature. His soul will be filled with intense longing to know the fullness of that love which passes knowledge. As he advances in the divine life, he will be better able to grasp the elevated, ennobling truths of the Word of God, until, by beholding, he becomes changed, and is enabled to reflect the likeness of his Redeemer.[94]

Child of God, angels are watching the character you develop, they are weighing your words and actions; therefore take heed to your ways, . . . prove whether you are in the love of God.[95]

To love God supremely and our neighbor as ourselves is genuine sanctification.[96]

JOY AND PEACE IN THE HOLY GHOST

For the kingdom of God is not meat and drink; but righteousness, and peace, and joy in the Holy Ghost. Rom. 14:17.

The promises are, "A new heart will I give you"; "I will put my Spirit within you." This provision is made for us through the merit of Christ's righteousness: "And the work of righteousness shall be peace; and the effect of righteousness quietness and assurance for ever." Isa. 32:17. Those who experience the change spoken of in these words will find that their restlessness and disquietude are all taken away, and they will find rest unto their souls in Christ. His merit, His righteousness, are imputed to the believing soul, and the believer has inward peace and joy in the Holy Ghost.[97]

The Lord would have all His sons and daughters happy, peaceful, and obedient. . . .

Happiness that is sought from selfish motives, outside of the path of duty, is ill-balanced, fitful, and transitory; it passes away, and the soul is filled with loneliness and sorrow; but there is joy and satisfaction in the service of God; the Christian is not left to walk in uncertain paths; he is not left to vain regrets and disappointments. If we do not have the pleasures of this life, we may still be joyful in looking to the life beyond.

But even here Christians may have the joy of communion with Christ; they may have the light of His love, the perpetual comfort of His presence. Every step in life may bring us closer to Jesus, may give us a deeper experience of His love, and may bring us one step nearer to the blessed home of peace.[98]

There is peace in believing, and joy in the Holy Ghost. Believing brings peace, and trusting in God brings joy. Believe, believe! my soul says, believe. Rest in God. He is able to keep that which you have committed to His trust. He will bring you off more than conqueror through Him who hath loved you.[99]

WHAT IS FAITH?

Now faith is the substance of things hoped for, the evidence of things not seen. Heb. 11:1.

It is not essential to the exercise of faith that the feelings should be wrought up to a high pitch of excitement; neither is it necessary, in order to gain the hearing of the Lord, that our petitions should be noisy, or attended with physical exercise.

It is true that Satan frequently creates in the heart of the suppliant such a conflict with doubt and temptation that strong cries and tears are involuntarily forced from him; and it is also true that the penitent's sense of guilt is sometimes so great that a repentance commensurate with his sin causes him to experience an agony that finds vent in cries and groans, which the compassionate Saviour hears with pity. But Jesus does not fail to answer the silent prayer of faith. He who simply takes God at His word, and reaches out to connect himself with the Saviour, will receive His blessing in return.[100]

Faith is not feeling. . . . True faith is in no sense allied to presumption. Only he who has true faith is secure against presumption, for presumption is Satan's counterfeit of faith.

Faith claims God's promises, and brings forth fruit in obedience. Presumption also claims the promises, but uses them as Satan did, to excuse transgression. Faith would have led our first parents to trust the love of God and to obey His commands. Presumption led them to transgress His law, believing that His great love would save them from the consequences of their sin. It is not faith that claims the favor of Heaven without complying with the conditions on which mercy is to be granted. Genuine faith has its foundation in the promises and provisions of the Scriptures.[101]

To abide in faith is to put aside feeling and selfish desires, to walk humbly with the Lord, to appropriate His promises, and apply them to all occasions, believing that God will work out His own plans and purposes in your heart and life.[102]

FAITH COMES THROUGH THE PROMISES

*So then faith cometh by hearing, and hearing by the word of God.
Rom. 10:17.*

The truths of the Word of God meet man's great practical necessity—the conversion of the soul through faith. These grand principles are not to be thought too pure and holy to be brought into
the daily life. They are truths which reach to heaven and compass
eternity, yet their vital influence is to be woven into human experience. They are to permeate all the great things and all the little
things of life.[103]

How far we come from representing the character of Christ! But
we must lay hold of His merits by living faith, and claim Him as our
Saviour. He died on Calvary to save us. Each should make it a personal work between God and his own soul, as though there were
no one in the world but himself. When we exercise personal faith,
our hearts will not be as cold as an iron wedge; we shall be able to
realize what is meant by the psalmist when he says, "Blessed is he
. . . whose sin is covered." Ps. 32:1.[104]

God invites us to prove for ourselves the reality of His Word, the
truth of His promises. He bids us "taste and see that the Lord is
good." Ps. 34:8. . . . He declares, "Ask, and ye shall receive." John
16:24. His promises will be fulfilled. They have never failed; they
never can fail.[105]

Our Saviour wants you to keep in close relation to Himself, that
He may make you happy. When Christ lets His blessing rest upon
us, we should offer thanksgiving and praise to His dear name. But,
you say, if I could only know that He is my Saviour! Well, what kind
of evidence do you want? Do you want a special feeling or emotion
to prove that Christ is yours? Is this more reliable than pure faith in
God's promises? Would it not be better to take the blessed promises
of God and apply them to yourself, bearing your whole weight upon
them? This is faith.[106]

THE GOOD FIGHT OF FAITH

Fight the good fight of faith, lay hold on eternal life, whereunto thou art also called, and hast professed a good profession before many witnesses. 1 Tim. 6:12.

The earnest counsel given by the apostle Paul to Timothy, that he might not fail in doing his duty, should be set before the youth of today: "Let no man despise thy youth; but be thou an example of the believers, in word, in conversation, in charity, in spirit, in faith, in purity." 1 Tim. 4:12. Besetting sins must be battled with and overcome. Objectionable traits of character, whether hereditary or cultivated, should be taken up separately, and compared with the great rule of righteousness; and in the light reflected from the Word of God, they should be firmly resisted and overcome, through the strength of Christ. . . .

Day by day, and hour by hour, there must be a vigorous process of self-denial and of sanctification going on within; and then the outward works will testify that Jesus is abiding in the heart by faith. Sanctification does not close the avenues of the soul to knowledge, but it comes to expand the mind, and to inspire it to search for truth, as for hidden treasure; and the knowledge of God's will advances the work of sanctification. There is a heaven, and O, how earnestly we should strive to reach it. I appeal to you . . . to believe in Jesus as your Saviour. Believe that He is ready to help you by His grace, when you come to Him in sincerity. You must fight the good fight of faith. You must be wrestlers for the crown of life. Strive, for the grasp of Satan is upon you; and if you do not wrench yourselves from him, you will be palsied and ruined. The foe is on the right hand, and on the left, before you, and behind you; and you must trample him under your feet. Strive, for there is a crown to be won.[107]

Soon we shall witness the coronation of our King. Those whose lives have been hidden with Christ, those who on this earth have fought the good fight of faith, will shine forth with the Redeemer's glory in the kingdom of God.[108]

THE JUST SHALL LIVE BY FAITH

As ye have therefore received Christ Jesus the Lord, so walk ye in him. Col. 2:6.

Our growth in grace, our joy, our usefulness—all depend upon our union with Christ. It is by communion with Him, daily, hourly—by abiding in Him—that we are to grow in grace. He is not only the author, but the finisher of our faith. It is Christ first and last and always. He is to be with us, not only at the beginning and the end of our course, but at every step of the way. . . .

Do you ask, "How am I to abide in Christ?" In the same way as you received Him at first. "As ye have therefore received Christ Jesus the Lord, so walk ye in him." Col. 2:6. "The just shall live by faith." Heb. 10:38. You gave yourself to God, to be His wholly, to serve and obey Him, and you took Christ as your Saviour. You could not yourself atone for your sins or change your heart; but having given yourself to God, you believe that He for Christ's sake did all this for you. By *faith* you became Christ's, and by faith you are to grow up in Him—by giving and taking. You are to *give* all—your heart, your will, your service—give yourself to Him to obey all His requirements; and you must *take* all—Christ, the fullness of all blessing, to abide in your heart, to be your strength, your righteousness, your everlasting helper—to give you power to obey.

Consecrate yourself to God in the morning; make this your very first work. Let your prayer be, "Take me, O Lord, as wholly Thine. I lay all my plans at Thy feet. Use me today in Thy service. Abide with me, and let all my work be wrought in Thee." This is a daily matter. Each morning consecrate yourself to God for that day. Surrender all your plans to Him, to be carried out or given up as His providence shall indicate. Thus day by day you may be giving your life into the hands of God, and thus your life will be molded more and more after the life of Christ.[109]

FAITH IS THE VICTORY

For whatsoever is born of God overcometh the world: and this is the victory that overcometh the world, even our faith. 1 John 5:4.

The Christian's life should be one of faith, of victory, and joy in God. "Whatsoever is born of God overcometh the world: and this is the victory that overcometh the world, even our faith." Truly spake God's servant Nehemiah, "The joy of the Lord is your strength." Neh. 8:10. And Paul says: "Rejoice in the Lord alway: and again I say, Rejoice." Phil. 4:4. "Rejoice evermore. Pray without ceasing. In every thing give thanks. . . ." 1 Thess. 5:16-18.[110]

God is able and willing to bestow upon His servants all the strength they need, and to give them the wisdom that their varied necessities demand. He will more than fulfill the highest expectations of those who put their trust in Him.

Jesus does not call on us to follow Him, and then forsake us. If we surrender our lives to His service, we can never be placed in a position for which God has not made provision. Whatever may be our situation, we have a Guide to direct our way; whatever our perplexities, we have a sure Counselor; whatever our sorrow, bereavement, or loneliness, we have a sympathizing Friend. If in our ignorance we make missteps, Christ does not leave us. . . . "He shall deliver the needy when he crieth; the poor also, and him that hath no helper." Ps. 72:12.[111]

Faith . . . enables us to look beyond the present, with its burdens and cares, to the great hereafter, where all that now perplexes us shall be made plain. Faith sees Jesus standing as our Mediator at the right hand of God. Faith beholds the mansions that Christ has gone to prepare for those who love Him. Faith sees the robe and crown prepared for the overcomer, and hears the song of the redeemed.[112]

We may claim much of our kind heavenly Father. . . . We may believe in God, we may trust Him, and by so doing glorify His name.[113]

The strength of those who, in faith, love and serve God, will be renewed day by day.[114]

CONVERSION AND THE NEW LIFE

TRUE SORROW FOR SIN

Repent ye therefore, and be converted, that your sins may be blotted out, when the times of refreshing shall come from the presence of the Lord. Acts 3:19.

The conditions of obtaining mercy of God are simple and just and reasonable. The Lord does not require us to do some grievous thing in order that we may have the forgiveness of sin. We need not make long and wearisome pilgrimages, or perform painful penances, to commend our souls to the God of heaven or to expiate our transgression; but he that confesseth and forsaketh his sin shall have mercy.[1]

Repentance includes sorrow for sin, and a turning away from it. We shall not renounce sin unless we see its sinfulness; until we turn away from it in heart, there will be no real change in the life.[2]

One ray of the glory of God, one gleam of the purity of Christ, penetrating the soul, makes every spot of defilement painfully distinct, and lays bare the deformity and defects of the human character. It makes apparent the unhallowed desires, the infidelity of the heart, the impurity of the lips. The sinner's acts of disloyalty in making void the law of God, are exposed to his sight, and his spirit is stricken and afflicted under the searching influence of the Spirit of God.[3]

The tears of the penitent are only the raindrops that precede the sunshine of holiness. This sorrow heralds a joy which will be a living fountain in the soul. "Only acknowledge thine iniquity, that thou hast transgressed against the Lord thy God"; "and I will not cause mine anger to fall upon you: for I am merciful, saith the Lord." Jer. 3:13, 12. "Unto them that mourn in Zion," He has appointed to give "beauty for ashes, the oil of joy for mourning, the garment of praise for the spirit of heaviness." Isa. 61:3.[4]

SINCERE CONFESSION ESSENTIAL

If we confess our sins, he is faithful and just to forgive us our sins,
and to cleanse us from all unrighteousness. 1 John 1:9.

The apostle says, "Confess your faults one to another, and pray
one for another, that ye may be healed." James 5:16. Confess your
sins to God, who only can forgive them, and your faults to one another. If you have given offense to your friend or neighbor, you are
to acknowledge your wrong, and it is his duty freely to forgive you.
Then you are to seek the forgiveness of God, because the brother
you have wounded is the property of God, and in injuring him you
have sinned against his Creator. . . .

True confession is always of a specific character, and acknowledges particular sins. They may be of such a nature as to be brought
before God only; they may be wrongs that should be confessed to
individuals who have suffered injury through them; or they may be
of a public character, and should then be as publicly confessed. But
all confession should be definite and to the point, acknowledging
the very sins of which you are guilty.[5]

Many, many confessions should never be spoken in the hearing
of mortals; for the result is that which the limited judgment of finite
beings does not anticipate. . . . God will be better glorified if we confess the secret, inbred corruption of the heart to Jesus alone than if we
open its recesses to finite, erring man, who cannot judge righteously
unless his heart is constantly imbued with the Spirit of God. . . . Do
not pour into human ears the story which God alone should hear.[6]

The confession that is the outpouring of the inmost soul finds its
way to the God of infinite pity.[7]

Your sins may be as mountains before you; but if you humble
your heart, and confess your sins, trusting in the merits of a crucified and risen Saviour, He will forgive, and will cleanse you from all
unrighteousness. . . . Desire the fullness of the grace of Christ. Let
your heart be filled with an intense longing for His righteousness.[8]

THE MEANING OF FORGIVENESS

Who is a God like unto thee, that pardoneth iniquity, and passeth by the transgression of the remnant of his heritage? he retaineth not his anger for ever, because he delighteth in mercy. Micah 7:18.

God's forgiveness is not merely a judicial act by which He sets us free from condemnation. It is not only forgiveness for sin but reclaiming from sin. It is the outflow of redeeming love that transforms the heart. David had the true conception of forgiveness when he prayed, "Create in me a clean heart, O God; and renew a right spirit within me." Ps. 51:10.[9]

If you take even one step toward Him in repentance, He will hasten to enfold you in His arms of infinite love. His ear is open to the cry of the contrite soul. The very first reaching out of the heart after God is known to Him. Never a prayer is offered, however faltering, never a tear is shed, however secret, never a sincere desire after God is cherished, however feeble, but the Spirit of God goes forth to meet it. Even before the prayer is uttered or the yearning of the heart made known, grace from Christ goes forth to meet the grace that is working upon the human soul.

Your heavenly Father will take from you the garments defiled by sin. In the beautiful parabolic prophecy of Zechariah, the high priest Joshua, standing clothed in filthy garments before the angel of the Lord, represents the sinner. And the word is spoken by the Lord, "Take away the filthy garments from him. And unto him he said, Behold, I have caused thine iniquity to pass from thee, and I will clothe thee with change of raiment. . . . So they set a fair mitre upon his head, and clothed him with garments." Zech. 3:4, 5. Even so God will clothe you with "the garments of salvation," and cover you with "the robe of righteousness." Isa. 61:10. . . .

"If thou wilt walk in my ways," He declares, "I will give thee places to walk among these that stand by" (Zech. 3:7)—even among the holy angels that surround His throne.[10]

THE SONS AND DAUGHTERS OF GOD

But as many as received him, to them gave he power to become the sons of God, even to them that believe on his name. John 1:12.

It is through faith in Jesus Christ that the truth is accepted in the heart, and the human agent is purified and cleansed. . . . He has an abiding principle in the soul, that enables him to overcome temptation. "Whosoever abideth in him sinneth not." 1 John 3:6. God has power to keep the soul that is in Christ who is under temptation. . . .

A mere profession of godliness is worthless. It is he that abideth in Christ that is a Christian. . . . Unless the mind of God becomes the mind of men, every effort to purify himself will be useless; for it is impossible to elevate man except through a knowledge of God.[11]

The question you need to put to yourselves is, "Am I a Christian?" To be a Christian is to be far more than many understand. It means more than simply having your name upon the church records. It means to be joined to Christ. It means to have simple faith, unwavering reliance upon God. It means to have childlike confidence in your heavenly Father through the name and merit of His dear Son. Do you love to keep the commandments of God, because the commandments of God are God's precepts, the transcript of His character, and can no more be altered than can the character of God? Do you respect and love the law of Jehovah?[12]

As sons and daughters of God, Christians should strive to reach the high ideal set before them in the gospel. They should be content with nothing less than perfection.[13]

To those who receive Him He gives power to become the sons of God, that at last God may receive them as His, to dwell with Him throughout eternity. If during this life they are loyal to God, they will at last "see his face; and his name shall be in their foreheads." Rev. 22:4. And what is the happiness of heaven but to see God? What greater joy could come to the sinner saved by the grace of Christ than to look upon the face of God and know Him as Father?[14]

FORGIVEN AS WE FORGIVE

For with what judgment ye judge, ye shall be judged: and with what measure ye mete, it shall be measured to you again. Matt. 7:2.

We can receive forgiveness from God only as we forgive others. It is the love of God that draws us unto Him, and that love cannot touch our hearts without creating love for our brethren.

After completing the Lord's Prayer, Jesus added: "If ye forgive men their trespasses, your heavenly Father will also forgive you: but if ye forgive not men their trespasses, neither will your Father forgive your trespasses." Matt. 6:14, 15. He who is unforgiving cuts off the very channel through which alone he can receive mercy from God. We should not think that unless those who have injured us confess the wrong we are justified in withholding from them our forgiveness. It is their part, no doubt, to humble their hearts by repentance and confession; but we are to have a spirit of compassion toward those who have trespassed against us, whether or not they confess their faults.[15]

Nothing can justify an unforgiving spirit. He who is unmerciful toward others shows that he himself is not a partaker of God's pardoning grace. In God's forgiveness the heart of the erring one is drawn close to the great heart of Infinite Love. The tide of divine compassion flows into the sinner's soul, and from him to the souls of others. . . .

We are not forgiven *because* we forgive, but *as* we forgive. The ground of all forgiveness is found in the unmerited love of God, but by our attitude toward others we show whether we have made that love our own. Wherefore Christ says, "With what judgment ye judge, ye shall be judged."[16]

Let Christ, the divine Life dwell in you and through you reveal the heaven-born love that will inspire hope in the hopeless and bring heaven's peace to the sin-stricken heart. As we come to God, this is the condition which meets us at the threshold, that, receiving mercy from Him, we yield ourselves to reveal His grace to others.[17]

RESTITUTION IS REQUIRED

If the wicked restore the pledge, give again that he had robbed, walk in the statutes of life, without committing iniquity; he shall surely live, he shall not die. Eze. 33:15.

No repentance is genuine that does not work reformation. . . .

The Christian in his business life is to represent to the world the manner in which our Lord would conduct business enterprises. In every transaction he is to make it manifest that God is his teacher. "Holiness unto the Lord" is to be written upon daybooks and ledgers, on deeds, receipts, and bills of exchange. Those who profess to be followers of Christ, and who deal in an unrighteous manner, are bearing false witness against the character of a holy, just, and merciful God. . . . If we have injured others through any unjust business transaction, if we have overreached in trade, or defrauded any man, even though it be within the pale of the law, we should confess our wrong, and make restitution as far as lies in our power. It is right for us to restore not only that which we have taken, but all that it would have accumulated if put to a right and wise use during the time it has been in our possession.[18]

If we have in any manner defrauded or injured our brother, we should make restitution. If we have unwittingly borne false witness, if we have misstated his words, if we have injured his influence in any way, we should go to the ones with whom we have conversed about him, and take back all our injurious misstatements.[19]

It will not be long before probation will close. If you do not now serve the Lord with fidelity, how will you meet the record of your unfaithful dealing? . . . If you have refused to deal honestly with God, I beseech you to think of your deficiency, and if possible to make restitution. If this cannot be done, in humble penitence pray that God for Christ's sake will pardon your great debt. Begin now to act like Christians. Make no excuse for failing to give the Lord His own. Now, . . . while it is not yet too late for wrongs to be righted, while it is called today, if ye will hear His voice, harden not your hearts.[20]

COME JUST AS YOU ARE

Can the Ethiopian change his skin, or the leopard his spots? then may ye also do good, that are accustomed to do evil. Jer. 13:23.

God does not regard all sins as of equal magnitude; there are degrees of guilt in His estimation, as well as in that of man; but however trifling this or that wrong act may seem in the eyes of men, no sin is small in the sight of God. Man's judgment is partial, imperfect; but God estimates all things as they really are. The drunkard is despised, and is told that his sin will exclude him from heaven; while pride, selfishness, and covetousness too often go unrebuked. But these are sins that are especially offensive to God; for they are contrary to the benevolence of His character, to that unselfish love which is the very atmosphere of the unfallen universe. He who falls into some of the grosser sins may feel a sense of his shame and poverty and his need of the grace of Christ; but pride feels no need, and so it closes the heart against Christ, and the infinite blessings He came to give. . . .

If you see your sinfulness, do not wait to make yourself better. How many there are who think they are not good enough to come to Christ. Do you expect to become better through your own efforts? . . . There is help for us only in God. We must not wait for stronger persuasions, for better opportunities, or for holier tempers. We can do nothing for ourselves. We must come to Christ just as we are.[21]

Yield yourself to Christ without delay; He alone, by the power of His grace, can redeem you from ruin. He alone can bring your moral and mental powers into a state of health. Your heart may be warm with the love of God; your understanding, clear and mature; your conscience, illuminated, quick, and pure; your will, upright and sanctified, subject to the control of the Spirit of God. You can make yourself what you choose. If you will now face rightabout, cease to do evil and learn to do well, then you will be happy indeed; you will be successful in the battles of life, and rise to glory and honor in the better life than this.[22]

A PERSONAL PARDON

Have mercy upon me, O God, according to thy lovingkindness: according unto the multitude of thy tender mercies blot out my transgressions. Ps. 51:1.

We should remember that all make mistakes; even men and women who have had years of experience sometimes err; but God does not cast them off because of their errors; to every erring son and daughter of Adam He gives the privilege of another trial.[23]

Jesus loves to have us come to Him just as we are, sinful, helpless, dependent. We may come with all our weakness, our folly, our sinfulness, and fall at His feet in penitence. It is His glory to encircle us in the arms of His love, and to bind up our wounds, to cleanse us from all impurity.

Here is where thousands fail: they do not believe that Jesus pardons them personally, individually. They do not take God at His word. It is the privilege of all who comply with the conditions to know for themselves that pardon is freely extended for every sin. Put away the suspicion that God's promises are not meant for you. They are for every repentant transgressor. Strength and grace have been provided through Christ to be brought by ministering angels to every believing soul. None are so sinful that they cannot find strength, purity, and righteousness in Jesus, who died for them. He is waiting to strip them of their garments stained and polluted with sin, and to put upon them the white robes of righteousness; He bids them live and not die. . . .

Can you believe that when the poor sinner longs to return, longs to forsake his sins, the Lord sternly withholds him from coming to His feet in repentance? Away with such thoughts! Nothing can hurt your own soul more than to entertain such a conception of our heavenly Father. . . . Come with your whole heart to Jesus, and you may claim His blessing.[24]

He who through His own atonement provided for man an infinite fund of moral power will not fail to employ this power in their behalf.[25]

UNION WITH CHRIST

Abide in me, and I in you. As the branch cannot bear fruit of itself, except it abide in the vine; no more can ye, except ye abide in me. John 15:4.

Every individual, by his own act, either puts Christ from him by refusing to cherish His spirit and follow His example, or he enters into a personal union with Christ by self-renunciation, faith, and obedience. We must, each for himself, choose Christ, because He has first chosen us. This union with Christ is to be formed by those who are naturally at enmity with Him. It is a relation of utter dependence, to be entered into by a proud heart. This is close work, and many who profess to be followers of Christ know nothing of it. They nominally accept the Saviour, but not as the sole ruler of their hearts.[26]

The evil tendencies of mankind are hard to overcome. The battles are tedious. Every soul in the strife knows how severe, how bitter, are these contests. Everything about growth in grace is difficult, because the standard and maxims of the world are constantly interposed between the soul and God's holy standard. The Lord would have us elevated, ennobled, purified, by carrying out the principles underlying His great moral standard, which will test every character in the great day of final reckoning.[27]

We must gain the victory over self, crucify the affections and lusts; and then begins the union of the soul with Christ. . . . After this union is formed, it can be preserved only by continual, earnest, painstaking effort. . . .

Every Christian must stand on guard continually, watching every avenue of the soul where Satan might find access. He must pray for divine help and at the same time resolutely resist every inclination to sin. By courage, by faith, by persevering toil, he can conquer. But let him remember that to gain the victory Christ must abide in him and he in Christ. . . . It is only by personal union with Christ, by communion with Him daily, hourly, that we can bear the fruits of the Holy Spirit.[28]

HELP FOR THE POOR IN SPIRIT

Blessed are the poor in spirit: for their's is the kingdom of heaven. Matt. 5:3.

All who have a sense of their deep soul poverty, who feel that they have nothing good in themselves, may find righteousness and strength by looking unto Jesus.[29]

"The sacrifices of God are a broken spirit: a broken and a contrite heart, O God, thou wilt not despise." Ps. 51:17. Man must be emptied of self before he can be, in the fullest sense, a believer in Jesus. When self is renounced, then the Lord can make man a new creature.[30]

When man has sinned against a holy and merciful God, he can pursue no course so noble as to repent sincerely, and confess his errors in tears and bitterness of soul. This God requires of him; He accepts nothing less than a broken heart and a contrite spirit.[31]

The proud heart strives to earn salvation; but both our title to heaven and our fitness for it are found in the righteousness of Christ. The Lord can do nothing toward the recovery of man until, convinced of his own weakness, and stripped of all self-sufficiency, he yields himself to the control of God. Then he can receive the gift that God is waiting to bestow. From the soul that feels his need, nothing is withheld. He has unrestricted access to Him in whom all fullness dwells.[32]

The only reason why we may not have remission of sins that are past is that we are not willing to humble our proud hearts and comply with the conditions.[33]

God is very pitiful, for He understands our weaknesses and our temptations; and when we come to Him with broken hearts and contrite spirits, He accepts our repentance, and promises that, as we take hold of His strength to make peace with Him, we shall make peace with Him. Oh, what gratitude, what joy, should we feel that God is merciful![34]

The offering most sweet and acceptable in God's sight is a heart made humble by self-denial, by lifting the cross and following Jesus.[35]

A CHANGE OF HEART NEEDED

Jesus answered and said unto him, Verily, verily, I say unto thee, Except a man be born again, he cannot see the kingdom of God. John 3:3.

Nicodemus held a high position of trust in the Jewish nation. . . . With others, he had been stirred by the teaching of Jesus. . . . The lessons that had fallen from the Saviour's lips had greatly impressed him, and he desired to learn more of these wonderful truths. . . .

Nicodemus had come to the Lord thinking to enter into a discussion with Him, but Jesus laid bare the foundation principles of truth. He said to Nicodemus, It is not theoretical knowledge you need so much as spiritual regeneration. You need not to have your curiosity satisfied, but to have a new heart. You must receive a new life from above before you can appreciate heavenly things.[36]

The change of heart represented by the new birth can be brought about only by the effectual working of the Holy Spirit. . . . Pride and self-love resist the Spirit of God; every natural inclination of the soul opposes the change from self-importance and pride to the meekness and lowliness of Christ. But if we would travel in the pathway to eternal life, we must not listen to the whispering of self. In humility and contrition we must beseech our heavenly Father, "Create in me a clean heart, O God; and renew a right spirit within me." Ps. 51:10. As we receive divine light, and cooperate with the heavenly intelligences, we are "born again," freed from the defilement of sin by the power of Christ.[37]

The mighty power of the Holy Spirit works an entire transformation in the character of the human agent, making him a new creature in Christ Jesus. . . . The words and actions express the love of the Saviour. There is no striving for the highest place. Self is renounced. The name of Jesus is written on all that is said and done.[38]

Is not this, the renewal of man, the greatest miracle that can be performed? What cannot the human agent do who by faith takes hold of the divine power?[39]

BLESSINGS ON THE HUMBLE

And Jesus called a little child unto him, and set him in the midst of them, and said, Verily I say unto you, Except ye be converted, and become as little children, ye shall not enter into the kingdom of heaven. Matt. 18:2, 3.

The helpless sinner must cling to Christ as his only hope. If he lets go his hold for a moment, he imperils his own soul and the souls of others. Only in the exercise of living faith are we safe. But the commission of any known sin, the neglect of known duties, at home or abroad, will destroy faith, and disconnect the soul from God.

Nothing is more offensive to God than a self-sufficient spirit. In the life of Peter is a sad lesson which should be a warning to all the professed followers of Christ. The Saviour had faithfully warned him of the approaching danger, but, self-confident and presumptuous, he asserted his constant fidelity and zeal, and declared himself willing to follow his Master to prison and to death. The test came for Peter when the storm burst upon the disciples by the humiliation of their Leader. Mournful are the words traced by the pen of inspiration: "Then all the disciples forsook him, and fled." Matt. 26:56. And the ardent, zealous, self-confident Peter repeatedly denied his Lord. He afterward bitterly repented; but this example should admonish all to beware of self-confidence and self-righteousness.[40]

The men who humble themselves even as a little child are the men who will be taught by God. The Lord is not dependent on any man's talents; for He is the Source of all perfect gifts. The very humblest man, if he loves and fears God, is the possessor of heavenly gifts. The Lord can use such a man, because he does not strive to work himself according to his own standard. He works with fear and trembling lest he will spoil the pattern. His life is an expression of the life of Christ.[41]

We must constantly cherish meekness and humility, if we would possess the spirit of Christ.[42]

A NEW LIFE ALTOGETHER

That ye put off concerning the former conversation the old man, which is corrupt according to the deceitful lusts; and be renewed in the spirit of your mind; and that ye put on the new man, which after God is created in righteousness and true holiness. Eph. 4:22-24.

Conversion is a work that most do not appreciate. It is not a small matter to transform an earthly, sin-loving mind and bring it to understand the unspeakable love of Christ, the charms of His grace, and the excellency of God, so that the soul shall be imbued with divine love and captivated with the heavenly mysteries. When he understands these things, his former life appears disgusting and hateful. He hates sin, and, breaking his heart before God, he embraces Christ as the life and joy of the soul. He renounces his former pleasures. He has a new mind, new affections, new interest, new will; his sorrows, and desires, and love are all new. . . . Heaven, which once possessed no charms, is now viewed in its riches and glory; and he contemplates it as his future home, where he shall see, love, and praise the One who hath redeemed him by His precious blood. The works of holiness, which appeared wearisome, are now his delight. The Word of God, which was dull and uninteresting, is now chosen as his study, the man of his counsel. It is as a letter written to him from God, bearing the inscription of the Eternal. His thoughts, his words, and his deeds are brought to this rule and tested. He trembles at the commands and threatenings which it contains, while he firmly grasps its promises and strengthens his soul by appropriating them to himself.[43]

When the transforming grace of Christ is upon the heart, a righteous indignation will take possession of the soul because the sinner has so long neglected the great salvation that God has provided for him. He will then surrender himself, body, soul, and spirit, to God and will withdraw from companionship with Satan, through the grace given him of God.[44]

All need to understand the process of conversion. The fruit is seen in the changed life.[45]

HOLINESS OF LIFE

Follow peace with all men, and holiness, without which no man shall see the Lord. Heb. 12:14.

No one who claims holiness is really holy. Those who are registered as holy in the books of heaven are not aware of the fact, and are the last ones to boast of their own goodness.[46]

It is not a conclusive evidence that a man is a Christian because he manifests spiritual ecstasy under extraordinary circumstances. Holiness is not rapture: it is an entire surrender of the will to God; it is living by every word that proceeds from the mouth of God; it is doing the will of our heavenly Father; it is trusting God in trial, in darkness as well as in the light; it is walking by faith and not by sight; it is relying on God with unquestioning confidence, and resting in His love.[47]

No one can be omnipotent, but all can cleanse themselves from filthiness of the flesh and spirit, perfecting holiness in the fear of the Lord. God requires every soul to be pure and holy. We have hereditary tendencies to wrong. This is a part of self that no one need carry about. It is a weakness of humanity to pet selfishness, because it is a natural trait of character. But unless all selfishness is put away, unless self is crucified, we can never be holy as God is holy. There is in humanity a tendency to suspicious imagining, which circumstances quicken into lively growth. If this trait is indulged, it spoils the character and ruins the soul.[48]

God requires moral perfection in all. Those who have been given light and opportunities should, as God's stewards, aim for perfection, and never, never lower the standard of righteousness to accommodate inherited and cultivated tendencies to wrong. Christ took upon Him our human nature, and lived our life, to show us that we may be like Him. . . . We ought to be holy even as God is holy; and when we comprehend the full significance of this statement, and set our heart to do the work of God, to be holy as He is holy, we shall approach the standard set for each individual in Christ Jesus.[49]

STRENGTHENED BY THE SPIRIT

That he would grant you, according to the riches of his glory, to be strengthened with might by his Spirit in the inner man. Eph. 3:16.

Jesus says, "What things soever ye desire, when ye pray, believe that ye receive them, and ye shall have them." Mark 11:24. There is a condition to this promise—that we pray according to the will of God. But it is the will of God to cleanse us from sin, to make us His children, and to enable us to live a holy life. So we may ask for these blessings, and believe that we receive them, and thank God that we have received them. It is our privilege to go to Jesus and be cleansed, and to stand before the law without shame or remorse. . . .

Through this simple act of believing God, the Holy Spirit has begotten a new life in your heart. You are as a child born into the family of God, and He loves you as He loves His Son.

Now that you have given yourself to Jesus, do not draw back, do not take yourself away from Him, but day by day say, "I am Christ's; I have given myself to Him;" and ask Him to give you His Spirit, and keep you by His grace. As it is by giving yourself to God, and believing Him, that you become His child, so you are to live in Him. The apostle says, "As ye have therefore received Christ Jesus the Lord, so walk ye in him." Col. 2:6.

Some seem to feel that they must be on probation, and must prove to the Lord that they are reformed, before they can claim His blessing. But they may claim the blessing of God even now. They must have His grace, the Spirit of Christ, to help their infirmities, or they cannot resist evil.[50]

The Spirit furnishes the strength that sustains striving, wrestling souls in every emergency, amidst the hatred of the world, and the realization of their own failures and mistakes. In sorrow and affliction, when the outlook seems dark and the future perplexing, and we feel helpless and alone—these are the times when, in answer to the prayer of faith, the Holy Spirit brings comfort to the heart.[51]

AMAZING TRANSFORMATION OF CHARACTER

As for me, I will behold thy face in righteousness: I shall be satisfied, when I awake, with thy likeness. Ps. 17:15.

Jesus came to restore in man the image of his Maker. None but Christ can fashion anew the character that has been ruined by sin. He came to expel the demons that had controlled the will.[52]

The Lord Jesus is making experiments on human hearts through the exhibition of His mercy and abundant grace. He is effecting transformations so amazing that Satan, with all his triumphant boasting, with all his confederacy of evil united against God and the laws of His government, stands viewing them as a fortress impregnable to his sophistries and delusions. They are to him an incomprehensible mystery. The angels of God, seraphim and cherubim, the powers commissioned to cooperate with human agencies, look on with astonishment and joy, that fallen men, once children of wrath, are through the training of Christ developing characters after the divine similitude, to be sons and daughters of God, to act an important part in the occupations and pleasures of heaven.[53]

They were purified in the furnace of affliction. For Jesus' sake they endured opposition, hatred, calumny. They followed Him through conflicts sore; they endured self-denial and experienced bitter disappointments. By their own painful experience they learned the evil of sin, its power, its guilt, its woe; and they look upon it with abhorrence. A sense of the infinite sacrifice made for its cure, humbles them in their own sight, and fills their hearts with gratitude and praise which those who have never fallen cannot appreciate. They love much, because they have been forgiven much. Having been partakers of Christ's sufferings, they are fitted to be partakers with Him of His glory.[54]

In their untainted purity and spotless perfection, Christ looks upon His people as the reward of all His suffering, His humiliation, and His love, and the supplement of His glory—Christ, the great center from which radiates all glory.[55]

OUR LORD'S EXAMPLE

Therefore we are buried with him by baptism into death: that like as Christ was raised up from the dead by the glory of the Father, even so we also should walk in newness of life. Rom. 6:4.

Jesus did not receive baptism as a confession of guilt on His own account. He identified Himself with sinners, taking the steps that we are to take, and doing the work that we must do. His life of suffering and patient endurance after His baptism was also an example to us.[56]

Christ as the head of humanity was to take the same steps that we are required to take. Although sinless, He was our example in fulfilling all the requirements for the redemption of the sinful race. He bore the sins of the whole world. His baptism was to embrace the whole sinful world who by repentance and faith would be pardoned. "After that the kindness and love of God our Saviour toward man appeared, not by works of righteousness which we have done, but according to his mercy he saved us, by the washing of regeneration, and renewing of the Holy Ghost; which he shed on us abundantly through Jesus Christ our Saviour; that being justified by his grace, we should be made heirs according to the hope of eternal life. This is a faithful saying, and these things I will that thou affirm constantly, that they which have believed in God might be careful to maintain good works. These things are good and profitable unto men." Titus 3:4-8. Man was brought again into favor with God by the washing of regeneration. The washing was the burial with Christ in the water in the likeness of His death, representing that all who repent of the transgression of the law of God receive purification, cleansing, through the work of the Holy Spirit. Baptism represents true conversion by the renewing of the Holy Spirit.[57]

Those who have been buried with Christ in baptism, and been raised in the likeness of His resurrection, have pledged themselves to live in newness of life. "If ye then be risen with Christ, seek those things which are above, where Christ sitteth on the right hand of God. Set your affection on things above, not on things on the earth." Col. 3:1, 2.[58]

"THIS IS MY BELOVED SON"

And Jesus, when he was baptized, went up straightway out of the water: and, lo, the heavens were opened unto him, and he saw the Spirit of God descending like a dove, and lighting upon him: and lo a voice from heaven, saying, This is my beloved Son, in whom I am well pleased. Matt. 3:16, 17.

As Jesus asked for baptism, John drew back, exclaiming, "I have need to be baptized of thee, and comest thou to me?" With firm yet gentle authority, Jesus answered, "Suffer it to be so now: for thus it becometh us to fulfil all righteousness." Matt. 3:14, 15. And John, yielding, led the Saviour down into the Jordan, and buried Him beneath the water. "And straightway coming up out of the water," Jesus "saw the heavens opened, and the Spirit like a dove descending upon him. Mark 1:10. . . . The solemnity of the divine Presence rested upon the assembly. The people stood silently gazing upon Christ. His form was bathed in the light that ever surrounds the throne of God. His upturned face was glorified as they had never before seen the face of man. From the open heavens a voice was heard saying, "This is my beloved Son, in whom I am well pleased." Matt. 3:17. . . .

The word that was spoken to Jesus at the Jordan . . . embraces humanity. God spoke to Jesus as our representative. With all our sins and weaknesses, we are not cast aside as worthless. "He hath made us accepted in the beloved." Eph. 1:6. The glory that rested upon Christ is a pledge of the love of God for us. . . . His love has encircled man, and reached the highest heaven. The light which fell from the open portals upon the head of our Saviour will fall upon us as we pray for help to resist temptation. The voice which spoke to Jesus says to every believing soul, This is My beloved child, in whom I am well pleased. . . .

Our Redeemer has opened the way so that the most sinful, the most needy, the most oppressed and despised, may find access to the Father. All may have a home in the mansions which Jesus has gone to prepare.[59]

BORN OF WATER AND THE SPIRIT

Jesus answered, Verily, verily, I say unto thee, Except a man be born of water and of the Spirit, he cannot enter into the kingdom of God. John 3:5.

Christ here referred to water baptism and the renewing of the heart by the Spirit of God.[60]

Repentance, faith, and baptism are the requisite steps in conversion. . . . As Christians submit to the solemn rite of baptism, He registers the vow that they make to be true to Him. This vow is their oath of allegiance.[61]

Christ has made baptism the sign of entrance to His spiritual kingdom. He has made this a positive condition with which all must comply who wish to be acknowledged as under the authority of the Father, the Son, and the Holy Spirit. Before man can find a home in the church, before passing the threshold of God's spiritual kingdom, he is to receive the impress of the divine name, "The Lord our Righteousness." Jer. 23:6. . . . Those who are baptized in the three-fold name of the Father, the Son, and the Holy Spirit, at the very entrance of their Christian life declare publicly that they have forsaken the service of Satan and have become members of the royal family, children of the heavenly King. They have obeyed the command: "Come out from among them, and be ye separate, . . . and touch not the unclean thing." And to them is fulfilled the promise: "I will receive you, and will be a Father unto you, and ye shall be my sons and daughters." 2 Cor. 6:17, 18.[62]

Henceforth the believer is to bear in mind that he is dedicated to God, to Christ, and to the Holy Spirit. He is to make all worldly considerations secondary to this new relation. . . .

The obligations in the spiritual agreement entered into at baptism are mutual. As human beings act their part with whole-hearted obedience, they have a right to pray, "Let it be known, Lord, that Thou art God in Israel." The fact that you have been baptized in the name of the Father, the Son, and the Holy Spirit, is an assurance that if you will claim their help, these powers will help you in every emergency.[63]

BAPTIZED INTO HIS DEATH AND RESURRECTION

Know ye not, that so many of us as were baptized into Jesus Christ were baptized into his death? Rom. 6:3.

Those who have taken part in the solemn rite of baptism have pledged themselves to seek for those things which are above, where Christ sitteth on the right hand of God; pledged themselves to labor earnestly for the salvation of sinners. God asks those who take His name, How are you using the powers that have been redeemed by the death of My Son? Are you doing all in your power to rise to a greater height in spiritual understanding? Are you adjusting your interest and actions in harmony with the momentous claims of eternity?[64]

Baptism is a most solemn renunciation of the world. Self is by profession dead to a life of sin. The waters cover the candidate, and in the presence of the whole heavenly universe the mutual pledge is made. In the name of the Father, and Son, and the Holy Spirit, man is laid in his watery grave, buried with Christ in baptism, and raised from the water to live the new life of loyalty to God. The three great powers in heaven are witnesses; they are invisible but present.[65]

We have died to the world. . . . We have been buried in the likeness of Christ's death and raised in the likeness of His resurrection, and we are to live a new life. Our life is to be bound up with the life of Christ.[66]

In the first chapter of Second Peter is presented the progressive work in the Christian life. The whole chapter is a lesson of deep importance. If man, in acquiring the Christian graces, works on the plan of addition, God has pledged Himself to work in his behalf upon the plan of multiplication. "Grace and peace be multiplied unto you through the knowledge of God, and of Jesus our Lord." 2 Peter 1:2. The work is laid out before every soul that has acknowledged his faith in Jesus Christ by baptism.[67]

If we are true to our vow, there is opened to us a door of communication with heaven—a door that no human hand or satanic agency can close.[68]

WALKING IN HIS STEPS

If ye then be risen with Christ, seek those things which are above, where Christ sitteth on the right hand of God. Col. 3:1.

All who enter upon the new life should understand, prior to their baptism, that the Lord requires the undivided affections. . . . The practicing of the truth is essential. The bearing of fruit testifies to the character of the tree. . . . There is need of a thorough conversion to the truth.[69]

There are children . . . who have been taught from their youth to observe the Sabbath. Some of these are very good children, faithful to duty as far as temporal matters are concerned; but they feel no deep conviction of sin and no need of repentance from sin. . . . As there are no outbreaking sins in their own lives, they flatter themselves they are about right. To these youth I am authorized to say: Repent ye and be converted, that your sins may be blotted out. . . . You are required to repent, believe, and be baptized. Christ was wholly righteous; yet He, the Saviour of the world, gave man an example by Himself taking the steps which He requires the sinner to take to become a child of God, and heir of heaven.

If Christ, the spotless and pure Redeemer of man, condescended to take the steps necessary for the sinner to take in conversion, why should any, with the light of truth shining upon their pathway, hesitate to submit their hearts to God, and in humility confess that they are sinners, and show their faith in the atonement of Christ by words and actions, identifying themselves with those who profess to be His followers?[70]

All who study the life of Christ and practice His teachings will become like Christ. Their influence will be like His. They will reveal soundness of character. As they walk in the humble path of obedience, doing the will of God, they exert an influence that tells for the advancement of the cause of God and the healthful purity of His work.[71]

WHEN REBAPTISM IS APPROPRIATE

*And now why tarriest thou? arise, and be baptized, and wash
away thy sins, calling on the name of the Lord. Acts 22:16.*

There are many at the present day who have unwittingly violated one of the precepts of God's law. When the understanding is
enlightened, and the claims of the fourth commandment are urged
upon the conscience, they see themselves sinners in the sight of
God. "Sin is the transgression of the law" and he that shall "offend
in one point, he is guilty of all." 1 John 3:4; James 2:10.

The honest seeker after truth will not plead ignorance of the law
as an excuse for transgression. Light was within his reach. God's
Word is plain, and Christ has bidden him search the Scriptures. He
reveres God's law as holy, just, and good, and he repents of his
transgression. By faith he pleads the atoning blood of Christ, and
grasps the promise of pardon. His former baptism does not satisfy
him now. He has seen himself a sinner, condemned by the law of
God. He has experienced anew a death to sin, and he desires again
to be buried with Christ by baptism, that he may rise to walk in newness of life. . . .

This is a subject which each individual must conscientiously take
his position upon in the fear of God. . . . The duty of urging belongs
to no one but God; give God a chance to work with His Holy Spirit
upon the minds, so that the individual will be perfectly convinced
and satisfied in regard to this advanced step. . . .

It [rebaptism] is a matter to be treated as a great privilege and
blessing, and all who are rebaptized, if they have the right ideas
upon this subject, will thus consider it.[72]

It is the privilege and the duty of every Christian to have a rich
and abundant experience in the things of God. "I am the light of the
world," said Jesus. "He that followeth me shall not walk in darkness,
but shall have the light of life." John 8:12. . . . Every step of faith and
obedience brings the soul into closer connection with the Light of
the world, in whom there "is no darkness at all."[73]

OUR LORD'S COMMAND

Go ye therefore, and teach all nations, baptizing them in the name of the Father, and of the Son, and of the Holy Ghost. Matt. 28:19.

Thus Christ gave His disciples their commission. He made full provision for the prosecution of the work, and took upon Himself the responsibility for its success. So long as they obeyed His word, and worked in connection with Him, they could not fail. Go to all nations, He bade them. Go to the farthest part of the habitable globe. . . . Labor in faith . . . , for the time will never come when I will forsake you.

The Saviour's commission to the disciples included all the believers. It includes all believers in Christ to the end of time. It is a fatal mistake to suppose that the work of saving souls depends alone on the ordained minister. All to whom the heavenly inspiration has come are put in trust with the gospel. All who receive the life of Christ are ordained to work for the salvation of their fellow men. For this work the church was established, and all who take upon themselves its sacred vows are thereby pledged to be co-workers with Christ.[74]

We are to be consecrated channels, through which the heavenly life is to flow to others. The Holy Spirit is to animate and pervade the whole church, purifying and cementing hearts. Those who have been buried with Christ in baptism are to rise to newness of life, giving a living representation of the life of Christ. . . . You are dedicated to the work of making known the gospel of salvation. Heaven's perfection is to be your power.[75]

The Duke of Wellington was once present where a party of Christian men were discussing the possibility of success in missionary effort among the heathen. They appealed to the duke to say whether in his judgment such efforts were likely to prove a success commensurate to the cost. The old soldier replied: "Gentlemen, what are your marching orders? Success is not the question for you to discuss. If I read your orders aright, they run thus, 'Go ye into all the world, and preach the gospel to every creature.' Gentlemen, obey your marching orders."[76]

CHANGED BY BEHOLDING

But we all, with open face beholding as in a glass the glory of the Lord, are changed into the same image from glory to glory even as by the Spirit of the Lord. 2 Cor. 3:18.

As the mind dwells upon Christ, the character is molded after the divine similitude. The thoughts are pervaded with a sense of His goodness, His love. We contemplate His character, and thus He is in all our thoughts. His love encloses us. If we gaze even a moment upon the sun in its meridian glory, when we turn away our eyes, the image of the sun will appear in everything upon which we look. Thus it is when we behold Jesus; everything we look upon reflects His image, the Sun of Righteousness. We cannot see anything else, or talk of anything else. His image is imprinted upon the eye of the soul, and affects every portion of our daily life, softening and sub-duing our whole nature. By beholding, we are conformed to the di-vine similitude, even the likeness of Christ. To all with whom we associate we reflect the bright and cheerful beams of His righteous-ness. We have become transformed in character; for heart, soul, mind, are irradiated by the reflection of Him who loved us, and gave Himself for us. . . .

Jesus Christ is everything to us—the first, the last, the best in everything. Jesus Christ, His Spirit, His character, colors every-thing; it is the warp and the woof, the very texture of our entire being. The words of Christ are spirit and life. We cannot, then, center our thoughts upon self; it is no more we that live, but Christ that liveth in us, and He is the hope of glory. Self is dead, but Christ is a living Saviour.[77]

If we keep our minds stayed upon Christ, He will come unto us as the rain, "as the latter and former rain unto the earth." Hosea 6:3. As the Sun of Righteousness, He will arise upon us "with healing in his wings." Mal. 4:2. We shall "grow as the lily." We shall "revive as the corn, and grow as the vine." Hosea 14:5, 7. By constantly rely-ing upon Christ as our personal Saviour, we shall grow up into Him in all things who is our head.[78]

TAKING UP OUR CROSS

And he said to them all, If any man will come after me, let him deny himself, and take up his cross daily, and follow me. Luke 9:23.

The foundation of the plan of salvation was laid in sacrifice. Jesus left the royal courts and became poor, that we through His poverty might be made rich. All who share this salvation, purchased for them at such an infinite sacrifice by the Son of God, will follow the example of the true Pattern. Christ was the chief Cornerstone, and we must build upon this Foundation. Each must have a spirit of self-denial and self-sacrifice. The life of Christ upon earth was unselfish; it was marked with humiliation and sacrifice. And shall men, partakers of the great salvation which Jesus came from heaven to bring them, refuse to follow their Lord and to share in His self-denial and sacrifice? . . . Is the servant greater than his Lord? . . .

"Then said Jesus unto his disciples, If any man will come after me, let him deny himself, and take up his cross, and follow me." Matt. 16:24. I lead the way in the path of self-denial. I require nothing of you, My followers, but that of which I, your Lord, give you an example in My own life.[79]

Self-denial and the cross lie directly in the pathway of every follower of Christ. The cross is that which crosses the natural affections and the will.[80]

Jesus is our pattern. If He would lay aside His humiliation and sufferings, and cry, "If any man will come after Me, let him please himself, and enjoy the world, and he shall be My disciple," the multitude would believe and follow Him. But Jesus will come to us in no other character than that of the meek, crucified One. If we would be with Him in heaven, we must be like Him on earth.[81]

Let us follow the Saviour in His simplicity and self-denial. Let us lift up the Man of Calvary by word and by holy living.[82]

And to all who lift it and bear it after Christ, the cross is a pledge of the crown of immortality that they will receive.[83]

DEVELOPING GOOD HABITS

I have refrained my feet from every evil way, that I might keep thy word. Ps. 119:101.

We are nearing the end of time, and we want now, not to meet the world's tastes and practices, but to meet the mind of God; to see what saith the Scriptures, and then to walk according to the light which God has given us.[84]

The youth are forming habits which will, in nine cases out of ten, decide their future. The influence of the company they keep, the associations they form, and the principles they adopt will be carried with them through life.[85]

We shall be individually, for time and eternity, what our habits make us. The lives of those who form right habits, and are faithful in the performance of every duty, will be as shining lights, shedding bright beams upon the pathway of others.[86]

There is no need of being spiritual dwarfs if the mind is continually exercised in spiritual things. But merely praying for this, and about this, will not meet the necessities of the case. You must habituate the mind to concentration upon spiritual things. Exercise will bring strength. Many professed Christians are in a fair way to lose both worlds. To be half a Christian and half a worldly man makes you about one-hundredth part a Christian and all the rest worldly.[87]

The mind must be educated and disciplined to love purity. A love for spiritual things should be encouraged; yea, must be encouraged, if you would grow in grace and in the knowledge of the truth. . . . The will must be exercised in the right direction. I *will* be a wholehearted Christian. I *will* know the length and breadth, the height and depth, of perfect love. Listen to the words of Jesus: "Blessed are they which do hunger and thirst after righteousness: for they shall be filled." Matt. 5:6. Ample provisions are made by Christ to satisfy the soul that hungers and thirsts for righteousness.[88]

UNASHAMED OF JESUS

For I am not ashamed of the gospel of Christ: for it is the power of God unto salvation to every one that believeth; to the Jew first, and also to the Greek. Rom. 1:16.

Many of the young have not the spirit of Jesus. The love of God is not in their hearts, therefore all the natural besetments hold the victory instead of the Spirit of God and salvation.

Those who really possess the religion of Jesus will not be ashamed nor afraid to bear the cross before those who have more experience than they. They will, if they earnestly long to be right, desire all the help they can get from older Christians. Gladly will they be helped by them; hearts that are warmed by love to God will not be hindered by trifles in the Christian course. They will talk out what the Spirit of God works in. They will sing it out, pray it out. It is the lack of religion, lack of holy living, that makes the young backward. Their life condemns them. They know they do not live as Christians should, therefore they have not confidence toward God, or before the church.[89]

We should speak of the mercy and loving-kindness of God, of the matchless depths of the Saviour's love. Our words should be words of praise and thanksgiving. If the mind and heart are full of the love of God, this will be revealed in the conversation. It will not be a difficult matter to impart that which enters into our spiritual life.[90]

Never be ashamed of your faith; never be found on the side of the enemy. "Ye are the light of the world." Matt. 5:14. Your faith is to be revealed as precious truth, truth which all should have and all must have if they are saved. . . . We should fight the good fight of faith, and be found "stedfast, unmoveable, always abounding in the work of the Lord." 1 Cor. 15:58.[91]

The unstudied, unconscious influence of a holy life is the most convincing sermon that can be given in favor of Christianity. Argument, even when unanswerable, may provoke only opposition; but a godly example has a power that it is impossible wholly to resist.[92]

THE RIGHT EXERCISE OF THE WILL

For it is God which worketh in you both to will and to do of his good pleasure. Phil. 2:13.

God's promise is, "Ye shall seek me, and find me, when ye shall search for me with all your heart." Jer. 29:13.

The whole heart must be yielded to God, or the change can never be wrought in us by which we are to be restored to His likeness.[93]

Pure religion has to do with the will. The will is the governing power in the nature of man, bringing all the other faculties under its sway. The will is not the taste or the inclination, but it is the deciding power which works in the children of men unto obedience to God or unto disobedience.[94]

The Saviour says, "Whosoever he be of you that forsaketh not all that he hath, he cannot be my disciple." Luke 14:33. Whatever shall draw away the heart from God must be given up. Mammon is the idol of many. The love of money, the desire for wealth, is the golden chain that binds them to Satan. Reputation and worldly honor are worshiped by another class. The life of selfish ease and freedom from responsibility is the idol of others. But these slavish bands must be broken. We cannot be half the Lord's and half the world's. We are not God's children unless we are such entirely. . . .

Desires for goodness and holiness are right as far as they go; but if you stop here, they will avail nothing. Many will be lost while hoping and desiring to be Christians. They do not come to the point of yielding the will to God. They do not now *choose* to be Christians.[95]

The Lord does not propose to save us in companies. Individually we are to make our choice. One by one we are to appropriate the grace of God to the soul, and one cannot decide for another what course he shall take.[96]

A pure and noble life, a life of victory over appetite and lust, is possible to everyone who will unite his weak, wavering human will to the omnipotent, unwavering will of God.[97]

THE SOWING TIME OF LIFE

Be not deceived, God is not mocked: for whatsoever a man soweth, that shall he also reap. Gal. 6:7.

In the laws of God in nature, effect follows cause with unerring certainty. The reaping will testify as to what the sowing has been. . . .

Every seed sown produces a harvest of its kind. So it is in human life. We all need to sow the seeds of compassion, sympathy, and love; for we shall reap what we sow. Every characteristic of selfishness, self-love, self-esteem, every act of self-indulgence, will bring forth a like harvest. He who lives for self is sowing to the flesh, and of the flesh he will reap corruption.

God destroys no man. Everyone who is destroyed will have destroyed himself. Everyone who stifles the admonitions of conscience is sowing the seeds of unbelief, and these will produce a sure harvest. By rejecting the first warning from God, Pharaoh of old sowed the seeds of obstinacy, and he reaped obstinacy.[98]

Each actor in history stands in his lot and place; for God's great work after His own plan will be carried out by men who have prepared themselves to fill positions for good or evil. In opposition to righteousness, men become instruments of unrighteousness. But they are not forced to take this course of action. They need not become instruments of unrighteousness, any more than Cain needed to.[99]

Men act out their own free will, either in accordance with a character placed under the molding of God or a character placed under the harsh rule of Satan.[100]

Every act, every word, is a seed that will bear fruit. Every deed of thoughtful kindness, of obedience, or of self-denial, will reproduce itself in others, and through them in still others. So every act of envy, malice, or dissension is a seed that will spring up in a "root of bitterness" (Heb. 12:15), whereby many shall be defiled.[101]

Dear young friends, that which you sow, you will also reap. Now is the sowing time for you. What will the harvest be?[102]

DON'T GET DISCOURAGED!

Have not I commanded thee? Be strong and of a good courage;
be not afraid, neither be thou dismayed: for the Lord thy God is with
thee whithersoever thou goest. Joshua 1:9.

After the passing of the time in 1844, a number of brethren and sisters were assembled in a meeting. All were very sad, for the disappointment had been sore. Presently a man came in, crying, "Courage in the Lord, brethren; courage in the Lord!" This he repeated again and again, till every face was aglow, and every voice lifted in praise to God.

Today I say to every worker for the Master, "Courage in the Lord!" . . .

Some look always at the objectionable and discouraging features, and therefore discouragement overtakes them. They forget that the heavenly universe is waiting to make them agencies of blessing to the world; and that the Lord Jesus is a never-failing storehouse from which human beings may draw strength and courage. There is no need for despondency and apprehension. The time will never come when the shadow of Satan will not be cast athwart our pathway. Thus the enemy seeks to hide the light shining from the Sun of Righteousness. But our faith should pierce this shadow.[103]

Hope and courage are essential to perfect service for God. These are the fruit of faith. Despondency is sinful and unreasonable. God is able and willing "more abundantly" to bestow upon His servants the strength they need for test and trial. . . .

For the disheartened there is a sure remedy—faith, prayer, work. Faith and activity will impart assurance and satisfaction that will increase day by day. . . . In the darkest days, when appearances seem most forbidding, fear not. Have faith in God.[104]

Christ did not fail, neither was He discouraged, and His followers are to manifest a faith of the same enduring nature. . . . They are to despair of nothing, and to hope for everything. With the golden chain of His matchless love Christ has bound them to the throne of God.[105]

A LIFE INSURANCE POLICY FOR YOU

Wherefore the rather, brethren, give diligence to make your calling and election sure: for if ye do these things, ye shall never fall. 2 Peter 1:10.

In the council of heaven, provision was made that men, though transgressors, should not perish in their disobedience, but, through faith in Christ as their substitute and surety, might become the elect of God, predestinated unto the adoption of children by Jesus Christ to Himself according to the good pleasure of His will. God wills that all men should be saved; for ample provision has been made, in giving His only-begotten Son to pay man's ransom. Those who perish will perish because they refuse to be adopted as children of God through Christ Jesus. . . .

There is no such thing in the Word of God as unconditional election—once in grace, always in grace. In the second chapter of Second Peter the subject is made plain and distinct. After a history of some who followed an evil course, the explanation is given: "Which have forsaken the right way, . . . following the way of Balaam the son of Bosor, who loved the wages of unrighteousness." 2 Peter 2:15. . . . Here is a class of whom the apostle warns, "For it had been better for them not to have known the way of righteousness, than, after they have known it, to turn from the holy commandment delivered unto them." 2 Peter 2:21. . . .

There is truth to be received if souls are saved. The keeping of the commandments of God is life eternal to the receiver. But the Scriptures make it plain that those who once knew the way of life and rejoiced in the truth are in danger of falling through apostasy, and being lost. Therefore there is need of a decided, daily conversion to God.

All who seek to sustain the doctrine of election, once in grace, always in grace, do this against a plain, "Thus saith the Lord." [106]

It depends upon *your* course of action as to whether or not you will secure the benefits bestowed upon those who, as the elect of God, receive an eternal life-insurance policy. [107]

155

HERE AND HEREAFTER

TIME A PRECIOUS TALENT

So teach us to number our days, that we may apply our hearts unto wisdom. Ps. 90:12.

Our time belongs to God. Every moment is His, and we are under the most solemn obligation to improve it to His glory. Of no talent He has given will He require a more strict account than of our time.

The value of time is beyond computation. Christ regarded every moment as precious, and it is thus that we should regard it. Life is too short to be trifled away. We have but a few days of probation in which to prepare for eternity. We have no time to waste, no time to devote to selfish pleasure, no time for the indulgence of sin. It is now that we are to form characters for the future, immortal life. It is now that we are to prepare for the searching judgment.

The human family have scarcely begun to live when they begin to die. . . . The man who appreciates time as his working day will fit himself for a mansion and for a life that is immortal. It is well that he was born. We are admonished to redeem the time. But time squandered can never be recovered. We cannot call back even one moment. The only way in which we can redeem our time is by making the most of that which remains, by being co-workers with God in His great plan of redemption. . . .

Every moment is freighted with eternal consequences. We are to stand as minute men, ready for service at a moment's notice. The opportunity that is now ours to speak to some needy soul the word of life may never offer again. God may say to that one, "This night thy soul shall be required of thee," and through our neglect he may not be ready. (Luke 12:20.) In the great judgment day, how shall we render our account to God?[1]

A CURE FOR IDLENESS

Not slothful in business; fervent in spirit; serving the Lord. Rom. 12:11.

The life of Christ from His earliest years was a life of earnest activity. He lived not to please Himself. He was the Son of the infinite God, yet He worked at the carpenter's trade with His father Joseph. His trade was significant. He had come into the world as the character builder, and as such all His work was perfect. Into all His secular labor He brought the same perfection as into the characters He was transforming by His divine power. He is our pattern.[2]

It is the duty of every Christian to acquire habits of order, thoroughness, and dispatch. There is no excuse for slow bungling at work of any character. When one is always at work and the work is never done, it is because mind and heart are not put into the labor. . . . The exercise of the will power will make the hands move deftly.[3]

The Bible gives no indorsement to idleness. It is the greatest curse that afflicts our world. Every man and woman who is truly converted will be a diligent worker.

Upon the right improvement of our time depends our success in acquiring knowledge and mental culture. The cultivation of the intellect need not be prevented by poverty, humble origin, or unfavorable surroundings. Only let the moments be treasured. A few moments here and a few there, that might be frittered away in aimless talk; the morning hours so often wasted in bed; the time spent in traveling on trams or railway cars, or waiting at the station; the moments of waiting for meals, waiting for those who are tardy in keeping an appointment—if a book were kept at hand, and these fragments of time were improved in study, reading, or careful thought, what might not be accomplished. A resolute purpose, persistent industry, and careful economy of time, will enable men to acquire knowledge and mental discipline which will qualify them for almost any position of influence and usefulness.[4]

THE TRUE VALUE OF MONEY

Honour the Lord with thy substance, and with the firstfruits of all thine increase: so shall thy barns be filled with plenty, and thy presses shall burst out with new wine. Prov. 3:9, 10.

This scripture teaches that God, as the giver of all our benefits, has a claim upon them all; that His claim should be our first consideration; and that a special blessing will attend all who honor this claim.

Herein is set forth a principle that is seen in all God's dealings with men. The Lord placed our first parents in the Garden of Eden. He surrounded them with everything that could minister to their happiness, and He bade them acknowledge Him as the possessor of all things. In the Garden He caused to grow every tree that was pleasant to the eye or good for food; but among them He made one reserve. Of all else, Adam and Eve might freely eat; but of this one tree God said, "Thou shalt not eat of it." Here was the test of their gratitude and loyalty to God.

So the Lord has imparted to us heaven's richest treasure in giving us Jesus. With Him He has given us all things richly to enjoy.[5]

God . . . entrusts men with means. He gives them power to get wealth. . . .

Our money has not been given us that we might honor and glorify ourselves. As faithful stewards we are to use it for the honor and glory of God. Some think that only a portion of their means is the Lord's. When they have set apart a portion for religious and charitable purposes, they regard the remainder as their own, to be used as they see fit. But in this they mistake. All we possess is the Lord's, and we are accountable to Him for the use we make of it. In the use of every penny, it will be seen whether we love God supremely and our neighbor as ourselves. Money has great value, because it can do great good. In the hands of God's children it is food for the hungry, drink for the thirsty, and clothing for the naked. . . . But money is of no more value than sand, only as it is put to use in providing for the necessities of life, in blessing others, and advancing the cause of Christ.[6]

AN AROUSED CONSCIENCE

Awake to righteousness, and sin not; for some have not the knowledge of God: I speak this to your shame. 1 Cor. 15:34.

A decided advancement in spirituality, piety, charity, and activity, has been made . . . in the ———— church. Discourses were preached on the sin of robbing God in tithes and offerings. . . .

Many confessed that they had not paid tithes for years; and we know that God cannot bless those who are robbing Him, and that the church must suffer in consequence of the sin of its individual members. . . .

One brother said that for two years he had not paid his tithes, and he was in despair; but as he confessed his sin, he began to gather hope. "What shall I do?" he asked.

I said, "Give your note to the treasurer of the church; that will be businesslike."

He thought that was a rather strange request; but he sat down, and began to write, "For value received, I promise to pay—" He looked up, as if to say, Is that the proper form in which to write out a note to the Lord?

"Yes," he continued, "for value received. Have I not been receiving the blessings of God day after day? Have not the angels guarded me? Has not the Lord blessed me with all spiritual and temporal blessings? For value received, I promise to pay the sum of $571.50 to the church treasurer." After doing all he could do on his part, he was a happy man. In a few days he took up his note, and paid his tithe into the treasury. He had also made a Christmas donation of $125.

Another brother gave a note for $1,000, expecting to meet it in a few weeks; and another gave a note for $300. . . .

If you have robbed the Lord, make restitution. As far as possible, make the past right, and then ask the Saviour to pardon you. Will you not return to the Lord His own, before this year, with its burden of record, has passed into eternity?[7]

A LIVING BENEVOLENCE

I have shewed you all things, how that so labouring ye ought to support the weak, and to remember the words of the Lord Jesus, how he said, It is more blessed to give than to receive. Acts 20:35.

We should regard ourselves as stewards of the Lord's property and God as the supreme proprietor, to whom we are to render His own when He shall require it. . . .

The servants of God should be making their wills every day in good works and liberal offerings to God.[8]

Dying legacies are a miserable substitute for living benevolence.[9]

Hoarded wealth is not merely useless, it is a curse. In this life it is a snare to the soul, drawing the affections away from the heavenly treasure. In the great day of God its witness to unused talents and neglected opportunities will condemn its possessor. . . . He who realizes that his money is a talent from God will use it economically, and will feel it a duty to save that he may give.[10]

It is utter folly to defer to make a preparation for the future life until nearly the last hour of the present life. It is also a great mistake to defer to answer the claims of God for liberality to His cause until the time comes when you are to shift your stewardship upon others. Those to whom you entrust your talents of means may not do as well with them as you have done. How dare rich men run so great risks! Those who wait till death before they make a disposition of their property, surrender it to death rather than to God. In so doing many are acting directly contrary to the plan of God plainly stated in His Word. If they would do good they must seize the present golden moments and labor with all their might, as if fearful that they may lose the favorable opportunity. . . .

We must all be rich in good works in this life if we would secure the future, immortal life. When the judgment shall sit and the books shall be opened, every man will be rewarded according to his works.[11]

FAITHFUL IN LITTLE THINGS

And he said unto him, Well, thou good servant: because thou hast been faithful in a very little, have thou authority over ten cities. Luke 19:17.

Talents used are talents multiplied. Success is not the result of chance or of destiny; it is the outworking of God's own providence, the reward of faith and discretion, of virtue and persevering effort. The Lord desires us to use every gift we have; and if we do this, we shall have greater gifts to use. He does not supernaturally endow us with the qualifications we lack; but while we use that which we have, He will work with us to increase and strengthen every faculty. . . .

Through faith in the power of God, it is wonderful how strong a weak man may become, how decided his efforts, how prolific of great results. He who begins with a little knowledge, in a humble way, and tells what he knows, while seeking diligently for further knowledge, will find the whole heavenly treasure awaiting his demand. The more he seeks to impart light, the more light he will receive. . . .

The man [in the parable] who received the one talent "went and digged in the earth, and hid his lord's money."

It was the one with the smallest gift who left his talent unimproved. In this is given a warning to all who feel that the smallness of their endowments excuses them from service for Christ. If they could do some great thing, how gladly would they undertake it; but because they can serve only in little things, they think themselves justified in doing nothing. In this they err. The Lord in His distribution of gifts is testing character. The man who neglected to improve his talent proved himself an unfaithful servant. Had he received five talents, he would have buried them as he buried the one. . . .

However small your talent, God has a place for it. That one talent, wisely used, will accomplish its appointed work. By faithfulness in little duties, we are to work on the plan of addition, and God will work for us on the plan of multiplication. These littles will become the most precious influence in His work.[12]

SOURCE OF ALL LIFE

For with thee is the fountain of life: in thy light shall we see light. Ps. 36:9.

All created beings live by the will and power of God. They are dependent recipients of the life of God. From the highest seraph to the humblest animate being, all are replenished from the Source of life.[13]

The youth need to understand the deep truth underlying the Bible statement that with God "is the fountain of life." Not only is He the originator of all, but He is the life of everything that lives. It is His life that we receive in the sunshine, in the pure, sweet air, in the food which builds up our bodies and sustains our strength. It is by His life that we exist, hour by hour, moment by moment. Except as perverted by sin, all His gifts tend to life, to health and joy.[14]

A mysterious life pervades all nature—a life that sustains the unnumbered worlds throughout immensity, that lives in the insect atom which floats in the summer breeze, that wings the flight of the swallow and feeds the young ravens which cry, that brings the bud to blossom and the flower to fruit.

The same power that upholds nature, is working also in man.

The laws that govern the heart's action, regulating the flow of the current of life to the body, are the laws of the mighty Intelligence that has the jurisdiction of the soul. From Him all life proceeds. Only in harmony with Him can be found its true sphere of action. For all the objects of His creation the condition is the same—a life sustained by receiving the life of God, a life exercised in harmony with the Creator's will. To transgress His law, physical, mental, or moral, is to place one's self out of harmony with the universe. . . .

To him who learns thus to interpret its teachings, all nature becomes illuminated; the world is a lesson book, life a school. The unity of man with nature and with God, the universal dominion of law, the results of transgression, cannot fail of impressing the mind and molding the character.[15]

HE CARES FOR US EVERY MINUTE

Know ye that the Lord he is God: it is he that hath made us, and not we ourselves; we are his people, and the sheep of his pasture. Ps. 100:3.

The work of creation cannot be explained by science. What science can explain the mystery of life?[16]

Life is a gift of God.[17]

The natural life is preserved moment by moment by divine power; yet it is not sustained by a direct miracle, but through the use of blessings placed within our reach.[18]

The Saviour in His miracles revealed the power that is continually at work in man's behalf, to sustain and to heal him. Through the agencies of nature, God is working, day by day, hour by hour, moment by moment, to keep us alive, to build up and restore us. When any part of the body sustains injury, a healing process is at once begun; nature's agencies are set at work to restore soundness. But the power working through these agencies is the power of God. All life-giving power is from Him. When one recovers from disease, it is God who restores him. Sickness, suffering, and death are work of an antagonistic power. Satan is the destroyer; God is the restorer.[19]

A great lesson is learned when we understand our relation to God, and His relation to us.[20]

We have an individuality and an identity that is our own. No one can submerge his identity in that of any other. All must act for themselves, according to the dictates of their own conscience. As regards our responsibility and influence, we are amenable to God as deriving our life from Him. This we do not obtain from humanity, but from God only. We are His by creation and by redemption. Our very bodies are not our own, to treat as we please, to cripple by habits that lead to decay, making it impossible to render to God perfect service. Our lives and all our faculties belong to Him. He is caring for us every moment; He keeps the living machinery in action; if we were left to run it for one moment, we should die. We are absolutely dependent upon God.[21]

THE GREAT OBJECT OF LIFE

I press toward the mark for the prize of the high calling of God in Christ Jesus. Phil. 3:14.

When Adam came from the Creator's hand, he bore, in his physical, mental, and spiritual nature, a likeness to his Maker. "God created man in his own image" (Gen. 1:27), and it was His purpose that the longer man lived the more fully he should reveal this image—the more fully reflect the glory of the Creator. All his faculties were capable of development; their capacity and vigor were continually to increase. Vast was the scope offered for their exercise, glorious the field opened to their research. The mysteries of the visible universe—the "wondrous works of him which is perfect in knowledge" (Job 37:16)—invited man's study. Face-to-face, heart-to-heart communion with his Maker was his high privilege. Had he remained loyal to God, all this would have been his forever. Throughout eternal ages he would have continued to gain new treasures of knowledge, to discover fresh springs of happiness, and to obtain clearer and yet clearer conceptions of the wisdom, the power, and the love of God. More and more fully would he have . . . reflected the Creator's glory.

But by disobedience this was forfeited. Through sin the divine likeness was marred, and well-nigh obliterated. Man's physical powers were weakened, his mental capacity was lessened, his spiritual vision dimmed. He had become subject to death. Yet the race was not left without hope. By infinite love and mercy the plan of salvation had been devised, and a life of probation was granted. To restore in man the image of his Maker, to bring him back to the perfection in which he was created, to promote the development of body, mind, and soul, that the divine purpose in his creation might be realized—this was to be the work of redemption. This is the object of education, the great object of life.[22]

To honor Christ, to become like Him, to work for Him, is . . . life's highest ambition and its greatest joy.[23]

ONE LEASE OF LIFE

Remember now thy Creator in the days of thy youth, while the evil days come not, nor the years draw nigh, when thou shalt say, I have no pleasure in them. Eccl. 12:1.

Life is mysterious and sacred. It is the manifestation of God Himself, the source of all life. Precious are its opportunities, and earnestly should they be improved. Once lost, they are gone forever.

Before us God places eternity, with its solemn realities, and gives us a grasp on immortal, imperishable themes. He presents valuable, ennobling truth, that we may advance in a safe and sure path, in pursuit of an object worthy of the earnest engagement of all our capabilities.

God looks into the tiny seed that He Himself has formed, and sees wrapped within it the beautiful flower, the shrub, or the lofty, wide-spreading tree. So does He see the possibilities in every human being. We are here for a purpose. God has given us His plan for our life, and He desires us to reach the highest standard of development.

He desires that we shall constantly be growing in holiness, in happiness, in usefulness. All have capabilities which they must be taught to regard as sacred endowments, to appreciate as the Lord's gifts, and rightly to employ. He desires the youth to cultivate every power of their being, and to bring every faculty into active exercise. He desires them to enjoy all that is useful and precious in this life, to be good and to do good, laying up a heavenly treasure for the future life.

It should be their ambition to excel in all things that are unselfish, high, and noble. Let them look to Christ as the pattern after which they are to be fashioned. The holy ambition that He revealed in His life they are to cherish—an ambition to make the world better for their having lived in it. This is the work to which they are called.[24]

Only one lease of life is granted us; and the inquiry with everyone should be, How can I invest my life so that it will yield the greatest profit? How can I do most for the glory of God and the benefit of my fellow men?[25]

BEHIND THE SCENES OF LIFE

And I will bring the blind by a way that they knew not; I will lead them in paths that they have not known: I will make darkness light before them, and crooked things straight. These things will I do unto them, and not forsake them. Isa. 42:16.

In the annals of human history the growth of nations, the rise and fall of empires, appear as dependent on the will and prowess of man. The shaping of events seems, to a great degree, to be determined by his power, ambition, or caprice. But in the Word of God the curtain is drawn aside, and we behold, behind, above, and through all the play and counterplay of human interests and power and passions, the agencies of the all-merciful One, silently, patiently working out the counsels of His own will. . . .

Amidst the strife and tumult of nations, He that sitteth above the cherubim still guides the affairs of the earth. . . . To every nation and to every individual . . . God has assigned a place in His great plan. . . . Men and nations are being measured by the plummet in the hand of Him who makes no mistake. All are by their own choice deciding their destiny, and God is overruling all for the accomplishment of His purposes.

The history which the great I AM has marked out in His Word, uniting link after link in the prophetic chain, from eternity in the past to eternity in the future, tells us where we are today in the procession of the ages, and what may be expected in the time to come.

All that prophecy has foretold as coming to pass, until the present time, has been traced on the pages of history, and we may be assured that all which is yet to come will be fulfilled in its order. . . .

We need to study the working out of God's purpose in the history of nations and in the revelation of things to come, that we may estimate at their true value things seen and things unseen; that we may learn what is the true aim of life; that, viewing the things of time in the light of eternity, we may put them to their truest and noblest use.[26]

LIVE WHILE YOU HAVE A CHANCE

Whatsoever thy hand findeth to do, do it with thy might; for there is no work, nor device, nor knowledge, nor wisdom, in the grave, whither thou goest. Eccl. 9:10.

It is a solemn thing to die, but a far more solemn thing to live. Every thought and word and deed of our lives will meet us again. What we make of ourselves in probationary time, that we must remain to all eternity. Death brings dissolution to the body, but makes no change in the character. The coming of Christ does not change our characters; it only fixes them forever beyond all change. . . .

I appeal to the members of the church to be Christians, to be Christlike. Jesus was a worker, not for Himself, but for others. . . . If you are Christians you will imitate His example. . . .

Awake , I beseech you, from the sleep of death. It is too late to devote the strength of brain, bone, and muscle to self-serving. Let not the last day find you destitute of heavenly treasure. Seek to push the triumphs of the cross, seek to enlighten souls, labor for the salvation of your fellow beings, and your work will abide the trying test of fire.[27]

Let us remember that while the work we have to do may not be our choice, it is to be accepted as God's choice for us. Whether pleasing or unpleasing, we are to do the duty that lies nearest. "Whatsoever thy hand findeth to do, do it with thy might; for there is no work, nor device, nor knowledge, nor wisdom, in the grave, whither thou goest."

If the Lord desires us to bear a message to Nineveh, it will not be as pleasing to Him for us to go to Joppa or to Capernaum. He has reasons for sending us to the place toward which our feet have been directed. At that very place there may be someone in need of the help we can give.[28]

Whatever the line of work in which we engage, the Word of God teaches us to be "not slothful in business; fervent in spirit; serving the Lord." Rom. 12:11. . . . Knowing that of the Lord ye shall receive the reward of the inheritance: for ye serve the Lord Christ." Col. 3:24.[29]

SEEKING THE HEAVENLY TREASURE

Set your affection on things above, not on things on the earth. Col. 3:2.

The Lord reveals man's relative estimate of time and eternity, of earth and heaven. He has admonished us: "If riches increase, set not your heart upon them." Ps. 62:10. They have a value when used for the good of others and the glory of God; but no earthly treasure is to be your portion, your god, or your savior.[30]

God tests men, some in one way, and some in another. He tests some by bestowing upon them His rich bounties, and others by withholding His favors. He proves the rich to see if they will love God, the Giver, and their neighbor as themselves. When man makes a right use of these bounties, God is pleased; He can then trust him with greater responsibilities.[31]

There is within the worldly man a craving for something that he does not have. He has, from force of habit, bent every thought, every purpose, in the direction of making provision for the future, and as he grows older, he becomes more eager than ever to acquire all that it is possible to gain. . . .

All this energy, this perseverance, this determination, this industry after earthly power, is the result of the perversion of his powers to a wrong object. Every faculty might have been cultivated to the highest possible elevation by exercise, for the heavenly, immortal life, and for the far more exceeding and eternal weight of glory. The customs and practices of the worldly man in his perseverance and his energies, and in availing himself of every opportunity to add to his store, should be a lesson to those who claim to be children of God, seeking for glory, honor, and immortality. The children of the world are wiser in their generation than the children of the light, and herein is seen their wisdom. Their object is for earthly gain, and to this end they direct all their energies. O that this zeal would characterize the toiler for heavenly riches![32]

THE ARROW OF DEATH

O that they were wise, that they understood this, that they would consider their latter end! Deut. 32:29.

The Lord "doth not afflict willingly nor grieve the children of men." Lam. 3:33. "Like as a father pitieth his children, so the Lord pitieth them that fear him. For he knoweth our frame; he remembereth that we are dust." Ps. 103:13, 14. He knows our heart, for He reads every secret of the soul. . . . He knows the end from the beginning. Many will be laid away to sleep before the fiery ordeal of the time of trouble shall come upon our world. . . .

If Jesus, the world's Redeemer, prayed, "O my Father, if it be possible, let this cup pass from me," and added, "nevertheless not as I will, but as thou wilt" (Matt. 26:39), how very appropriate it is for finite mortals to make the same surrender to the wisdom and will of God.[33]

We have but a brief lifetime here, and we know not how soon the arrow of death may strike our hearts. We know not how soon we may be called to give up the world and all its interests. Eternity stretches before us. The curtain is about to be lifted. But a few short years, and for everyone now numbered with the living the mandate will go forth: "He that is unjust, let him be unjust still: . . . and he that is righteous, let him be righteous still: and he that is holy, let him be holy still." Rev. 22:11.

Are we prepared? Have we become acquainted with God, the Governor of heaven, the Lawgiver, and with Jesus Christ whom He sent into the world as His representative? When our lifework is ended, shall we be able to say, as did Christ our example:

"I have glorified thee on the earth: I have finished the work which thou gavest me to do. . . . I have manifested thy name"? John 17:4-6.

The angels of God are seeking to attract us from ourselves and from earthly things. Let them not labor in vain.[34]

LIGHT IN THE SHADOWS

But though he cause grief, yet will he have compassion according to the multitude of his mercies. For he doth not afflict willingly nor grieve the children of men. Lam. 3:32, 33.

When my eldest son was sixteen years old, he was stricken down in sickness.* His case was considered critical, and he called us to his bedside, and said, "Father, Mother, it will be hard for you to part with your eldest son. If the Lord sees fit to spare my life, for your sake I will be pleased. If it is for my good and His name's glory for my life to close now, I will say, It is well with my soul. Father, go by yourself, and Mother, go by yourself; and pray. Then you will receive an answer according to the will of my Saviour, whom you love and I love." He was afraid that if we should bow together, our sympathies would strengthen, and we would ask for that which it would not be best for the Lord to grant. . . . We received no evidence that our son would recover. He died, putting his full trust in Jesus our Saviour. His death was a great blow to us, but it was a victory even in death; for his life was hid with Christ in God.

Before the death of my eldest boy, my babe was sick unto death. We prayed, and thought that the Lord would spare us our darling; but we closed his eyes in death, and laid him away to rest in Jesus, until the Life-giver shall come to awaken His precious loved ones to a glorious immortality.

Then my husband, the faithful servant of Jesus Christ, who had stood by my side for thirty-six years, was taken from me, and I was left to labor alone. He sleeps in Jesus. I have no tears to shed over his grave. But how I miss him! . . .

The Lord has often instructed me that many little ones are to be laid away before the time of trouble. We shall see our children again. We shall meet them and know them in the heavenly courts. Put your trust in the Lord, and be not afraid.[35]

*Mrs. White's personal experience with sorrow is presented here for the encouragement of all who must suffer the loss of dear ones.—COMPILERS.

OUR BLESSED DEAD

And I heard a voice from heaven saying unto me, Write, Blessed are the dead which die in the Lord from henceforth: Yea, saith the Spirit, that they may rest from their labours; and their works do follow them. Rev. 14:13.

I hardly know what to say to you.* The news of your wife's death was to me overwhelming. I could hardly believe it and can hardly believe it now. God gave me a view last Sabbath night which I will write. . . .

I saw that she was sealed and would come up at the voice of God and stand upon the earth, and would be with the 144,000. I saw we need not mourn for her; she would rest in the time of trouble, and all that we could mourn for was our loss in being deprived of her company. I saw her death would result in good.

I warn F and the rest of the children to prepare to meet Jesus, and then they will meet their mother again, never more to be parted. O children, will you heed her faithful warning that she gave you while she was with you, and let not all her prayers that she has offered up to God for you be as water spilt upon the ground? Get ready to meet Jesus, and all will be well. Give your hearts to God and do not rest a day unless you know that you love Jesus. Dear Brother, we have prayed to God to gird you up and strengthen you to sustain your loss. God will be with you and uphold you. Only have faith. . . .

Sorrow not as those who have no hope. The grave can hold her but a little while. Hope thou in God and cheer up, dear brother, and you will meet her in a little while. We will not cease to pray for the blessings of God to rest upon your family and you. God will be your sun and your shield. He will stand by you in this your deep affliction and trial. Endure the trial well and you will receive a crown of glory with your companion at the appearing of Jesus. Hold fast truth, and you with her will be crowned with glory, honor, immortality, and eternal life.[36]

---

*Words to a husband and children on the loss of a wife and mother.

MAN A MERE MORTAL

Shall mortal man be more just than God? shall a man be more pure than his maker? Job 4:17.

Man is only mortal, and while he feels himself too wise to accept Jesus, he will remain only mortal.[37]

Physical life is . . . not eternal or immortal; for God, the Life-giver, takes it again. Man has no control over his life.[38]

The Word of God nowhere teaches that the soul of man is immortal. Immortality is an attribute of God only.[39]

Upon the fundamental error of natural immortality rests the doctrine of consciousness in death—a doctrine, like eternal torment, opposed to the teachings of the Scriptures, to the dictates of reason, and to our feelings of humanity. . . . What say the Scriptures concerning these things? David declares that man is not conscious in death. "His breath goeth forth, he returneth to his earth; in that very day his thoughts perish." Ps. 146:4. . . .

When, in answer to his prayer, Hezekiah's life was prolonged fifteen years, the grateful king rendered to God a tribute of praise for His great mercy. In this song he tells the reason why he thus rejoices: "The grave cannot praise thee, death can not celebrate thee: they that go down into the pit cannot hope for thy truth. The living, the living, he shall praise thee, as I do this day." Isa. 38:18, 19. Popular theology represents the righteous dead as in heaven, entered into bliss, and praising God with an immortal tongue: but Hezekiah could see no such glorious prospect in death. . . .

Peter, on the day of Pentecost, declared that the patriarch David "is both dead and buried, and his sepulchre is with us unto this day." "For David is not ascended into the heavens." Acts 2:29, 34. The fact that David remains in the grave until the resurrection, proves that the righteous do not go to heaven at death. It is only through the resurrection, and by virtue of the fact that Christ has risen, that David can at last sit at the right hand of God.[40]

OUR STATE IN DEATH

For the living know that they shall die: but the dead know not any thing, neither have they any more a reward; for the memory of them is forgotten. Also their love, and their hatred, and their envy, is now perished; neither have they any more a portion for ever in any thing that is done under the sun. Eccl. 9:5, 6.

The theory of the immortality of the soul was one of those false doctrines that Rome, borrowing from paganism, incorporated into the religion of Christendom. Martin Luther classed it with the "monstrous fables that form part of the Roman dunghill of decretals." Commenting on the words of Solomon in Ecclesiastes, that the dead know not anything, the Reformer says: ". . . Solomon judgeth that the dead are asleep, and feel nothing at all. For the dead lie there, accounting neither days nor years, but when they are awakened, they shall seem to have slept scarce one minute." [41]

The martyr Tyndale, referring to the state of the dead, declared: "I confess openly, that I am not persuaded that they be already in the full glory that Christ is in, or the elect angels of God are in. Neither is it any article of my faith; for if it were so, I see not but then the preaching of the resurrection of the flesh were a thing in vain." [42]

According to the popular belief, the redeemed in heaven are acquainted with all that takes place on the earth, and especially with the lives of the friends whom they have left behind. But how could it be a source of happiness to the dead to know the troubles of the living, . . . to see them enduring all the sorrows, disappointments and anguish of life? . . . And how utterly revolting is the belief that as soon as the breath leaves the body, the soul of the impenitent is consigned to the flames of hell! To what depths of anguish must those be plunged who see their friends passing to the grave unprepared, to enter upon an eternity of woe and sin! [43]

Christ represents death as a sleep to His believing children. Their life is hid with Christ in God, and until the last trump shall sound those who die will sleep in Him. [44]

A GOODNESS IN GOD'S JUSTICE

And fear not them which kill the body, but are not able to kill the soul: but rather fear him which is able to destroy both soul and body in hell. Matt. 10:28.

How repugnant to every emotion of love and mercy, and even to our sense of justice, is the doctrine that the wicked dead are tormented with fire and brimstone in an eternally burning hell; that for the sins of a brief earthly life they are to suffer torture as long as God shall live. . . .

Where, in the pages of God's Word, is such teaching to be found? Will the redeemed in heaven be lost to all emotions of pity and compassion, and even to feelings of common humanity? Are these to be exchanged for the indifference of the stoic, or the cruelty of the savage? No, no; such is not the teaching of the Book of God. . . .

The theory of eternal torment is one of the false doctrines that constitute the wine of the abominations of Babylon.[45]

When we consider in what false colors Satan has painted the character of God, can we wonder that our merciful Creator is feared, . . . even hated?[46]

The principles of kindness, mercy, and love, taught and exemplified by our Saviour, are a transcript of the will and character of God. . . . God executes justice upon the wicked, for the good of the universe, and even for the good of those upon whom His judgments are visited. . . .

Those who have chosen Satan as their leader, and have been controlled by his power, are not prepared to enter the presence of God. . . .

Could they endure the glory of God and the Lamb? No, no; years of probation were granted them, that they might form characters for heaven; but thcy have never trained the mind to love purity; they have never learned the language of heaven, and now it is too late.[47]

To sin, wherever found, "our God is a consuming fire." Heb. 12:29. In all who submit to His power the Spirit of God will consume sin. But if men cling to sin, they become identified with it. Then the glory of God, which destroys sin, must destroy them.[48]

THE PORTION OF THE WICKED

Behold, all souls are mine; as the soul of the father, so also the soul of the son is mine: the soul that sinneth, it shall die. Eze. 18:4.

While life is the inheritance of the righteous, death is the portion of the wicked.[49]

The soul that sinneth it shall die an everlasting death—a death that will last forever, from which there will be no hope of a resurrection; and then the wrath of God will be appeased.[50]

It was a marvel to me that Satan could succeed so well in making men believe that the words of God, "The soul that sinneth, it shall die," mean that the soul that sinneth it shall not die, but live eternally in misery. Said the angel, "Life is life, whether it is in pain or happiness. Death is without pain, without joy, without hatred.[51]

Christ endured an agonizing death under the most humiliating circumstances that we might have life. He gave up His precious life that He might vanquish death. But He rose from the tomb, and the myriads of angels who came to behold Him take up the life He had laid down heard His words of triumphant joy as He stood above Joseph's rent sepulcher proclaiming: "I am the resurrection, and the life." John 11:25.

The question, "If a man die, shall he live again?" has been answered. By bearing the penalty of sin, by going down into the grave, Christ has brightened the tomb for all who die in faith. God in human form has brought life and immortality to light through the gospel. In dying, Christ secured eternal life for all who believe in Him. In dying, He condemned the originator of sin and disloyalty to suffer the penalty of sin—eternal death.

The possessor and giver of eternal life, Christ was the only one who could conquer death. He is our Redeemer.[52]

Christ is life itself. He who passed through death to destroy him that had the power of death is the Source of all vitality. There is balm in Gilead, and a Physician there.[53]

NATURAL IMMORTALITY A LIE

The getting of treasures by a lying tongue is a vanity tossed to and fro of them that seek death. Prov. 21:6.

The great original lie which he [Satan] told to Eve in Eden, "Ye shall not surely die," was the first sermon ever preached on the immortality of the soul. That sermon was crowned with success, and terrible results followed. He has brought minds to receive that sermon as truth, and ministers preach it, sing it, and pray it.[54]

After the Fall, Satan bade his angels make a special effort to inculcate the belief in man's natural immortality; and having induced the people to receive this error, they were to lead them on to conclude that the sinner would live in eternal misery. Now the prince of darkness, working through his agents, represents God as a revengeful tyrant, declaring that He plunges into hell all those who do not please Him, and causes them ever to feel His wrath. . . .

A large class to whom the doctrine of eternal torment is revolting, are driven to the opposite error. They see that the Scriptures represent God as a being of love and compassion, and they cannot believe that He will consign His creatures to the fires of an eternally burning hell. But holding that the soul is naturally immortal, they see no alternative but to conclude that all mankind will finally be saved. Many regard the threatenings of the Bible as designed merely to frighten men into obedience, and not to be literally fulfilled. Thus the sinner can live in selfish pleasure, disregarding the requirements of God, and yet expect to be finally received into His favor. . . .

God has given to men a declaration of His character, and of His method of dealing with sin. . . . "All the wicked will he destroy." Ps. 145:20. . . . Yet all the manifestations of retributive justice will be perfectly consistent with the character of God as a merciful, long-suffering, benevolent being. . . .

And all who have a just conception of these qualities will love Him because they are drawn toward Him in admiration of His attributes.[55]

NOW IS GOD'S TIME

For he saith, I have heard thee in a time accepted, and in the day of salvation have I succoured thee: behold, now is the accepted time; behold, now is the day of salvation. 2 Cor. 6:2.

God has ordained laws for the government, not only of living beings, but of all the operations of nature. Everything is under fixed laws, which cannot be disregarded. . . .

Like the angels, the dwellers in Eden had been placed upon probation; their happy estate could be retained only on condition of fidelity to the Creator's law. They could obey and live, or disobey and perish. God had made them the recipients of rich blessings; but should they disregard His will, He who spared not the angels that sinned, could not spare them; transgression would forfeit His gifts, and bring upon them misery and ruin.[56]

Adam and Eve transgressed the law of God. This made it necessary for them to be driven from Eden and be separated from the tree of life, to eat of which after their transgression would perpetuate sin. . . .

Death entered the world because of transgression. But Christ gave His life that man should have another trial. He did not die on the cross to abolish the law of God, but to secure for man a second probation. He did not die to make sin an immortal attribute; He died to secure the right to destroy him that had the power of death, that is, the devil.[57]

It is impossible for men to secure the salvation of the soul after death. . . . This life is the only time given to man in which to prepare for eternity.[58]

Probation is granted to all, that all may form characters for eternal life. An opportunity will be given to all to decide for life or death. . . .

The probation of those who choose to live a life of sin, and neglect the great salvation offered, closes when Christ's ministration ceases just previous to His appearing in the clouds of heaven.[59]

Now is the hour of probation. Now is the day of salvation. Now, now, is God's time.[60]

CHRIST THE FIRST FRUITS

If in this life only we have hope in Christ, we are of all men most miserable. But now is Christ risen from the dead, and become the firstfruits of them that slept. 1 Cor. 15:19, 20.

Christ arose from the dead as the first fruits of those that slept. He was the antitype of the wave sheaf, and His resurrection took place on the very day when the wave sheaf was to be presented before the Lord. For more than a thousand years this symbolic ceremony had been performed. From the harvest fields the first heads of ripened grain were gathered, and when the people went up to Jerusalem to the Passover, the sheaf of first fruits was waved as a thank offering before the Lord. Not until this was presented could the sickle be put to the grain, and it be gathered into sheaves. The sheaf dedicated to God represented the harvest. So Christ the first fruits represented the great spiritual harvest to be gathered for the kingdom of God. His resurrection is the type and pledge of the resurrection of all the righteous dead.[61]

The resurrection of Jesus was a sample of the final resurrection of all who sleep in Him. The risen body of the Saviour, His deportment, the accents of His speech, were all familiar to His followers. In like manner will those who sleep in Jesus rise again. We shall know our friends even as the disciples knew Jesus. Though they may have been deformed, diseased, or disfigured in this mortal life, yet in their resurrected and glorified body their individual identity will be perfectly preserved, and we shall recognize, in the face radiant with the light shining from the face of Jesus, the lineaments of those we love.[62]

At His second coming all the precious dead shall hear His voice, and shall come forth to glorious, immortal life. The same power that raised Christ from the dead will raise His church, and glorify it with Him, above all principalities, above all powers, above every name that is named, not only in this world, but also in the world to come.[63]

He will receive us with honor. To us will be given a crown of glory that fadeth not away.[64]

DEATH SWALLOWED UP IN VICTORY

For we that are in this tabernacle do groan, being burdened: not for that we would be unclothed, but clothed upon, that mortality might be swallowed up of life. 2 Cor. 5:4.

The Life-giver is coming to break the fetters of the tomb. He is to bring forth the captives and proclaim, "I am the resurrection and the life."[65]

Nowhere in the Sacred Scriptures is found the statement that the righteous go to their reward or the wicked to their punishment at death. The patriarchs and prophets have left no such assurance. Christ and His apostles have given no hint of it. The Bible clearly teaches that the dead do not go immediately to heaven. They are represented as sleeping until the resurrection. In the very day when the silver cord is loosed and the golden bowl broken, man's thoughts perish. They that go down to the grave are in silence. They know no more of anything that is done under the sun. Blessed rest for the weary righteous! Time, be it long or short, is but a moment to them. They sleep; they are awakened by the trump of God to a glorious immortality. "For the trumpet shall sound, and the dead shall be raised incorruptible. . . . So when . . . this mortal shall have put on immortality, then shall be brought to pass the saying that is written, Death is swallowed up in victory." 1 Cor. 15:52-54. As they are called forth from their deep slumber, they begin to think just where they ceased. The last sensation was the pang of death, the last thought that they were falling beneath the power of the grave. When they arise from the tomb, their first glad thought will be echoed in the triumphal shout, "O death, where is thy sting? O grave, where is thy victory?" 1 Cor. 15:55.[66]

The pangs of death were the last things they felt. . . . When they awake the pain is all gone. . . . The gates of the city of God swing back upon their hinges, . . . and the ransomed of God walk in through the cherubims and seraphims. Christ bids them welcome and puts upon them His benediction. "Well done, thou good and faithful servant: . . . enter thou into the joy of thy lord." Matt. 25:21.[67]

A SPECIAL RESURRECTION

And many of them that sleep in the dust of the earth shall awake,
some to everlasting life, and some to shame and everlasting contempt.
Dan. 12:2.

It is at midnight that God manifests His power for the deliverance of His people. The sun appears, shining in its strength. Signs and wonders follow in quick succession. The wicked look with terror and amazement upon the scene, while the righteous behold with solemn joy the tokens of their deliverance. Everything in nature seems turned out of its course. The streams cease to flow. Dark, heavy clouds come up, and clash against each other. In the midst of the angry heavens is one clear space of indescribable glory, whence comes the voice of God like the sound of many waters, saying, "It is done." Rev. 16:17. . . .

That voice shakes the heavens and the earth. There is a mighty earthquake, "such as was not since men were upon the earth, so mighty an earthquake, and so great." Rev. 16:18. . . . The whole earth heaves and swells like the waves of the sea. Its surface is breaking up. Its very foundations seem to be giving way. . . .

Graves are opened, and "many of them that sleep in the dust of the earth . . . awake, some to everlasting life, and some to shame and everlasting contempt." Dan. 12:2. All who have died in the faith of the third angel's message come forth from the tomb glorified, to hear God's covenant of peace with those who have kept His law.[68]

Those who had died in faith under the third angel's message, keeping the Sabbath, came forth from their dusty beds.[69]

"They also which pierced him" (Rev. 1:7), those that mocked and derided Christ's dying agonies, and the most violent opposers of His truth and His people, are raised to behold Him in His glory, and to see the honor placed upon the loyal and obedient. . . .

The voice of God is heard from heaven, declaring the day and hour of Jesus' coming, and delivering the everlasting covenant to His people. . . . And when the blessing is pronounced on those who have honored God by keeping His Sabbath holy, there is a mighty shout of victory.[70]

THE RESURRECTION TO IMMORTALITY

For if we believe that Jesus died and rose again, even so them also which sleep in Jesus will God bring with him. 1 Thess. 4:14.

To the believer, Christ is the resurrection and the life. In our Saviour the life that was lost through sin is restored; for He has life in Himself to quicken whom He will. He is invested with the right to give immortality. The life that He laid down in humanity, He takes up again, and gives to humanity.[71]

When Christ comes to gather to Himself those who have been faithful, the last trump will sound, and the whole earth, from the summits of the loftiest mountains to the lowest recesses of the deepest mines, will hear. The righteous dead will hear the sound of the last trump, and will come forth from their graves.[72]

All come forth from their graves the same in stature as when they entered the tomb. Adam, who stands among the risen throng, is of lofty height and majestic form, in stature but little below the Son of God. He presents a marked contrast to the people of later generations; in this one respect is shown the great degeneracy of the race. But all arise with the freshness and vigor of eternal youth. . . . The mortal, corruptible form, devoid of comeliness, once polluted with sin, becomes perfect, beautiful, and immortal. . . . Restored to the tree of life in the long-lost Eden, the redeemed will "grow up" to the full stature of the race in its primeval glory. . . .

The living righteous are changed "in a moment, in the twinkling of an eye." 1 Cor. 15:52. At the voice of God they were glorified; now they are made immortal, and with the risen saints are caught up to meet their Lord in the air. . . . Little children are borne by holy angels to their mothers' arms. Friends long separated by death are united, nevermore to part, and with songs of gladness ascend together to the city of God.[73]

All the precious dead, from righteous Abel to the last saint that dies, shall awake to glorious, immortal life.[74]

THE RESURRECTION TO DAMNATION

For evildoers shall be cut off: but those that wait upon the Lord, they shall inherit the earth. Ps. 37:9.

At the close of the thousand years the second resurrection will take place. Then the wicked will be raised from the dead, and appear before God. . . . Thus the revelator, after describing the resurrection of the righteous, says, "The rest of the dead lived not again until the thousand years were finished." Rev. 20:5.[75]

At the first resurrection all came forth in immortal bloom; but at the second the marks of the curse are visible on all. The kings and noblemen of the earth, the mean and low, the learned and unlearned, come forth together. All behold the Son of man; and those very men who despised and mocked Him, who put the crown of thorns upon His sacred brow, and smote Him with the reed, behold Him in all His kingly majesty. Those who spit upon Him in the hour of His trial now turn from His piercing gaze and from the glory of His countenance. Those who drove the nails through His hands and feet now look upon the marks of His crucifixion. Those who thrust the spear into His side behold the marks of their cruelty on His body. And they know that He is the very one whom they crucified and derided in His expiring agony. And then there arises one long protracted wail of agony, as they flee to hide from the presence of the King of kings and Lord of lords.

All are seeking to hide in the rocks, to shield themselves from the terrible glory of Him whom they once despised. And, overwhelmed and pained with His majesty and exceeding glory, they with one accord raise their voices, and with terrible distinctness exclaim, "Blessed is he that cometh in the name of the Lord." Ps. 118:26.[76]

Fire will come down from God out of heaven and devour them [the wicked]—burn them up root and branch. Satan is the root, and his children are the branches.[77]

The destiny of the wicked is fixed by their own choice. Their exclusion from heaven is voluntary with themselves, and just and merciful on the part of God.[78]

182

THE LIFE-GIVER IS COMING

If a man die, shall he live again? all the days of my appointed time will I wait, till my change come. Job 14:14.

The Life-giver will call up His purchased possession in the first resurrection, and until that triumphant hour, when the last trump shall sound and the vast army shall come forth to eternal victory, every sleeping saint will be kept in safety and will be guarded as a precious jewel, who is known to God by name. By the power of the Saviour that dwelt in them while living and because they were partakers of the divine nature, they are brought forth from the dead.[79]

Our fondest hopes are often blighted here. Our loved ones are torn from us by death. We close their eyes and habit them for the tomb, and lay them away from our sight. But hope bears our spirits up. We are not parted forever, but shall meet the loved ones who sleep in Jesus. They shall come again from the land of the enemy. The Life-giver is coming. Myriads of holy angels escort Him on His way. He bursts the bands of death, breaks the fetters of the tomb, the precious captives come forth in health and immortal beauty.[80]

Our personal identity is preserved in the resurrection, though not the same particles of matter or material substance as went into the grave. . . . In the resurrection every man will have his own character. God in His own time will call forth the dead, giving again the breath of life, and bidding the dry bones live.[81]

There will be a relinking of the family chain. When we look upon our dead, we may think of the morning when the trump of God shall sound, when "the dead shall be raised incorruptible, and we shall be changed." 1 Cor. 15:52.[82]

The last lingering traces of the curse of sin will be removed, and Christ's faithful ones will appear in "the beauty of the Lord our God," in mind and soul and body reflecting the perfect image of their Lord.[83]

Are we ready so that if we shall fall asleep, we can do so with hope in Jesus Christ?[84]

SORROW WITH HOPE

But I would not have you to be ignorant, brethren, concerning them which are asleep, that ye sorrow not, even as others which have no hope. 1 Thess. 4:13.

To the afflicted ones I would say, be of good comfort in the hope of the resurrection morning. The waters of which you have been drinking are as bitter to your taste as were the waters of Marah to the children of Israel in the wilderness, but Jesus can make them so sweet with His love. . . .

God has provided a balm for every wound. There is a balm in Gilead, there is a Physician there. Will you not now as never before study the Scriptures? Seek the Lord for wisdom in every emergency. In every trial plead with Jesus to show you a way out of your troubles, then your eyes will be opened to behold the remedy and to apply to your case the healing promises that have been recorded in His Word. In this way the enemy will find no place to lead you into mourning and unbelief, but instead you will have faith and hope and courage in the Lord. The Holy Spirit will give you clear discernment that you may see and appropriate every blessing that will act as an antidote to grief, as a branch of healing to every draught of bitterness that is placed to your lips. Every draught of bitterness will be mingled with the love of Jesus, and in place of complaining of the bitterness, you will realize that Jesus' love and grace are so mingled with sorrow that it has been turned into subdued, holy, sanctified joy.

When Henry White, our eldest son, lay dying, he said, "A bed of pain is a precious place when we have the presence of Jesus." When we are obliged to drink of the bitter waters, turn away from the bitter to the precious and the bright. In trial grace can give the human soul assurance, and when we stand at the deathbed and see how the Christian can bear suffering and go through the valley of death, we gather strength . . . and we fail not, neither are we discouraged in leading souls to Jesus.[85]

WHEN ETERNAL LIFE BEGINS

And this is the record, that God hath given to us eternal life, and this life is in his Son. He that hath the Son hath life; and he that hath not the Son of God hath not life. 1 John 5:11, 12.

Jesus declared, "I am the resurrection, and the life." In Christ is life, original, unborrowed, underived. "He that hath the Son hath life." The divinity of Christ is the believer's assurance of eternal life. "He that believeth in me," said Jesus, "though he were dead, yet shall he live: and whosoever liveth and believeth in me shall never die." John 11:25, 26.[86]

To the believer, death is but a small matter. Christ speaks of it as if it were of little moment. "If a man keep my saying, he shall never see death," "he shall never taste of death." John 8:51, 52. To the Christian, death is but a sleep, a moment of silence and darkness. The life is hid with Christ in God, and "when Christ, who is our life, shall appear, then shall ye also appear with him in glory." Col. 3:4.[87]

He who Himself was soon to die upon the cross stood . . . a conqueror of the grave, and asserted His right and power to give eternal life.[88]

"I will raise him up at the last day." John 6:40. Christ became one flesh with us, in order that we might become one spirit with Him. It is by virtue of this union that we are to come forth from the grave— not merely as a manifestation of the power of Christ, but because, through faith, His life has become ours. Those who see Christ in His true character, and receive Him into the heart, have everlasting life. It is through the Spirit that Christ dwells in us; and the Spirit of God, received into the heart by faith, is the beginning of the life eternal.[89]

Jesus is . . . crying, "If any man thirst, let him come unto me, and drink." "Let him that is athirst come. And whosoever will, let him take the water of life freely." "Whosoever drinketh of the water that I shall give him shall never thirst; but the water that I shall give him shall be in him a well of water springing up into everlasting life." John 7:37; Rev. 22:17; John 4:14.[90]

THE SANCTUARY OF GOD

THE LORD IS IN THIS PLACE

And Jacob awaked out of his sleep, and he said, Surely the Lord is in this place; and I knew it not. And he was afraid, and said, How dreadful is this place! this is none other but the house of God, and this is the gate of heaven. Gen. 28:16, 17.

True reverence for God is inspired by a sense of His infinite greatness and a realization of His presence. With this sense of the Unseen, every heart should be deeply impressed. The hour and place of prayer are sacred, because God is there. And as reverence is manifested in attitude and demeanor, the feeling that inspires it will be deepened. "Holy and reverend is his name," the psalmist declares (Ps. 111:9). Angels, when they speak that name, veil their faces. With what reverence, then, should we, who are fallen and sinful, take it upon our lips! Well would it be for old and young to ponder those words of Scripture that show how the place marked by God's special presence should be regarded. "Put off thy shoes from off thy feet," He commanded Moses at the burning bush, "for the place whereon thou standest is holy ground." Ex. 3:5.[1]

God is high and holy; and to the humble, believing soul, His house on earth, the place where His people meet for worship, is as the gate of heaven. The song of praise, the words spoken by Christ's ministers, are God's appointed agencies to prepare a people for the church above, for that loftier worship into which there can enter nothing that is impure. . . . God sees every irreverent thought or action, and it is registered in the books of heaven. . . . Nothing is hid from His all-searching eye. If you have formed in any degree the habit of inattention and indifference in the house of God, exercise the powers you have to correct it. . . . Practice reverence until it becomes a part of yourself.[2]

KEEP SILENCE BEFORE HIM

The Lord is in his holy temple: let all the earth keep silence before him. Hab. 2:20.

From the sacredness which was attached to the earthly sanctuary, Christians may learn how they should regard the place where the Lord meets with His people. There has been a great change, not for the better, but for the worse, in the habits and customs of the people in reference to religious worship. The precious, the sacred, things which connect us with God are fast losing their hold upon our minds and hearts, and are being brought down to the level of common things. The reverence which the people had anciently for the sanctuary where they met with God in sacred service has largely passed away. Nevertheless, God Himself gave the order of His service, exalting it high above everything of a temporal nature.

The house is the sanctuary for the family, and the closet or the grove the most retired place for individual worship; but the church is the sanctuary for the congregation.[3]

In the name of Jesus we may come before Him with confidence, but we must not approach Him with the boldness of presumption, as though He were on a level with ourselves. There are those who address the great and all-powerful and holy God, who dwelleth in light unapproachable, as they would address an equal, or even an inferior. There are those who conduct themselves in His house as they would not presume to do in the audience-chamber of an earthly ruler. These should remember that they are in His sight whom seraphim adore.[4]

Those who assemble to worship Him should put away every evil thing. Unless they worship Him in spirit and truth and in the beauty of holiness, their coming together will be of no avail.[5]

It is your privilege, dear young friends, to glorify God upon the earth. In order to do this, you must direct your minds away from things that are superficial, frivolous, and unimportant, to those that are of eternal worth.[6]

PURGING FROM SIN

Then said I, Woe is me! for I am undone; because I am a man of unclean lips, and I dwell in the midst of a people of unclean lips: for mine eyes have seen the King, the Lord of hosts. Isa. 6:5.

As the prophet Isaiah beheld the glory of the Lord, he was amazed, and, overwhelmed with a sense of his own weakness and unworthiness, he cried, "Woe is me! . . ."

Isaiah had denounced the sin of others; but now he sees himself exposed to the same condemnation he had pronounced upon them. He had been satisfied with a cold, lifeless ceremony in his worship of God. He had not known this until the vision was given him of the Lord. How little now appeared his wisdom and talents as he looked upon the sacredness and majesty of the sanctuary. . . . His view of himself might be expressed in the language of the apostle Paul, "O wretched man that I am! who shall deliver me from the body of this death?" Rom. 7:24. . . .

"Then flew one of the seraphims unto me, having a live coal in his hand, which he had taken with the tongs from off the altar: and he laid it upon my mouth, and said, Lo, this hath touched thy lips; and thine iniquity is taken away, and thy sin purged." Isa. 6:6, 7.

The vision given to Isaiah represents the condition of God's people in the last days. They are privileged to see by faith the work that is going forward in the heavenly sanctuary. . . . As they look by faith into the holy of holies, and see the work of Christ in the heavenly sanctuary, they perceive that they are a people of unclean lips—a people whose lips have often spoken vanity, and whose talents have not been sanctified and employed to the glory of God. Well may they despair as they contrast their own weakness and unworthiness with the purity and loveliness of the glorious character of Christ. But if they, like Isaiah, will receive the impression the Lord designs shall be made upon the heart, if they will humble their souls before God, there is hope for them. The bow of promise is above the throne, and the work done for Isaiah will be performed in them.[7]

THE SPIRIT IN THE SOUL TEMPLE

Know ye not that ye are the temple of God, and that the Spirit of God dwelleth in you? 1 Cor. 3:16.

From eternal ages it was God's purpose that every created being, from the bright and holy seraph to man, should be a temple for the indwelling of the Creator. Because of sin, humanity ceased to be a temple for God. Darkened and defiled by evil, the heart of man no longer revealed the glory of the Divine One. But by the incarnation of the Son of God, the purpose of Heaven is fulfilled. God dwells in humanity, and through saving grace the heart of man becomes again His temple.

God designed that the temple at Jerusalem should be a continual witness to the high destiny open to every soul. But the Jews had not understood the significance of the building they regarded with so much pride. They did not yield themselves as holy temples for the Divine Spirit. The courts of the temple at Jerusalem, filled with the tumult of unholy traffic, represented all too truly the temple of the heart. . . . In cleansing the temple from the world's buyers and sellers, Jesus announced His mission to cleanse the heart from the defilement of sin—from . . . the selfish lusts, the evil habits, that corrupt the soul. . . .

No man can of himself cast out the evil throng that have taken possession of the heart. Only Christ can cleanse the soul temple. But He will not force an entrance. He comes not into the heart as to the temple of old; but He says, "Behold, I stand at the door, and knock: if any man hear my voice, and open the door, I will come in to him." Rev. 3:20. He will come, not for one day merely; for He says, "I will dwell in them, and walk in them; . . . and they shall be my people." 2 Cor. 6:16. . . . His presence will cleanse and sanctify the soul, so that it may be a holy temple unto the Lord, and "an habitation of God through the Spirit." Eph. 2:22.[8]

The Lord is more willing to give the Holy Spirit to those who serve Him than parents are to give good gifts to their children.[9]

THE PURPOSE OF THE SANCTUARY

And let them make me a sanctuary; that I may dwell among them. Ex. 25:8.

"I will dwell among the children of Israel, and will be their God," "and the tabernacle shall be sanctified by my glory" (Ex. 29:45, 43), was the assurance given to Moses.[10]

In the building of the sanctuary as a dwelling place for God, Moses was directed to make all things according to the pattern of things in the heavens. God called him into the mount, and revealed to him the heavenly things, and in their similitude the tabernacle, with all that pertained to it, was fashioned.

So to Israel, whom He desired to make His dwelling place, He revealed His glorious ideal of character. The pattern was shown them in the mount when the law was given from Sinai. . . .

But this ideal they were, in themselves, powerless to attain. The revelation at Sinai could only impress them with their need and helplessness. Another lesson the tabernacle, through its service of sacrifice, was to teach—the lesson of pardon of sin, and power through the Saviour for obedience unto life.

Through Christ was to be fulfilled the purpose of which the tabernacle was a symbol—that glorious building, its walls of glistening gold reflecting in rainbow hues the curtains inwrought with cherubim, the fragrance of ever-burning incense pervading all, the priests robed in spotless white, and in the deep mystery of the inner place, above the mercy seat, between the figures of the bowed, worshiping angels, the glory of the Holiest. In all, God desired His people to read His purpose for the human soul. It was the same purpose long afterward set forth by the apostle Paul, speaking by the Holy Spirit:

"Know ye not that ye are the temple of God, and that the Spirit of God dwelleth in you? If any man defile the temple of God, him shall God destroy; for the temple of God is holy, which temple ye are." 1 Cor. 3:16, 17.[11]

A TEMPLE BUILT BY SACRIFICE

Speak unto the children of Israel, that they bring me an offering: of every man that giveth it willingly with his heart ye shall take my offering. Ex. 25:2.

God Himself gave to Moses the plan of that structure [the sanctuary], with particular directions as to its size and form, the materials to be employed, and every article of furniture which it was to contain. The holy places made with hands were to be "figures of the true" (Heb. 9:24), "patterns of things in the heavens" (Heb. 9:23)—a miniature representation of the heavenly temple where Christ, our great high priest, after offering His life as a sacrifice, was to minister in the sinner's behalf. . . .

For the building of the sanctuary, great and expensive preparations were necessary; a large amount of the most precious and costly material was required; yet the Lord accepted only freewill offerings. "Of every man that giveth it willingly with his heart ye shall take my offering," was the divine command repeated by Moses to the congregation. Devotion to God and a spirit of sacrifice were the first requisites in preparing a dwelling place for the Most High.

All the people responded with one accord. "They came, every one whose heart stirred him up, and every one whom his spirit made willing, and they brought the Lord's offering to the work of the tabernacle of the congregation, and for all his service, and for the holy garments. And they came, both men and women, as many as were willing hearted, and brought bracelets . . . : and every man that offered an offering of gold unto the Lord." Ex. 35:21, 22. . . .

The people, old and young—men, women, and children—continued to bring their offerings, until those in charge of the work found that they had enough, and even more than could be used. . . .

All who love the worship of God, and prize the blessing of His sacred presence, will manifest the same spirit of sacrifice in preparing a house where He may meet with them.[12]

If there was ever a time when sacrifices should be made, it is now.[13]

STRENGTH AND BEAUTY IN HIS SANCTUARY

Honour and majesty are before him: strength and beauty are in his sanctuary. Ps. 96:6.

From the creation and fall of man to the present time, there has been a continual unfolding of the plan of God for the redemption, through Christ, of the fallen race. The tabernacle and temple of God on earth were patterned after the original in heaven. Around the sanctuary and its solemn services mystically gathered the grand truths which were to be developed through succeeding generations.

There has been no time when God has granted greater evidences of His grandeur and exalted majesty than while He was the acknowledged governor of Israel. The manifestations of an invisible King were grand and unspeakably awful. A scepter was swayed, but it was held by no human hand. The sacred ark, covered by the mercy seat, and containing the holy law of God, was symbolical of Jehovah Himself. It was the power of the Israelites to conquer in battle. Before it idols were thrown down, and for rashly looking into it thousands perished. Never in our world has the Lord given such open manifestations of His supremacy as when He alone was the acknowledged king of Israel.[14]

The law of God, enshrined within the ark, was the great rule of righteousness and judgment. That law pronounced death upon the transgressor; but above the law was the mercy seat, upon which the presence of God was revealed, and from which, by virtue of the atonement, pardon was granted to the repentant sinner. Thus in the work of Christ for our redemption, symbolized by the sanctuary service, "mercy and truth are met together; righteousness and peace have kissed each other." Ps. 85:10.[15]

While we rejoice today that our Saviour has come, that the sacrifices of the former dispensation have given place to the perfect offering for sin, we are not excusable in showing contempt for that period.[16]

REDEEMER, PRIEST, AND KING

For such an high priest became us, who is holy, harmless, undefiled, separate from sinners, and made higher than the heavens. Heb. 7:26.

By divine direction the tribe of Levi was set apart for the service of the sanctuary. In the earliest times every man was the priest of his own household. In the days of Abraham, the priesthood was regarded as the birthright of the eldest son. Now, instead of the first-born of all Israel, the Lord accepted the tribe of Levi for the work of the sanctuary. . . . The priesthood, however, was restricted to the family of Aaron. Aaron and his sons alone were permitted to minister before the Lord; the rest of the tribe were entrusted with the charge of the tabernacle. . . .

In accordance with their office, a special dress was appointed for the priests. "Thou shalt make holy garments for Aaron thy brother for glory and for beauty" (Ex. 28:2), was the divine direction to Moses. . . . Everything connected with the apparel and deportment of the priests was to be such as to impress the beholder with a sense of the holiness of God, the sacredness of His worship, and the purity required of those who came into His presence. Not only the sanctuary itself, but the ministration of the priests, was to "serve unto the example and shadow of heavenly things." Heb. 8:5.[17]

The people were taught each day, by means of types and shadows, the great truths relative to the advent of Christ as Redeemer, Priest, and King; and once each year their minds were carried forward to the closing events of the great controversy between Christ and Satan, the final purification of the universe from sin and sinners. The sacrifices and offerings of the Mosaic ritual were ever pointing toward a better service, even a heavenly.[18]

The merits of His [Jesus'] sacrifice are sufficient to present to the Father in our behalf.[19]

We are to have free access to the atoning blood of Christ. This we must regard as the most precious privilege, the greatest blessing, ever granted to sinful man.[20]

A DAILY CONSECRATION TO GOD

I beseech you therefore, brethren, by the mercies of God, that ye present your bodies a living sacrifice, holy, acceptable unto God, which is your reasonable service. Rom. 12:1.

The ministration of the sanctuary consisted of two divisions, a daily and a yearly service. The daily service was performed at the altar of burnt offering in the court of the tabernacle, and in the holy place; while the yearly service was in the most holy. . . .

The daily service consisted of the morning and evening burnt offering, the offering of sweet incense on the golden altar, and the special offerings for individual sins. And there were also offerings for sabbaths, new moons, and special feasts.

Every morning and evening a lamb of a year old was burned upon the altar, with its appropriate meat offering, thus symbolizing the daily consecration of the nation to Jehovah, and their constant dependence upon the atoning blood of Christ. God expressly directed that every offering presented for the service of the sanctuary should be "without blemish." . . . Only an offering "without blemish" could be a symbol of His perfect purity who was to offer Himself as "a lamb without blemish and without spot." 1 Peter 1:19. The apostle Paul points to these sacrifices as an illustration of what the followers of Christ are to become. He says, "I beseech you therefore, brethren, by the mercies of God, that ye present your bodies a living sacrifice, holy, acceptable unto God, which is your reasonable service." . . .

The hours appointed for the morning and the evening sacrifice were regarded as sacred, and they came to be observed as the set time for worship throughout the Jewish nation. . . . In this custom, Christians have an example for morning and evening prayer. While God condemns a mere round of ceremonies, without the spirit of worship, He looks with great pleasure upon those who love Him, bowing morning and evening to seek pardon for sins committed, and to present their requests for needed blessings.[21]

THE INCENSE OF RIGHTEOUSNESS

And walk in love, as Christ also hath loved us, and hath given himself for us an offering and a sacrifice to God for a sweetsmelling savour. Eph. 5:2.

The showbread was kept ever before the Lord as a perpetual offering. . . . It was called showbread, or "bread of the presence," because it was ever before the face of the Lord. It was an acknowledgment of man's dependence upon God for both temporal and spiritual food, and that it is received only through the mediation of Christ. . . . Both the manna and the showbread pointed to Christ, the living bread who is ever in the presence of God for us.[22]

In the offering of incense the priest was brought more directly into the presence of God than in any other act of the daily ministration. As the inner veil of the sanctuary did not extend to the top of the building, the glory of God, which was manifested above the mercy seat, was partially visible from the first apartment. When the priest offered incense before the Lord, he looked toward the ark; and as the cloud of incense arose, the divine glory descended upon the mercy seat and filled the most holy place, and often so filled both apartments that the priest was obliged to retire to the door of the tabernacle. As in that typical service the priest looked by faith to the mercy seat which he could not see, so the people of God are now to direct their prayers to Christ, their great high priest, who, unseen by human vision, is pleading in their behalf in the sanctuary above.

The incense, ascending with the prayers of Israel, represents the merits and intercession of Christ, His perfect righteousness, which through faith is imputed to His people, and which can alone make the worship of sinful beings acceptable to God. Before the veil of the most holy place, was an altar of perpetual intercession, before the holy, an altar of continual atonement. By blood and by incense, God was to be approached—symbols pointing to the great Mediator, through whom sinners may approach Jehovah, and through whom alone mercy and salvation can be granted to the repentant, believing soul.[23]

CHRIST DIED FOR THE INDIVIDUAL

This is a faithful saying, and worthy of all acceptation, that Christ Jesus came into the world to save sinners; of whom I am chief. 1 Tim. 1:15.

The most important part of the daily ministration was the service performed in behalf of individuals. The repentant sinner brought his offering to the door of the tabernacle, and placing his hand upon the victim's head, confessed his sins, thus in figure transferring them from himself to the innocent sacrifice. By his own hand the animal was then slain, and the blood was carried by the priest into the holy place and sprinkled before the veil, behind which was the ark containing the law that the sinner had transgressed. By this ceremony the sin was, through the blood, transferred in figure to the sanctuary. In some cases the blood was not taken into the holy place; but the flesh was then to be eaten by the priest. . . . Both ceremonies alike symbolized the transfer of the sin from the penitent to the sanctuary.

Such was the work that went on day by day throughout the year. The sins of Israel being thus transferred to the sanctuary, the holy places were defiled, and a special work became necessary for the removal of the sins. God commanded that an atonement be made for each of the sacred apartments, as for the altar, to "cleanse it, and hallow it from the uncleanness of the children of Israel." Lev. 16:19.

Once a year, on the great Day of Atonement, the priest entered the most holy place for the cleansing of the sanctuary. The work there performed, completed the yearly round of ministration. . . .

The earthly sanctuary was built . . . according to the pattern shown . . . in the mount. It was "a figure for the time then present, in which were offered both gifts and sacrifices"; its two holy places were "patterns of things in the heavens"; Christ, our great high priest, is "a minister of the sanctuary, and of the true tabernacle, which the Lord pitched, and not man." Heb. 9:9, 23; 8:2.[24]

He appears in the presence of God, . . . ready to accept the repentance and to answer the prayers of His people.[25]

THE VOLUNTARY SACRIFICE OF JESUS

Then said I, Lo, I come: in the volume of the book it is written of me, I delight to do thy will, O my God: yea, thy law is within my heart. Ps. 40:7, 8.

The children of Israel were anciently commanded to make an offering for the entire congregation to purify them from ceremonial defilement. This sacrifice was a red heifer and represented the more perfect offering that should redeem from the pollution of sin. This was an occasional sacrifice for the purification of all those who had necessarily or accidentally touched the dead. All who came in contact with death in any way were considered ceremonially unclean. This was to forcibly impress the minds of the Hebrews with the fact that death came in consequence of sin and therefore is a representative of sin. The *one* heifer, the *one* ark, the *one* brazen serpent, impressively point to the *one* great offering, the sacrifice of Christ.

This heifer was to be red, which was a symbol of blood. It must be without spot or blemish, and one that had never borne a yoke. Here, again, Christ was typified. The Son of God came voluntarily to accomplish the work of atonement. There was no obligatory yoke upon Him, for He was independent and above all law. The angels, as God's intelligent messengers, were under the yoke of obligation; no personal sacrifice of theirs could atone for the guilt of fallen man. Christ alone was free from the claims of the law to undertake the redemption of the sinful race. . . .

Jesus might have remained at His Father's right hand, wearing His kingly crown and royal robes. But He chose to exchange all the riches, honor, and glory of heaven for the poverty of humanity, and His station of high command for the horrors of Gethsemane and the humiliation and agony of Calvary. . . .

The wounded hands, the pierced side, the marred feet, plead eloquently for fallen man, whose redemption is purchased at such an infinite cost. Oh, matchless condescension! Neither time nor events can lessen the efficacy of the atoning sacrifice.[26]

THE BLOOD APPLIED CONTINUALLY

For if the blood of bulls and of goats, and the ashes of an heifer sprinkling the unclean, sanctifieth to the purifying of the flesh: how much more shall the blood of Christ, . . . purge your conscience from dead works to serve the living God? Heb. 9:13, 14.

The sacrificial [red] heifer was conducted without the camp and slain in the most imposing manner. Thus Christ suffered without the gates of Jerusalem, for Calvary was outside the city walls. This was to show that Christ did not die for the Hebrews alone, but for all mankind. He proclaims to a fallen world that He has come to be their Redeemer and urges them to accept the salvation He offers them. The heifer having been slain in a most solemn manner, the priest, clothed in pure white garments, took the blood in his hands as it issued from the body of the victim and cast it toward the temple seven times. . . .

The body of the heifer was burned to ashes, which signified a whole and ample sacrifice. The ashes were then gathered up by a person uncontaminated by contact with the dead and placed in a vessel containing water from a running stream. This clean and pure person then took a cedar stick with scarlet cloth and a bunch of hyssop, and sprinkled the contents of the vessel upon the tent and the people assembled. This ceremony was repeated several times and was done as a purification from sin.

Thus Christ, in His own spotless righteousness, after shedding His precious blood, enters into the holy place to cleanse the sanctuary. And there the crimson current is brought into the service of reconciling God to man. Some may look upon this slaying of the heifer as a meaningless ceremony, but it was done by the command of God and bears a deep significance that has not lost its application to the present time. . . .

The blood of Christ is efficacious, but it needs to be applied continually. . . .

If it was necessary in ancient times for the unclean to be purified by the blood of sprinkling, how essential for those living in the perils of the last days, and exposed to the temptations of Satan, to have the blood of Christ applied to their hearts daily.[27]

INTO THE HOLY PLACE

Neither by the blood of goats and calves, but by his own blood he entered in once into the holy place, having obtained eternal redemption for us. Heb. 9:12.

In the spring of A.D. 31, Christ, the true Sacrifice, was offered on Calvary.[28]

When Christ on the cross cried out, "It is finished," the veil of the temple was rent in twain. This veil was significant to the Jewish nation. It was of most costly material, of purple and gold, and was of great length and breadth. At the moment when Christ breathed His last, there were witnesses in the temple who beheld the strong, heavy material rent by unseen hands from top to bottom. This act signified to the heavenly universe, and to a world corrupted by sin, that a new and living way had been opened to the fallen race, that all sacrificial offerings terminated in the one great offering of the Son of God.[29]

Type . . . met antitype in the death of God's Son. . . . The way into the holiest is laid open. A new and living way is prepared for all. No longer need sinful, sorrowing humanity await the coming of the high priest. Henceforth the Saviour was to officiate as priest and advocate in the heaven of heavens. . . . There is now an end to all sacrifices and offerings for sin. The Son of God is come according to His word, "Lo, I come (in the volume of the book it is written of me,) to do thy will, O God." "By his own blood" He entereth "in once into the holy place, having obtained eternal redemption for us." Heb. 10:7; 9:12.[30]

The Holy Spirit which descended on the day of Pentecost carried the minds of the disciples from the earthly sanctuary to the heavenly, where Jesus had entered by His own blood, to shed upon His disciples the benefits of His atonement.[31]

The eyes of men were turned to the true sacrifice for the sins of the world. The earthly priesthood ceased; but we look to Jesus, the minister of the new covenant.[32]

The Elder Brother of our race is by the eternal throne.[33]

THE VERY CENTER OF HIS WORK

Now of the things which we have spoken this is the sum: We have such an high priest, who is set on the right hand of the throne of the Majesty in the heavens; a minister of the sanctuary, and of the true tabernacle, which the Lord pitched, and not man. Heb. 8:1, 2.

The question, What is the sanctuary? is clearly answered in the Scriptures. The term "sanctuary," as used in the Bible, refers, first, to the tabernacle built by Moses, as a pattern of heavenly things; and, secondly, to the "true tabernacle" in heaven, to which the earthly sanctuary pointed. At the death of Christ the typical service ended. The "true tabernacle" in heaven is the sanctuary of the new covenant.[34]

The holy places of the sanctuary in heaven are represented by the two apartments in the sanctuary on earth. As in vision the apostle John was granted a view of the temple of God in heaven, he beheld there "seven lamps of fire burning before the throne." Rev. 4:5. He saw an angel "having a golden censer; and there was given unto him much incense, that he should offer it with the prayers of all saints upon the golden altar which was before the throne." Rev. 8:3. Here the prophet was permitted to behold the first apartment of the sanctuary in heaven; and he saw there the "seven lamps of fire" and the "golden altar," represented by the golden candlestick and the altar of incense in the sanctuary on earth. Again, "the temple of God was opened" (Rev. 11:19), and he looked within the inner veil, upon the holy of holies. Here he beheld "the ark of his testament," represented by the sacred chest constructed by Moses to contain the law of God. . . .

Moses made the earthly sanctuary after a pattern which was shown him. Paul teaches that that pattern was the true sanctuary which is in heaven. And John testifies that he saw it in heaven.[35]

The sanctuary in heaven is the very center of Christ's work in behalf of men. It concerns every soul living upon the earth.[36]

When Christ ascended to heaven, He ascended as our Advocate. We always have a Friend at court.[37]

APPEARS IN HEAVEN FOR US

For Christ is not entered into the holy places made with hands, which are the figures of the true; but into heaven itself, now to appear in the presence of God for us. Heb. 9:24.

The subject of the sanctuary . . . should be clearly understood by the people of God. All need a knowledge for themselves of the position and work of their great High Priest. . . .

The intercession of Christ in man's behalf in the sanctuary above is as essential to the plan of salvation as was His death upon the cross. By His death He began that work which after His resurrection He ascended to complete in heaven. We must by faith enter within the veil, "whither the forerunner is for us entered." Heb. 6:20. There the light from the cross of Calvary is reflected. There we may gain a clearer insight into the mysteries of redemption. The salvation of man is accomplished at an infinite expense to heaven; the sacrifice made is equal to the broadest demands of the broken law of God. Jesus has opened the way to the Father's throne, and through His mediation the sincere desire of all who come to Him in faith may be presented before God.

"He that covereth his sins shall not prosper: but whoso confesseth and forsaketh them shall have mercy." Prov. 28:13. If those who hide and excuse their faults could see how Satan exults over them, how he taunts Christ and holy angels with their course, they would make haste to confess their sins and to put them away. Through defects in the character, Satan works to gain control of the whole mind, and he knows that if these defects are cherished, he will succeed. Therefore he is constantly seeking to deceive the followers of Christ with his fatal sophistry that it is impossible for them to overcome. But Jesus pleads in their behalf His wounded hands, His bruised body; and He declares to all who would follow Him, "My grace is sufficient for thee." 2 Cor. 12:9. . . . Let none, then, regard their defects as incurable. God will give faith and grace to overcome them.[38]

UTTERMOST SALVATION FOR HIS CHILDREN

But this man, because he continueth ever, hath an unchangeable priesthood. Wherefore he is able also to save them to the uttermost that come unto God by him, seeing he ever liveth to make intercession for them. Heb. 7:24, 25.

Every provision has been made for our infirmities, every encouragement offered us to come to Christ.

Christ offered up His broken body to purchase back God's heritage, to give man another trial. . . . By His spotless life, His obedience, His death on the cross of Calvary, Christ interceded for the lost race. And now, not as a mere petitioner does the Captain of our salvation intercede for us, but as a Conqueror claiming His victory. His offering is complete, and as our Intercessor He executes His self-appointed work, holding before God the censer containing His own spotless merits and the prayers, confessions, and thanksgiving of His people. Perfumed with the fragrance of His righteousness, these ascend to God as a sweet savor. The offering is wholly acceptable, and pardon covers all transgression.

Christ has pledged Himself to be our substitute and surety, and He neglects no one. He who could not see human beings exposed to eternal ruin without pouring out His soul unto death in their behalf, will look with pity and compassion upon every soul who realizes that he cannot save himself.

He will look upon no trembling suppliant without raising him up. He who through His own atonement provided for man an infinite fund of moral power, will not fail to employ this power in our behalf. We may take our sins and sorrows to His feet; for He loves us. His every look and word invites our confidence. He will shape and mold our characters according to His own will.

In the whole satanic force there is not power to overcome one soul who in simple trust casts himself on Christ. "He giveth power to the faint; and to them that have no might he increaseth strength." Isa. 40:29.[39]

THE TRUE MEDIATOR

For there is one God, and one mediator between God and men, the man Christ Jesus. 1 Tim. 2:5.

In the mediatorial work of Christ, the love of God was revealed in its perfection to men and angels.[40]

He stands to mediate for you. He is the great High Priest who is pleading in your behalf; and you are to come and present your case to the Father through Jesus Christ. Thus you can find access to God; and though you sin, your case is not hopeless. "If any man sin, we have an advocate with the Father, Jesus Christ the righteous." 1 John 2:1.[41]

Christ is your Redeemer; He will take no advantage of your humiliating confessions. If you have sin of a private character, confess it to Christ, who is the only mediator between God and man.[42]

He presents us to the Father clothed in the white raiment of His own character. He pleads before God in our behalf, saying: I have taken the sinner's place. Look not upon this wayward child, but look on Me. Does Satan plead loudly against our souls, . . . claiming us as his prey, the blood of Christ pleads with greater power.[43]

The work of Christ in the sanctuary above, presenting His own blood each moment before the mercy seat, as He makes intercession for us, should have its full impression upon the heart, that we may realize the worth of each moment. Jesus ever liveth to make intercession for us; but one moment carelessly spent can never be recovered.[44]

Think of Jesus. He is in His holy place, not in a state of solitude, but surrounded by ten thousand times ten thousand of heavenly angels who wait to do His bidding. And He bids them go and work for the weakest saint who puts his trust in God. High and low, rich and poor, have the same help provided.[45]

Consider this great fact that Christ ceases not to engage in His solemn work in the heavenly sanctuary, and if you wear Christ's yoke, if you lift Christ's burden, you will be engaged in a work of like character with that of your living Head.[46]

THE HEAVENLY THINGS PURIFIED

And almost all things are by the law purged with blood; and without shedding of blood is no remission. It was therefore necessary that the patterns of things in the heavens should be purified with these; but the heavenly things themselves with better sacrifices than these. Heb. 9:22, 23.

What is the cleansing of the sanctuary? That there was such a service in connection with the earthly sanctuary, is stated in the Old Testament Scriptures. But can there be anything in heaven to be cleansed? In Hebrews 9 the cleansing of both the earthly and the heavenly sanctuary is plainly taught. . . .

The cleansing, both in the typical and in the real service, must be accomplished with blood: in the former, with the blood of animals; in the latter, with the blood of Christ.[47]

The cleansing was not a removal of physical impurities, for it was to be accomplished with blood, and therefore must be a cleansing from sin.[48]

But how could there be sin connected with the sanctuary, either in heaven or upon the earth?[49]

As the sins of the people were anciently transferred, in figure, to the earthly sanctuary by the blood of the sin offering, so our sins are, in fact, transferred to the heavenly sanctuary by the blood of Christ. And as the typical cleansing of the earthly was accomplished by the removal of the sins by which it had been polluted, so the actual cleansing of the heavenly is to be accomplished by the removal, or blotting out, of the sins which are there recorded. This necessitates an examination of the books of record to determine who, through repentance of sin and faith in Christ, are entitled to the benefits of His atonement.[50]

Then [in the great day of final award] by virtue of the atoning blood of Christ, the sins of all the truly penitent will be blotted from the books of heaven.[51]

He [Christ] asks for His people not only pardon and justification, full and complete, but a share in His glory and a seat upon His throne.[52]

CHRIST BEFORE THE ANCIENT OF DAYS

I saw in the night visions, and, behold, one like the Son of man came with the clouds of heaven, and came to the Ancient of days, and they brought him near before him. Dan. 7:13.

After His ascension, our Saviour began His work as our high priest. Says Paul, "Christ is not entered into the holy places made with hands, which are the figures of the true; but into heaven itself, now to appear in the presence of God for us." Heb. 9:24. . . .

For eighteen centuries this work of ministration continued in the first apartment of the sanctuary. The blood of Christ, pleaded in behalf of penitent believers, secured their pardon and acceptance with the Father, yet their sins still remained upon the books of record. As in the typical service there was a work of atonement at the close of the year, so before Christ's work for the redemption of men is completed, there is a work of atonement for the removal of sin from the sanctuary. This is the service which began when the 2300 days ended. At that time . . . our High Priest entered the most holy, to perform the last division of His solemn work—to cleanse the sanctuary. . . .

The coming of Christ as our high priest to the most holy place, for the cleansing of the sanctuary, brought to view in Daniel 8:14; the coming of the Son of man to the Ancient of days, as presented in Daniel 7:13; and the coming of the Lord to His temple, foretold by Malachi, are descriptions of the same event; and this is also represented by the coming of the bridegroom to the marriage, described by Christ in the parable of the ten virgins, of Matthew 25.[53]

The cleansing of the sanctuary . . . involves a work of investigation—a work of judgment. This work must be performed prior to the coming of Christ to redeem His people; for when He comes, His reward is with Him to give to every man according to his works.[54]

In the day of final reckoning, position, rank, or wealth will not alter by a hair's breadth the case of any one. By the all-seeing God, men will be judged by what they are in purity, in nobility, in love for Christ.[55]

THE SIGNAL TO BEGIN

And he said unto me, Unto two thousand and three hundred days; then shall the sanctuary be cleansed. Dan. 8:14.

We should be earnest students of prophecy; we should not rest until we become intelligent in regard to the subject of the sanctuary, which is brought out in the visions of Daniel and John. This subject sheds great light on our present position and work, and gives us unmistakable proof that God has led us in our past experience. It explains our disappointment in 1844, showing us that the sanctuary to be cleansed was not the earth, as we had supposed, but that Christ then entered into the most holy apartment of the heavenly sanctuary, and is there performing the closing work of His priestly office, in fulfillment of the words of the angel to the prophet Daniel.[56]

The 2300 days had been found to begin when the commandment of Artaxerxes for the restoration and building of Jerusalem, went into effect, in the autumn of B.C. 457. Taking this as the starting point, there was perfect harmony in the application of all the events foretold in the explanation of that period in Daniel 9:25-27. . . . The seventy weeks, or 490 years, were to pertain especially to the Jews. At the expiration of this period, the nation sealed its rejection of Christ by the persecution of His disciples, and the apostles turned to the Gentiles, A.D. 34. The first 490 years of the 2300 having then ended, 1810 years would remain. From A.D. 34, 1810 years extend to 1844. "Then," said the angel, "shall the sanctuary be cleansed."[57]

Our faith in reference to the messages of the first, second, and third angels was correct. The great waymarks we have passed are immovable. Although the hosts of hell may try to tear them from their foundation, and triumph in the thought that they have succeeded, yet they do not succeed. These pillars of truth stand firm as the eternal hills, unmoved by all the efforts of men combined with those of Satan and his host. We can learn much, and should be constantly searching the Scriptures to see if these things are so.[58]

OUR EYES FIXED ON CHRIST

O our God, wilt thou not judge them? for we have no might against this great company that cometh against us; neither know we what to do: but our eyes are upon thee. 2 Chron. 20:12.

"I beheld," says the prophet Daniel, "till thrones were placed, and one that was ancient of days did sit. . . . Thousand thousands ministered unto him, and ten thousand times ten thousand stood before him: the judgment was set, and the books were opened." Dan. 7:9, 10, RV.

Thus was presented to the prophet's vision the great and solemn day when the characters and the lives of men should pass in review before the judge of all the earth, and to every man should be rendered "according to his works." The Ancient of days is God the Father. . . . It is He, the source of all being, and the fountain of all law, that is to preside in the judgment. And holy angels, as ministers and witnesses, in number "ten thousand times ten thousand, and thousands of thousands" (Rev. 5:11), attend this great tribunal.

"And, behold, one like the Son of man came with the clouds of heaven, and came to the Ancient of days, and they brought him near before him." Dan. 7:13. . . . The coming of Christ here described is not His second coming to the earth. He comes to the Ancient of days in heaven to receive dominion, and glory, and a kingdom, which will be given Him at the close of His work as a mediator. It is this coming, and not His second advent to the earth, that was foretold in prophecy to take place at the termination of the 2300 days in 1844. Attended by heavenly angels, our great High Priest enters the holy of holies, and there appears in the presence of God . . . to perform the work of investigative judgment, and to make an atonement for all who are shown to be entitled to its benefits.[59]

God's people are now to have their eyes fixed on the heavenly sanctuary, where . . . our great High Priest . . . is interceding for His people.[60]

Soon we shall be weighed in the balances of the sanctuary, and over against our names will be recorded the judgment rendered.[61]

JUDGED FROM THE RECORDS

For God shall bring every work into judgment, with every secret thing, whether it be good, or whether it be evil. Eccl. 12:14.

In the great day of final atonement and investigative judgment, the only cases considered are those of the professed people of God. The judgment of the wicked is a distinct and separate work, and takes place at a later period. . . . The books of record in heaven, in which the names and the deeds of men are registered, are to determine the decisions of the judgment. . . .

The book of life contains the names of all who have ever entered the service of God. Jesus bade His disciples, "Rejoice, because your names are written in heaven." Luke 10:20. Paul speaks of his faithful fellow workers, "Whose names are in the book of life." Phil. 4:3. . . .

"A book of remembrance" is written before God, in which are recorded the good deeds of "them that feared the Lord, and that thought upon his name." Mal. 3:16. Their words of faith, their acts of love, are registered in heaven. . . .

There is a record also of the sins of men. The secret purposes and motives appear in the unerring register.

Every man's work passes in review before God. . . . Opposite each name in the books of heaven is entered, with terrible exactness, every wrong word, every selfish act, every unfulfilled duty, and every secret sin, with every artful dissembling. Heaven-sent warnings or reproofs neglected, wasted moments, unimproved opportunities, the influence exerted for good or for evil, with its far-reaching results, all are chronicled by the recording angel.[62]

If your name is registered in the Lamb's book of life, then all will be well with you. Be ready and anxious to confess your faults and forsake them, that your mistakes and sins may go beforehand to judgment and be blotted out.[63]

EACH LIFE PASSES IN REVIEW

Rejoice, O young man, in thy youth; and let thy heart cheer thee in the days of thy youth, and walk in the ways of thine heart, and in the sight of thine eyes: but know thou, that for all these things God will bring thee into judgment. Eccl. 11:9.

At the time appointed for the judgment—the close of the 2300 days, in 1844—began the work of investigation and blotting out of sins. All who have ever taken upon themselves the name of Christ must pass its searching scrutiny. Both the living and the dead are to be judged "out of those things which were written in the books, according to their works." Rev. 20:12.[64]

Said the judge: "All will be justified by their faith and judged by their works."[65]

Sins that have not been repented of and forsaken will not be pardoned, and blotted out of the books of record, but will stand to witness against the sinner in the day of God. . . .

There is earnest warfare before all who would subdue the evil tendencies that strive for the mastery. The work of preparation is an individual work. We are not saved in groups. The purity and devotion of one will not offset the want of these qualities in another. Though all nations are to pass in judgment before God, yet He will examine the case of each individual with as close and searching scrutiny as if there were not another being upon the earth. Every one must be tested, and found without spot or wrinkle or any such thing.

The judgment is now passing in the sanctuary above. For many years this work has been in progress. Soon—none know how soon—it will pass to the cases of the living. In the awful presence of God our lives are to come up in review. At this time above all others it behooves every soul to heed the Saviour's admonition, "Watch and pray: for ye know not when the time is." Mark 13:33. "If therefore thou shalt not watch, I will come on thee as a thief, and thou shalt not know what hour I will come upon thee." Rev. 3:3.[66]

THE BLOTTING OUT OF SINS

He that overcometh, the same shall be clothed in white raiment;
and I will not blot out his name out of the book of life, but I will
confess his name before my Father, and before his angels. Rev. 3:5.

As the books of record are opened in the judgment, the lives of
all who have believed on Jesus come in review before God.
Beginning with those who first lived upon the earth, our Advocate
presents the cases of each successive generation, and closes with the
living. Every name is mentioned, every case closely investigated.
Names are accepted, names rejected. When any have sins remaining
upon the books of record, unrepented of and unforgiven, their names
will be blotted out of the book of life, and the record of their good
deeds will be erased from the book of God's remembrance. . . .

All who have truly repented of sin, and by faith claimed the blood
of Christ as their atoning sacrifice, have had pardon entered against
their names in the books of heaven; as they have become partakers
of the righteousness of Christ, and their characters are found to be in
harmony with the law of God, their sins will be blotted out, and they
themselves will be accounted worthy of eternal life. . . .

The divine Intercessor presents the plea that all who have overcome through faith in His blood be forgiven their transgressions, that
they be restored to their Eden home, and crowned as joint heirs with
Himself to the "first dominion." . . .

While Jesus is pleading for the subjects of His grace, Satan ac-
cuses them before God as transgressors. . . .

Jesus does not excuse their sins, but shows their penitence and
faith, and, claiming for them forgiveness, He lifts His wounded
hands before the Father and the holy angels, saying, "I know them
by name." . . . Their names stand enrolled in the book of life, and
concerning them it is written, "They shall walk with me in white: for
they are worthy." Rev. 3:4.[67]

Christians may daily cultivate faith by contemplating the One who
has undertaken their cause, their "merciful and faithful high priest."[68]

A PRIOR JUDGMENT

Some men's sins are open beforehand, going before to judgment;
and some men they follow after. 1 Tim. 5:24.

The work of the investigative judgment and the blotting out of sins is to be accomplished before the second advent of the Lord. Since the dead are to be judged out of the things written in the books, it is impossible that the sins of men should be blotted out until after the judgment at which their cases are to be investigated. . . . When the investigative judgment closes, Christ will come, and His reward will be with Him to give to every man as his work shall be.[69]

All are to be judged according to the things written in the books, and to be rewarded as their works have been. This judgment does not take place at death.[70]

In the typical service the high priest, having made the atonement for Israel, came forth and blessed the congregation. So Christ, at the close of His work as mediator, will appear, "without sin unto salvation," to bless His waiting people with eternal life. As the priest, in removing the sins from the sanctuary, confessed them upon the head of the scapegoat, so Christ will place all these sins upon Satan, the originator and instigator of sin. The scapegoat, bearing the sins of Israel, was sent away "unto a land not inhabited;" so Satan, bearing the guilt of all the sins which he has caused God's people to commit, will be for a thousand years confined to the earth, which will then be desolate, without inhabitant, and he will at last suffer the full penalty of sin in the fires that shall destroy all the wicked.[71]

A few, yes, only a few, of the vast number who people the earth will be saved unto life eternal, while the masses who have not perfected their souls in obeying the truth will be appointed to the second death.[72]

While the sins of penitent believers are being removed from the sanctuary, there is to be a special work of purification, of putting away of sin, among God's people upon earth.[73]

211

TIME IS RUNNING OUT!

Redeeming the time, because the days are evil. Eph. 5:16.

On the morning of October 23, 1879, about two o'clock, the Spirit of the Lord rested upon me, and I beheld scenes in the coming judgment. . . . The great day of the execution of God's judgment seemed to have come. Ten thousand times ten thousand were assembled before a large throne, upon which was seated a person of majestic appearance. Several books were before Him, and upon the covers of each was written in letters of gold, which seemed like a burning flame of fire: "Ledger of Heaven." One of these books, containing the names of those who claim to believe the truth, was then opened. . . . As these persons were named, one by one, and their good deeds mentioned, their countenances would light up with a holy joy. . . .

Another book was opened, wherein were recorded the sins of those who profess the truth. Under the general heading of selfishness came every other sin. . . . As the Holy One upon the throne slowly turned the leaves of the ledger, and His eyes rested for a moment upon individuals, His glance seemed to burn into their very souls, and at the same moment every word and action of their lives passed before their minds as clearly as though traced before their vision in letters of fire. . . .

One class were registered as cumberers of the ground. . . . This class had made *self* supreme, laboring only for selfish interests. . . .

The question was then asked: "Why have you not washed your robes of character and made them white in the blood of the Lamb? . . . You would not be partaker of His sufferings, and you cannot now be partaker with Him of His glory." . . . The book then closed, and the mantle fell from the Person on the throne, revealing the terrible glory of the Son of God.

The scene then passed away, and I found myself still upon the earth, inexpressibly grateful that the day of God had not yet come, and that precious probationary time is still granted us in which to prepare for eternity.[74]

WHEN PROBATION CLOSES

He that is unjust let him be unjust still: and he which is filthy, let him be filthy still: and he that is righteous, let him be righteous still: and he that is holy, let him be holy still. Rev. 22:11.

God has not revealed to us the time when this message [the third angel's] will close, or when probation will have an end. . . . Letters have come to me asking me if I have any special light as to the time when probation will close; and I answer that I have only this message to bear, that it is now time to work while the day lasts, for the night cometh in which no man can work.[75]

When Jesus rises up in the most holy place, and lays off His mediatorial garments, and clothes Himself with the garments of vengeance in place of the priestly attire, the work for sinners will be done. . . . The probation of all closes when the pleading for sinners is ended and the garments of vengeance are put on.[76]

The case of every soul will have been decided, and there will be no atoning blood to cleanse from sin. . . . Then the restraining Spirit of God is withdrawn from the earth.[77]

In that fearful time the righteous must live in the sight of a holy God without an intercessor. The restraint which has been upon the wicked is removed, and Satan has entire control of the finally impenitent. . . . Satan will then plunge the inhabitants of the earth into one great, final trouble. As the angels of God cease to hold in check the fierce winds of human passion, all the elements of strife will be let loose. The whole world will be involved in ruin more terrible than that which came upon Jerusalem of old.[78]

We have no time to lose. We know not how soon our probation may close. . . . Christ is soon to come.[79]

When probation ends, it will come suddenly, unexpectedly—at a time when we are least expecting it. But we can have a clean record in heaven today, and know that God accepts us; and finally, if faithful, we shall be gathered into the kingdom of heaven.[80]

THE SAINTS SHALL JUDGE THE WORLD

Therefore judge nothing before the time, until the Lord come, who both will bring to light the hidden things of darkness, and will make manifest the counsels of the hearts: and then shall every man have praise of God. 1 Cor. 4:5.

During the thousand years between the first and the second resurrection, the judgment of the wicked takes place. The apostle Paul points to this judgment as an event that follows the Second Advent. "Judge nothing before the time, until the Lord come. . . ." Daniel declares that when the Ancient of days came, "judgment was given to the saints of the most High." Dan. 7:22.

At this time the righteous reign as kings and priests unto God. John in the Revelation says: "I saw thrones, and they sat upon them, and judgment was given unto them." Rev. 20:4. . . . It is at this time that, as foretold by Paul, "the saints shall judge the world." 1 Cor. 6:2, 3. In union with Christ they judge the wicked, comparing their acts with the statute book, the Bible, and deciding every case according to the deeds done in the body. Then the portion which the wicked must suffer is meted out, according to their works; and it is recorded against their names in the book of death.[81]

We shall not hear a charge against us on the ground of the outbreaking sins we have committed, but the charge will be made against us for the neglect of good and noble duties enjoined upon us by the God of love. The deficiencies of our characters will be held up to view. It will then be known that all who are so condemned had light and knowledge, were entrusted with their Lord's goods, and were found unfaithful to their trust.[82]

Satan also and evil angels are judged by Christ and His people. Says Paul, "Know ye not that we shall judge angels?" 1 Cor. 6:3.[83]

When the judge of all the earth shall demand of Satan, "Why hast thou rebelled against Me, and robbed Me of the subjects of My kingdom?" the originator of evil can render no excuse. Every mouth will be stopped, and all the hosts of rebellion will be speechless.[84]

SCHEMES OF SATAN

Be sober, be vigilant; because your adversary the devil, as a roaring lion, walketh about, seeking whom he may devour. 1 Peter 5:8.

It is unsafe to trust to feelings or impressions; these are unreliable guides. God's law is the only correct standard of holiness. It is by this law that character is to be judged. If an inquirer after salvation were to ask, "What must I do to inherit eternal life?" the modern teachers of sanctification would answer, "Only believe that Jesus saves you." But when Christ was asked this question He said, "What is written in the law? how readest thou?" And when the questioner replied, "Thou shalt love the Lord thy God with all thy heart, . . . and thy neighbour as thyself," Jesus said, "Thou hast answered right: this do, and thou shalt live." Luke 10:26-28.[85]

No value is attached to a mere profession of faith in Christ; only the love which is shown by works is counted genuine. Yet it is love alone which in the sight of Heaven makes any act of value. . . .

The hidden selfishness of men stands revealed in the books of heaven. . . . Sad is the record which angels bear to heaven. Intelligent beings, professed followers of Christ, are absorbed in the acquirement of worldly possessions or the enjoyment of earthly pleasures. Money, time, and strength are sacrificed for display and self-indulgence; but few are the moments devoted to prayer, to the searching of the Scriptures, to humiliation of soul and confession of sin.

Satan invents unnumbered schemes to occupy our minds, that they may not dwell upon the very work with which we ought to be best acquainted. The archdeceiver hates the great truths that bring to view an atoning sacrifice and an all-powerful Mediator. He knows that with him everything depends on his diverting minds from Jesus and His truth.

Those who would share the benefits of the Saviour's mediation should permit nothing to interfere with their duty to perfect holiness in the fear of God.[86]

ESTABLISHED IN THE PRESENT TRUTH

Wherefore I will not be negligent to put you always in remembrance of these things, though ye know them, and be established in the present truth. 2 Peter 1:12.

We believe without a doubt that Christ is soon coming. This is not a fable to us; it is a reality. We have no doubt, neither have we had a doubt for years, that the doctrines we hold today are present truth, and that we are nearing the judgment. We are preparing to meet Him who, escorted by a retinue of holy angels, is to appear in the clouds of heaven to give the faithful and the just the finishing touch of immortality. When He comes He is not to cleanse us of our sins, to remove from us the defects in our characters, or to cure us of the infirmities of our tempers and dispositions. If wrought for us at all, this work will all be accomplished before that time.

When the Lord comes, those who are holy will be holy still. Those who have preserved their bodies and spirits in holiness, in sanctification and honor, will then receive the finishing touch of immortality. But those who are unjust, unsanctified, and filthy will remain so forever. No work will then be done for them to remove their defects and give them holy characters. The Refiner does not then sit to pursue His refining process and remove their sins and their corruption. . . . It is *now* that this work is to be accomplished for us.[87]

God is now testing and proving His people. Character is being developed. Angels are weighing moral worth, and keeping a faithful record of all the acts of the children of men. . . . That God who reads the hearts of everyone, will bring to light hidden things of darkness where they are often least suspected, that stumbling blocks which have hindered the progress of truth may be removed.[88]

There will be no future probation in which to prepare for eternity. It is in this life that we are to put on the robe of Christ's righteousness. This is our only opportunity to form characters for the home which Christ has made ready for those who obey His commandments.[89]

WALKING AS CHRIST WALKED

Imitating Christ   *August 1*

JESUS OUR PERFECT PATTERN

*He that saith he abideth in him ought himself also so to walk,
even as he walked. 1 John 2:6.*

We have before us the highest, holiest example. In thought,
word, and deed Jesus was sinless. Perfection marked all that He did.
He points us to the path that He trod, saying, "If any man will come
after me, let him deny himself, and take up his cross, and follow
me." Matt. 16:24.[1]

Christ unites in His person the fullness and perfection of the
Godhead and the fullness and perfection of sinless humanity. He met
all the temptations by which Adam was assailed, and overcame these
temptations because in His humanity He relied upon divine power.
This subject demands far more contemplation than it receives.
Christians strike too low. They are content with a superficial spiritual
experience, and therefore they have only the glimmerings of light,
when . . . they might discern more clearly the wonderful perfection of
Christ's humanity, which rises far above all human greatness, all human
power. Christ's life is a revelation of what fallen human beings may become through union and fellowship with the divine nature. . . .

Men and women frame many excuses for their proneness to sin.
Sin is represented as a necessity, an evil that cannot be overcome.
But sin is not a necessity. Christ lived in this world from infancy to
manhood, and during that time He met and resisted all the temptations by which man is beset. He is a perfect pattern of childhood, of
youth, of manhood.[2]

The life of Christ has shown what humanity can do by being partaker of the divine nature. All that Christ received from God we too
may have. Then ask and receive. . . . Let your life be knit by hidden
links to the life of Jesus.[3]

RELIGION TO BE SUPREME

Jesus said unto him, Thou shalt love the Lord thy God with all thy heart, and with all thy soul, and with all thy mind. This is the first and great commandment. Matt. 22:37, 38.

The youth need to realize that they need a deep experience in the things of God. A mere surface work will be of no benefit to them. You need to bring the light of God's Word into your heart, that you may search it as with a lighted candle.[4]

Many profess to be on the Lord's side, but they are not; the weight of all their actions is on Satan's side. By what means shall we determine whose side we are on? Who has the heart? With whom are our thoughts? Upon whom do we love to converse? Who has our warmest affections and our best energies? If we are on the Lord's side, our thoughts are with Him, and our sweetest thoughts are of Him. We have no friendship with the world; we have consecrated all that we have and are to Him. We long to bear His image, breathe His spirit, do His will, and please Him in all things.[5]

Bible religion is not one influence among many others, but its influence is supreme, pervading and controlling every other influence. Bible religion is to exercise control over life and conduct. It is not to be like a dash of color, brushed here and there upon the canvas, but its influence is to pervade the whole life, as though the canvas were dipped into color until every thread of the fabric was dyed in a deep, fast, unfading hue.[6]

The religion of Christ is a firm fabric, composed of innumerable threads, woven together with tact and skill. Only by the wisdom that God gives can we weave this fabric. Trusting to ourselves, we draw into it threads of selfishness, and the pattern is spoiled.[7]

Let everyone inquire seriously, "Am I a genuine Christian? Am I bearing the true marks of a Christian? Am I doing my best to perfect a character after the divine model?"[8]

Pure religion is an imitation of Christ.[9]

SEPARATED FROM THE WORLD

I pray not that thou shouldest take them out of the world, but that thou shouldest keep them from the evil. John 17:15.

Many professed Christians are well represented by the vine that is trailing upon the ground and entwining its tendrils about the roots and rubbish that lie in its path. To all such the message comes, "Come out from among them, and be ye separate, saith the Lord." 2 Cor. 6:17. . . . Your tendrils must be severed from everything earthly. . . . It is impossible for you to unite with those who are corrupt, and still remain pure.[10]

O that the young might realize that they may be as precious plants in the Lord's garden. . . . Let the delicate tendrils of the affections twine about Jesus, to receive nourishment from Him; and instead of creeping upon the earth, turn the face toward the Sun of Righteousness, that you may catch divine rays of light. Day by day grow up into His likeness, and become a partaker of His divine nature, that you may at last be found perfect in the paradise of God. . . .

Rivet the soul to the eternal Rock; for in Christ alone there will be safety.[11]

A union with Christ by living faith is enduring; every other union must perish. . . . But this union costs us something. . . . There must be a painful work of detachment, as well as a work of attachment. Pride, selfishness, vanity, worldliness—sin in all its forms—must be overcome, if we would enter into a union with Christ. The reason why many find the Christian life so deplorably hard, why they are so fickle, so variable, is, they try to attach themselves to Christ without detaching themselves from these cherished idols.[12]

Will we accept the condition laid down in His Word—separation from the world? . . . Our consecration to God must be a living principle, interwoven with the life, and leading to self-denial and self-sacrifice. It must underlie all our thoughts, and be the spring of every action. This will elevate us above the world, and separate us from its polluting influence.[13]

SECURITY ONLY IN RIGHT THINKING

*Keep thy heart with all diligence; for out of it are the issues of life.
Prov. 4:23.*

As a man "thinketh in his heart, so is he." Prov. 23:7. Many
thoughts make up the unwritten history of a single day; and these
thoughts have much to do with the formation of character. Our
thoughts are to be strictly guarded; for one impure thought makes a
deep impression on the soul. An evil thought leaves an evil impress
on the mind. If the thoughts are pure and holy, the man is better for
having cherished them. By them the spiritual pulse is quickened,
and the power for doing good is increased. And as one drop of rain
prepares the way for another in moistening the earth, so one good
thought prepares the way for another.[14]

Wrong habits of thought, when once accepted, become a
despotic power that fastens the mind as in a grasp of steel.[15]

The thoughts are not to be allowed to run riot. They must be re-
strained, brought into captivity to the obedience of Christ. Let them be
placed upon holy things. Then, through the grace of Christ, they will
be pure and true. We need a constant sense of the ennobling power
of pure thoughts. The only security for any soul is right thinking.[16]

Our minds take the level of the things on which our thoughts
dwell, and if we think upon earthly things, we shall fail to take the impress of that which is heavenly. We would be greatly benefited by contemplating the mercy, goodness, and love of God; but we sustain great
loss by dwelling upon those things which are earthly and temporal.[17]

Although there may be a tainted, corrupted atmosphere around
us, we need not breathe its miasma, but may live in the pure air of
heaven. We may close every door to impure imaginings and unholy
thoughts by lifting the soul into the presence of God through sincere
prayer. Those whose hearts are open to receive the support and
blessing of God will walk in a holier atmosphere than that of earth
and will have constant communion with Heaven.[18]

TRANSFORMED BY SEARCHING THE WORD

As newborn babes, desire the sincere milk of the word, that ye may grow thereby. 1 Peter 2:2.

No man, woman, or youth can attain to Christian perfection and neglect the study of the Word of God. By carefully and closely searching His Word we shall obey the injunction of Christ, "Search the scriptures; for in them ye think ye have eternal life: and they are they which testify of me." John 5:39. This search enables the student to observe closely the divine Model. . . . The Pattern must be inspected often and closely in order to imitate it. As one becomes acquainted with the history of the Redeemer, he discovers in himself defects of character; his unlikeness to Christ is so great that he sees he cannot be a follower without a very great change in his life. Still he studies, with a desire to be like his great Exemplar; he catches the looks, the spirit, of his beloved Master; by beholding he becomes changed.[19]

All the philosophies of human nature have led to confusion and shame when God has not been recognized as all in all. But the precious faith inspired of God imparts strength and nobility of character. As His goodness, His mercy, and His love are dwelt upon, clearer and still clearer will be the perception of truth; higher, holier, the desire for purity of heart and clearness of thought. The soul dwelling in the pure atmosphere of holy thought is transformed by intercourse with God through the study of His Word. Truth is so large, so far-reaching, so deep, so broad, that self is lost sight of. The heart is softened and subdued into humility, kindness, and love.[20]

The Bible . . . trains the mind to grapple with the deepest problems and to pursue the broadest explorations. It exalts the intellect. It saves the soul. . . . Take it as your mirror. It will be a faithful monitor, detecting the faults and errors of your character. It will strengthen every good trait.[21]

That Word which reveals the guilt of sin, has a power upon the human heart to make man right and keep him so.[22]

221

WATCH AND PRAY

Praying always with all prayer and supplication in the Spirit, and watching thereunto with all perseverance and supplication for all saints. Eph. 6:18.

Prayer and watching thereunto are necessary for advancement in the divine life. . . . Your only safety is to live like a watchman. Watch and pray always. Oh, what a preventive against yielding to temptation and falling into the snares of the world![23]

"Take ye heed, watch and pray." Mark 13:33. . . .

First, you are to watch. Watch, lest you should speak hastily, fretfully, and impatiently. Watch, lest pride should find a place in your heart. Watch, lest evil passions should overcome you, instead of your subduing them. Watch, lest . . . you . . . become light and trifling, and your influence savor of death, rather than life.

Second, you are to pray. Jesus would not have enjoined this upon you, unless there was actual necessity for it. It is well known to Him that of yourself you cannot overcome the many temptations of the enemy, and the many snares laid for your feet. He has not left you alone to do this; but has provided a way that you can obtain help. Therefore He has bid you to pray.

To pray aright is to ask God in faith for the very things you need. Go to your chamber, or in some retired place, and ask your Father for Jesus' sake to help you. There is power in that prayer that is sent up from a heart convinced of its own weakness, yet earnestly longing for that strength that comes of God. The earnest, fervent prayer will be heard and answered. . . .

Faint not. Cast yourself at the feet of Jesus, who has been tempted, and knows how to help such as are tempted. . . . Plead your case before God, through Jesus, until your soul can with confidence rely upon Him for strength, and you feel that you are not left to do the work of overcoming alone. God will help you. Angels will watch over you. But before you can expect this help, you must do what you can on your part. Watch and pray.[24]

HEART COMMUNION WITH GOD

Wait on the Lord: be of good courage, and he shall strengthen thine heart: wait, I say, on the Lord. Ps. 27:14.

An intensity such as never before was seen is taking possession of the world. In amusement, in moneymaking, in the contest for power, in the very struggle for existence, there is a terrible force that engrosses body and mind and soul. In the midst of this maddening rush, God is speaking. He bids us come apart and commune with Him. "Be still, and know that I am God." Ps. 46:10.

Many, even in their seasons of devotion, fail of receiving the blessing of real communion with God. They are in too great haste. With hurried steps they press through the circle of Christ's loving presence, pausing perhaps a moment within the sacred precincts, but not waiting for counsel. They have no time to remain with the divine Teacher. With their burdens they return to their work. . . .

Not a pause for a moment in His presence, but personal contact with Christ, to sit down in companionship with Him—this is our need.[25]

We may bring Him our little cares and perplexities as well as our greater troubles. Whatever arises to disturb or distress us, we should take it to the Lord in prayer.[26]

Calmly, yet fervently, the soul is to reach out after God; and sweet and abiding will be the influence emanating from Him who sees in secret, whose ear is open to the prayer arising from the heart. He who in simple faith holds communion with God will gather to himself divine rays of light to strengthen and sustain him in the conflict with Satan.[27]

If we keep the Lord ever before us, allowing our hearts to go out in thanksgiving and praise to Him, we shall have a continual freshness in our religious life. Our prayers will take the form of a conversation with God as we would talk with a friend. He will speak His mysteries to us personally. Often there will come to us a sweet, joyful sense of the presence of Jesus. . . . Prayer turns aside the attacks of Satan.[28]

FULLNESS OF JOY

Thou wilt shew me the path of life: in thy presence is fulness of joy; at thy right hand there are pleasures for evermore. Ps. 16:11.

The religion of Jesus is joy, peace, and happiness.[29]

All Heaven is interested in the happiness of man. Our heavenly Father does not close the avenues of joy to any of His creatures. The divine requirements call upon us to shun those indulgences that would bring suffering and disappointment, that would close to us the door of happiness and heaven. . . . He [the world's Redeemer] requires us to perform only those duties that will lead our steps to heights of bliss to which the disobedient can never attain. The true, joyous life of the soul is to have Christ formed within, the hope of glory.[30]

Those who abide in Jesus will be happy, cheerful, and joyful in God. A subdued gentleness will mark the voice, reverence for spiritual and eternal things will be expressed in the actions, and music, joyful music, will echo from the lips, for it is wafted from the throne of God. This is the mystery of godliness, not easily explained, but nonetheless felt and enjoyed.[31]

Words cannot describe the peace and joy possessed by him who takes God at His word. Trials do not disturb him, slights do not vex him. Self is crucified. Day by day his duties may become more taxing, his temptations stronger, his trials more severe; but he does not falter; for he receives strength equal to his need.[32]

In those who possess it, the religion of Christ will reveal itself as a vitalizing, pervading principle, a living, working, spiritual energy. There will be manifest the freshness and power and joyousness of perpetual youth. The heart that receives the Word of God is not as a pool that evaporates, not like a broken cistern that loses its treasure. It is like the mountain stream fed by unfailing springs, whose cool, sparkling waters leap from rock to rock, refreshing the weary, the thirsty, the heavy laden.[33]

GOD'S DWELLING PLACE

Know ye not that your body is the temple of the Holy Ghost which is in you, which ye have of God, and ye are not your own? 1 Cor. 6:19.

By a most beautiful and impressive figure, God's Word shows the regard He places upon our physical organism and the responsibility resting on us to preserve it in the best condition. . . .

The body is a temple in which God desires to dwell, . . . it must be kept pure, the abiding place of high and noble thoughts.[34]

The knowledge that man is to be a temple for God, a habitation for the revealing of His glory, should be the highest incentive to the care and development of our physical powers. Fearfully and wonderfully has the Creator wrought in the human frame, and He bids us make it our study, understand its needs, and act our part in preserving it from harm and defilement.[35]

Our first duty toward God and our fellow beings is that of self-development. Every faculty with which the Creator has endowed us, should be cultivated to the highest degree of perfection, that we may be able to do the greatest amount of good of which we are capable. Hence that time is spent to good account which is used in the establishment and preservation of physical and mental health. We cannot afford to dwarf or cripple any function of body or mind. As surely as we do this we must suffer the consequences.[36]

The desire of God for every human being is expressed in the words, "Beloved, I wish above all things that thou mayest prosper and be in health, even as thy soul prospereth." 3 John 2.

He it is who "forgiveth all thine iniquities; who healeth all thy diseases; who redeemeth thy life from destruction; who crowneth thee with lovingkindness and tender mercies." Ps. 103:3, 4. . . .

"Above all things," God desires us to "be in health"—health of body and of soul. And we are to be workers together with Him for the health of both soul and body.[37]

HEALTH THE REWARD OF RIGHT HABITS

My son, forget not my law; but let thine heart keep my commandments; for length of days, and long life, and peace, shall they add to thee. Prov. 3:1, 2.

The laws of nature are the laws of God—as truly divine as are the precepts of the Decalogue. The laws that govern our physical organism, God has written upon every nerve, muscle, and fiber of the body. Every careless or willful violation of these laws is a sin against our Creator.[38]

There is an intimate relation between the mind and the body, and in order to reach a high standard of moral and intellectual attainment, the laws that control our physical being must be heeded. To secure a strong, well-balanced character, both the mental and the physical powers must be exercised and developed. What study can be more important for the young than that which treats of this wonderful organism that God has committed to us, and of the laws by which it may be preserved in health?"[39]

Health may be earned by proper habits of life and may be made to yield interest and compound interest. But this capital, more precious than any bank deposit, may be sacrificed by intemperance in eating and drinking, or by leaving the organs to rust from inaction. Pet indulgences must be given up; laziness must be overcome.[40]

The health should be as sacredly guarded as the character.[41]

Our bodies are Christ's purchased possession, and we are not at liberty to do with them as we please. All who understand the laws of health should realize their obligation to obey these laws which God has established in their being. Obedience to the laws of health is to be made a matter of personal duty. We ourselves must suffer the results of violated law. We must individually answer to God for our habits and practices. Therefore the question with us is not, "What is the world's practice?" but, "How shall I as an individual treat the habitation that God has given me?"[42]

HEALTH IN OBEYING GOD'S LAW

For bodily exercise profiteth little: but godliness is profitable unto all things, having promise of the life that now is, and of that which is to come. 1 Tim. 4:8.

There is health in obedience to God's law.[43]

The wise man says that wisdom's "ways are ways of pleasantness, and all her paths are peace." Prov. 3:17. Many cherish the impression that devotion to God is detrimental to health and to cheerful happiness in the social relations of life. But those who walk in the path of wisdom and holiness find that "godliness is profitable unto all things, having promise of the life that now is, and of that which is to come." They are alive to the enjoyment of life's real pleasures, while they are not troubled with vain regrets over misspent hours, nor with gloom or horror of mind, as the worldling too often is when not diverted by some exciting amusement. . . . Godliness does not conflict with the laws of health, but is in harmony with them. Had men ever been obedient to the law of Ten Commandments, . . . the curse of disease that now floods the world would not be.[44]

The assurance of God's approval will promote physical health. It fortifies the soul against doubt, perplexity, and excessive grief, that so often sap the vital forces and induce nervous diseases.[45]

The consciousness of rightdoing is the best medicine for diseased bodies and minds. The special blessing of God resting upon the receiver is health and strength.

A person whose mind is quiet and satisfied in God is in the pathway to health. To have a consciousness that the eyes of the Lord are upon us, and His ears open to hear our prayers, is a satisfaction indeed. To know that we have a never-failing Friend in whom we can confide all the secrets of the soul, is a privilege which words can never express.[46]

Courage, hope, faith, sympathy, love, promote health and prolong life. A contented mind, a cheerful spirit, is health to the body and strength to the soul.[47]

EATING FOR HEALTH AND HAPPINESS

Whether therefore ye eat, or drink, or whatsoever ye do, do all to the glory of God. 1 Cor. 10:31.

Here is a principle which lies at the foundation of every act, thought, and motive; the consecration of the entire being, both physical and mental, to the control of the Spirit of God.[48]

Even the natural act of eating or drinking, should be done . . . "to the glory of God."[49]

If the indulgence of appetite was so strong upon the race that, in order to break its power, the divine Son of God, in behalf of man, was required to fast nearly six weeks, what a work is before the Christian in order that he may overcome even as Christ overcame! The strength of the temptation to indulge perverted appetite can be measured only by the inexpressible anguish of Christ in that long fast in the wilderness.[50]

As our first parents lost Eden through the indulgence of appetite, our only hope of regaining Eden is through the firm denial of appetite.[51]

God has furnished man with abundant means for the gratification of an unperverted appetite. He has spread before him the products of the earth—a bountiful variety of food that is palatable to the taste and nutritious to the system. Of these our benevolent heavenly Father says we may freely eat. Fruits, grains, and vegetables, prepared in a simple way, free from spice and grease of all kinds, make, with milk or cream, the most healthful diet. They . . . give a power of endurance and vigor of intellect that are not produced by a stimulating diet.[52]

We do not mark out any precise line to be followed in diet; but we do say that in countries where there are fruits, grains, and nuts in abundance, flesh food is not the right food for God's people. . . . If meat eating was ever healthful, it is not safe now.[53]

Again and again I have been shown that God is trying to lead us back, step by step, to His original design—that man should subsist upon the natural products of the earth.[54]

ABSTAINING FROM HARMFUL INDULGENCES

Dearly beloved, I beseech You as strangers and pilgrims, abstain from fleshly lusts, which war against the soul. 1 Peter 2:11.

The Word of God plainly warns us that unless we abstain from fleshly lusts, the physical nature will be brought into conflict with the spiritual nature. Lustful eating wars against health and peace. Thus a warfare is instituted between the higher and the lower attributes of the man. The lower propensities, strong and active, oppress the soul. The highest interests of the being are imperiled by the indulgence of appetites unsanctioned by Heaven.[55]

Health, character, and even life, are endangered by the use of stimulants, which excite the exhausted energies to unnatural, spasmodic effort.[56]

Condiments are injurious in their nature. Mustard, pepper, spices, pickles, and other things of a like character, irritate the stomach and make the blood feverish and impure. . . .

Tea and coffee do not nourish the system. . . . The continued use of these nerve irritants is followed by headache, wakefulness, palpitation of the heart, indigestion, trembling, and many other evils; for they wear away the life forces. . . .

Tobacco is a slow, insidious, but most malignant poison. In whatever form it is used, it tells upon the constitution; it is all the more dangerous because its effects are slow and at first hardly perceptible. . . . Its use excites a thirst for strong drink and in many cases lays the foundations for the liquor habit.[57]

In relation to tea, coffee, tobacco, and alcoholic drinks, the only safe course is to touch not, taste not, handle not.[58]

True temperance teaches us to dispense entirely with everything hurtful, and to use judiciously that which is healthful.[59]

The Spirit of God cannot come to our help, and assist us in perfecting Christian characters, while we are indulging our appetites to the injury of health.[60]

BLESSING IN PHYSICAL ACTIVITY

And the Lord God took the man, and put him into the garden of Eden to dress it and to keep it. Gen. 2:15.

One of the first laws of the being is that of action. Every organ of the body has its appointed work, upon the development of which depends its strength. The normal action of all the organs gives vigor and life; inaction brings decay and death.[61]

To the dwellers in Eden was committed the care of the garden, "to dress it and to keep it." . . . God appointed labor as a blessing to man, to occupy his mind, to strengthen his body, and to develop his facilities. In mental and physical activity, Adam found one of the highest pleasures of his holy existence.[62]

A proportionate exercise of all the organs and faculties of the body is essential to the best work of each. When the brain is constantly taxed while the other organs of the living machinery are inactive, there is a loss of strength, physical and mental.[63]

Those whose habits are sedentary should, when the weather will permit, exercise in the open air every day, summer or winter. Walking is preferable to riding or driving, for it brings more of the muscles into exercise. The lungs are forced into healthy action, since it is impossible to walk briskly without inflating them. . . .

Full, deep inspirations of pure air, which fill the lungs with oxygen, purify the blood. They impart to it a bright color and send it, a life-giving current, to every part of the body. A good respiration soothes the nerves; it stimulates the appetite and renders digestion more perfect; and it induces sound, refreshing sleep.[64]

Jesus was an earnest, constant worker. Never lived there among men another so weighted with responsibilities. . . . Yet His was a life of health. Physically as well as spiritually He was represented by the sacrificial lamb, "without blemish and without spot." 1 Peter 1:19. In body as in soul He was an example of what God designed all humanity to be through obedience to His laws.[65]

COME APART AND REST

And he said unto them, Come ye yourselves apart into a desert place, and rest a while: for there were many coming and going, and they had no leisure so much as to eat. Mark 6:31.

He [Jesus] did not urge upon His disciples the necessity of ceaseless toil. . . . "Come ye yourselves apart, . . . and rest a while," He says to those who are worn and weary. It is not wise to be always under the strain of work and excitement, . . . for in this way personal piety is neglected, and the powers of mind and soul and body are overtaxed.[66]

Care needs to be exercised in regard to the regulation of hours for sleeping and laboring. We must take periods of rest, periods of recreation, periods for contemplation.[67]

There are modes of recreation which are highly beneficial to both mind and body. . . . Recreation in the open air, the contemplation of the works of God in nature, will be of the highest benefit.[68]

It is for our health and happiness to go out of our houses, and spend as much of our time as possible in the open air. . . . We should invite our minds to be interested in all the glorious things God has provided for us with a liberal hand. And in reflecting upon these rich tokens of His love and care, we may forget infirmities, be cheerful, and make melody in our hearts unto the Lord.[69]

Pure air, sunlight, abstemiousness, rest, exercise, proper diet, the use of water, trust in divine power—these are the true remedies. . . . Nature, untrammeled, does her work wisely and well. Those who persevere in obedience to her laws will reap the reward in health of body and health of mind.[70]

He [Jesus] found recreation amidst the scenes of nature. . . . His hours of greatest happiness were found when He could turn aside from His labors to go into the fields, to meditate in the quiet valleys, to hold communion with God on the mountainside or amid the trees of the forest.[71]

We may . . . make our seasons of recreation what the name implies—seasons of true upbuilding for body and mind and soul.[72]

231

FRIENDSHIP OF CHRIST'S FRIENDS

I am a companion of all them that fear thee, and of them that keep thy precepts. Ps. 119:63.

It is natural to seek companionship. Everyone will find companions or make them. And just in proportion to the strength of the friendship, will be the amount of influence which friends will exert over one another for good or for evil. . . .

Young persons who are thrown into one another's society may make their association a blessing or a curse. They may edify, bless, and strengthen one another, improving in deportment, in disposition, in knowledge; or, by permitting themselves to become careless and unfaithful, they may exert only a demoralizing influence.[73]

It is by leading the followers of Christ to associate with the ungodly and unite in their amusements, that Satan is most successful in alluring them into sin. . . . The followers of Christ are to separate themselves from sinners, choosing their society only when there is opportunity to do them good. We cannot be too decided in shunning the company of those who exert an influence to draw us away from God. While we pray, "Lead us not into temptation," we are to shun temptation, so far as possible.[74]

By the choice of evil companions many have been led step by step from the path of virtue into depths of disobedience and dissipation to which at one time they would have thought it impossible for them to sink.[75]

We may refuse to be corrupted, and place ourselves where evil association shall not corrupt our hearts. Individually the youth should seek for association with those who are toiling upward with unfaltering steps.[76]

Better than all the friendship of the world is the friendship of Christ's redeemed.[77]

The warmth of true friendship, the love that binds heart to heart, is a foretaste of the joys of heaven.[78]

YOUR INFLUENCE COUNTS!

This is my commandment, That ye love one another, as I have loved you. John 15:12.

What quality is this love? . . . A love for the soul that would part with selfish gratifications and practice stern self-denial in order to elevate, ennoble, and sanctify those with whom we associate. "And for their sakes I sanctify myself, that they also might be sanctified through the truth." John 17:19. Do you love those with whom you associate well enough to forgo your desire for amusement and self-pleasing that you will not place these souls in the path of temptation, that you will not beckon them to pursue a course of fun and frolic which leads to the extinguishment of serious thoughts in regard to the salvation of their souls? Do you cultivate personal piety, . . . that your youthful friends may follow where you lead the way, upward and forward to obedience to God? . . . What is the quality of your love? Is it of a character to make your associates more Christlike? Will it have a tendency to bring solid timbers into their character building?[79]

God enjoins upon all His followers to bear a living testimony in unmistakable language by their conduct, their dress and conversation, in all the pursuits of life, that the power of true godliness is profitable to all in this life and in the life to come.[80]

A cheap Christian character works more harm in the world than the character of a worldling, for professed Christians mislead others by professing to represent Him whose name they assume.[81]

God is love. Whoso dwelleth in God, dwelleth in love. All who have indeed become acquainted . . . with the love and tender compassion of our heavenly Father will impart light and joy wherever they may be. Their presence and influence will be to their associates as the fragrance of sweet flowers, because they are linked to God and heaven, and the purity and exalted loveliness of heaven are communicated through them to all that are brought within their influence.[82]

You can surround your souls with an atmosphere that will be like zephyrs from the heavenly Eden.[83]

WORDS OF GRACE

Let your speech be alway with grace, seasoned with salt, that ye may know how ye ought to answer every man. Col. 4:6.

How is it that many who profess the name of Christ utter so many vain, idle words? Satan watches to obtain an advantage over those who speak in a reckless manner. . . . When we utter meaningless and silly words we encourage others to indulge in the same kind of conversation. . . . The only words that should come from our lips should be pure, clean words. No one can tell how much sin is created by careless, foolish, unmeaning words. . . . Every word you speak is as a seed that will germinate and produce either good or bad fruit.[84]

When in the company of those who indulge in foolish talk, it is our duty to change the subject of conversation if possible. By the help of the grace of God we should quietly drop words or introduce a subject that will turn the conversation into a profitable channel.[85]

He [God] desires us to be cheerful, but not trifling. He says to each one of us, "But as he which hath called you is holy, so be ye holy in all manner of conversation." 1 Peter 1:15. God wants us to be happy. He desires to put a new song on our lips, even praise to our God.[86]

When you take the hand of a friend, let praise to God be on your lips and in your heart. This will attract his thoughts to Jesus.[87]

How pleased the Saviour would be to hear His followers talking of His precious lessons of instruction, and to know that they had a relish for holy things! . . . That which is in the heart will flow from the lips. It cannot be repressed. The things that God has prepared for those that love Him will be the theme of conversation. The love of Christ is in the soul as a well of water, springing up into everlasting life, sending forth living streams, that bring life and gladness wherever they flow.[88]

We lose much by not talking more of Jesus and of heaven, the saints' inheritance. The more we contemplate heavenly things, the more new delights we shall see, and the more will our hearts be brimful of thanks to our beneficent Creator.[89]

SOMETHING BETTER!

I have set the Lord always before me: because he is at my right hand, I shall not be moved. Ps. 16:8.

Whatever Christ asks us to renounce, He offers in its stead something better. Often the youth cherish objects, pursuits, and pleasures that may not appear to be evil, but that fall short of the highest good. They divert the life from its noblest aim.[90]

Never let amusements, or the companionship of others, come between you and Jesus, your best Friend . . . When natural inclination draws you in the direction of fulfilling some selfish desire, set the Lord before you as your counselor, and ask, "Will this please Jesus? Will this increase my love for my best Friend? Will this course grieve my dear Saviour? Will it separate me from His company? Will Jesus accompany me to the pleasure party, where all will be lightness and gaiety, where there will be nothing of a religious nature, nothing serious, no thought of the things of God?"[91]

Christians have many sources of happiness at their command, and they may tell with unerring accuracy what pleasures are lawful and right. They may enjoy such recreations as will not dissipate the mind or debase the soul, such as will not disappoint, and leave a sad after influence to destroy self-respect or bar the way to usefulness. If they can take Jesus with them, and maintain a prayerful spirit, they are perfectly safe.[92]

An enlightened, discriminating mind will find abundant means for entertainment and diversion, from sources not only innocent, but instructive.[93]

In all our seasons of recreation we may gather from the Divine Source of strength fresh courage and power, that we may the more successfully elevate our lives to purity, true goodness, and holiness.[94]

Those who really enjoy the love of God will have joy and peace. Religion was never designed to make one pleasureless. What can be productive of greater happiness than to enjoy the peace of Christ, the bright sunshine of His presence?[95]

CLOSING THE DOOR OF TEMPTATION

Love not the world, neither the things that are in the world. If any man love the world, the love of the Father is not in him. 1 John 2:15.

Between the associations of the followers of Christ for Christian recreation, and worldly gatherings for pleasure and amusement, will exist a marked contrast. Instead of prayer and the mentioning of Christ and sacred things, will be heard from the lips of worldlings the silly laugh and the trifling conversation. The idea is to have a general high time.[96]

Worldly pleasures are infatuating; and for their momentary enjoyment many sacrifice the friendship of Heaven, with the peace, love, and joy that it affords. But these chosen objects of delight soon become disgusting, unsatisfying.[97]

Some of the most popular amusements, such as football and boxing, have become schools of brutality. . . . Other athletic games, though not so brutalizing, are scarcely less objectionable because of the excess to which they are carried. They stimulate the love of pleasure and excitement, thus fostering a distaste for useful labor, a disposition to shun practical duties and responsibilities. . . . Thus the door is opened to dissipation and lawlessness, with their terrible results.[98]

The true Christian will not desire to enter any place of amusement or engage in any diversion upon which he cannot ask the blessing of God. He will not be found at the theater, the billiard hall, or the bowling saloon. He will not unite with the gay waltzes or indulge in any other bewitching pleasure that will banish Christ from the mind. To those who plead for these diversions we answer, We cannot indulge in them in the name of Jesus of Nazareth. . . . No Christian would wish to meet death in such a place. No one would wish to be found there when Christ shall come.[99]

If we venture on Satan's ground we have no assurance of protection from his power. So far as in us lies, we should close every avenue by which the tempter may find access to us.[100]

DEPOSITS IN THE BANK OF HEAVEN

Pure religion and undefiled before God and the Father is this, To visit the fatherless and widows in their affliction, and to keep himself unspotted from the world. James 1:27.

The tender sympathies of our Saviour were aroused for fallen and suffering humanity. If you would be His followers, you must cultivate compassion and sympathy. . . . The widow, the orphan, the sick, and the dying will always need help. Here is an opportunity to proclaim the gospel—to hold up Jesus, the hope and consolation of all men. When the suffering body has been relieved, . . . the heart is opened, and you can pour in the heavenly balm.[101]

A company of believers may be poor, uneducated, and unknown; yet in Christ they may do a work in the home, the neighborhood, the church, and even in "the regions beyond," whose results will be as far-reaching as eternity. It is because this work is neglected that so many young disciples never advance beyond the mere alphabet of Christian experience. The light which was glowing in their own hearts when Jesus spoke to them, "Thy sins be forgiven thee," they might have kept alive by helping those in need. The restless energy that is so often a source of danger to the young might be directed into channels through which it would flow out in streams of blessing.[102]

The hours so often spent in amusement that refreshes neither body nor soul should be spent in . . . seeking to help someone who is in need.[103]

Every opportunity to help a brother in need, or to aid the cause of God in the spread of the truth, is a pearl that you can send beforehand, and deposit in the bank of heaven for safe-keeping.[104]

Love, courtesy, self-sacrifice—these are never lost. When God's chosen ones are changed from mortality to immortality, their words and deeds of goodness will be made manifest, and will be preserved through the eternal ages. . . . Through the merits of Christ's imputed righteousness, the fragrance of such words and deeds is forever preserved.[105]

GOD AND CAESAR

Is it lawful for us to give tribute unto Caesar, or no? . . . And he said unto them, Render therefore unto Caesar the things which be Caesar's, and unto God the things which be God's. Luke 20:22-25.

Christ's reply was . . . a candid answer to the question. Holding in His hand the Roman coin, upon which were stamped the name and image of Caesar, He declared that since they were living under the protection of the Roman power, they should render to that power the support it claimed, so long as this did not conflict with a higher duty. But while peaceably subject to the laws of the land, they should at all times give their first allegiance to God.[106]

We are to recognize human government as an ordinance of divine appointment, and teach obedience to it as a sacred duty, within its legitimate sphere. But when its claims conflict with the claims of God, we must obey God rather than men. God's Word must be recognized as above all human legislation. A "Thus saith the Lord" is not to be set aside for a "Thus saith the church" or a "Thus saith the state." The crown of Christ is to be lifted above the diadems of earthly potentates.[107]

The wisdom and authority of the divine law are supreme. . . . The ten precepts of Jehovah are the foundation of all righteous and good laws. Those who love God's commandments will conform to every good law of the land.[108]

We are not required to defy authorities. . . . We are to go forward in Christ's name, advocating the truths committed to us. If we are forbidden by men to do this work, then we may say, as did the apostles, "Whether it be right in the sight of God to hearken unto you more than unto God, judge ye. For we cannot but speak the things which we have seen and heard." Acts 4:19, 20.[109]

Our kingdom is not of this world. We are waiting for our Lord from heaven to come to earth to . . . set up His everlasting kingdom.[110]

CHRISTIAN YOUTH AND THEIR BOOKS

Finally, brethren, whatsoever things are true, whatsoever things are honest, whatsoever things are just, whatsoever things are pure, whatsoever things are lovely, whatsoever things are of good report; if there be any virtue, and if there be any praise, think on these things. Phil. 4:8.

Those who would not fall a prey to Satan's devices, must guard well the avenues of the soul; they must avoid reading, seeing, or hearing that which will suggest impure thoughts.[111]

Many of the popular publications of the day are filled with sensational stories that are educating the youth in wickedness and leading them in the path to perdition. Mere children in years are old in a knowledge of crime. They are incited to evil by the tales they read. . . . The seeds of lawlessness are sown broadcast. None need marvel that a harvest of crime is the result.[112]

The readers of fiction are indulging an evil that destroys spirituality, eclipsing the beauty of the sacred page. It creates an unhealthy excitement, fevers the imagination, unfits the mind for usefulness, weans the soul from prayer, and disqualifies it for any spiritual exercise.[113]

Suffer not yourselves to open the lids of a book that is questionable. There is a hellish fascination in the literature of Satan. It is the powerful battery by which he tears down a simple religious faith. Never feel that you are strong enough to read infidel books; for they contain a poison like that of asps.[114]

Young men and young women, read the literature that will give you true knowledge, and that will be a help to the entire family. Say firmly: "I will not spend precious moments in reading that which will be of no profit to me, and which only unfits me to be of service to others. . . . I will close my eyes to frivolous and sinful things."[115]

The oftener and more diligently you study the Bible, the more beautiful will it appear, and the less relish you will have for light reading. Bind this precious volume to your hearts. It will be to you a friend and guide.[116]

MELODY IN THE HEART

Speaking to yourselves in psalms and hymns and spiritual songs, singing and making melody in your heart to the Lord. Eph. 5:19.

The melody of praise is the atmosphere of heaven; and when heaven comes in touch with the earth, there is music and song. . . .

Above the new-created earth, as it lay, fair and unblemished, under the smile of God, "the morning stars sang together, and all the sons of God shouted for joy." Job 38:7. So human hearts, in sympathy with heaven, have responded to God's goodness in notes of praise.[117]

Young men and women . . . have a keen ear for music, and Satan knows what organs to excite to animate, engross, and charm the mind so that Christ is not desired. . . . Frivolous songs and the popular sheet music of the day seem congenial to their taste. The instruments of music have taken time which should have been devoted to prayer. Music, when not abused, is a great blessing; but when put to a wrong use, it is a terrible curse. It excites, but does not impart that strength and courage which the Christian can find only at the throne of grace. . . . Satan is leading the young captive. . . . He is a skillful charmer, luring them on to perdition.[118]

Musical entertainments which, if conducted properly, will do no harm, are often a source of evil. . . . Musical talent too often fosters pride and ambition for display, and singers have but little thought of the worship of God.[119]

Let all take time to cultivate the voice so that God's praise can be sung in clear, soft tones. . . . The ability to sing is the gift of God; let it be used to His glory.[120]

Let us remember that our praises are supplemented by the choirs of the angelic hosts above.[121]

Those who in heaven join with the angelic choir in their anthem of praise must learn on earth the song of heaven, the keynote of which is thanksgiving.[122]

BEAUTY THAT ENDURES

Whose adorning let it not be that outward adorning of plaiting the hair, and of wearing of gold, or of putting on of apparel; but let it be the hidden man of the heart, in that which is not corruptible, even the ornament of a meek and quiet spirit, which is in the sight of God of great price. 1 Peter 3:3, 4.

In dress, as in all things else, it is our privilege to honor our Creator. He desires our clothing to be not only neat and healthful, but appropriate and becoming. . . . Our appearance in every respect should be characterized by neatness, modesty, and purity. . . .

Our clothing, while modest and simple, should be of good quality, of becoming colors, and suited for service.[123]

Chaste simplicity in dress, when united with modesty of demeanor, will go far toward surrounding a young woman with that atmosphere of sacred reserve which will be to her a shield from a thousand perils.[124]

It is right to buy good material and have it carefully made. This is economy. But rich trimmings are not needed, and to indulge in them is to spend for self-gratification money that should be put into God's cause. . . . Practice economy in your outlay of means for dress.[125]

When the mind is fixed upon pleasing God alone, all the needless embellishments of the person disappear.[126]

He [Jesus] will send the bright beams of the Sun of Righteousness into the soul, which will impart beauty and fragrance to the spiritual life. He will give to the character the ornament of a meek and quiet spirit, which in the sight of God is of great price.[127]

It is right to love beauty and to desire it; but God desires us to love and seek first the highest beauty, that which is imperishable. No outward adorning can compare in value or loveliness with that "meek and quiet spirit," the "fine linen, white and clean," which all the holy ones of earth will wear. This apparel will make them beautiful and beloved here, and will hereafter be their badge of admission to the palace of the King.[128]

A TENTH FOR GOD

And all the tithe of the land, whether of the seed of the land, or of the fruit of the tree, is the Lord's: it is holy unto the Lord. Lev. 27:30.

The Lord has imparted to us heaven's richest treasure in giving us Jesus. With Him He has given us all things richly to enjoy. The productions of the earth, the bountiful harvests, the treasures of gold and silver, are His gifts. Houses and lands, food and clothing, He has placed in the possession of men. He asks us to acknowledge Him as the Giver of all things; and for this reason He says, Of all your possessions I reserve a tenth for Myself, besides gifts and offerings, which are to be brought into My storehouse.[129]

God's plan in the tithing system is beautiful in its simplicity and equality. . . . All may feel that they can act a part in carrying forward the precious work of salvation. Every man, woman, and youth may become a treasurer for the Lord and may be an agent to meet the demands upon the treasury. Says the apostle: "Let every one of you lay by him in store, as God hath prospered him." 1 Cor. 16:2.[130]

Let each regularly examine his income, which is all a blessing from God, and set apart the tithe as a separate fund, to be sacredly the Lord's. This fund should not in any case be devoted to any other use; it is to be devoted solely to support the ministry of the gospel.[131]

A tithe of our income is "holy unto the Lord." The New Testament does not re-enact the law of the tithe, as it does not that of the Sabbath; for the validity of both is assumed.[132]

I speak of the tithing system, yet how meager it looks to my mind! How small the estimate! How vain the endeavor to measure with mathematical rules, time, money and love against a love and sacrifice that is measureless and incomputable! Tithes for Christ! Oh, meager pittance, shameful recompense for that which cost so much! From the cross of Calvary, Christ calls for an unconditional surrender. . . . All we have should be consecrated to God.[133]

THE OFFERINGS OF GRATITUDE

Every man according as he purposeth in his heart, so let him give; not grudgingly, or of necessity: for God loveth a cheerful giver. 2 Cor. 9:7.

Not only should we faithfully render to God our tithes, which He claims as His own, but we should bring a tribute to His treasury as an offering of gratitude. Let us with joyful hearts bring to our Creator the first fruits of all His bounties—our choicest possessions, our best and holiest service.[134]

The Lord requires gifts to be made at stated times, being so arranged that giving will become a habit and benevolence be felt to be a Christian duty. The heart, opened by one gift, is not to have time to become selfishly cold and to close before the next is bestowed. The stream is to be continually flowing, thus keeping open the channel by acts of benevolence.[135]

The contributions required of the Hebrews for religious and charitable purposes amounted to fully one fourth of their income. So heavy a tax upon the resources of the people might be expected to reduce them to poverty; but, on the contrary, the faithful observance of these regulations was one of the conditions of their prosperity.[136]

It is not the greatness of the gift that makes the offering acceptable to God; it is the purpose of the heart, the spirit of gratitude and love that it expresses. Let not the poor feel that their gifts are so small as to be unworthy of notice.[137]

The small sums saved by deeds of sacrifice will do more for the upbuilding of the cause of God than larger gifts will accomplish that have not called for denial of self.[138]

There is nothing too precious for us to give to Jesus. If we return to Him the talents of means He has entrusted to our keeping, He will give more into our hands. Every effort we make for Christ will be rewarded by Him; and every duty we perform in His name will minister to our own happiness.[139]

IN THE CHANNEL OF BLESSING

Not forsaking the assembling of ourselves together, as the manner of some is; but exhorting one another: and so much the more, as ye see the day approaching. Heb. 10:25.

Never entertain the thought that you can be Christians and yet withdraw within yourselves. Each one is a part of the great web of humanity, and the nature and quality of your experience will be largely determined by the experiences of those with whom you associate. . . . Then let us not forsake the assembling of ourselves together.[140]

Many declare that it is certainly no harm to go to a concert and neglect the prayer meeting, or absent themselves from meetings where God's servants are to declare a message from heaven. It is safe for you to be just where Christ has said He would be. . . . Jesus has said, "Where two or three are gathered together in my name, there am I in the midst of them." Matt. 18:20. Can you afford to choose your pleasure and miss the blessing?[141]

If Christians would associate together, speaking to each other of the love of God, and of the precious truths of redemption, their own hearts would be refreshed, and they would refresh one another.[142]

All should have something to say for the Lord, for by so doing they will be blest. A book of remembrance is written of those who do not forsake the assembling of themselves together, but speak often one to another. The remnant are to overcome by the blood of the Lamb and the word of their testimony. . . . We should not come together to remain silent; those only are remembered of the Lord who assemble to speak of His honor and glory and tell of His power; upon such the blessing of God will rest, and they will be refreshed.[143]

We should improve every opportunity of placing ourselves in the channel of blessing. . . . The convocations of the church, as in camp meetings, the assemblies of the home church, and all occasions where there is personal labor for souls, are God's appointed opportunities for giving the early and the latter rain.[144]

GOD'S HELPING HAND

And he said unto them, Go ye into all the world, and preach the gospel to every creature. Mark 16:15.

"God so loved the world, that he gave his only begotten Son." He "sent not his Son into the world to condemn the world; but that the world through him might be saved." John 3:16, 17. The love of God embraces all mankind. Christ, in giving the commission to the disciples, said: "Go ye into all the world, and preach the gospel to every creature." [145]

All who are ordained unto the life of Christ are ordained to work for the salvation of their fellow men. Their hearts will throb in unison with the heart of Christ. The same longing for souls that He has felt will be manifest in them. Not all can fill the same place in the work, but there is a place and a work for all. . . . Every gift is to be employed for the advancement of His kingdom and the glory of His name. [146]

Christ desires to use the youth in His service. He needs missionaries. The barren fields all over the world call to heaven for laborers. If the youth will give themselves to God, He will give them wisdom and knowledge, preparing them for service. If they will consecrate themselves to Him, He will make them vessels unto honor, into which He can pour the precious oil of the Spirit, to be imparted to others. God's helping hand—this is what you may be if you will yield yourselves to His keeping. [147]

To everyone who offers himself to the Lord for service, withholding nothing, is given power for the attainment of measureless results. For these God will do great things. [148]

To young men and young women, as well as to those who are older, God will give power from above. With converted minds, converted hands, converted feet, and converted tongues, their lips touched with a living coal from the divine altar, they will go forth into the Master's service, moving steadily onward and upward, carrying the work forward to completion. [149]

KEEP LOOKING UP!

Looking unto Jesus the author and finisher of our faith; who for the joy that was set before him endured the cross, despising the shame, and is set down at the right hand of the throne of God. Heb. 12:2.

Several years ago, while journeying from Christiania, Norway, to Göteborg, Sweden, I was favored with the sight of the most glorious sunset it was ever my privilege to behold. Language is inadequate to picture its beauty. The last beams of the setting sun, silver and gold, purple, amber, and crimson, shed their glories athwart the sky, growing brighter and brighter, rising higher and higher in the heavens, until it seemed that the gates of the city of God had been left ajar, and gleams of the inner glory were flashing through. For two hours the wondrous splendor continued to light up the cold northern sky—a picture painted by the great Master Artist upon the shifting canvas of the heavens. Like the smile of God it seemed, above all earthly homes, above the rock-bound plains, the rugged mountains, the lonely forests, through which our journey lay.

Angels of mercy seemed whispering: "Look up! This glory is but a gleam of the light which flows from the throne of God. Live not for earth alone. Look up, and behold by faith the mansions of the heavenly home." This scene was to me as the bow of promise to Noah, enabling me to grasp the assurance of God's unfailing care, and to look forward to the haven of rest awaiting the faithful worker. . . .

As God's children, it is our privilege ever to look up, keeping the eye of faith fixed on Christ. As we constantly keep Him in view, the sunshine of His presence floods the chambers of the mind. The light of Christ in the soul-temple brings peace. The soul is stayed on God. All perplexities and anxieties are committed to Jesus. As we continue to behold Him, His image becomes engraved on the heart, and is revealed in the daily life. . . .

My dear young friends, ever keep Christ in view. Thus only can you keep the eye single to God's glory. Jesus is your light and life and peace and assurance forever.[150]

THE HAND THAT NEVER LETS GO

For I the Lord thy God will hold thy right hand, saying unto thee, Fear not; I will help thee. Isa. 41:13.

The sun shone brilliantly on the dazzling snow of one of the highest mountains of the Alps, as a traveler followed his guide along the narrow path. . . . He had confidence in his guide, and followed fearlessly in his footsteps, though the track was entirely new to him. Suddenly he hesitated; for the bold mountaineer stepped across a narrow but very deep chasm, and then, holding out his hand, asked . . . [him] to take it, and step across. Still the traveler hesitated, but the guide encouraged him to obey, saying reassuringly, "Take my hand; that hand never lets go."

Dear young friends, One greater than any human guide calls upon you to follow Him over the heights of patience and self-sacrifice. The path is not an easy one. . . . All the way along, Satan has prepared pitfalls for the feet of the unwary. But following our Guide, we may walk with perfect security; for the path is consecrated by His footsteps. It may be steep and rugged, but He has traveled it; His feet have pressed down the thorns to make the way easier for us. Every burden we are called upon to bear, He Himself has borne. Personal contact with Him brings light and hope and power. Of those who follow Him, He says, "They shall never perish, neither shall any man pluck them out of my hand." John 10:28.[151]

We are to live only one day at a time. We do not have to do the work of a lifetime in a few hours. We need not look into the future with anxiety; for God has made it possible for us to be overcomers every day.[152]

By the exercise of living faith today, we are to conquer the enemy. We must today seek God, and be determined that we will not rest satisfied without His presence. We should watch and work and pray as though this were the last day that would be granted us.[153]

If you are right with God today, you are ready if Christ should come today.[154]

THE CHRIST-CENTERED HOME

THE EDEN HOME

And the Lord God planted a garden eastward in Eden; and there he put the man whom he had formed. Gen. 2:8.

That home [the home of our first parents], beautified by the hand of God Himself, was not a gorgeous palace. Men, in their pride, delight in magnificent and costly edifices, and glory in the works of their own hands; but God placed Adam in a garden. This was his dwelling. The blue heavens were its dome; the earth, with its delicate flowers and carpet of living green, was its floor; and the leafy branches of the goodly trees were its canopy. Its walls were hung with the most magnificent adornings—the handiwork of the great Master Artist.[1]

It was the design of God that man should find happiness in the employment of tending the things He had created, and that his wants should be met with the fruits of the trees of the garden.[2]

In the surroundings of the holy pair was a lesson for all time—that true happiness is found, not in the indulgence of pride and luxury, but in communion with God through His created works. If men would . . . cultivate greater simplicity, they would come far nearer to answering the purpose of God in their creation. . . . What are the possessions of even the most wealthy, in comparison with the heritage given to the lordly Adam?[3]

The Garden of Eden was a representation of what God desired the whole earth to become, and it was His purpose that, as the human family increased in numbers, they should establish other homes . . . like the one He had given. Thus in course of time the whole earth might be occupied with homes and schools where the words and the works of God should be studied, and where the students should thus be fitted more and more fully to reflect, throughout endless ages, the light of the knowledge of His glory.[4]

THE FIRST MARRIAGE

And the Lord God said, It is not good that the man should be alone; I will make him an help meet for him. Gen. 2:18.

Man was not made to dwell in solitude; he was to be a social being. Without companionship, the beautiful scenes and delightful employments of Eden would have failed to yield perfect happiness. Even communion with angels could not have satisfied his desire for sympathy and companionship. There was none of the same nature to love, and to be loved.

God Himself gave Adam a companion. He provided "an help meet for him"—a helper corresponding to him—one who was fitted to be his companion, and who could be one with him in love and sympathy. Eve was created from a rib taken from the side of Adam, signifying that she was not to control him as the head, nor to be trampled under his feet as an inferior, but to stand by his side as an equal, to be loved and protected by him. A part of man, bone of his bone, and flesh of his flesh, she was his second self; showing the close union and the affectionate attachment that should exist in this relation. "For no man ever yet hated his own flesh; but nourisheth and cherisheth it." Eph. 5:29. . . .

God celebrated the first marriage. Thus the institution has for its originator the Creator of the universe. "Marriage is honourable" (Heb. 13:4); it was one of the first gifts of God to man, and it is one of the two institutions that, after the Fall, Adam brought with him beyond the gates of Paradise. When the divine principles are recognized and obeyed in this relation, marriage is a blessing; it guards the purity and happiness of the race, it provides for man's social needs, it elevates the physical, the intellectual, and the moral nature.[5]

The family tie is the closest, the most tender and sacred, of any on earth. It was designed to be a blessing to mankind. And it is a blessing wherever the marriage covenant is entered into intelligently, in the fear of God, and with due consideration for its responsibilities.[6]

BLENDING OF TWO LIVES

Therefore shall a man leave his father and his mother, and shall cleave unto his wife: and they shall be one flesh. Gen. 2:24.

God has ordained that there should be perfect love and harmony between those who enter into the marriage relation. Let bride and bridegroom, in the presence of the heavenly universe, pledge themselves to love each other as God has ordained they should.[7]

Around each family there is a sacred circle that should be kept unbroken. Within this circle no other person has a right to come. Let not the husband or the wife permit another to share the confidences that belong solely to themselves. Let each give love rather than exact it. Cultivate what is noblest in yourselves, and be quick to recognize the good qualities in each other.[8]

Affection may be as clear as crystal and beauteous in its purity, yet it may be shallow because it has not been tested and tried. Make Christ first and last and best in everything. Constantly behold Him, and your love for Him will daily become deeper and stronger as it is submitted to the test of trial. And as your love for Him increases, your love for each other will grow deeper and stronger.[9]

If Christ indeed is formed within, the hope of glory, there will be union and love in the home. Christ abiding in the heart of the wife will be at agreement with Christ abiding in the heart of the husband. They will be striving together for the mansions Christ has gone to prepare for those who love Him.[10]

Only where Christ reigns can there be deep, true, unselfish love. Then soul will be knit with soul, and the two lives will blend in harmony. Angels of God will be guests in the home, and their holy vigils will hallow the marriage chamber.*[11]

The sweetest type of heaven is a home where the Spirit of the Lord presides.[12]

---

* See *The Adventist Home,* chapter 18, "Marital Duties and Privileges," pages 121-128.

A UNION FOR LIFE

Wherefore they are no more twain, but one flesh. What therefore God hath joined together, let not man put asunder. Matt. 19:6.

The marriage vow . . . links the destinies of the two individuals with bonds which nought but the hand of death should sever.[13]

In the Sermon on the Mount Jesus declared plainly that there could be no dissolution of the marriage tie, except for unfaithfulness to the marriage vow. "Every one," He said, "that putteth away his wife, saving for the cause of fornication, maketh her an adulteress: and whosoever shall marry her when she is put away committeth adultery." Matt. 5:32, RV. . . .

Jesus pointed His hearers back to the marriage institution as ordained at creation. . . . Then marriage and the Sabbath had their origin, twin institutions for the glory of God in the benefit of humanity. Then, as the Creator joined the hands of the holy pair in wedlock, . . . He enunciated the law of marriage for all the children of Adam to the close of time. That which the Eternal Father Himself had pronounced good was the law of highest blessing and development for man. Like every other one of God's good gifts entrusted to the keeping of humanity, marriage has been perverted by sin; but it is the purpose of the gospel to restore its purity and beauty.[14]

Men and women, at the beginning of married life, should reconsecrate themselves to God. . . .

Where the Spirit of God reigns, there will be no talk of unsuitability in the marriage relation.[15]

Though difficulties, perplexities, and discouragements may arise, let neither husband nor wife harbor the thought that their union is a mistake or a disappointment. Determine to be all that it is possible to be to each other. Continue the early attentions. In every way encourage each other in fighting the battles of life. Study to advance the happiness of each other. Let there be mutual love, mutual forbearance. Then marriage, instead of being the end of love, will be as it were the very beginning of love.[16]

LET GOD CONTROL

Except the Lord build the house, they labour in vain that build it: except the Lord keep the city, the watchman waketh but in vain. Ps. 127:1.

God . . . desired that the earth should be filled with joy and peace. He created man for happiness, and He longs to fill human hearts with the peace of heaven. He desires that the families below shall be a symbol of the great family above.[17]

Christian homes, established and conducted in accordance with God's plan, are among His most effective agencies for the formation of Christian character and for the advancement of His work.[18]

Home should be made all that the word implies. It should be a little heaven upon earth, a place where the affections are cultivated instead of being studiously repressed. Our happiness depends upon this cultivation of love, sympathy, and true courtesy to one another.[19]

Let your home be such that Christ can enter it as an abiding guest. Let it be such that people will take knowledge of you that you have been with Jesus, and have learned of Him.

The home in which the members are kindly, courteous Christians exerts a far-reaching influence for good. Other families mark the results attained by such a home, and follow the example set, in their turn guarding their homes against evil influences.

Angels of heaven often visit the home in which the will of God bears sway. Under the power of divine grace, such a home becomes a place of refreshing to worn, weary pilgrims. Self is kept from asserting itself. Right habits are formed. There is a careful recognition of the rights of others. The faith that works by love and purifies the soul stands at the helm, presiding over the entire household.[20]

The greatest evidence of the power of Christianity that can be presented to the world is a well-ordered, well-disciplined family. This will recommend the truth as nothing else can, for it is a living witness of its practical power upon the heart.[21]

THE LOVE THAT LASTS

Many waters cannot quench love, neither can the floods drown it: if a man would give all the substance of his house for love, it would utterly be contemned. S. of Sol. 8:7.

Love is a precious gift, which we receive from Jesus. Pure and holy affection is not a feeling, but a principle. Those who are actuated by true love, are neither unreasonable nor blind.[22]

The divine love emanating from Christ never destroys human love, but includes it. By it human love is refined and purified, elevated and ennobled. Human love can never bear its precious fruit until it is united with the divine nature and trained to grow heavenward.[23]

True love is not a strong, fiery, impetuous passion. On the contrary, it is calm and deep in its nature. It looks beyond mere externals, and is attracted by qualities alone. It is wise and discriminating, and its devotion is real and abiding.[24]

Hearts that are filled with the love of Christ can never get very far apart. Religion is love, and a Christian home is one where love reigns and finds expression in words and acts of thoughtful kindness and gentle courtesy.[25]

Our homes must be made a Bethel, our hearts a shrine. Wherever the love of God is cherished in the soul, there will be peace, there will be light and joy.[26]

Jesus wants to see happy marriages, happy firesides.[27]

Men and women can reach God's ideal for them if they will take Christ as their helper. What human wisdom cannot do, His grace will accomplish for those who give themselves to Him in loving trust. His providence can unite hearts in bonds that are of heavenly origin. Love will not be a mere exchange of soft and flattering words. The loom of heaven weaves with warp and woof finer, yet more firm, than can be woven by the looms of earth. The result is not a tissue fabric, but a texture that will bear test and trial. Heart will be bound to heart in the golden bonds of a love that is enduring.[28]

FAR ABOVE RUBIES

Who can find a virtuous woman? for her price is far above rubies. The heart of her husband doth safely trust in her, so that he shall have no need of spoil. Prov. 31:10, 11.

The happiness of the family depends much upon the wife and mother.[29]

Let a young man seek one to stand by his side who is fitted to bear her share of life's burdens, one whose influence will ennoble and refine him, and who will make him happy in her love.[30]

Married life is not all romance; it has its real difficulties and its homely details. The wife must not consider herself a doll, to be tended, but a woman; one to put her shoulder under real, not imaginary, burdens, and live an understanding, thoughtful life, considering that there are other things to be thought of than herself.[31]

A knowledge of domestic duties is beyond price to every woman. There are families without number whose happiness is wrecked by the inefficiency of the wife and mother.[32]

Every girl should learn to take charge of the domestic affairs of home, should be a cook, a housekeeper, a seamstress. She should understand all those things which it is necessary that the mistress of a house should know.[33]

If need be, a young woman can dispense with a knowledge of French and algebra, or even of the piano; but it is indispensable that she learn to make good bread, to fashion neatly fitting garments, and to perform efficiently the many duties that pertain to homemaking.[34]

"A prudent wife is from the Lord." Prov. 19:14. "The heart of her husband doth safely trust in her. . . ." "She openeth her mouth with wisdom; and in her tongue is the law of kindness. She looketh well to the ways of her household, and eateth not the bread of idleness. Her children arise up, and call her blessed; her husband also, and he praiseth her," saying, "Many daughters have done virtuously, but thou excellest them all." Prov. 31:11, 12, 26-29. He who gains such a wife "findeth a good thing, and obtaineth favour of the Lord."[35]

LOVE STANDS THE TEST

He brought me to the banqueting house, and his banner over me was love." S. of Sol. 2:4.

Before giving her hand in marriage, every woman should en-quire whether he with whom she is about to unite her destiny is worthy. What has been his past record? Is his life pure? Is the love which he expresses of a noble, elevated character, or is it a mere emotional fondness? Has he traits of character that will make her happy? Can she find true peace and joy in his affection? Will she be allowed to preserve her individuality, or must her judgment and con-science be surrendered to the control of her husband? As a disciple of Christ, she is not her own; she has been bought with a price. Can she honor the Saviour's claims as supreme? Will body and soul, thoughts and purposes, be preserved pure and holy? These ques-tions have a vital bearing upon the well-being of every woman who enters the marriage relation.[36]

If you are blessed with God-fearing parents, seek counsel of them. Open to them your hopes and plans, learn the lessons which their life experiences have taught, and you will be saved many a heartache, Above all, make Christ your counselor. Study His Word with prayer.

Under such guidance let a young woman accept as a life com-panion only one who possesses pure, manly traits of character, one who is diligent, aspiring, and honest, one who loves and fears God.[37]

The heart yearns for human love, but this love is not strong enough, or pure enough, or precious enough, to supply the place of the love of Jesus. Only in her Saviour can the wife find wisdom, strength, and grace to meet the cares, responsibilities, and sorrows of life. She should make Him her strength and her guide. Let woman give herself to Christ before giving herself to any earthly friend, and enter into no relation which shall conflict with this.[38]

It is only in Christ that a marriage alliance can be safely formed. Human love should draw its closest bonds from divine love. Only where Christ reigns can there be a deep, true, unselfish affection.[39]

255

SUNSHINE OR SHADOWS?

Be ye not unequally yoked together with unbelievers: for what fellowship hath righteousness with unrighteousness? and what communion hath light with darkness? 2 Cor. 6:14.

One of the greatest dangers that besets the people of God today, is that of association with the ungodly; especially in uniting themselves in marriage with unbelievers.[40]

Hundreds have sacrificed Christ and heaven in consequence of marrying unconverted persons. . . . The happiness and prosperity of the married life depend upon the unity of the parties. How can the carnal mind harmonize with the mind that is assimilated to the mind of Christ? . . . There is a perpetual difference of taste, of inclination, and of purpose. Unless the believer shall, through his steadfast adherence to principle, win the impenitent, he will, as is much more common, become discouraged and sell his religious principles for the poor companionship of one who has no connection with Heaven.[41]

Those who profess the truth trample on the will of God in marrying unbelievers; they lose His favor and make bitter work for repentance. The unbelieving may possess an excellent moral character; but the fact that he or she has not answered to the claims of God, and has neglected so great salvation, is sufficient reason why such a union should not be consummated.[42]

Of Solomon the Inspired Record says, "His wives turned away his heart after other gods: and his heart was not perfect with the Lord his God." 1 Kings 11:4. . . . Let the sad memory of Solomon's apostasy warn every soul to shun the same precipice.[43]

If men and women are in the habit of praying twice a day before they contemplate marriage, they should pray four times a day when such a step is anticipated. Marriage is something that will influence and affect your life, both in this world and in the world to come.[44]

Unless you would have a home where the shadows are never lifted, do not unite yourself with one who is an enemy of God.[45]

A PARTNERSHIP THAT WORKS

For the husband is the head of the wife, even as Christ is the head of the church: and he is the saviour of the body. Eph. 5:23.

The Lord has constituted the husband the head of the wife to be her protector; he is the house-band of the family, binding the members together, even as Christ is the head of the church and the Saviour of the mystical body. Let every husband who claims to love God carefully study the requirements of God in his position. Christ's authority is exercised in wisdom, in all kindness and gentleness; so let the husband exercise his power and imitate the great Head of the church.[46]

The husband should remember that much of the burden of training his children rests upon the mother. . . . This should call into exercise his tenderest feelings, and with care should he lighten her burdens. He should encourage her to lean upon his large affections.[47]

Neither the husband nor the wife should attempt to exercise over the other an arbitrary control. Do not try to compel each other to yield to your wishes. You cannot do this and retain each other's love. Be kind, patient, and forbearing, considerate, and courteous. By the grace of God you can succeed in making each other happy, as in your marriage vow you promised to do.[48]

Marriage, a union for life, is a symbol of the union between Christ and His church. The spirit that Christ manifests toward His church is the spirit that the husband and wife are to manifest toward each other. If they love God supremely, they will love each other in the Lord. . . . In their mutual self-denial and self-sacrifice they will be a blessing to each other. . . .

God wants the home to be the happiest place on earth, the very symbol of the home in heaven. Bearing the marriage responsibilities in the home, linking their interests with Jesus Christ, leaning upon His arm and His assurance, husband and wife may share a happiness in this union that angels of God commend. Marriage does not lessen their usefulness, but strengthens it.[49]

KINGS AND QUEENS

Through wisdom is an house builded, and by understanding is it established. Prov. 24:3.

In God's plan for Israel every family had a home on the land, with sufficient ground for tilling. Thus were provided both the means and the incentive for a useful, industrious, and self-supporting life. And no devising of men has ever improved upon that plan.[50]

The earth has blessings hidden in her depths for those who have courage and will and perseverance to gather her treasures. Fathers and mothers who possess a piece of land and a comfortable home are kings and queens.[51]

An expensive dwelling, elaborate furnishings, display, luxury, and ease, do not furnish the conditions essential to a happy, useful life. Jesus came to this earth to accomplish the greatest work ever accomplished among men. He came as God's ambassador, to show us how to live so as to secure life's best results. What were the conditions chosen by the infinite Father for His Son? A secluded home in the Galilean hills; a household sustained by honest, self-respecting labor; a life of simplicity; daily conflict with difficulty and hardship; self-sacrifice, economy, and patient, gladsome service; the hour of study at His mother's side, with the open scroll of Scripture; the quiet of dawn or twilight in the green valley; the holy ministries of nature; the study of creation and providence; and the soul's communion with God—these were the conditions and opportunities of the early life of Jesus. . . .

Let it be your first aim to make a pleasant home. Be sure to provide the facilities that will lighten labor and promote health and comfort. . . .

Furnish your home with things plain and simple, things that will bear handling, that can be easily kept clean, and that can be replaced without great expense. By exercising taste, you can make a very simple home attractive and inviting, if love and contentment are there.[52]

THE CROWNING TREASURE OF THE HOME

Thy wife shall be as a fruitful vine by the sides of thine house: thy children like olive plants round about thy table. Ps. 128:3.

Children and youth are God's peculiar treasure.[53]

When two compose a family, . . . and there are no children to call into exercise patience, forbearance, and true love, there is need of constant watchfulness lest selfishness obtain the supremacy, lest you yourselves become the center, and you require attention, care, and interest, which you feel under no obligation to bestow upon others.[54]

Care and affection for dependent children removes the roughness from our natures, makes us tender and sympathetic, and has an influence to develop the nobler elements of our character.[55]

After the birth of his first son, Enoch reached a higher experience; he was drawn into a closer relationship with God. He realized more fully his own obligations and responsibility as a son of God. And as he saw the child's love for its father, its simple trust in his protection; as he felt the deep, yearning tenderness of his own heart for that first-born son, he learned a precious lesson of the wonderful love of God to men in the gift of His Son, and the confidence which the children of God may repose in their heavenly Father.[56]

I have a very tender interest in all children. . . . I have taken many children to care for, and I have always felt that association with the simplicity of childhood was a great blessing to me. . . .

The sympathy, forbearance, and love required in dealing with children would be a blessing in any household. They would soften and subdue set traits of character in those who need to be more cheerful and restful. The presence of a child in a home sweetens and refines. A child brought up in the fear of the Lord is a blessing. . . .

Your sons and daughters are younger members of God's family. He has committed them to your care, to train and educate for heaven.[57]

The soul of the little child that believes in Christ is as precious in His sight as are the angels about His throne.[58]

WHAT KIND OF INHERITANCE?

And Manoah said, Now let thy words come to pass. How shall we order the child, and how shall we do unto him? Judges 13:12.

The words spoken to the wife of Manoah contain a truth that the mothers of today would do well to study.[59]

The child will be affected for good or for evil by the habits of the mother. She must herself be controlled by principle, and must practice temperance and self-denial, if she would seek the welfare of her child.[60]

If before the birth of her child she is unstable, if she is selfish, peevish, and exacting, the disposition of her child will bear the marks of her wrong course. . . . But if she unswervingly adheres to the right, if she is kind, gentle, and unselfish, she will give her child these traits of character.[61]

And fathers as well as mothers are involved in this responsibility. Both parents transmit their own characteristics, mental and physical, their dispositions and appetites, to their children. . . . The inquiry of every father and mother should be, "What shall we do unto the child that shall be born unto us?" The effect of prenatal influences has been by many lightly regarded; but the instruction sent from heaven to those Hebrew parents shows how the matter is looked upon by our Creator.[62]

The mother who is a fit teacher for her children must, before their birth, form habits of self-denial and self-control; for she transmits to them her own qualities, her own strong or weak traits of character. The enemy of souls understands this matter much better than do many parents. He will bring temptations upon the mother, knowing that if she does not resist him, he can through her affect her child. The mother's only hope is in God. She may flee to Him for grace and strength. She will not seek help in vain. He will enable her to transmit to her offspring qualities that will help them to gain success in this life and to win eternal life.[63]

PATTERN FOR CHILDREN AND YOUTH

And the child grew, and waxed strong in spirit, filled with wisdom: and the grace of God was upon him. Luke 2:40.

Jesus is our example. . . . It is in His home life that He is the pattern for all children and youth.[64]

His mother was His first human teacher. From her lips and from the scrolls of the prophets, He learned of heavenly things. . . . His intimate acquaintance with the Scriptures shows how diligently His early years were given to the study of God's Word. . . . From His earliest years He was possessed of one purpose; He lived to bless others.[65]

In His youth He worked with His father at the carpenter's trade. . . . From His childhood He was a pattern of obedience and industry. He was as a pleasant sunbeam in the home circle. Faithfully and cheerfully He acted His part, doing the humble duties that He was called to do in His lowly life.[66]

The life of Christ was humble, free from affectation or display. He lived mostly in the open air. . . . The birds, the natural flowers that decked the fields with their glowing beauty, the majestic trees and lofty mountains, the ragged rocks and perpetual hills, all had special charms for Him. . . . Secluded from every human eye, He communed with His heavenly Father. His moral powers were strengthened by His meditation and communion with God.[67]

It is the precious privilege of . . . parents to cooperate in teaching the children how to drink in the gladness of Christ's life by learning to follow His example. The Saviour's early years were useful years. He was His mother's helper in the home; and He was just as verily fulfilling His commission when performing the duties of the home and working at the carpenter's bench as when He engaged in His public work of ministry.[68]

Every youth who follows Christ's example of faithfulness and obedience in His lowly home may claim those words spoken of Him by the Father through the Holy Spirit, "Behold my servant, whom I uphold; mine elect, in whom my soul delighteth." Isa. 42:1.[69]

THE GRANDEST WORK OF ALL

That our sons may be as plants grown up in their youth; that our daughters may be as corner stones, polished after the similitude of a palace. Ps. 144:12.

The tenderest earthly tie is that between the mother and her child.[70]

In the children committed to her care, every mother has a sacred charge from God. "Take this son, this daughter," He says; "train it for Me; give it a character polished after the similitude of a palace, that it may shine in the courts of the Lord forever."[71]

This work of molding, refining, and polishing is the mother's. The character of the child is to be developed. The mother must engrave upon the tablet of the heart lessons as enduring as eternity.[72]

Child training is the grandest work ever committed to mortals. The child belongs to the Lord, and from the time it is an infant in its mother's arms, it is to be trained for Him.[73]

The home should be to the children the most attractive place in the world, and the mother's presence should be its greatest attraction. . . . By gentle discipline, in loving words and acts, mothers may bind their children to their hearts.[74]

There is a God above, and the light and glory from His throne rests upon the faithful mother as she tries to educate her children to resist the influence of evil. No other work can equal hers in importance. She has not, like the artist, to paint a form of beauty upon canvas, nor, like the sculptor, to chisel it from marble. She has not, like the author, to embody a noble thought in words of power, nor, like the musician, to express a beautiful sentiment in melody. It is hers, with the help of God, to develop in a human soul the likeness of the divine.[75]

The king upon his throne has no higher work than has the mother. The mother is queen of her household. She has in her power the molding of her children's characters, that they may be fitted for the higher, immortal life. An angel could not ask for a higher mission.[76]

HOUSE-BAND OF THE FAMILY

And, ye fathers, provoke not your children to wrath: but bring them up in the nurture and admonition of the Lord. Eph. 6:4.

Great as is the work of the mother, it should never be forgotten that the father also has a part to act in the education and training of his children. . . . Especially as the children advance in years is the father's influence needed, in union with that of the mother, to restrain, control, and guide.[77]

A Christian father is the house-band of his family, binding them close to the throne of God. Never is his interest in his children to flag. The father who has a family of boys should not leave these restless boys wholly to the care of the mother. . . . He should make himself their companion and friend. He should exert himself to keep them from evil associates. . . . He should take more of the burden upon himself, doing all in his power to lead his boys to God.[78]

When children lose their self-control and speak passionate words, the parents should for a time keep silent. . . . Silence is golden, and will do more to bring repentance than any words that can be uttered. Satan is well pleased when parents irritate their children by speaking harsh, angry words. . . . "Fathers, provoke not your children to anger, lest they be discouraged." Col. 3:21. . . . Let your calmness help to restore them to a proper frame of mind.[79]

By kind and judicious management, fathers as well as mothers should bind their children to them by the strong ties of reverence, gratitude, and love, and should kindle in their young hearts an earnest longing for righteousness and truth. While the mother seeks to implant good principles, the father should see that the precious seed is not choked by the growth of evil. His sterner discipline is needed that his children may learn firmness and self-control. . . .

Christian father, labor kindly, patiently, for the welfare of your children. Seek to turn their hearts to the bright beams of the Sun of Righteousness. Teach them by precept and example that the spirit of Christ is the spirit of doing good.[80]

HOLDING THE REINS OF GOVERNMENT

Children, obey your parents in the Lord: for this is right. Eph. 6:1.

The will of God is the law of heaven. As long as that law was the rule of life, all the family of God were holy and happy. But when the divine law was disobeyed, then envy, jealousy, and strife were introduced, and a part of the inhabitants of heaven fell. As long as God's law is revered in our earthly homes, the family will be happy.[81]

One of the first lessons a child needs to learn is the lesson of obedience. Before he is old enough to reason, he may be taught to obey.[82]

The mother is the queen of the home, and the children are her subjects. She is to rule her household wisely, in the dignity of her motherhood. Her influence in the home is to be paramount.[83]

Self-will should never be permitted to go unrebuked. The future well-being of the child requires kindly, loving, but firm discipline. . . . It is impossible to depict the evil that results from leaving a child to its own will.[84]

A fitful government—at one time holding the lines firmly, and at another allowing that which has been condemned—is ruination to a child.[85]

Uniform firmness and unimpassioned control are necessary to the discipline of every family. Say what you mean calmly, move with consideration, and carry out what you say without deviation.[86]

The requirements of the parents should always be reasonable; kindness should be expressed, not by foolish indulgence, but by wise direction. Parents are to teach their children pleasantly, without scolding or faultfinding, seeking to bind the hearts of the little ones to them by silken cords of love.[87]

The combined influence of authority and love will make it possible to hold firmly and kindly the reins of family government. An eye single to the glory of God and to what our children owe Him will keep us from looseness and from sanctioning evil.[88]

SILKEN CORDS OF AFFECTION

And be ye kind one to another, tenderhearted, forgiving one another, even as God for Christ's sake hath forgiven you. Eph. 4:32.

The principle inculcated by the injunction, "Be kindly affectioned one to another" (Rom. 12:10), lies at the very foundation of domestic happiness.[89]

Unkindness, complaining, and anger shut Jesus from the dwelling. I saw that angels of God will flee from a house where there are unpleasant words, fretfulness, and strife.[90]

Gentle manners, cheerful conversation, and loving acts will bind the hearts of children to their parents by the silken cords of affection and will do more to make home attractive than the rarest ornaments that can be bought for gold.[91]

Tender affection should ever be cherished between husband and wife, parents and children, brothers and sisters. Every hasty word should be checked, and there should not be even the appearance of the lack of love one for another. . . . Children are to respect and reverence their parents, and parents are to manifest patience, kindness, and affection for their children. Each one should seek in every possible way to please and make happy the members of the family circle.[92]

Acts of kindness . . . will bind hearts together, and will draw them closer to the heart of Him from whom every generous impulse springs. The little attentions, the small acts of love and self-sacrifice, that flow out from the life as quietly as the fragrance from a flower—these constitute no small share of the blessings and happiness of life.[93]

Oh, what rays of softness and beauty shone forth in the daily life of our Saviour! What sweetness flowed from His very presence! The same spirit will be revealed in His children. Those with whom Christ dwells will be surrounded with a divine atmosphere. Their white robes of purity will be fragrant with perfume from the garden of the Lord. Their faces will reflect light from His, brightening the path for stumbling and weary feet.[94]

WORKING TOGETHER

Bear ye one another's burdens, and so fulfil the law of Christ. Gal. 6:2.

Children as well as parents have important duties in the home. They should be taught that they are a part of the home firm. They are fed and clothed and loved and cared for; and they should respond to these many mercies by bearing their share of the home burdens, and bringing all the happiness possible into the family.[95]

Even the little ones should be trained to share in the daily work, and should be made to feel that their help is needed and is appreciated. The older ones should be their parents' assistants, entering into their plans, and sharing their responsibilities and burdens. Let fathers and mothers take time to teach their children, let them show that they value their help, desire their confidence, and enjoy their companionship, and the children will not be slow to respond. Not only will the parents' burden be lightened, and the children receive a practical training of inestimable worth, but there will be a strengthening of the home ties and a deepening of the very foundations of character.[96]

Work is good for children; they are happier to be usefully employed a large share of the time; their innocent amusements are enjoyed with a keener zest after the successful completion of their tasks. Labor strengthens both the muscles and the mind. Mothers may make precious little helpers of their children.[97]

The approval of God rests with loving assurance upon the children who cheerfully take their part in the duties of domestic life, sharing the burdens of father and mother.[98]

If children were taught to regard the humble round of everyday duties as the course marked out for them by the Lord, . . . how much more pleasant and honorable would their work appear. To perform every duty as unto the Lord, throws a charm around the humblest employment, and links the workers on earth with the holy beings who do God's will in heaven.[99]

"I WILL SAVE THY CHILDREN"

But thus saith the Lord, even the captives of the mighty shall be taken away, and the prey of the terrible shall be delivered: for I will contend with him that contendeth with thee, and I will save thy children. Isa. 49:25.

The youth are the objects of Satan's special attacks.[100]

Wherever we turn, the battle goes on unceasingly. . . . Multitudes of the youth are swept away by the overwhelming tide of evil. In every earnest Christian heart the question rises, "Why, oh, why, in a land of Bibles and Christian teaching, can the adversary of souls exert over our youth a power so mighty, so unrestrained?" The reason is apparent. Parents are neglecting their solemn responsibility.[101]

If a field is left uncultivated, a crop of weeds is sure to appear. So it is with children. If the soil of the heart is uncultivated, Satan sows his seeds of anger and hatred, selfishness and pride, and they quickly spring up, to bear a harvest that parents reap with bitter regret. Too late they see their terrible mistake.[102]

One of the signs of the "last days" is the disobedience of children to their parents.[103]

The sin of rebellion against parental authority, lies at the very foundation of the misery and crime in the world today.[104]

Jesus loves children and youth. He rejoices when He sees Satan repulsed in his efforts to overcome them. Many a youth is in imminent peril through manifold temptations, but the Saviour has the tenderest sympathy for him, and sends His angels to guard and protect him. He is the Good Shepherd, ever ready to . . . seek for the lost, straying sheep.[105]

Parents stand in the place of God to their children, and they will have to render an account, whether they have been faithful to the charge committed to their trust.[106]

[Christian parents,] be true to your trust. God will help you. Guided by Him, your children will grow up to bless and honor you in this life and in the life to come.[107]

267

LITTLE CHILDREN MAY BE CHRISTIANS

Jesus said, Suffer little children, and forbid them not, to come unto me: for of such is the kingdom of heaven. Matt. 19:14.

God wants every child of tender age to be His child, to be adopted into His family. Young though they may be, the youth may be members of the household of faith, and have a most precious experience.[108]

I was eleven years old when the light broke into my heart. I had pious parents, who in every way tried to make their children acquainted with their heavenly Father. We sang the praises of God in our household. Every morning and evening we had family prayer. There were eight children in the family, and every opportunity was improved by our parents to lead us to give our hearts to Jesus.[109]

Children are most susceptible to the teachings of the gospel; their hearts are open to divine influences, and strong to retain the lessons received. The little children may be Christians, having an experience in accordance with their years.[110]

Happy are the parents whose lives are a true reflection of the divine, so that the promises and commands of God awaken in the child gratitude and reverence; the parents whose tenderness and justice and long-suffering interpret to the child the love and justice and long-suffering of God; and who, by teaching the child to love and trust and obey them, are teaching him to love and trust and obey his Father in heaven. Parents who impart to a child such a gift have endowed him with a treasure more precious than the wealth of all the ages—a treasure as enduring as eternity.[111]

Never allow your children to suppose that they are not children of God until they are old enough to be baptized.[112]

If properly instructed, very young children may have correct views of their state as sinners and of the way of salvation through Christ.[113]

In love, faith, and prayer let parents work for their households, until with joy they can come to God saying, "Behold, I and the children whom the Lord hath given me." Isa. 8:18.[114]

FEASTING ON GOD'S WORD

And these words, which I command thee this day, shall be in thine heart: and thou shalt teach them diligently unto thy children, and shalt talk of them when thou sittest in thine house, and when thou walkest by the way, and when thou liest down, and when thou risest up. Deut. 6:6, 7.

Our heavenly Father, in giving His Word, did not overlook the children. In all that men have written, where can be found anything that has such a hold upon the heart, anything so well adapted to awaken the interest of the little ones, as the stories of the Bible? In these simple stories may be made plain the great principles of the law of God.[115]

The Sabbath school affords to parents and children a precious opportunity for the study of God's Word. . . . Parents, set apart a little time each day for the study of the Sabbath school lesson with your children. . . . Parents, as well as children, will receive benefit from this study. Let the more important passages of Scripture connected with the lesson be committed to memory, not as a task, but as a privilege. . . .

Observe system in the study of the Scriptures in your families. Neglect anything of a temporal nature; . . . but be sure that the soul is fed with the bread of life.[116]

Many are the benefits derived from feasting on His Word. . . . Habits of self-control are formed and strengthened. The infirmities of childhood—fretfulness, willfulness, selfishness, hasty words, passionate acts—disappear, and in their place are developed the graces of Christian manhood and womanhood.[117]

We need to recognize the Holy Spirit as our enlightener. That Spirit loves to address the children, and discover to them the treasures and beauties of the Word. The promises spoken by the Great Teacher will captivate the senses and animate the soul of the child with a spiritual power that is divine. There will grow in the receptive mind a familiarity with divine things which will be as a barricade against the temptations of the enemy.[118]

SWEETEST HOUR OF THE DAY

My voice shalt thou hear in the morning, O Lord; in the morning will I direct my prayer unto thee, and will look up. Ps. 5:3.

If ever there was a time when every house should be a house of prayer, it is now.[119]

In every Christian home God should be honored by the morning and evening sacrifices of prayer and praise. Children should be taught to respect and reverence the hour of prayer. It is the duty of Christian parents, morning and evening, by earnest prayer and persevering faith, to make a hedge about their children.[120]

The hours of morning and evening worship should be the sweetest and most helpful of the day. Let it be understood that into these hours no troubled, unkind thoughts are to intrude; that parents and children assemble to meet with Jesus, and to invite into the home the presence of holy angels. Let the services be brief and full of life, adapted to the occasion, and varied from time to time. Let all join in the Bible reading, and learn and often repeat God's law.[121]

In the church at home the children are to learn to pray and to trust in God. . . . Come in humility, with a heart full of tenderness, and with a sense of the temptations and dangers before yourselves and your children; by faith bind them to the altar, entreating for them the care of the Lord. Train the children to offer their simple words of prayer. Tell them that God delights to have them call upon Him.

Will the Lord of heaven pass by such homes, and leave no blessing there? Nay, verily. Ministering angels will guard the children who are thus dedicated to God. They hear the offering of praise and the prayer of faith, and they bear the petitions to Him who ministers in the sanctuary for His people, and offers His merits in their behalf.[122]

The beautiful lessons of the Bible stories and parables, the pure, simple instruction of God's Holy Word, is the spiritual food for you and your children. Oh, what a work is before you! Will you take hold of it in the love and fear of God?[123]

SINGING ON LIFE'S WAY

Blessed is the people that know the joyful sound: they shall walk, O Lord, in the light of thy countenance. Ps. 89:15.

As the children of Israel, journeying through the wilderness, cheered their way by the music of sacred song, so God bids His children today gladden their pilgrim life. There are few means more effective for fixing His words in the memory than repeating them in song. And such song has wonderful power. It has power to subdue rude and uncultivated natures; power to quicken thought and . . . to promote harmony of action. . . . It is one of the most effective means of impressing the heart with spiritual truth. How often to the soul hard-pressed and ready to despair, memory recalls some word of God's—the long-forgotten burden of a childhood song—and temptations lose their power. . . . Let there be singing in the home, of songs that are sweet and pure, and there will be fewer words of censure, and more of cheerfulness and hope and joy.[124]

Jesus carried into His labor cheerfulness and tact. . . . Often He expressed the gladness of His heart by singing psalms and heavenly songs. Often the dwellers in Nazareth heard His voice raised in praise and thanksgiving to God. He held communion with heaven in song; and as His companions complained of weariness from labor, they were cheered by the sweet melody from His lips. His praise seemed to banish the evil angels, and, like incense, fill the place with fragrance.[125]

With the voice of singing He welcomed the morning light. He listened to the lark caroling forth music to its God, and joined His voice with the voice of praise and thanksgiving.[126]

Song is a weapon that we can always use against discouragement.[127]

The voice of thanksgiving, praise, and rejoicing is heard in heaven. The voices of the angels in heaven unite with the voices of the children of God on earth as they ascribe honor and glory and praise to God and to the Lamb for the great salvation provided.[128]

Let us learn the song of the angels now, that we may sing it when we join their shining ranks.[129]

DAY OF DAYS

And hallow my sabbaths; and they shall be a sign between me and you, that ye may know that I am the Lord your God. Eze. 20:20.

The Sabbath should be made so interesting to our families that its weekly return will be hailed with joy.[130]

The Sabbath school and the meeting for worship occupy only a part of the Sabbath. The portion remaining to the family may be made the most sacred and precious season of all the Sabbath hours.[131]

In the minds of the children the very thought of the Sabbath should be bound up with the beauty of natural things. . . . Happy the father and mother who can teach their children God's written word with illustrations from the open pages of the book of nature; who can gather under the green trees, in the fresh, pure air, to study the Word and to sing the praise of the Father above.[132]

In pleasant weather let parents walk with their children in the fields and groves. Amid the beautiful things of nature tell them the reason for the institution of the Sabbath. Describe to them God's great work of creation. Tell them that when the earth came from His hand, it was holy and beautiful. Every flower, every shrub, every tree, answered the purpose of its Creator. . . . Show that it was sin which marred God's perfect work; that thorns and thistles, sorrow and pain and death, are all the result of disobedience to God. Bid them see how the earth, though marred with the curse of sin, still reveals God's goodness.[133]

If we can cultivate within us a beauty of soul corresponding to the beauty of nature around us, there will be a blending of the divine and human agencies.[134]

As the sun goes down, let the voice of prayer and the hymn of praise mark the close of the sacred hours and invite God's presence through the cares of the week of labor.

Thus parents can make the Sabbath, as it should be, the most joyful day of the week. They can lead their children to regard it as a delight, the day of days, the holy of the Lord, honorable.[135]

THE ROYAL ROBE OF HEAVEN

Even a child is known by his doings, whether his work be pure, and whether it be right. Prov. 20:11.

Better than any other inheritance of wealth you can give to your children will be the gift of a healthy body, a sound mind, and a noble character.[136]

The lessons learned, the habits formed, during the years of infancy and childhood have more to do with the formation of the character and the direction of the life than have all the instruction and training of after years.[137]

God has withheld no blessing that is necessary for shaping the character of children and youth after the divine pattern given them in the youth of Jesus.[138]

The physical constitution of Jesus, as well as His spiritual development, is brought before us in these words, "the child grew," and "increased in stature." In childhood and youth attention should be given to physical development. Parents should so train their children in good habits of eating and drinking, dressing, and exercise, that a good foundation will be laid for sound health in afterlife. . . . This places the children and youth in a favorable position, so that, with proper religious training, they may, like Christ, wax strong in spirit.[139]

Let the youth and the little children be taught to choose for themselves that royal robe woven in heaven's loom, the "fine linen, clean and white" (Rev. 19:8), which all the holy ones of earth will wear. This robe, Christ's own spotless character, is freely offered to every human being. But all who receive it will receive and wear it here.

Let the children be taught that as they open their minds to pure, loving thoughts and do loving and helpful deeds, they are clothing themselves with His beautiful garment of character. This apparel will make them beautiful and beloved here, and will hereafter be their title of admission to the palace of the King. His promise is: "They shall walk with me in white: for they are worthy" (Rev. 3:4).[140]

A PLACE OF REFUGE

Be not forgetful to entertain strangers: for thereby some have entertained angels unawares. Heb. 13:2.

Our sympathies are to overflow the boundaries of self and the enclosure of family walls. There are precious opportunities for those who will make their homes a blessing to others.[141]

We are in a world of sin and temptation; all around us are souls perishing out of Christ, and God wants us to labor for them in every way possible. If you have a pleasant home, invite to it the youth who have no home, those who are in need of help, who long for sympathy and kind words, for respect and courtesy.[142]

Our homes should be a place of refuge for the tempted youth. Many there are who stand at the parting of the ways. Every influence, every impression, is determining the choice that shapes their destiny both here and hereafter. Evil invites them. Its resorts are made bright and attractive. They have a welcome for every comer. All about us are youth who have no home, and many whose homes have no helpful, uplifting power, and the youth drift into evil. . . .

These youth need a hand stretched out to them in sympathy. . . . If we would . . . invite them to our homes, and surround them with cheering, helpful influences, there are many who would gladly turn their steps into the upward path.[143]

The season of prayer makes its impression on those who receive entertainment, and even one visit may mean the saving of a soul from death.[144]

Let visitors see that we are striving to conform to the will of Christ. . . . The very atmosphere of a truly Christian home is that of peace and restfulness. Such an example will not be without effect.[145]

As you open your door to Christ's needy and suffering ones, you are welcoming unseen angels. You invite the companionship of heavenly beings. They bring a sacred atmosphere of joy and peace. They come with praises upon their lips, and an answering strain is heard in heaven. Every deed of mercy makes music there.[146]

AN EVER-WIDENING CIRCLE

Train up a child in the way he should go: and when he is old, he will not depart from it. Prov. 22:6.

Fathers and mothers should feel that a duty devolves upon them to guide the affections of the youth, that they may be placed upon those who will be suitable companions. They should . . . so mold the character of the children from their earliest years that they will be pure and noble, and will be attracted to the good and true. . . .

True love is a high and holy principle, altogether different in character from that love which is awakened by impulse, and which suddenly dies when severely tested. It is by faithfulness to duty in the parental home that the youth are to prepare themselves for homes of their own. Let them here practice self-denial, and manifest kindness, courtesy, and Christian sympathy. Thus love will be kept warm in the heart, and he who goes out from such a household to stand at the head of a family of his own, will know how to promote the happiness of her whom he has chosen as a companion for life.[147]

Fathers and mothers, you are to build up in this life characters which will help you to fit your children for the future, immortal life, which will help them to form such characters that you will not be ashamed to see them, as parents, taking the charge of their own children, and transferring to them your own attributes.[148]

Let those who are contemplating marriage weigh every sentiment and watch every development of character in the one with whom they think to unite their life destiny.[149]

Take God and your God-fearing parents into your counsel, young friends. Pray over the matter. . . . The step you are about to take is one of the most important in your life, and should not be taken hastily. While you may love, do not love blindly.[150]

Let every step toward a marriage alliance be characterized by modesty, simplicity, sincerity, and an earnest purpose to please and honor God.[151]

A BRIGHT AND HOLY LIGHT

That ye may be blameless and harmless, the sons of God, without rebuke, in the midst of a crooked and perverse nation, among whom ye shine as lights in the world. Phil. 2:15.

The mission of the home extends beyond its own members. The Christian home is to be an object lesson, illustrating the excellence of the true principles of life. . . . Far more powerful than any sermon that can be preached is the influence of a true home upon human hearts and lives. As the youth go out from such a home, the lessons they have learned are imparted. Nobler principles of life are introduced into other households, and an uplifting influence works in the community.[152]

From every Christian home a holy light should shine forth. Love should be revealed in action. It should flow out in all home intercourse, showing itself in thoughtful kindness, in gentle, unselfish courtesy. There are homes where this principle is carried out—homes where God is worshiped, and truest love reigns. From these homes, morning and evening prayer ascends to God as sweet incense, and His mercies and blessings descend upon the suppliants like the morning dew. . . . All can see that there is an influence at work in the family that affects the children, and that the God of Abraham is with them. If the homes of professed Christians had a right religious mold, they would exert a mighty influence for good. They would indeed be the "light of the world." [153]

He who lives Christianity in the home will be a bright and shining light everywhere.[154]

A lamp, however small, if kept steadily burning, may be the means of lighting many other lamps. Our sphere of influence may seem narrow, . . . yet wonderful possibilities are ours through a faithful use of the opportunities of our own homes. If we will open our hearts and homes to the divine principles of life we shall become channels for currents of life-giving power. From our homes will flow streams of healing, bringing life and beauty and fruitfulness where now are barrenness and dearth.[155]

A WELCOME TO THE HEAVENLY HOME

Open ye the gates, that the righteous nation which keepeth the truth may enter in. Isa. 26:2.

The life on earth is the beginning of the life in heaven.[156]

We are children of the heavenly King, members of the royal family, heirs of God, and joint heirs with Christ. The mansions Jesus has gone to prepare are to receive only those who are true, who are pure, who love and obey His words. . . . If we would enjoy eternal bliss, we must cultivate religion in the home. . . . Peace, harmony, affection, and happiness should be perseveringly cherished every day, until these precious things abide in the hearts of those who compose the family.[157]

That which will make the character lovely in the home is that which will make it lovely in the heavenly mansions.[158]

If we manifest the character of Christ here, keeping all the commandments of God, we shall be cheered and blessed with glimpses of the pleasant home in the mansions Jesus has gone to prepare.[159]

Let all that is beautiful in our earthly home remind us of the crystal river and green fields, the waving trees and the living fountains, the shining city and the white-robed singers, of our heavenly home—that world of beauty which no artist can picture, no mortal tongue describe.[160]

There the loves and sympathies that God has planted in the soul will find truest and sweetest exercise. The pure communion with holy beings, the harmonious social life with the blessed angels and with the faithful ones of all ages, the sacred fellowship that binds together "the whole family in heaven and earth"—all are among the experiences of the hereafter. . . . With unutterable delight we shall enter into the joy and the wisdom of unfallen beings.[161]

It is the privilege of parents to take their children with them to the gates of the city of God, saying, "I have tried to instruct my children to love the Lord, to do His will, and to glorify Him." To such the gate will be thrown open, and parents and children will enter in.[162]

A PURIFIED CHURCH

Object of Heaven's Supreme Regard — October 1

DEAR TO THE HEART OF GOD

Can a woman forget her sucking child, that she should not have compassion on the son of her womb? yea, they may forget, yet will I not forget thee. Behold, I have graven thee upon the palms of my hands; thy walls are continually before me. Isa. 49:15, 16.

The church of Christ is very precious in His sight. It is the case which contains His jewels, the fold which encloses His flock.[1]

Christ "loved the church, and gave himself for it." Eph. 5:25. It is the purchase of His blood. The divine Son of God is seen walking amid the seven golden candlesticks. Jesus Himself supplies the oil to these burning lamps. He it is that kindles the flame. "In him was life; and the life was the light of men." John 1:4. No candlestick, no church, shines of itself. From Christ emanates all its light. . . . The Lord God Almighty and the Lamb are the light thereof.[2]

At times the Lord may seem to have forgotten the perils of His church, and the injury done her by her enemies. But God has not forgotten. Nothing in this world is so dear to the heart of God as His church. It is not His will that worldly policy shall corrupt her record. He does not leave His people to be overcome by Satan's temptations.[3]

God declares that even a mother may forget her child, "yet will I not forget thee." . . . God thinks of His children with the tenderest solicitude and keeps a book of remembrance before Him, that He may never forget the children of His care.

> "Every human tie may perish,
> Friend to friend unfaithful prove,
> Mothers cease their own to cherish,
> Heaven and earth at last remove;
> But no changes
> Can attend Jehovah's love."[4]

A CITY OF REFUGE

For the Lord hath chosen Zion: he hath desired it for his habitation. This is my rest for ever: here will I dwell; for I have desired it. Ps. 132:13, 14.

Through centuries of persecution, conflict, and darkness, God has sustained His church. Not one cloud has fallen upon it that He has not prepared for; not one opposing force has risen to counter-work His work, that He has not foreseen. All has taken place as He predicted. He has not left His church forsaken, but has traced in prophetic declarations what would occur, and that which His Spirit inspired the prophets to foretell has been brought about. All His purposes will be fulfilled. His law is linked with His throne, and no power of evil can destroy it. Truth is inspired and guarded by God; and it will triumph over all opposition.

During ages of spiritual darkness, the church of God has been as a city set on a hill. From age to age, through successive generations, the pure doctrines of heaven have been unfolding within its borders. . . . It is the theater of His grace, in which He delights to reveal His power to transform hearts.[5]

The church is God's fortress, His city of refuge, which He holds in a revolted world. Any betrayal of the church is treachery to Him who has bought mankind with the blood of His only-begotten Son. From the beginning, faithful souls have constituted the church on earth. In every age the Lord has had His watchmen, who have borne a faithful testimony to the generation in which they lived. These sentinels gave the message of warning; and when they were called to lay off their armor, others took up the work. God brought these witnesses into covenant relation with Himself, uniting the church on earth with the church in heaven. He has sent forth His angels to minister to His church, and the gates of hell have not been able to prevail against His people.[6]

God loves His children with infinite love. To Him the dearest object on earth is His church.[7]

279

GOD WILL TAKE CARE OF HIS CHURCH

When thou passest through the waters, I will be with thee; and through the rivers, they shall not overflow thee: when thou walkest through the fire, thou shalt not be burned; neither shall the flame kindle upon thee. Isa. 43:2.

God has a church upon the earth, who are His chosen people, who keep His commandments. He is leading, not stray offshoots, not one here and one there, but a people.[8]

There is no need to doubt, to be fearful that the work will not succeed. God is at the head of the work, and He will set everything in order. If matters need adjusting at the head of the work, God will attend to that, and work to right every wrong. Let us have faith that God is going to carry the noble ship which bears the people of God safely into port.

When I voyaged from Portland, Maine, to Boston, many years ago, a storm came upon us, and the great waves dashed us to and fro. The chandeliers fell, and the trunks were rolled from side to side, like balls. The passengers were frightened, and many were screaming, waiting in expectation of death.

After a while the pilot came on board. The captain stood near the pilot as he took the wheel, and expressed fear about the course in which the ship was directed. "Will you take the wheel?" asked the pilot. The captain was not ready to do that, for he knew that he lacked experience. Then some of the passengers grew uneasy, and said they feared the pilot would dash them upon the rocks. "Will you take the wheel?" asked the pilot; but they knew that they could not manage the wheel.

When you think that the work is in danger, pray, "Lord, stand at the wheel. Carry us through the perplexity. Bring us safely into port." Have we not reason to believe that the Lord will bring us through triumphantly? . . .

You cannot with your finite minds understand the working of all the providences of God. Let God take care of His own work.[9]

THE JUDGMENT-HOUR MESSAGE

And I saw another angel fly in the midst of heaven, having the everlasting gospel to preach unto them that dwell on the earth . . . , saying with a loud voice, Fear God, and give glory to him; for the hour of his judgment is come. Rev. 14:6, 7.

An upright, honesthearted farmer, who had been led to doubt the divine authority of the Scriptures, yet who sincerely desired to know the truth, was the man specially chosen of God to lead out in the proclamation of Christ's second coming.[10]

God sent His angel . . . to lead him to search the prophecies. . . . He saw that the inhabitants of the earth were living in the closing scenes of this world's history, yet they knew it not. . . . God called him to leave his farm. . . . With trembling, William Miller began to unfold to the people the mysteries of the kingdom of God, carrying his hearers down through the prophecies to the second advent.

Thousands were led to embrace the truth preached by William Miller, and servants of God were raised up in the spirit and power of Elijah to proclaim the message. . . . And as the solemn warning to flee from the wrath to come was sounded, many who were united with the churches received the healing message; they saw their backslidings, and with bitter tears of repentance and deep agony of soul, humbled themselves before God.[11]

The special blessing of the Lord, both in the conversion of sin ners and the revival of spiritual life among Christians, . . . testified that the message was of Heaven.[12]

With clearness the believers . . . gave the reasons why they expected their Lord in 1844. Their opposers could bring no arguments against the powerful reasons offered.[13]

The announcement, "The hour of his judgment is come," points to the closing work of Christ's ministration for the salvation of men. It heralds a truth which must be proclaimed until the Saviour's intercession shall cease, and He shall return to the earth to take His people to Himself.[14]

LIGHT THROUGH THE DARKNESS

Cast not away therefore your confidence, which hath great recompence of reward. For ye have need of patience, that, after ye have done the will of God, ye might receive the promise. Heb. 10:35, 36.

The subject of the sanctuary was the key which unlocked the mystery of the disappointment of 1844. It opened to view a complete system of truth, connected and harmonious, showing that God's hand had directed the great Advent Movement.[15]

Adventists then held that the earth, or some portion of it, was the sanctuary. They understood that the cleansing of the sanctuary was the purification of the earth by the fires of the last great day, and that this would take place at the Second Advent. Hence the conclusion that Christ would return to the earth in 1844.

But the appointed time had passed, and the Lord had not appeared. The believers knew that God's Word could not fail; their interpretation of the prophecy must be at fault; but where was the mistake? . . .

In their investigation they learned that there is no Scripture evidence sustaining the popular view that the earth is the sanctuary; but they found in the Bible a full explanation of the subject of the sanctuary, its nature, location, and services.[16]

Those who followed in the light of the prophetic word saw that, instead of coming to the earth at the termination of the 2300 days in 1844, Christ then entered the most holy place of the heavenly sanctuary, to perform the closing work of atonement, preparatory to His coming. . . .

Now in the holy of holies they again beheld Him, their compassionate high priest, soon to appear as their king and deliverer.[17]

Following Him by faith, they were led to see also the closing work of the church. They had a clearer understanding of the first and second angels' messages, and were prepared to receive and give to the world the solemn warning of the third angel of Revelation 14.[18]

BABYLON IS FALLEN

And there followed another angel, saying, Babylon is fallen, is fallen, that great city, because she made all nations drink of the wine of the wrath of her fornication. Rev. 14:8.

The second angel's message of Revelation 14 was first preached in the summer of 1844, and it then had a more direct application to the churches of the United States, where the warning of the judgment had been most widely proclaimed and most generally rejected, and where the declension in the churches had been most rapid. But the message of the second angel did not reach its complete fulfillment in 1844. The churches then experienced a moral fall, in consequence of their refusal of the light of the Advent message; but that fall was not complete. As they have continued to reject the special truths for this time, they have fallen lower and lower. Not yet, however, can it be said that "Babylon is fallen, . . . because she made *all nations* drink of the wine of the wrath of her fornication." She has not yet made all nations do this. . . . The work of apostasy has not yet reached its culmination.

The Bible declares that before the coming of the Lord, Satan will work "with *all* power and signs and lying wonders, and with all deceivableness of unrighteousness;" and they that "received not the love of the truth, that they might be saved," will be left to receive "strong delusion, that they should believe a lie." 2 Thess. 2:9-11. Not until this condition shall be reached, and the union of the church with the world shall be fully accomplished throughout Christendom, will the fall of Babylon be complete. The change is a progressive one, and the perfect fulfillment of Revelation 14:8 is yet future.

Notwithstanding the spiritual darkness and alienation from God that exist in the churches which constitute Babylon, the great body of Christ's true followers are still to be found in their communion. There are many of these who have never seen the special truths for this time.[19]

THE LAST SOLEMN WARNING

And the third angel followed them, saying with a loud voice, If any man worship the beast and his image, and receive his mark in his forehead, or in his hand, the same shall drink of the wine of the wrath of God, which is poured out without mixture into the cup of his indignation. Rev. 14.9, 10.

As the ministration of Jesus closed in the holy place, and He passed into the holiest, and stood before the ark containing the law of God, He sent another mighty angel with a third message to the world. . . . This message was designed to put the children of God upon their guard, by showing them the hour of temptation and anguish that was before them.[20]

This symbol [the beast], as most Protestants have believed, represents the Papacy. . . .

The "image to the beast" represents that form of apostate Protestantism which will be developed when the Protestant churches shall seek the aid of the civil power for the enforcement of their dogmas. . . .

As the sign of the authority of the Catholic Church, papist writers cite "the very act of changing the Sabbath into Sunday." . . . What then is the change of the Sabbath, but the sign, or mark, of the authority of the Roman Church—"the mark of the beast"?[21]

Sundaykeeping is not yet the mark of the beast, and will not be until the decree goes forth causing men to worship this idol sabbath.[22]

And it is not until the issue is . . . plainly set before the people, and they are brought to choose between the commandments of God and the commandments of men, that those who continue in transgression will receive "the mark of the beast."[23]

When God sends to men warnings so important that they are represented as proclaimed by holy angels flying in the midst of heaven, He requires every person endowed with reasoning powers to heed the message.[24]

WHO SHALL RECEIVE GOD'S SEAL?

And I saw another angel ascending from the east, having the seal of the living God: and he cried with a loud voice to the four angels, to whom it was given to hurt the earth and the sea, saying, Hurt not the earth, neither the sea, nor the trees, till we have sealed the servants of our God in their foreheads. Rev. 7:2, 3.

The seal of the living God will be placed upon those only who bear a likeness to Christ in character.[25]

As wax takes the impression of the seal, so the soul is to take the impression of the Spirit of God and retain the image of Christ.[26]

It is obedience to the principles of the commandments of God, that molds the character after the divine similitude.[27]

The seal of God's law is found in the fourth commandment. This only, of all the ten, brings to view both the name and the title of the Lawgiver. It declares Him to be the Creator of the heavens and the earth, and thus shows His claim to reverence and worship above all others. Aside from this precept, there is nothing in the Decalogue to show by whose authority the law is given.[28]

The Israelites placed over their doors a signature of blood, to show that they were God's property. So the children of God in this age will bear the signature God has appointed. They will place themselves in harmony with God's holy law. A mark is placed upon every one of God's people just as verily as a mark was placed over the doors of the Hebrew dwellings, to preserve the people from the general ruin. God declares, "I gave them my sabbaths, to be a sign between me and them, that they might know that I am the Lord that sanctify them." Eze. 20:12.[29]

Just as soon as the people of God are sealed in their foreheads— it is not any seal or mark that can be seen, but a settling into the truth, both intellectually and spiritually, so they cannot be moved— just as soon as God's people are sealed and prepared for the shaking, it will come. Indeed, it has begun already; the judgments of God are now upon the land, . . . that we may know what is coming.[30]

GOD'S IDEAL FOR HIS CHURCH

That he might present it to himself a glorious church, not having spot, or wrinkle, or any such thing; but that it should be holy and without blemish. Eph. 5:27.

The Lord God is a jealous God; yet He bears long with the sins and transgressions of His people in this generation. If the people of God had walked in His counsel, the work of God would have advanced, the messages of truth would have been borne to all people that dwell on the face of the whole earth. . . . But because the people are disobedient, unthankful, unholy, as were ancient Israel, time is prolonged that all may hear the last message of mercy proclaimed with a loud voice. The Lord's work has been hindered, the sealing time delayed. Many have not heard the truth. But the Lord will give them a chance to hear and be converted.[31]

What are you doing . . . in the great work of preparation? Those who are uniting with the world are receiving the worldly mold and preparing for the mark of the beast. Those who are distrustful of self, who are humbling themselves before God and purifying their souls by obeying the truth—these are receiving the heavenly mold and preparing for the seal of God in their foreheads. When the decree goes forth and the stamp is impressed, their character will remain pure and spotless for eternity. Now is the time to prepare. The seal of God will never be placed upon the forehead of an impure man or woman. It will never be placed upon the forehead of the ambitious, world-loving man or woman. It will never be placed upon the forehead of men or women of false tongues or deceitful hearts. All who receive the seal must be without spot before God—candidates for heaven.[32]

Every individual soul, if he would receive the seal of the living God, must hear the Word of the Lord, and do it with exactitude. There must be no such thing as haphazard religion if men would have a place in the family of God.[33]

Now is the time, while the four angels are holding the four winds, to make our calling and election sure.[34]

THE TRIAL OF THE CHURCH

Therefore rejoice, ye heavens, and ye that dwell in them. Woe to the inhabiters of the earth and of the sea! for the devil is come down unto you, having great wrath, because he knoweth that he hath but a short time. Rev. 12:12.

Those who keep the commandments of God and the faith of Jesus will feel the ire of the dragon and his hosts. Satan numbers the world as his subjects, he has gained control of the apostate churches; but here is a little company that are resisting his supremacy. If he could blot them from the earth, his triumph would be complete. As he influenced the heathen nations to destroy Israel, so in the near future he will stir up the wicked powers of earth to destroy the people of God. . . . Their only hope is in the mercy of God; their only defense will be prayer.[35]

The trying experiences that came to God's people in the days of Esther were not peculiar to that age alone. The revelator, looking down the ages to the close of time, has declared, "The dragon was wroth with the woman, and went to make war with the remnant of her seed, which keep the commandments of God, and have the testimony of Jesus Christ." Rev. 12:17. Some who today are living on the earth will see these words fulfilled.[36]

The wrath of Satan increases as his time grows short, and his work of deceit and destruction will reach its culmination in the time of trouble.

Fearful sights of a supernatural character will soon be revealed in the heavens, in token of the power of miracle-working demons. The spirits of devils will go forth to the kings of the earth and to the whole world, to fasten them in deception, and urge them on to unite with Satan in his last struggle against the government of heaven. By these agencies, rulers and subjects will be alike deceived.[37]

Those who are seeking for truth, that they may obey it in the love of it, are the ones who excite his (Satan's) malice and stir his ire. He can never weaken them while they keep close to Jesus.[38]

ELIJAH AND THE MODERN CHURCH

Behold, I will send you Elijah the prophet before the coming of the great and dreadful day of the Lord: and he shall turn the heart of the fathers to the children, and the heart of the children to their fathers, lest I come and smite the earth with a curse. Mal. 4:5, 6.

The closing words of Malachi are a prophecy regarding the work that should be done preparatory to the first and the second advent of Christ.[39]

Those who are to prepare the way for the second coming of Christ are represented by faithful Elijah, as John came in the spirit of Elijah to prepare the way for Christ's first advent.[40]

Our message must be as direct as was that of John. He rebuked kings for their iniquity. Notwithstanding the peril his life was in, he never allowed truth to languish on his lips. . . .

In this time of well-nigh universal apostasy, God calls upon His messengers to proclaim His law in the spirit and power of Elias. As John the Baptist, in preparing a people for Christ's first advent, called their attention to the Ten Commandments, so we are to give, with no uncertain sound, the message: "Fear God, and give glory to him; for the hour of his judgment is come." With the earnestness that characterized Elijah the prophet and John the Baptist, we are to strive to prepare the way for Christ's second advent.[41]

The hour of God's judgment has come, and upon the members of His church on earth rests the solemn responsibility of giving warning to those who are standing as it were on the very brink of eternal ruin.[42]

All can do something in the work. None will be pronounced guiltless before God unless they have worked earnestly and unselfishly for the salvation of souls.[43]

Your duty cannot be shifted upon another. No one but yourself can do your work. If you withhold your light, someone must be left in darkness through your neglect.[44]

The Lord has a place for everyone in His great plan.[45]

A SABBATHKEEPING CHURCH

And the dragon was wroth with the woman, and went to make war with the remnant of her seed, which keep the commandments of God, and have the testimony of Jesus Christ. Rev. 12:17.

In the twelfth chapter of Revelation is represented the great conflict between the obedient and the disobedient.[46]

The sign of obedience is the observance of the Sabbath of the fourth commandment.[47]

The Sabbath is a test to this generation. In obeying the fourth commandment in spirit and truth, men will obey all the precepts of the Decalogue. To fulfill this commandment one must love God supremely, and exercise love toward all the creatures that He has made.[48]

The time is coming when God's people will feel the hand of persecution because they keep holy the seventh day. . . . The man of sin, who thought to change times and laws, and who has always oppressed the people of God, will cause laws to be made enforcing the observance of the first day of the week. But God's people are to stand firm for Him.[49]

Let no one yield to temptation and become less fervent in his attachment to God's law because of the contempt placed upon it; for that is the very thing that should make us pray with all our heart, and soul, and voice, "It is time for thee, Lord, to work: for they have made void thy law." Ps. 119:126. Therefore, because of the universal contempt, I will not turn traitor when God will be most glorified and most honored by my loyalty. . . .

Shall Seventh-day Adventists relax their devotedness when all their capabilities and powers should be placed on the Lord's side; when an unflinching testimony, noble and uplifting, should come from their lips? "Therefore I love thy commandments above gold; yea, above fine gold." Ps. 119:127. When the law of God is most derided and brought into the most contempt, then it is time for every true follower of Christ . . . to stand unflinchingly for the faith once delivered to the saints.[50]

THE GIFTS OF THE SPIRIT

Now concerning spiritual gifts, brethren, I would not have you ignorant. . . . The manifestation of the Spirit is given to every man to profit withal. 1 Cor. 12:1, 7.

Paul declares that the gifts and manifestations of the Spirit were set in the church . . . "till we all come in the unity of the faith, and of the knowledge of the Son of God, unto a perfect man, unto the measure of the stature of the fulness of Christ." Eph. 4:13.[51]

All men do not receive the same gifts, but to every servant of the Master some gift of the Spirit is promised.[52]

The Lord has need of all kinds of skillful workmen. "He gave some, apostles; and some, prophets; and some, evangelists; and some, pastors and teachers; for the perfecting of the saints, for the work of the ministry, for the edifying of the body of Christ." Eph. 4:11, 12.[53]

In immediate connection with the scenes of the great day of God, the Lord by the prophet Joel has promised a special manifestation of His Spirit. Joel 2:28. This prophecy received a partial fulfillment in the outpouring of the Spirit on the day of Pentecost; but it will reach its full accomplishment in the manifestation of divine grace which will attend the closing work of the gospel. . . .

At this time the special endowment of divine grace and power is not less needful to the church than in apostolic days.[54]

God will today endow men and women with power from above, as He endowed those who on the day of Pentecost heard the word of salvation. At this very hour His Spirit and His grace are for all who need them and will take Him at His word.[55]

The gifts are already ours in Christ, but their actual possession depends upon our reception of the Spirit of God. . . .

If they are connected with Christ, if the gifts of the Spirit are theirs, the poorest and most ignorant of His disciples will have a power that will tell upon hearts. God makes them the channel for the outworking of the highest influence in the universe.[56]

A PROPHET'S VOICE IN OUR TIME

And it shall come to pass afterward, that I will pour out my spirit upon all flesh; and your sons and your daughters shall prophesy, your old men shall dream dreams, your young men shall see visions. Joel 2:28.

In His Word, God has committed to men the knowledge necessary for salvation. The Holy Scriptures are to be accepted as an authoritative, infallible revelation of His will. They are the standard of character, the revealer of doctrines, and the test of experience. . . .

Yet the fact that God has revealed His will to men through His Word, has not rendered needless the continued presence and guiding of the Holy Spirit. . . .

During the ages while the Scriptures of both the Old and the New Testament were being given, the Holy Spirit did not cease to communicate light to individual minds, apart from the revelations to be embodied in the Sacred Canon. . . . And mention is made of prophets in different ages, of whose utterances nothing is recorded. In like manner, after the close of the canon of Scripture, the Holy Spirit was still to continue its work, to enlighten, warn, and comfort the children of God.[57]

God has . . . promised to give visions in the "last days"; not for a new rule of faith, but for the comfort of His people, and to correct those who err from Bible truth.[58]

As the Spirit of God has opened to my mind the great truths of His Word, and the scenes of the past and the future, I have been bidden to make known to others that which has thus been revealed.[59]

There are those who will be glad to lull you to sleep in your carnal security, but I have a different work. My message is to alarm you, to bid you reform your lives and cease your rebellion against the God of the universe. Take the Word of God, and see if you are in harmony with it. Is your character such as will bear the search of the heavenly investigation?[60]

"FEAR THOU NOT . . . I AM WITH THEE"

Fear thou not; for I am with thee: be not dismayed; for I am thy God: I will strengthen thee; yea, I will help thee; yea, I will uphold thee with the right hand of my righteousness. Isa. 41:10.

It was not long after the passing of the time in 1844 that my first vision was given me. I was visiting a dear sister in Christ, whose heart was knit with mine; five of us, all women, were kneeling quietly at the family altar. While we were praying, the power of God came upon me as I had never felt it before. I seemed to be surrounded with light, and to be rising higher and higher from the earth. I turned to look for the Advent people in the world, but could not find them, when a voice said to me: "Look again, and look a little higher." At this I raised my eyes and saw a straight and narrow path, cast up high above the world. On this path the Advent people were traveling toward the city. . . .

I related this vision to the believers . . . , who had full confidence that it was from God. The Spirit of the Lord attended the testimony, and the solemnity of eternity rested upon us. An unspeakable awe filled me, that I, so young and feeble, should be chosen as the instrument by which God would give light to His people. . . .

In a second vision, which soon followed the first, I was shown the trials through which I must pass, and that it was my duty to go and relate to others what God had revealed to me. . . .

I prayed earnestly for several days, and far into the night, that this burden might be removed from me and laid upon someone more capable of bearing it. But the light of duty did not change.[61]

My Saviour declared me to be His messenger. "Your work," He instructed me, "is to bear My word. . . . My Spirit and My power shall be with you. . . . It is the Lord that giveth the messages."[62]

I do not write . . . expressing merely my own ideas. They are what God has opened before me in vision—the precious rays of light shining from the throne.[63]

THE TESTIMONY OF JESUS

And I fell at his feet to worship him. And he said unto me, See thou do it not: I am thy fellowservant, and of thy brethren that have the testimony of Jesus: worship God: for the testimony of Jesus is the spirit of prophecy. Rev. 19:10.

Above all other books, the Word of God must be our study, the great textbook, the basis of all education.[64]

The *Testimonies* are not to belittle the Word of God, but to exalt it and attract minds to it, that the beautiful simplicity of truth may impress all.[65]

I took the precious Bible and surrounded it with the several *Testimonies for the Church*. . . . Here, said I, the cases of nearly all are met. The sins they are to shun are pointed out. The counsel that they desire can be found here, given for other cases situated similarly to themselves. God has been pleased to give you line upon line and precept upon precept. But there are not many of you that really know what is contained in the *Testimonies*. You are not familiar with the Scriptures. If you had made God's Word your study, with a desire to reach the Bible standard and attain to Christian perfection, you would not have needed the *Testimonies*. . . .

The Lord designs to warn you, to reprove, to counsel, through the testimonies given, and to impress your minds with the importance of the truth of His Word. The written testimonies are not to give new light, but to impress vividly upon the heart the truths of inspiration already revealed. Man's duty to God and to his fellow man has been distinctly specified in God's Word; yet but few of you are obedient to the light given. Additional truth is not brought out; but God has through the *Testimonies* simplified the great truths already given and in His own chosen way brought them before the people to awaken and impress the mind with them, that all may be left without excuse.[66]

If we disregard them [the warnings in the *Testimonies*], what excuse can we offer?[67]

293

PROVE ALL THINGS

Quench not the Spirit. Despise not prophesyings. Prove all things; hold fast that which is good. 1 Thess. 5:19-21.

"In ancient times God spoke to men by the mouth of prophets and apostles. In these days He speaks to them by the testimonies of His Spirit. There was never a time when God instructed His people more earnestly than He instructs them now concerning His will and the course that He would have them pursue." [68]

The instruction that was given in the early days of the message is to be held as safe instruction to follow in these its closing days. [69]

Let the *Testimonies* be judged by their fruits. What is the spirit of their teaching? What has been the result of their influence? "All who desire to do so can acquaint themselves with the fruits of these visions. . . ."

"This work is of God, or it is not. God does nothing in partnership with Satan. My work . . . bears the stamp of God or the stamp of the enemy. There is no halfway work in the matter. The *Testimonies* are of the Spirit of God, or of the devil." [70]

The very last deception of Satan will be to make of none effect the testimony of the Spirit of God. "Where there is no vision, the people perish." Prov. 29:18. Satan will work ingeniously, in different ways and through different agencies, to unsettle the confidence of God's remnant people in the true testimony. He will bring in spurious visions, to mislead and mingle the false with the true, and so disgust people that they will regard everything that bears the name of visions, as a species of fanaticism; but honest souls, by contrasting false and true, will be enabled to distinguish between them. [71]

"When the *Testimonies,* which were once believed, are doubted and given up, Satan knows the deceived ones will not stop at this; and he redoubles his efforts till he launches them into open rebellion, which becomes incurable and ends in destruction." [72]

THE SERVANT OF MAN

Verily, verily, I say unto you, The servant is not greater than his lord; neither he that is sent greater than he that sent him. John 13:16.

In His life and lessons, Christ has given a perfect exemplification of the unselfish ministry which has its origin in God. God does not live for Himself. By creating the world, and by upholding all things, He is constantly ministering for others. . . . This ideal of ministry God has committed to His Son. Jesus was given to stand at the head of humanity, that by His example He might teach what it means to minister. His whole life was under a law of service. . . . Thus He lived the law of God, and by His example showed how we are to obey it.

Again and again Jesus had tried to establish this principle among His disciples. When James and John made their request for preeminence, He had said, "Whosoever will be great among you, let him be your minister." Matt. 20:26. In My kingdom the principle of preference and supremacy has no place. The only greatness is the greatness of humility. The only distinction is found in devotion to the service of others.[73]

The ordinance of feet washing is an ordinance of service. This is the lesson the Lord would have all learn and practice. When this ordinance is rightly celebrated, the children of God are brought into holy relationship with each other, to help and bless each other.

That His people might not be misled by the selfishness which dwells in the natural heart, and which strengthens by self-serving, Christ Himself set us an example of humility. He would not leave this great subject in man's charge. Of so much consequence did He regard it that He Himself, One equal with God, washed the feet of His disciples. . . . This ceremony means much to us. God would have us take in the whole scene, not only the single act of outward cleansing. This lesson does not merely refer to the one act. It is to reveal the great truth that Christ is an example of what we through His grace are to be in our intercourse with each other. It shows that the entire life should be one of humble, faithful ministry.[74]

JESUS' EXAMPLE IN HUMILITY

If I then, your Lord and Master, have washed your feet; ye also ought to wash one another's feet. For I have given you an example, that ye should do as I have done to you. John 13:14, 15.

There is in man a disposition to esteem himself more highly than his brother, to work for self, to seek the highest place; and often this results in evil surmisings and bitterness of spirit. The ordinance preceding the Lord's Supper is to clear away these misunderstandings, to bring man out of his selfishness, down from his stilts of self-exaltation, to the humility of heart that will lead him to serve his brother.[75]

The ordinance of feet washing most forcibly illustrates the necessity of true humility. While the disciples were contending for the highest place, in the promised kingdom, Christ girded Himself, and performed the office of a servant by washing the feet of those who called Him Lord.[76]

Reconciliation one with another is the work for which the ordinance of feet washing was instituted. . . . Whenever it is celebrated, Christ is present by His Holy Spirit. It is this Spirit that brings conviction to hearts.

As Christ celebrated this ordinance with His disciples, conviction came to the hearts of all save Judas. So we shall be convicted as Christ speaks to our hearts. The fountains of the soul will be broken up. The mind will be energized, and, springing into activity and life, will break down every barrier that has caused disunion and alienation. Sins that have been committed will appear with more distinctness than ever before; for the Holy Spirit will bring them to our remembrance.[77]

Having washed the disciples' feet, He [Jesus] said, "I have given you an example, that ye should do as I have done to you." . . . Christ was here instituting a religious service. By the act of our Lord this humiliating ceremony was made a consecrated ordinance. It was to be observed by the disciples, that they might ever keep in mind His lessons of humility and service.[78]

A PROOF OF LOYALTY

If ye know these things, happy are ye if ye do them. John 13:17.

This ordinance of feet washing was made a religious service. . . . It was given as something to test and prove the loyalty of the children of God. When modern Israel observes the sacramental ordinance, this ceremony should precede the partaking of the emblems of the Lord's death.

This ordinance was given for the benefit of Christ's disciples. And Christ meant all that He said when His lips uttered the words, "I have given you an example, that ye should do as I have done to you. . . . If ye know these things, happy are ye if ye do them." He designed by this to test the true state of the heart and mind of those who participated.[79]

Christ gave His disciples to understand that the washing of their feet did not cleanse away their sin, but that the cleansing of their heart was tested in this humble service. If the heart was cleansed, this act was all that was essential to reveal the fact. He had washed the feet of Judas; but He said, "Ye are not all clean." Judas brought a traitor's heart to this scene, and Christ revealed to all that He knew him to be the betrayer of his Lord, and that the washing of his feet was not an ordinance to cleanse the soul from its moral defilement.[80]

When believers assemble to celebrate the ordinances, there are present messengers unseen by human eyes. . . . Heavenly angels . . . are present. These unseen visitants are present on every such occasion. . . .

Christ by the Holy Spirit is there to set the seal to His own ordinance. He is there to convict and soften the heart. Not a look, not a thought of contrition, escapes His notice. For the repentant, brokenhearted one He is waiting. All things are ready for that soul's reception. He who washed the feet of Judas longs to wash every heart from the stain of sin. . . . All who come with their faith fixed upon Him will be greatly blessed.[81]

IN REMEMBRANCE OF ME

And he took bread, and gave thanks, and brake it, and gave unto them, saying, This is my body which is given for you: this do in remembrance of me. Luke 22:19.

In the last Passover our Lord observed with His disciples, He instituted the Lord's Supper in place of the Passover, to be observed in memory of His death.[82]

The national festival of the Jews was to pass away forever. The service which Christ established was to be observed by His followers in all lands and through all ages.[83]

God has not left it with men to say who shall present themselves on these occasions. For who can read the heart? Who can distinguish the tares from the wheat? "Let a man examine himself, and so let him eat of that bread, and drink of that cup." For "whosoever shall eat this bread, and drink this cup of the Lord, unworthily, shall be guilty of the body and blood of the Lord." "He that eateth and drinketh unworthily, eateth and drinketh damnation to himself, not discerning the Lord's body." 1 Cor. 11:28, 27, 29. . . .

In partaking with His disciples of the bread and wine, Christ pledged Himself to them as their Redeemer. . . . As we receive the bread and wine symbolizing Christ's broken body and spilled blood, we in imagination join in the scene of Communion in the upper chamber. We seem to be passing through the garden consecrated by the agony of Him who bore the sins of the world. We witness the struggle by which our reconciliation with God was obtained. Christ is set forth crucified among us.

Looking upon the crucified Redeemer, we more fully comprehend the magnitude and meaning of the sacrifice made by the Majesty of heaven. The plan of salvation is glorified before us, and the thought of Calvary awakens living and sacred emotions in our hearts. Praise to God and the Lamb will be in our hearts and on our lips; for pride and self-worship cannot flourish in the soul that keeps fresh in memory the scenes of Calvary.[84]

"THE NEW TESTAMENT IN MY BLOOD"

Likewise also the cup after supper, saying, This cup is the new testament in my blood, which is shed for you. Luke 22:20.

In partaking with His disciples of the bread and wine, Christ pledged Himself to them as their Redeemer. He committed to them the new covenant, by which all who receive Him become children of God, and joint heirs with Christ. By this covenant every blessing that Heaven could bestow for this life and the life to come was theirs. This covenant deed was to be ratified with the blood of Christ. And the administration of the sacrament was to keep before the disciples the infinite sacrifice made for each of them individually as a part of the great whole of fallen humanity.

But the communion service was not to be a season of sorrowing. This was not its purpose. As the Lord's disciples gather about His table, they are not to remember and lament their shortcomings. They are not to dwell upon their past religious experience, whether that experience has been elevating or depressing. They are not to recall the differences between them and their brethren. The preparatory service has embraced all this. The self-examination, the confession of sin, the reconciling of differences, has all been done. Now they come to meet with Christ. They are not to stand in the shadow of the cross, but in its saving light. They are to open the soul to the bright beams of the Sun of Righteousness. With hearts cleansed by Christ's most precious blood, in full consciousness of His presence, although unseen, they are to hear His words, "Peace I leave with you, my peace I give unto you: not as the world giveth, give I unto you." John 14:27.[85]

The atoning sacrifice is full and sufficient. It is the new covenant, sealed with His blood, which was shed for many for the remission of sins. This Christ declared at the Last Supper. In this cup there is to those who drink in faith, peace-making, soul-cleansing efficacy. It is the balm of Gilead, which God has provided to restore health and soundness to the sin-stricken soul.[86]

AS OFT AS YE EAT AND DRINK

For as often as ye eat this bread, and drink this cup, ye do shew the Lord's death till he come. 1 Cor. 11:26.

The salvation of men depends upon a continual application to their hearts of the cleansing blood of Christ. Therefore, the Lord's Supper was not to be observed only occasionally or yearly, but more frequently than the annual Passover. This solemn ordinance commemorates a far greater event than the deliverance of the children of Israel from Egypt. That deliverance was typical of the great atonement which Christ made by the sacrifice of His own life for the final deliverance of His people.[87]

This ordinance is not to be exclusive, as many would make it. Each must participate in it publicly, and thus bear witness: I accept Christ as my personal Saviour. He gave His life for me, that I might be rescued from death.[88]

The communion service points to Christ's second coming. It was designed to keep this hope vivid in the minds of the disciples. Whenever they met together to commemorate His death, they recounted how "he took the cup, and gave thanks, and gave it to them, saying, Drink ye all of it: for this is my blood of the new testament, which is shed for many for the remission of sins. But I say unto you, I will not drink henceforth of this fruit of the vine, until that day when I drink it new with you in my father's kingdom." Matt. 26:27-29. In their tribulation they found comfort in the hope of their Lord's return. Unspeakably precious to them was the thought, "As often as ye eat this bread, and drink this cup, ye do shew the Lord's death till he come." . . .

Christ has instituted this service that it may speak to our senses of the love of God. . . . There can be no union between our souls and God except through Christ. The union and love between brother and brother must be cemented and rendered eternal by the love of Jesus. And nothing less than the death of Christ could make His love efficacious for us. It is only because of His death that we can look with joy to His second coming. His sacrifice is the center of our hope.[89]

BAPTISM AND THE PASSION OF CHRIST

Buried with him in baptism, wherein also ye are risen with him through the faith of the operation of God, who hath raised him from the dead. Col. 2:12.

Christ rested in the tomb on the Sabbath day, and when holy beings of both heaven and earth were astir on the morning of the first day of the week, He rose from the grave to renew His work of teaching His disciples. But this fact does not consecrate the first day of the week, and make it a Sabbath. Jesus, prior to His death, established a memorial of the breaking of His body and the spilling of His blood for the sins of the world, in the ordinance of the Lord's Supper, saying, "For as often as ye eat this bread, and drink this cup, ye do shew the Lord's death till he come." 1 Cor. 11:26. And the repentant believer, who takes the steps required in conversion, commemorates in his baptism the death, burial, and resurrection of Christ. He goes down into the water in the likeness of Christ's death and burial, and he is raised out of the water in the likeness of His resurrection to live a new life in Christ Jesus.[90]

The angelic host were filled with amazement as they beheld the sufferings and death of the King of glory. But . . . it was no marvel to them that the Lord of life and glory . . . should break the bands of death, and walk forth from His prison house, a triumphant conqueror. Therefore, if either of these events should be commemorated by a day of rest, it is the crucifixion. But I saw that neither of these events was designed to alter or abrogate God's law; on the contrary, they give the strongest proof of its immutability. . . .

The Sabbath was instituted in Eden before the Fall, and was observed by Adam and Eve, and all the heavenly host. God rested on the seventh day, and blessed and hallowed it. I saw that the Sabbath never will be done away; but that the redeemed saints, and all the angelic host, will observe it in honor of the great Creator to all eternity.[91]

301

THE NAME THE LORD HAS GIVEN US

The Lord shall establish thee an holy people unto himself, . . . if thou shalt keep the commandments of the Lord thy God, and walk in his ways. And all people of the earth shall see that thou art called by the name of the Lord; and they shall be afraid of thee. Deut. 28:9, 10.

If we would come into possession of the heavenly inheritance, the glorious, eternal substance, we must be in covenant relation with God, and employ every faculty of our being to win souls to Christ. . . . God's people must be a peculiar, holy people, distinct in character and practice from the world, distinguished from all the religionists of the day. They must be patterns in personal piety and good works. There is higher, holier work for us to do than we have yet done. Christ has said, "My kingdom is not of this world." It has no principles that will meet the principles of the world. The Lord has set His church as a light in the world, to guide the world to heaven. It is to be a part of heaven on the earth, flashing divine light on the pathway of benighted souls.[92]

You are a spectacle to the world, to angels, and to men. God's people should now receive the light and diffuse it. They need not try to shine; if their hearts are enlightened by Christ, they cannot help shining. The brightness will appear; every true disciple will reveal Christ to the world as the sin-pardoning Saviour.[93]

We are Seventh-day Adventists. Are we ashamed of our name? We answer, No, no! We are not. It is the name the Lord has given us. It points out the truth that is to be the test of the churches. That this may be, we must look ever to Jesus.[94]

The name Seventh-day Adventist carries the true features of our faith in front, and will convict the inquiring mind. Like an arrow from the Lord's quiver, it will wound the transgressors of God's law, and will lead to repentance toward God and faith in our Lord Jesus Christ.[95]

There are many who are looking to you, to see what religion can do for you. If you are faithful in your God-given work, you will make right impressions, and will lead souls in the way of righteousness.[96]

BUILDERS, NOT DESTROYERS

And they that shall be of thee shall build the old waste places:
thou shalt raise up the foundations of many generations; and thou
shalt be called, The repairer of the breach, The restorer of paths to
dwell in. Isa. 58:12.

Has God no living church? He has a church, but it is the church
militant, not the church triumphant. We are sorry that there are de-
fective members. . . . While the Lord brings into the church those
who are truly converted, Satan at the same time brings persons who
are not converted into its fellowship. While Christ is sowing the
good seed, Satan is sowing the tares. There are two opposing influences continually exerted on the members of the church. One influence is working for the purification of the church, and the other for
the corrupting of the people of God. . . .

Although there are evils existing in the church, and will be until
the end of the world, the church in these last days is to be the light
of the world that is polluted and demoralized by sin. . . .

There is but one church in the world who are at the present time
standing in the breach, and making up the hedge, building up the
old waste places; and for any man to call the attention of the world
and other churches to this church, denouncing her as Babylon, is to
do a work in harmony with him who is the accuser of the brethren.
. . . The whole world is filled with hatred of those who proclaim the
binding claims of the law of God, and the church who are loyal to
Jehovah must engage in no ordinary conflict. . . . Those who have
any realization of what this warfare means, will not turn their
weapons against the church militant, but with all their powers will
wrestle with the people of God against the confederacy of evil.

Those who start up to proclaim a message on their own individual responsibility, who, while claiming to be taught and led of
God, still make it their special work to tear down that which God
has been for years building up, are not doing the will of God. Be it
known that these men are on the side of the great deceiver. Believe
them not.[97]

RICHES FOR THE LAODICEANS

I counsel thee to buy of me gold tried in the fire, that thou mayest be rich; and white raiment, that thou mayest be clothed, and that the shame of thy nakedness do not appear; and anoint thine eyes with eyesalve, that thou mayest see. Rev. 3:18.

The message to the Laodicean church is applicable to all who have had great light and many opportunities, and yet have not appreciated them.[98]

There are a large number of professing Christians who do not really follow Jesus. They do not bear the cross by proper self-denial and self-sacrifice. Although making a great profession of being earnest Christians, they weave into the fabric of their character so many of the threads of their own imperfections that the beautiful pattern is spoiled. Of them Christ says: "You boast of being rich and increased with supposed spiritual attainments. In reality you are neither cold nor hot, but are filled with vain conceit. Unless converted, you cannot be saved; for you would mar heaven with your unsanctified wisdom. I cannot endorse your spirit and your work. You do not act according to the divine Example. You are following a pattern merely of your own invention. Because you are lukewarm, I must spue you out of My mouth."[99]

The True Witness has said, "Buy of me gold tried in the fire, that thou mayest be rich; and white raiment, that thou mayest be clothed, and that the shame of thy nakedness do not appear."[100]

Jesus is going from door to door, standing in front of every soul temple, proclaiming, "I stand at the door, and knock." As a heavenly merchantman, He opens His treasures. . . . "Open your doors," says the great Merchantman, the possessor of spiritual riches, "and transact your business with Me. It is I, your Redeemer, who counsels you to buy of Me."[101]

The counsel of the True Witness is full of encouragement and comfort. The churches may yet obtain the gold of truth, faith, and love, and be rich in heavenly treasure.[102]

A PEOPLE WHO KEEP GOD'S LAW

Here is the patience of the saints: here are they that keep the commandments of God, and the faith of Jesus. Rev. 14:12.

We are standing upon the threshold of great and solemn events. Prophecies are fulfilling. Strange, eventful history is being recorded in the books of heaven. Everything in our world is in agitation. . . . Only a moment of time, as it were, yet remains. . . .

Satan is busily laying his plans for the last mighty conflict, when all will take sides. . . .

Men in their blindness boast of wonderful progress and enlightenment; but to the eye of Omniscience are revealed the inward guilt and depravity. The heavenly watchers see the earth filled with violence and crime. Wealth is obtained by every species of robbery, not robbery of men only, but of God. Men are using His means to gratify their selfishness. Everything they can grasp is made to minister to their greed. Avarice and sensuality prevail. Men cherish the attributes of the first great deceiver. They . . . have become imbued with his spirit.

But the cloud of judicial wrath hangs over them, containing the elements that destroyed Sodom. In his visions of things to come the prophet John beheld this scene. This demon worship was revealed to him, and it seemed to him as if the whole world were standing on the brink of perdition. But as he looked with intense interest he beheld the company of God's commandment-keeping people. They had upon their foreheads the seal of the living God, and he said: "Here is the patience of the saints: here are they that keep the commandments of God, and the faith of Jesus." [103]

This distinctive banner . . . [Rev. 14:12 quoted] is to be borne through the world to the close of probation. [104]

This is not a time to haul down our colors, to be ashamed of our faith. [105]

Every man is to stand in his lot and place, thinking, speaking, and acting in harmony with the Spirit of God. [106]

THE GOSPEL TO ALL THE WORLD

And this gospel of the kingdom shall be preached in all the world for a witness unto all nations; and then shall the end come. Matt. 24:14.

Not upon the ordained minister only rests the responsibility of going forth to fulfill this commission. Every one who has received Christ is called to work for the salvation of his fellow men. "The Spirit and the bride say, Come. And let him that heareth say, Come." Rev. 22:17. The charge to give this invitation includes the entire church. Every one who has heard the invitation is to echo the message from hill and valley, saying, "Come."

It is a fatal mistake to suppose that the work of soulsaving depends alone upon the ministry. The humble, consecrated believer upon whom the Master of the vineyard places a burden for souls, is to be given encouragement by the men upon whom the Lord has laid larger responsibilities. Those who stand as leaders in the church of God are to realize that the Saviour's commission is given to all who believe in His name. God will send forth into His vineyard many who have not been dedicated to the ministry by the laying on of hands.

Hundreds, yea, thousands, who have heard the message of salvation, are still idlers in the market place, when they might be engaged in some line of active service. To these Christ is saying, "Why stand ye here all the day idle?" and He adds, "Go ye also into the vineyard." Matt. 20:6, 7. Why is it that many more do not respond to the call? Is it because they think themselves excused in that they do not stand in the pulpit? Let them understand that there is a large work to be done outside the pulpit, by thousands of consecrated lay members.

Long has God waited for the spirit of service to take possession of the whole church, so that every one shall be working for Him according to his ability. When the members of the church of God do their appointed work in the needy fields at home and abroad, in fulfillment of the gospel commission, the whole world will soon be warned, and the Lord Jesus will return to this earth with power and great glory.[107]

LOVE BEGETS LOVE

He that spared not his own Son, but delivered him up for us all, how shall he not with him also freely give us all things? Rom. 8:32.

Those who are truly converted will . . . dispense, for the advancement of the work, the means He has placed in their hands. . . .

We are Christ's witnesses, and we are not to allow worldly interests and plans to absorb our time and attention. There are higher interests at stake. . . .

We plead for the money that is spent on needless things. . . . Waste not your money in purchasing unnecessary things. You may think these little sums do not amount to much, but many littles will make a great whole. Cut off every extravagant expenditure. Indulge in nothing that is simply for display. Your money means the salvation of souls. Let there be systematic giving on the part of all. Some may be unable to give a large sum, but all can lay aside each week something for the Master. Let the children act their part. Let parents teach their children to save their pennies to give to the Lord. The gospel ministry is to be supported by self-denial and sacrifice. . . .

Let not our church members complain because they are so often called upon to give. What is it that makes the frequent calls a necessity? Is it not the rapid increase of missionary enterprises? . . .

So long as there are souls to save, our interest in the work of soul-saving is to know no abating. The church cannot abridge her task without denying her Master. . . .

Love for lost souls brought Christ to Calvary's cross. Love for souls will lead us to self-denial and sacrifice, for the saving of that which is lost. And as Christ's followers give back to the Lord His own, they are accumulating treasure which will be theirs when they hear the words: "Well done, thou good and faithful servant: . . . enter thou into the joy of thy lord." Matt. 25:21. . . . The joy of seeing souls eternally saved will be the reward of all who follow in the steps of the Redeemer.[108]

BUILT ON THE ROCK

And I say also unto thee, That thou art Peter, and upon this rock I will build my church; and the gates of hell shall not prevail against it. Matt. 16:18.

The word Peter signifies a stone—a rolling stone. Peter was not the rock upon which the church was founded. The gates of hell did prevail against him when he denied his Lord with cursing and swearing. The church was built upon One against whom the gates of hell could not prevail. . . . The church is built upon Christ as its foundation; it is to obey Christ as its head.[109]

If Jesus had delegated any special authority to one of the disciples above the others, we should not find them so often contending as to who should be the greatest. They would have submitted to the wish of their Master, and honored the one whom He had chosen.

Instead of appointing one to be their head, Christ said to the disciples, "Be not ye called Rabbi;" "neither be ye called masters: for one is your Master, even Christ." Matt. 23:8, 10.

"The head of every man is Christ." God, who put all things under the Saviour's feet, "gave him to be the head over . . . the church." 1 Cor. 11:3; Eph. 1:22.[110]

In the presence of God, and all the heavenly intelligences, in the presence of the unseen army of hell, Christ founded His church upon the living Rock. That Rock is Himself—His own body, for us broken and bruised. Against the church built upon this foundation, the gates of hell shall not prevail. . . .

For six thousand years, faith has builded upon Christ. For six thousand years the floods and tempests of satanic wrath have beaten upon the Rock of our salvation. but it stands unmoved. . . .

The Rock of faith is the living presence of Christ in the church. Upon this the weakest may depend, and those who think themselves the strongest will prove to be the weakest, unless they make Christ their efficiency. . . . The Lord "is the Rock, his work is perfect." "Blessed are all they that put their trust in him." Deut. 32:4; Ps. 2:122.[111]

FACING THE FINAL TEST

FOR SUCH A TIME AS THIS!

For if thou altogether holdest thy peace at this time, then shall there enlargement and deliverance arise to the Jews from another place; but thou and thy father's house shall be destroyed: and who knoweth whether thou art come to the kingdom for such a time as this? Esther 4:14.

Whoever sees the repulsive character of sin, and in strength from above resists temptation, will assuredly arouse the wrath of Satan.[1]

The same spirit that in ages past led men to persecute the true church, will in the future lead to the pursuance of a similar course toward those who maintain their loyalty to God. . . .

The decree that will finally go forth against the remnant people of God will be very similar to that issued by Ahasuerus against the Jews. Today the enemies of the true church see in the little company keeping the Sabbath commandment, a Mordecai at the gate. . . .

Satan will arouse indignation against the minority who refuse to accept popular customs and traditions. . . . Persecuting rulers, ministers, and church members will conspire against them. With voice and pen, by boasts, threats, and ridicule, they will seek to overthrow their faith. . . . Not having a "Thus saith the Scriptures" to bring against the advocates of the Bible Sabbath, they will resort to oppressive enactments to supply the lack. To secure popularity and patronage, legislators will yield to the demand for Sunday laws. But those who fear God cannot accept an institution that violates a precept of the Decalogue. On this battlefield will be fought the last great conflict in the controversy between truth and error.[2]

The words of Mordecai to Esther may apply to the men and youth of today: "Who knoweth whether thou art come to the kingdom for such a time as this?"[3]

CRUEL POWER OF THE ENEMY

Submit yourselves therefore to God. Resist the devil, and he will flee from you. Draw nigh to God, and he will draw nigh to you. Cleanse your hands, ye sinners; and purify your hearts, ye double minded. James 4:7, 8.

There are multitudes today as truly under the power of evil spirits as was the demoniac of Capernaum. All who willfully depart from God's commandments are placing themselves under the control of Satan. Many a man tampers with evil, thinking that he can break away at pleasure; but he is lured on and on, until he finds himself controlled by a will stronger than his own. He cannot escape its mysterious power. Secret sin or master passion may hold him a captive as helpless as was the demoniac of Capernaum.[4]

Satan is the god of the world; his influence is to pervert the senses, control the human mind for evil, and drive his victims to violence and crime. He sows discord and darkens the intellect. The work of Christ is to break his power over the children of men. Yet how many in every department of life, in the home, in business transactions, and in the church, turn Jesus from their doors but let the hateful monster in.[5]

Satan's path is the broadest and the most deceptive. It is made to appear the most attractive, while it is hard, mystifying, and full of disappointment.[6]

He who feels his own danger is on the watch lest he shall grieve the Holy Spirit and then draw away from God because he knows that He is not pleased with his course of action. How much better and safer it is to draw nigh to God, that the pure light shining from His Word may heal the wounds that sin has made in the soul. The closer we are to God, the safer we are, for Satan hates and fears the presence of God.[7]

The subtlety of Satan will not decrease, but the wisdom given to men through a living connection with the Source of all light and divine knowledge will be proportionate to his arts and wiles.[8]

THE DEVICE OF WORLDLINESS

Lest Satan should get an advantage of us: for we are not ignorant of his devices. 2 Cor. 2:11.

Solomon says, "He that trusteth in his own heart is a fool" (Prov. 28:26); and there are hundreds of such to be found among professors of godliness. Says the apostle: "We are not ignorant of his [Satan's] devices." Oh, what art, what skill, what cunning, is exercised to lead the professed followers of Christ to a union with the world by seeking for happiness in the amusements of the world, under the delusion that some good is to be gained! And thus the unguarded walk right into the net, flattering themselves that there is no evil in the way. . . .

How can I endure the thought that most of the youth in this age will come short of everlasting life! Oh, that the sound of instrumental music might cease and they no more while away so much precious time in pleasing their own fancy. Oh, that they would devote less time to dress and vain conversation, and send forth their earnest, agonizing prayers to God for a sound experience. There is great necessity for close self-examination in the light of God's Word; let each one raise the inquiry: "Am I sound, or am I rotten at heart? Am I renewed in Christ, or am I still carnal at heart, with a new dress put on the outside?" Rein yourself up to the great tribunal, and in the light of God examine to see if there be any secret sin that you are cherishing, any idol that you have not sacrificed. Pray, yes, pray as you have never prayed before, that you may not be deluded by Satan's devices. . . . Surely the foundation of your hope of everlasting life cannot be laid too sure. . . . While those around us may be vain and engaged in pleasure seeking and folly, our conversation is in heaven, whence we look for the Saviour; the soul is reaching out after God for pardon and peace, for righteousness and true holiness.[9]

Expel sin from your hearts, for sin caused the death of the Son of God.[10]

Jesus died, dear youth, not to save you in your sins, but from your sins.[11]

TESTING THE VOICE OF THE SHEPHERDS

I am the good shepherd, and know my sheep, and am known of mine. John 10:14.

Every one of us will be sorely tempted; our faith will be tried to the uttermost.[12]

We need to be anchored in Christ, rooted and grounded in the faith. Satan works through agents. He selects those who have not been drinking of the living waters, whose souls are athirst for something new and strange, and who are ever ready to drink at any fountain that may present itself. Voices will be heard, saying, "Lo, here is Christ," or "Lo, there;" but we must believe them not. We have unmistakable evidence of the voice of the True Shepherd, and He is calling upon us to follow Him. He says, "I have kept my Father's commandments." He leads His sheep in the path of humble obedience to the law of God. . . .

"The voice of a stranger" is the voice of one who neither respects nor obeys God's holy, just, and good law. Many make great pretensions to holiness, and boast of the wonders they perform in healing the sick, when they do not regard this great standard of righteousness. But through whose power are these cures wrought? Are the eyes of either party opened to their transgressions of the law? and do they take their stand as humble, obedient children, ready to obey all of God's requirements? John testifies of the professed children of God: "He that saith, I know him, and keepeth not his commandments, is a liar, and the truth is not in him." 1 John 2:4. . . . If those through whom cures are performed, are disposed, on account of these manifestations, to excuse their neglect of the law of God, and continue in disobedience, though they have power to any and every extent, it does not follow that they have the great power of God. On the contrary, it is the miracle-working power of the great deceiver. . . . We must beware of the pretended holiness that permits transgression of the law of God. Those cannot be sanctified who trample that law under their feet, and judge themselves by a standard of their own devising.[13]

PRAYER FOR THE SICK

Confess your faults one to another, and pray one for another, that ye may be healed. The effectual fervent prayer of a righteous man availeth much. James 5:16.

Christ is the same compassionate physician now that He was during His earthly ministry. In Him there is healing balm for every disease.[14]

Why is it that men are so unwilling to trust Him who created man, and who can, by a touch, a word, a look, heal all manner of disease? Who is more worthy of our confidence than the One who has made so great a sacrifice for our redemption? Our Lord has given us definite instruction, through the apostle James, as to our duty in case of sickness. When human help fails, God will be the helper of His people. "Is any sick among you? let him call for the elders of the church; and let them pray over him, anointing him with oil in the name of the Lord: and the prayer of faith shall save the sick, and the Lord shall raise him up." James 5:14, 15.[15]

But the offering of such prayer is a most solemn act, and should not be entered upon without careful consideration. . . .

To those who desire prayer for their restoration to health, it should be made plain that the violation of God's law, either natural or spiritual, is sin, and that in order for them to receive His blessing, sin must be confessed and forsaken. . . .

We know that God hears us if we ask according to His will. But to press our petitions without a submissive spirit is not right; our prayers must take the form, not of command, but of intercession.

There are cases where God works decidedly by His divine power in the restoration of health. But not all the sick are healed. Many are laid away to sleep in Jesus. . . .

Our desires and interests should be lost in His will. These experiences that test faith are for our benefit. . . . Faith is strengthened by exercise. We must let patience have its perfect work, remembering that there are precious promises in the Scriptures for those who wait upon the Lord.[16]

THE SPIRIT OF TRUE HEROISM

For the Lord God will help me; therefore shall I not be confounded: therefore have I set my face like a flint, and I know that I shall not be ashamed. Isa. 50:7.

Strength of character consists of two things—power of will and power of self-control. Many youth mistake strong, uncontrolled passion for strength of character; but the truth is that he who is mastered by his passions is a weak man. The real greatness and nobility of the man is measured by the power of the feelings that he subdues, not by the power of the feelings that subdue him. The strongest man is he, who, while sensitive to abuse, will yet restrain passion and forgive his enemies. Such men are true heroes.[17]

The example of an energetic person is far reaching; he has an electric power over others. He meets obstacles in his work; but he has the push in him, and instead of allowing his way to be hedged up, he breaks down every barrier. . . .

There are thorns in every path. All who follow the Lord's leading must expect to meet with disappointments, crosses, and losses. But a spirit of true heroism will help them to overcome these. Many greatly magnify seeming difficulties, and then begin to pity themselves and give way to despondency. Such need to make an entire change in themselves. They need to discipline themselves to put forth exertion, and to overcome all childish feelings. They should determine that life shall not be spent in working at trifles. Let them resolve to accomplish something, and then do it. Many make good resolutions, but they are always going to do something and never get at it. About all their resolutions amount to is talk. . . .

Every one should have an aim, an object, in life. The loins of the mind should be girded up, and the thoughts be trained to keep to the point, as the compass to the pole. . . . Worthy purposes should be kept constantly in view, and every thought and act should tend to their accomplishment. Let there ever be a fixedness of purpose to carry out that which is undertaken.[18]

TESTING OUR METTLE

Beloved, think it not strange concerning the fiery trial which is to try you, as though some strange thing happened unto you: but rejoice, inasmuch as ye are partakers of Christ's sufferings, that, when his glory shall be revealed, ye may be glad also with exceeding joy. 1 Peter 4:12, 13.

The followers of Christ know little of the plots which Satan and his hosts are forming against them. But He who sitteth in the heavens will overrule all these devices for the accomplishment of His deep designs. The Lord permits His people to be subjected to the fiery ordeal of temptation, not because He takes pleasure in their distress and affliction, but because this process is essential to their final victory.[19]

By God's mighty cleaver of truth we have been taken from the quarry of the world and brought into the workshop of the Lord to be prepared for a place in His temple. In this work the hammer and chisel must act their part, and then comes the polishing. Rebel not under this process of grace. You may be a rough stone, on which much work must be done before you are prepared for the place God designs you to fill. You need not be surprised if with the hammer and the chisel of trial God cuts away your defects of character. He alone can accomplish this work. And be assured that He will not strike one useless blow.[20]

God has shown me that He gave His people a bitter cup to drink, to purify and cleanse them. . . . This bitter cup can be sweetened by patience, endurance, and prayer, and . . . it will have its designed effect upon the hearts of those who thus receive it, and God will be honored and glorified. It is no small thing to be a Christian and to be owned and approved of God.[21]

His grace is sufficient for all our trials; and although they are greater than ever before, yet if we trust wholly in God, we can overcome every temptation and through His grace come off victorious. . . . We must have on the whole armor of God and be ready at any moment for a conflict with the powers of darkness.[22]

SAFETY IN VIGILANCE

Therefore let us not sleep, as do others; but let us watch and be sober. 1 Thess. 5:6.

I was shown Satan as he once was, a happy, exalted angel. Then I was shown him as he now is. He still bears a kingly form. His features are still noble, for he is an angel fallen. But the expression of his countenance is full of anxiety, care, unhappiness, malice, hate, mischief, deceit, and every evil. That brow which was once so noble, I particularly noticed. His forehead commenced from his eyes to recede. I saw that he had so long bent himself to evil that every good quality was debased, and every evil trait was developed. His eyes were cunning, sly, and showed great penetration. His frame was large, but the flesh hung loosely about his hands and face. As I beheld him, his chin was resting upon his left hand. He appeared to be in deep thought. A smile was upon his countenance, which made me tremble, it was so full of evil and satanic slyness. This smile is the one he wears just before he makes sure of his victim, and as he fastens the victim in his snare, this smile grows horrible.[23]

The people of God must be prepared to withstand the wily foe. It is this resistance that Satan dreads. He knows better than we do the limit of his power and how easily he can be overcome if we resist and face him. Through divine strength the weakest saint is more than a match for him and all his angels, and if brought to the test he [the weakest saint] would be able to prove his superior power. Therefore Satan's step is noiseless, his movements stealthy, and his batteries masked. . . .

Man is Satan's captive and is naturally inclined to follow his suggestions and do his bidding. He has in himself no power to oppose effectual resistance to evil. It is only as Christ abides in him by living faith, influencing his desires and strengthening him with strength from above, that man may venture to face so terrible a foe. Every other means of defense is utterly vain.[24]

MYSTIC VOICES OF TODAY

And the soul that turneth after such as have familiar spirits, and after wizards, to go a whoring after them, I will even set my face against that soul, and will cut him off from among his people. Lev. 20:6.

The magicians of heathen times have their counterpart in the spiritualistic mediums, the clairvoyants, and the fortune tellers of today. The mystic voices that spoke at Endor and at Ephesus are still by their lying words misleading the children of men. Could the veil be lifted from before our eyes, we should see evil angels employing all their arts to deceive and to destroy.[25]

Spiritual beings sometimes appear to persons in the form of their deceased friends, and relate incidents connected with their lives, and perform acts which they performed while living. In this way they lead men to believe that their dead friends are angels, hovering over them, and communicating with them. Those who thus assume to be the spirits of the departed, are regarded with a certain idolatry, and with many their word has greater weight than the Word of God.[26]

I saw the rapidity with which this delusion [spiritualism] was spreading. A train of cars was shown me, going with the speed of lightning. The angel bade me look carefully. I fixed my eyes upon the train. It seemed that the whole world was on board. Then he showed me the conductor, a fair, stately person, whom all the passengers looked up to and reverenced. I was perplexed and asked my attending angel who it was. He said, "It is Satan. He is the conductor, in the form of an angel of light. He has taken the world captive. And they are all going with lightning speed to perdition."[27]

This delusion will spread, and we shall have to contend with it face to face; and unless we are prepared for it, we shall be ensnared and overcome.[28]

The people of God must be prepared to withstand these spirits with the Bible truth that the dead know not anything, and that they who thus appear are the spirits of devils.[29]

A DANGEROUS FORM OF MIND CURE

Beware lest any man spoil you through philosophy and vain deceit, after the tradition of men, after the rudiments of the world, and not after Christ. Col. 2:8.

There is . . . a form of mind cure that is one of the most effective agencies for evil. Through this so-called science, one mind is brought under the control of another so that the individuality of the weaker is merged in that of the stronger mind. One person acts out the will of another. . . .

But the so-called science is based upon false principles. It is foreign to the nature and spirit of Christ. It does not lead to Him who is life and salvation. The one who attracts minds to himself leads them to separate from the true Source of their strength.[30]

In these days when skepticism and infidelity so often appear in a scientific garb, we need to be guarded on every hand. Through this means our great adversary is deceiving thousands, and leading them captive according to his will. The advantage he takes of the sciences, sciences which pertain to the human mind, is tremendous. Here, serpentlike, he imperceptibly creeps in to corrupt the work of God. . . .

While it is believed that one human mind so wonderfully affects another, Satan, who is ready to press every advantage, insinuates himself, and works on the right hand and on the left. And while those who are devoted to these sciences, laud them to the heavens because of the great and good works which they affirm are wrought by them, they little know what a power for evil they are cherishing. . . . Mark the influence of these sciences, dear reader; for the conflict between Christ and Satan is not yet ended. . . .

Neglect of prayer leads men to rely on their own strength, and opens the door to temptation. In many cases the imagination is captivated by scientific research, and men are flattered through the consciousness of their own powers.[31]

Cut away from yourselves everything that savors of hypnotism, the science by which satanic agencies work.[32]

"SCIENCE FALSELY SO CALLED"

O Timothy, keep that which is committed to thy trust, avoiding profane and vain babblings, and oppositions of science falsely so called. 1 Tim. 6:20.

Human knowledge of both material and spiritual things is partial and imperfect; therefore many are unable to harmonize their views of science with Scripture statements. Many accept mere theories and speculations as scientific facts, and they think that God's Word is to be tested by the teachings of "science falsely so called." . . .

Men have endeavored to be wiser than their Creator; human philosophy has attempted to search out and explain mysteries which will never be revealed, through the eternal ages.[33]

To many, scientific research has become a curse. God has permitted a flood of light to be poured upon the world in discoveries in science and art; but even the greatest minds, if not guided by the Word of God in their research, become bewildered in their attempts to investigate the relations of science and revelation.[34]

God is the foundation of everything. All true science is in harmony with His works; all true education leads to obedience to His government. Science opens new wonders to our view; she soars high, and explores new depths; but she brings nothing from her research that conflicts with divine revelation.[35]

God is the author of science. . . . Rightly understood, science and the Written Word agree, and each sheds light on the other. Together they lead us to God, by teaching us something of the wise and beneficent laws through which He works.[36]

A knowledge of true science is power. . . . But while the knowledge of science is power, the knowledge that Jesus came in person to impart is still greater power. The science of salvation is the most important science to be learned in the preparatory school of earth. The wisdom of Solomon is desirable, but the wisdom of Christ is far more desirable and more essential.[37]

WOLVES IN SHEEP'S CLOTHING

For the time will come when they will not endure sound doctrine; but after their own lusts shall they heap to themselves teachers, having itching ears. 2 Tim. 4:3.

Rapidly are men ranging themselves under the banner they have chosen, restlessly waiting and watching the movements of their leaders. There are those who are watching and waiting and working for our Lord's appearing; while the other party are rapidly falling into line under the generalship of the first great apostate. They look for a God in humanity, and Satan personifies the one they seek. Multitudes will be so deluded through their rejection of truth, that they will accept the counterfeit. Humanity is hailed as God.[38]

Satan is ever on the alert to deceive and mislead. He is using every enchantment to allure men into the broad road of disobedience. He is working to confuse the senses with erroneous sentiments, and remove the landmarks by placing his false inscription on the signposts which God has established to point the right way.[39]

Teachers of falsehood will arise to draw you away from the narrow path and the strait gate. Beware of them; though concealed in sheep's clothing, inwardly they are ravening wolves. . . .

We are not bidden to prove them by their fair speeches and exalted professions. They are to be judged by the Word of God. . . . "Cease, my son, to hear the instruction that causeth to err from the words of knowledge." Prov. 19:27. What message do these teachers bring? Does it lead you to reverence and fear God? Does it lead you to manifest your love for Him by loyalty to His commandments? [40]

These false teachers, arising in the church and accounted true by many of their brethren in the faith, the apostle compared to "wells without water, clouds that are carried with a tempest; to whom the mist of darkness is reserved for ever." 2 Peter 2:17.[41]

Are our feet planted on the rock of God's immutable word? Are we prepared to stand firm in defense of the commandments of God and the faith of Jesus?[42]

ARE YOU IN DANGER?

Who is among you that feareth the Lord, that obeyeth the voice of his servant, that walketh in darkness, and hath no light? let him trust in the name of the Lord, and stay upon his God. Isa. 50:10.

There are many youth who walk in darkness, and have no light. . . .

The Lord's hand has been reached out in tenderest compassion and love; but they do not care to trust Him. They want to feel fully able to devise and plan for themselves. . . . The Lord marks out a way in which He would have them walk. He has lent them talents to be used for His glory, to do a certain work for the Master; but Satan says, "I will countermand the order of Christ. I will find another line of work for active brain and busy hands, whereby they shall serve me. I will eclipse eternal interests before this youth, and attract his mind by worldly interests. . . . I will bind him about with worldly allurements like the finest threads, whose power to bind will become at last like ropes of steel, and he shall be bound in my service. . . ."

Let the youth critically examine their motives, by prayer and searching of the Scriptures, and see if their own will and inclinations do not lead away from God's requirements. . . .

Young men and women, inquire in your business relations, Am I where God would have me to be? . . . Am I in the line of my duty? The blessing of God will be upon those who are just where God's plans would have them be. Has the Lord given you light that He requires you to do a certain work? If so, it is not safe for you to be disobedient. Let there be serious thinking on your part. Ask yourself, Am I serving my Master, Jesus Christ? Or am I pleasing myself, and failing to please God, and to bring honor to His holy name?

Do you want to change this order of things without delay? Would you choose to serve God? Then Jesus invites you to believe. . . . Grasp the hand of infinite power. Faith grows by exercise. Feed upon the promises; be content to rely on the simple promise of God's Word. Wait no longer in unbelief; for you are in danger of losing your souls.[43]

TAKING HOLD OF GOD'S STRENGTH

Let him take hold of my strength, that he may make peace with me; and he shall make peace with me. Isa. 27:5.

In the Revelation he [Satan] is declared to be the "accuser of our brethren," "which accused them before our God day and night." Rev. 12:10. The controversy is repeated over every soul that is rescued from the power of evil and whose name is registered in the Lamb's book of life. Never is one received from the family of Satan into the family of God without exciting the determined resistance of the wicked one. . . . He leads men into skepticism, causing them to lose confidence in God and to separate from His love; he tempts them to break His law, and then he claims them as his captives and contests the right of Christ to take them from him. He knows that those who seek God earnestly for pardon and grace will obtain it; therefore he presents their sins before them to discourage them. . . . By countless devices, the most subtle and the most cruel, he endeavors to secure their condemnation.

Man cannot meet these charges himself. In his sin-stained garments, confessing his guilt, he stands before God. But Jesus our Advocate presents an effectual plea in behalf of all who by repentance and faith have committed the keeping of their souls to Him. He pleads their cause and vanquishes their accuser by the mighty arguments of Calvary. His perfect obedience to God's law, even unto the death of the cross, has given Him all power in heaven and in earth, and He claims of His Father mercy and reconciliation for guilty man. . . .

Not one soul that in penitence and faith has claimed His protection will Christ permit to pass under the enemy's power. His word is pledged: "Let him take hold of my strength, that he may make peace with me; and he shall make peace with me." The promise . . . is made to all: "If thou wilt keep my charge, . . . I will give thee places to walk among these that stand by." Zech. 3:7. Angels of God will walk on either side of them, even in this world, and they will stand at last among the angels that surround the throne of God.[44]

SEEN AND UNSEEN FOES

Many shall be purified, and made white, and tried; but the wicked shall do wickedly: and none of the wicked shall understand; but the wise shall understand. Dan. 12:10.

The church must and will fight against seen and unseen foes. Satan's agencies in human form are on the ground. Men have confederated to oppose the Lord of hosts. These confederacies will continue until Christ shall leave His place of intercession before the mercy seat and shall put on the garments of vengeance. Satanic agencies are in every city, busily organizing into parties those opposed to the law of God. Professed saints and avowed unbelievers take their stand with these parties.[45]

God has revealed what is to take place in the last days, that His people may be prepared to stand against the tempest of opposition and wrath. Those who have been warned of the events before them are not to sit in calm expectation of the coming storm, comforting themselves that the Lord will shelter His faithful ones in the day of trouble. . . .

It is no time now* to allow our minds to be engrossed with things of minor importance. . . . The Sunday movement is now making its way in darkness. The leaders are concealing the true issue, and many who unite in the movement do not themselves see whither the undercurrent is tending. Its professions are mild and apparently Christian, but when it shall speak it will reveal the spirit of the dragon. It is our duty to do all in our power to avert the threatened danger.[46]

The time is coming when God's people will feel the hand of persecution because they keep holy the seventh day. . . . The man of sin, who thought to change times and laws, and who has always oppressed the people of God, will cause laws to be made enforcing the observance of the first day of the week. But God's people are to stand firm for Him. And the Lord will work in their behalf, showing plainly that He is the God of gods.[47]

---

* Written in 1885, at a time when religious liberty was threatened, much as it is today.

REVIVALS TRUE AND COUNTERFEIT

Ye shall know them by their fruits. Do men gather grapes of thorns, or figs of thistles? Even so every good tree bringeth forth good fruit; but a corrupt tree bringeth forth evil fruit. Matt. 7:16, 17.

Before the final visitation of God's judgments upon the earth, there will be, among the people of the Lord, such a revival of primitive godliness as has not been witnessed since apostolic times. The Spirit and power of God will be poured out upon His children. At that time many will separate themselves from those churches in which the love of this world has supplanted love for God and His Word. Many, both of ministers and people, will gladly accept those great truths which God has caused to be proclaimed at this time, to prepare a people for the Lord's second coming. The enemy of souls desires to hinder this work; and before the time for such a movement shall come, he will endeavor to prevent it, by introducing a counterfeit. In those churches which he can bring under his deceptive power, he will make it appear that God's special blessing is poured out; there will be manifest what is thought to be great religious interest. . . .

Wherever men neglect the testimony of the Bible, turning away from those plain, soul-testing truths which require self-denial and renunciation of the world, there we may be sure that God's blessing is not bestowed. . . .

A wrong conception of the character, the perpetuity, and the obligation of the divine law, has led to errors in relation to conversion and sanctification, and has resulted in lowering the standard of piety in the church. Here is to be found the secret of the lack of the Spirit and power of God in the revivals of our time. . . .

It is only as the law of God is restored to its rightful position that there can be a revival of primitive faith and godliness among His professed people. "Thus saith the Lord, Stand ye in the ways, and see, and ask for the old paths, where is the good way, and walk therein, and ye shall find rest for your souls." Jer. 6:16.[48]

TEARS AND CONFLICT

Serving the Lord with all humility of mind, and with many tears, and temptations, which befell me by the lying in wait of the Jews. Acts 20:19.

From the days of Adam to our own time, our great enemy has been exercising his power to oppress and destroy. He is now preparing for his last campaign against the church.[49]

The better to disguise his real character and purposes, he has caused himself to be so represented as to excite no stronger emotion than ridicule or contempt. He is well pleased to be painted as a ludicrous or loathsome object, misshapen, half animal and half human.[50]

If Satan was so cunning at first, what must he be now, after gaining an experience of many thousands of years? Yet God and holy angels, and all those who abide in obedience to all the Lord's will, are wiser than he.[51]

All who are actively engaged in the cause of God, seeking to unveil the deceptions of the evil one and to present Christ before the people, will be able to join in the testimony of Paul, in which he speaks of serving the Lord with all humility of mind, with many tears and temptations. . . .

The tempter has no power to control the will or to force the soul to sin. He may distress, but he cannot contaminate. He can cause agony, but not defilement.[52]

Satan cannot read our thoughts, but he can see our actions, hear our words; and from his long knowledge of the human family, he can shape his temptations to take advantage of our weak points of character. And how often do we let him into the secret of how he may obtain the victory over us. Oh, that we might control our words and actions![53]

Satan assailed Christ with his fiercest and most subtle temptations; but he was repulsed in every conflict. Those battles were fought in our behalf; those victories make it possible for us to conquer. Christ will give strength to all who seek it.[54]

PHYSICAL ATTACKS OF SATAN

And the Lord said unto Satan, Whence comest thou? Then Satan answered the Lord, and said, From going to and fro in the earth, and from walking up and down in it. Job 1:7.

Satan was "a murderer from the beginning." John 8:44.[55]

His temptations are leading multitudes to ruin. Intemperance dethrones reason; sensual indulgence, strife, and bloodshed follow. Satan delights in war; for it excites the worst passions of the soul, and then sweeps into eternity its victims steeped in vice and blood. It is his object to incite the nations to war against one another; for he can thus divert the minds of the people from the work of preparation to stand in the day of God.

Satan works through the elements also to garner his harvest of unprepared souls. He has studied the secrets of the laboratories of nature, and he uses all his power to control the elements as far as God allows. When he was suffered to afflict Job, how quickly flocks and herds, servants, houses, children, were swept away, one trouble succeeding another as in a moment. It is God that shields His creatures, and hedges them in from the power of the destroyer. . . .

In accidents and calamities by sea and by land, in great conflagrations, in fierce tornadoes and terrific hailstorms, in tempests, floods, cyclones, tidal waves, and earthquakes, in every place and in a thousand forms, Satan is exercising his power. He sweeps away the ripening harvest, and famine and distress follow. He imparts to the air a deadly taint, and thousands perish by the pestilence. These visitations are to become more and more frequent and disastrous.[56]

The power and malice of Satan and his host might justly alarm us, were it not that we may find shelter and deliverance in the superior power of our Redeemer. . . . Those who follow Christ are ever safe under His watchcare. Angels that excel in strength are sent from heaven to protect them. The wicked one cannot break through the guard which God has stationed about His people.[57]

IN THE HOUR OF DECISION

Multitudes, multitudes in the valley of decision: for the day of the Lord is near in the valley of decision. Joel 3:14.

The prophecy of Revelation 13 declares that the power represented by the beast with lamblike horns shall cause "the earth and them which dwell therein" to worship the Papacy—there symbolized by the beast "like unto a leopard." The beast with two horns is also to say "to them that dwell on the earth, that they should make an image to the beast;" and, furthermore, it is to command all, "both small and great, rich and poor, free and bond," to receive "the mark of the beast." . . .

The United States is the power represented by the beast with lamblike horns, and . . . this prophecy will be fulfilled when the United States shall enforce Sunday observance, which Rome claims as the special acknowledgment of her supremacy. But in this homage to Papacy the United States will not be alone. The influence of Rome in the countries that once acknowledged her dominion, is still far from being destroyed. And prophecy foretells a restoration of her power. "I saw one of his heads as it were wounded to death; and his deadly wound was healed: and all the world wondered after the beast." Rev. 13:3.

The infliction of the deadly wound points to the downfall of the Papacy in 1798. After this, says the prophet, "His deadly wound was healed: and all the world wondered after the beast." Paul states plainly that the man of sin will continue until the Second Advent. . . . In both the Old and the New World, the Papacy will receive homage in the honor paid to the Sunday institution, that rests solely upon the authority of the Roman Church. . . .

God's Word has given warning of the impending danger; let this be unheeded, and the Protestant world will learn what the purposes of Rome really are, only when it is too late to escape the snare.[58]

We should now seek a deep and living experience in the things of God. We have not a moment to lose.[59]

327

HARD DAYS OF PERSECUTION

Yea, and all that will live godly in Christ Jesus shall suffer persecution. 2 Tim. 3:12.

As the time comes for it [the third angel's message] to be given with greatest power, the Lord will work through humble instruments, leading the minds of those who consecrate themselves to His service. The laborers will be qualified rather by the unction of His Spirit than by the training of literary institutions. Men of faith and prayer will be constrained to go forth with holy zeal, declaring the words which God gives them. The sins of Babylon will be laid open. The fearful results of enforcing the observances of the church by civil authority, the inroads of spiritualism, the stealthy but rapid progress of the papal power—all will be unmasked. By these solemn warnings the people will be stirred. . . .

The power attending the message will only madden those who oppose it. . . . The church appeals to the strong arm of civil power, and in this work, papists and Protestants unite. As the movement for Sunday enforcement becomes more bold and decided, the law will be invoked against commandment keepers. . . .

The words of Paul will be literally fulfilled, "All that will live godly in Christ Jesus shall suffer persecution." As the defenders of truth refuse to honor the Sunday-sabbath, some of them will be thrust into prison, some will be exiled, some will be treated as slaves. To human wisdom, all this now seems impossible; but as the restraining Spirit of God shall be withdrawn from men: and they shall be under the control of Satan, . . . there will be strange developments. . . .

No man can serve God without enlisting against himself the opposition of the hosts of darkness.[60]

What was the strength of those who in the past have suffered persecution for Christ's sake? It was union with God, union with the Holy Spirit, union with Christ. It is this fellowship with the Saviour that will enable God's people to endure to the end.[61]

SAFETY ONLY IN OBEDIENCE

For the eyes of the Lord are over the righteous, and his ears are open unto their prayers: but the face of the Lord is against them that do evil. 1 Peter 3:12.

No man is safe for a day or an hour without prayer. Especially should we entreat the Lord for wisdom to understand His Word. Here are revealed the wiles of the tempter, and the means by which he may be successfully resisted. Satan is an expert in quoting Scripture, placing his own interpretation upon passages, by which he hopes to cause us to stumble. We should study the Bible with humility of heart, never losing sight of our dependence upon God. While we must constantly guard against the devices of Satan, we should pray in faith continually, "Lead us not into temptation."[62]

When Balaam, allured by the promise of rich rewards, practiced enchantments against Israel, and by sacrifices to the Lord sought to invoke a curse upon His people, the Spirit of God forbade the evil which he longed to pronounce, and Balaam was forced to exclaim: "How shall I curse, whom God hath not cursed?" Num. 23:8. . . .

The people of Israel were at this time loyal to God; and so long as they continued in obedience to His law, no power in earth or hell could prevail against them. But the curse which Balaam had not been permitted to pronounce against God's people, he finally succeeded in bringing upon them by seducing them into sin. When they transgressed God's commandments, then they separated themselves from Him, and they were left to feel the power of the destroyer.

Satan is well aware that the weakest soul who abides in Christ is more than a match for the hosts of darkness. . . . Only in humble reliance upon God, and obedience to all His commandments, can we be secure.[63]

Let none deceive themselves with the belief that God will pardon and bless them while they are trampling upon one of His requirements. The willful commission of a known sin silences the witnessing voice of the Spirit, and separates the soul from God.[64]

ANOTHER PENTECOST COMING!

And I will make them and the places round about my hill a blessing; and I will cause the shower to come down in his season; there shall be showers of blessing. Eze. 34:26.

The Lord has appointed the youth to be His helping hand.[65]

Many a lad of today, growing up as did Daniel in his Judean home, studying God's Word and His works, and learning the lessons of faithful service, will yet stand in legislative assemblies, in halls of justice, or in royal courts, as a witness for the King of kings. . . .

With such an army of workers as our youth, rightly trained, might furnish, how soon the message of a crucified, risen, and soon-coming Saviour might be carried to the whole world![66]

The great work of the gospel is not to close with less manifestation of the power of God than marked its opening. The prophecies which were fulfilled in the outpouring of the former rain at the opening of the gospel, are again to be fulfilled in the latter rain at its close. . . .

Servants of God, with their faces lighted up and shining with holy consecration, will hasten from place to place to proclaim the message from heaven. By thousands of voices, all over the earth, the warning will be given. Miracles will be wrought, the sick will be healed, and signs and wonders will follow the believers. Satan also works with lying wonders, even bringing down fire from heaven in the sight of men. Thus the inhabitants of the earth will be brought to take their stand.

The message will be carried not so much by argument as by the deep conviction of the Spirit of God. . . . The rays of light penetrate everywhere, the truth is seen in its clearness, and the honest children of God sever the bands which have held them.[67]

God has a work for His people to do for the world, and if they will work in harmony with one another and with heaven, He will demonstrate His power in their behalf as He did for His first disciples on the day of Pentecost.[68]

THE EARLY RAIN OF GOD'S SPIRIT

Be glad then, ye children of Zion, and rejoice in the Lord your God: for he hath given you the former rain moderately, and he will cause to come down for you the rain, the former rain, and the latter rain in the first month. Joel 2:23.

Under the figure of the early and the latter rain, that falls in Eastern lands at seedtime and harvest, the Hebrew prophets foretold the bestowal of spiritual grace in extraordinary measure upon God's church. The outpouring of the Spirit in the days of the apostles was the beginning of the early, or former, rain, and glorious was the result. . . . But near the close of earth's harvest, a special bestowal of spiritual grace is promised to prepare the church for the coming of the Son of man. This outpouring of the Spirit is likened to the falling of the latter rain.[69]

The latter rain, ripening earth's harvest, represents the spiritual grace that prepares the church for the coming of the Son of man. But unless the former rain has fallen, there will be no life; the green blade will not spring up. Unless the early showers have done their work, the latter rain can bring no seed to perfection. . . .

There must be a constant development of Christian virtue, a constant advancement in Christian experience. . . .

Every individual must realize his own necessity. The heart must be emptied of every defilement, and cleansed for the indwelling of the Spirit. It was by the confession and forsaking of sin, by earnest prayer and consecration of themselves to God, that the early disciples prepared for the outpouring of the Holy Spirit on the day of Pentecost. The same work, only in greater degree, must be done now. . . .

There must be no neglect of the grace represented by the former rain. Only those who are living up to the light they have, will receive greater light. Unless we are daily advancing in the exemplification of the active Christian virtues, we shall not recognize the manifestations of the Holy Spirit in the latter rain. It may be falling on hearts all around us, but we shall not discern or receive it.[70]

OUTPOURING OF THE LATTER RAIN

Ask ye of the Lord rain in the time of the latter rain; so the Lord shall make bright clouds, and give them showers of rain, to every one grass in the field. Zech. 10:1.

In the East the former rain falls at the sowing time. It is necessary in order that the seed may germinate. Under the influence of the fertilizing showers, the tender shoot springs up. The latter rain, falling near the close of the season, ripens the grain, and prepares it for the sickle. The Lord employs these operations of nature to represent the work of the Holy Spirit. . . .

While we cherish the blessing of the early rain, we must not, on the other hand, lose sight of the fact that without the latter rain, to fill out the ears and ripen the grain, the harvest will not be ready for the sickle, and the labor of the sower will have been in vain. Divine grace is needed at the beginning, divine grace at every step of advance, and divine grace alone can complete the work. . . .

Do not rest satisfied that in the ordinary course of the season, rain will fall. Ask for it. . . . We must seek His favors with the whole heart if the showers of grace are to come to us. We should improve every opportunity of placing ourselves in the channel of blessing. Christ has said, "Where two or three are gathered together in my name, there am I in the midst." Matt. 18:20. The convocations of the church, as in camp meetings, the assemblies of the home church, and all occasions where there is personal labor for souls, are God's appointed opportunities for giving the early and the latter rain. . . .

At every meeting we attend our prayers should ascend that at this very time, God will impart warmth and moisture to our souls. As we seek God for the Holy Spirit, it will work in us meekness, humbleness of mind, a conscious dependence upon God for the perfecting latter rain. If we pray for the blessing in faith, we shall receive it as God has promised.[71]

The Holy Spirit will come to all who are begging for the bread of life to give to their neighbors.[72]

LOUD CRY OF THE THIRD ANGEL

And after these things I saw another angel come down from heaven, having great power; and the earth was lightened with his glory. Rev. 18:1.

I saw another mighty angel commissioned to descend to the earth, to unite his voice with the third angel, and give power and force to his message.[73]

A work of worldwide extent and unwonted power is here foretold.[74]

Great power and glory were imparted to the angel, and as he descended, the earth was lightened with his glory. The light which attended this angel penetrated everywhere, as he cried mightily, with a strong voice, "Babylon the great is fallen, is fallen, and is become the habitation of devils, and the hold of every foul spirit, and a cage of every unclean and hateful bird." Rev. 18:2. The message of the fall of Babylon, as given by the second angel, is repeated, with the additional mention of the corruptions which have been entering the churches since 1844. The work of this angel comes in at the right time to join in the last great work of the third angel's message as it swells to a loud cry. And the people of God are thus prepared to stand in the hour of temptation, which they are soon to meet. I saw a great light resting upon them, and they united to fearlessly proclaim the third angel's message.

Angels were sent to aid the mighty angel from heaven, and I heard voices which seemed to sound everywhere, "Come out of her, my people." . . . The glory of God rested upon the patient, waiting saints, and they fearlessly gave the last solemn warning, proclaiming the fall of Babylon and calling upon God's people to come out of her that they might escape her fearful doom.

The light that was shed upon the waiting ones penetrated everywhere, and those in the churches who had any light, who had not heard and rejected the three messages, obeyed the call and left the fallen churches.[75]

UNMOVED IN THE SHAKING TIME

Wherefore we receiving a kingdom which cannot be moved, let us have grace, whereby we may serve God acceptably with reverence and godly fear. Heb. 12:28.

Those who accept Christ, and in their first confidence say, I am saved, are in danger of trusting to themselves. They lose sight of their own weakness and their constant need of divine strength. They are unprepared for Satan's devices. . . . Our only safety is in constant distrust of self, and dependence on Christ.[76]

Man's great danger is in being self-deceived, indulging self-sufficiency, and thus separating from God, the source of his strength.[77]

The Lord is coming very soon, and we are entering into scenes of calamity.[78]

We need not say: The perils of the last days are soon to come upon us. Already they have come. We need now the sword of the Lord to cut to the very soul and marrow of fleshly lusts, appetites, and passions.

Minds that have been given up to loose thought need to change. . . . The thoughts must be centered upon God. Now is the time to put forth earnest effort to overcome the natural tendencies of the carnal heart.[79]

As the storm approaches, a large class who have professed faith in the third angel's message, but have not been sanctified through obedience to the truth, abandon their position, and join the ranks of the opposition. By uniting with the world and partaking of its spirit, they have come to view matters in nearly the same light; and when the test is brought, they are prepared to choose the easy, popular side. Men of talent and pleasing address, who once rejoiced in the truth, employ their powers to deceive and mislead souls. They become the most bitter enemies of their former brethren.[80]

We are in the shaking time, the time when everything that can be shaken will be shaken. The Lord will not excuse those who know the truth if they do not in word and deed obey His commands.[81]

PREPARE TO MEET THY GOD

Therefore thus will I do unto thee, O Israel: and because I will do this unto thee, prepare to meet thy God, O Israel. Amos 4:12.

Many do not realize what they must be in order to live in the sight of the Lord without a high priest in the sanctuary through the time of trouble. Those who receive the seal of the living God and are protected in the time of trouble must reflect the image of Jesus fully.[82]

Their robes must be spotless, their characters must be purified from sin by the blood of sprinkling. Through the grace of God and their own diligent effort, they must be conquerors in the battle with evil. While the investigative judgment is going forward in heaven, while the sins of penitent believers are being removed from the sanctuary, there is to be a special work of purification, of putting away of sin, among God's people upon earth.[83]

I saw that many were neglecting the preparation so needful and were looking to the time of "refreshing" and the "latter rain" to fit them to stand in the day of the Lord and to live in His sight. Oh, how many I saw in the time of trouble without a shelter! They had neglected the needful preparation; therefore they could not receive the refreshing that all must have to fit them to live in the sight of a holy God.

Those who refuse to be hewed by the prophets and fail to purify their souls in obeying the whole truth, and who are willing to believe that their condition is far better than it really is, will come up to the time of the falling of the plagues, and then see that they needed to be hewed and squared for the building. . . .

I saw that none could share the "refreshing" unless they obtain the victory over every besetment, over pride, selfishness, love of the world, and over every wrong word and action. We should, therefore, be drawing nearer and nearer to the Lord and be earnestly seeking that preparation necessary to enable us to stand in the battle in the day of the Lord. Let all remember that God is holy and that none but holy beings can ever dwell in His presence.[84]

THE STRANGE ACT OF GOD

For the Lord shall rise up as in mount Perazim, he shall be wroth as in the valley of Gibeon, that he may do his work, his strange work; and bring to pass his act, his strange act. Isa. 28:21.

With unerring accuracy the Infinite One still keeps an account with all nations. While His mercy is tendered, with calls to repentance, this account will remain open; but when the figures reach a certain amount which God has fixed, the ministry of His wrath commences. The account is closed. Divine patience ceases. There is no more pleading of mercy in their behalf.

The prophet, looking down the ages, had this time presented before his vision. The nations of this age have been the recipients of unprecedented mercies. . . . But increased pride, covetousness, idolatry, contempt of God, and base ingratitude are written against them. They are fast closing up their account with God. . . .

The crisis is fast approaching. The rapidly swelling figures show that the time for God's visitation has about come.[85]

To our merciful God the act of punishment is a strange act. "As I live, saith the Lord God, I have no pleasure in the death of the wicked." Eze. 33:11. . . . Yet He will "by no means clear the guilty." "The Lord is slow to anger, and great in power, and will not at all acquit the wicked." Ex. 34:6, 7; Nahum 1:3. By terrible things in righteousness He will vindicate the authority of His downtrodden law. The severity of the retribution awaiting the transgressor may be judged by the Lord's reluctance to execute justice. The nation with which He bears long, and which He will not smite until it has filled up the measure of its iniquity in God's account, will finally drink the cup of wrath unmixed with mercy.[86]

After God has done all that could be done to save men, if they still show by their lives that they slight offered mercy, death will be their portion; and it will be a dreadful death, for they will have to feel the agony that Christ felt upon the cross. They will then realize what they have lost—eternal life and the immortal inheritance.[87]

"A TIME OF TROUBLE"

And at that time shall Michael stand up, the great prince which standeth for the children of thy people: and there shall be a time of trouble, such as never was since there was a nation even to that same time: and at that time thy people shall be delivered, every one that shall be found written in the book. Dan. 12:1.

When the third angel's message closes, mercy no longer pleads for the guilty inhabitants of the earth. The people of God have accomplished their work. . . . The final test has been brought upon the world, and all who have proved themselves loyal to the divine precepts have received "the seal of the living God." Then Jesus ceases His intercession in the sanctuary above. He lifts His hands, and with a loud voice says, "It is done." . . .

God's long-suffering has ended. The world has rejected His mercy, despised His love, and trampled upon His law. The wicked have passed the boundary of their probation; the Spirit of God, persistently resisted, has been at last withdrawn. Unsheltered by divine grace, they have no protection from the wicked one. Satan will then plunge the inhabitants of the earth into one great, final trouble. . . . The people of God will then be plunged into those scenes of affliction and distress described by the prophet as the time of Jacob's trouble.[88]

Those only who have clean hands and pure hearts will stand in that trying time. Now is the time for the law of God to be in our minds, foreheads, and written in our hearts. . . . What leisure time we have should be spent in searching the Bible, which is to judge us in the last day. . . .

Let the commandments of God and the testimony of Jesus Christ be in your minds continually and let them crowd out worldly thoughts and cares. When you lie down and when you rise up, let them be your meditation. Live and act wholly in reference to the coming of the Son of man. The sealing time is very short, and will soon be over. Now is the time, while the four angels are holding the four winds, to make our calling and election sure.[89]

SEVEN LAST PLAGUES

When the poor and needy seek water, and there is none, and their tongue faileth for thirst, I the Lord will hear them, I the God of Israel will not forsake them. Isa. 41:17.

When Christ ceases His intercession in the sanctuary, the unmingled wrath threatened against those who worship the beast and his image and receive his mark, will be poured out. The plagues upon Egypt when God was about to deliver Israel, were similar in character to those more terrible and extensive judgments which are to fall upon the world just before the final deliverance of God's people. Says the revelator, in describing those terrific scourges: "There fell a noisome and grievous sore upon the men which had the mark of the beast, and upon them which worshipped his image." The sea "became as the blood of a dead man: and every living soul died in the sea." And "the rivers and fountains of waters . . . became blood." Rev. 16:2-4. Terrible as these inflictions are, God's justice stands fully vindicated. . . .

These plagues are not universal, or the inhabitants of the earth would be wholly cut off. Yet they will be the most awful scourges that have ever been known to mortals. All the judgments upon men, prior to the close of probation, have been mingled with mercy. The pleading blood of Christ has shielded the sinner from receiving the full measure of his guilt; but in the final judgment, wrath is poured out unmixed with mercy.[90]

It is impossible to give any idea of the experience of the people of God who will be alive on the earth when past woes and celestial glory will be blended. They will walk in the light proceeding from the throne of God. By the means of the angels there will be constant communication between heaven and earth.[91]

The people of God will not be free from suffering; but . . . they will not be left to perish. . . . While the wicked are dying from hunger and pestilence, angels will shield the righteous, and supply their wants. To him that "walketh righteously" is the promise. "Bread shall be given him; his waters shall be sure." Isa. 33:16.[92]

THE TRIUMPH OF THE GOSPEL

The Prophecies Are Fulfilling!   *December 1*

AS IT WAS IN NOAH'S DAY

And as it was in the days of Noe, so shall it be also in the days of the Son of man. Luke 17:26.

From age to age the warnings which God has sent to the world by His servants have been received with . . . incredulity and unbelief. When the iniquity of the antediluvians moved Him to bring a flood of waters upon the earth, He first made known to them His purpose, that they might have opportunity to turn from their evil ways. For a hundred and twenty years was sounded in their ears the warning to repent, lest the wrath of God be manifested in their destruction. But the message seemed to them an idle tale, and they believed it not. . . .

Scoffers pointed to the things of nature—to the unvarying succession of the seasons, to the blue skies that had never poured out rain, to the green fields refreshed by the soft dews of night—and they cried out, "Doth he not speak parables?" In contempt they declared the preacher of righteousness to be a wild enthusiast; and they went on, more eager in their pursuit of pleasure, more intent upon their evil ways, than ever before. But their unbelief did not hinder the predicted event. . . .

Christ declares that there will exist similar unbelief concerning His second coming. As the people of Noah's day "knew not until the flood came, and took them all away; so," in the words of our Saviour, "shall also the coming of the Son of man be." Matt. 24:39.[1]

Solemnly there come to us down through the centuries the warning words of our Lord from the Mount of Olives: "Take heed to yourselves, lest at any time your hearts be overcharged with surfeiting, and drunkenness, and cares of this life, and so that day come upon you unawares." "Watch ye therefore, and pray always, that ye may be accounted worthy to escape all these things. . . ."[2]

THE CRIERS OF PEACE

For when they shall say, Peace and safety; then sudden destruction cometh upon them, as travail upon a woman with child; and they shall not escape. 1 Thess. 5:3.

The evil servant says in his heart, "My lord delayeth his coming." He does not say that Christ will not come. He does not scoff at the idea of His second coming. But in his heart and by his actions and words he declares that the Lord's coming is delayed. He banishes from the minds of others the conviction that the Lord is coming quickly. His influence leads men to presumptuous, careless delay. They are confirmed in their worldliness and stupor. Earthly passions, corrupt thoughts, take possession of the mind. The evil servant eats and drinks with the drunken, unites with the world in pleasure seeking. He smites his fellow servants, accusing and condemning those who are faithful to their Master. . . .

The advent of Christ will surprise the false teachers. They are saying, "Peace and safety." Like the priests and teachers before the fall of Jerusalem, they look for the church to enjoy earthly prosperity and glory. The signs of the times they interpret as foreshadowing this. But what saith the Word of Inspiration? "Sudden destruction cometh upon them." . . .

Men are putting afar off the coming of the Lord. They laugh at warnings. The proud boast is made, "All things continue as they were from the beginning." "To morrow shall be as this day and much more abundant." 2 Peter 3:4; Isa. 56:12. We will go deeper into pleasure loving. But Christ says, "Behold, I come as a thief." Rev. 16:15. At the very time when the world is asking in scorn, "Where is the promise of his coming?" the signs are fulfilling. While they cry, "Peace and safety," sudden destruction is coming. When the scorner, the rejecter of truth, has become presumptuous; when the routine of work in the various money-making lines is carried on without regard to principle; when the student is eagerly seeking knowledge of everything but his Bible, Christ comes as a thief.[3]

340

SIGNS BY LAND AND SEA

The great day of the Lord is near, it is near, and hasteth greatly, even the voice of the day of the Lord: the mighty man shall cry there bitterly. Zeph. 1:14.

We are near the close of time. I have been shown that the re-tributive judgments of God are already in the land. The Lord has given us warning of the events about to take place. . . . Those who are drinking from the same fountain of blessing will draw nearer to-gether. Truth dwelling in the hearts of believers will lead to blessed and happy assimilation. Thus will be answered the prayer of Christ that His disciples might be one even as He is one with the Father. For this oneness every truly converted heart will be striving.

With the ungodly there will be a deceptive harmony that but partially conceals a perpetual discord. In their opposition to the will and the truth of God they are united, while on every other point they are rent with hatred, emulation, jealousy, and deadly strife.[4]

The Lord is removing His restrictions from the earth, and soon there will be death and destruction, increasing crime, and cruel, evil working against the rich who have exalted themselves against the poor. Those who are without God's protection will find no safety in any place or position. Human agents are being trained and are using their inventive power to put into operation the most powerful machinery to wound and to kill.[5]

The Lord will arise to shake terribly the earth. We shall see troubles on all sides. Thousands of ships will be hurled into the depths of the sea. Navies will go down, and human lives will be sacrificed by millions. Fires will break out unexpectedly, and no human effort will be able to quench them. The palaces of earth will be swept away in the fury of the flames. Disasters by rail will become more and more frequent; confusion, collision, and death without a moment's warning will occur on the great lines of travel. The end is near, probation is closing. Oh, let us seek God while He may be found, call upon Him while He is near![6]

SIGNS IN THE HEAVENS

Now learn a parable of the fig tree; when his branch is yet tender, and putteth forth leaves, ye know that summer is nigh: so likewise ye, when ye shall see all these things, know that it is near, even at the doors. Matt. 24:32, 33.

The Saviour gives signs of His coming, and more than this, He fixes the time when the first of these signs shall appear: "Immediately after the tribulation of those days shall the sun be darkened, and the moon shall not give her light, and the stars shall fall from heaven, and the powers of the heavens shall be shaken: and then shall appear the sign of the Son of man in heaven: and then shall all the tribes of the earth mourn, and they shall see the Son of man coming in the clouds of heaven with power and great glory. . . ." Matt. 24:29-31.

At the close of the great papal persecution, Christ declared, the sun should be darkened, and the moon should not give her light. Next, the stars should fall from heaven.[7]

Thus was displayed the last of those signs of His coming, concerning which Jesus bade His disciples, "When ye shall see all these things, know that it is near, even at the doors." After these signs, John beheld, as the great event next impending, the heavens departing as a scroll, while the earth quaked, mountains and islands removed out of their places, and the wicked in terror sought to flee from the presence of the Son of man.[8]

But the day and the hour of His coming Christ has not revealed. . . . The exact time of the second coming of the Son of man is God's mystery.[9]

A little longer, and we shall see the King in His beauty. A little longer, and He will wipe all tears from our eyes. A little longer, and He will present us "faultless before the presence of his glory with exceeding joy." Jude 24. Wherefore, when He gave the signs of His coming He said, "When these things begin to come to pass, then look up, and lift up your heads; for your redemption draweth nigh." Luke 21:28.[10]

STUDY THE PROPHECIES

Blessed is he that readeth, and they that hear the words of this prophecy, and keep those things which are written herein: for the time is at hand. Rev. 1:3.

From the rise and fall of nations as made plain in the books of Daniel and the Revelation, we need to learn how worthless is mere outward and worldly glory. Babylon, with all its power and magnificence, the like of which our world has never since beheld—power and magnificence which to the people of that day seemed so stable and enduring—how completely has it passed away! As "the flower of the grass," it has perished. So perished the Medo-persian kingdom, and the kingdoms of Grecia and Rome. And so perishes all that has not God for its foundation. Only that which is bound up with His purpose, and expresses His character, can endure. His principles are the only steadfast things our world knows.[11]

When the books of Daniel and Revelation are better understood, believers will have an entirely different religious experience. They will be given such glimpses of the open gates of heaven that heart and mind will be impressed with the character that all must develop in order to realize the blessedness which is to be the reward of the pure in heart. The Lord will bless all who will seek humbly and meekly to understand that which is revealed in the Revelation. This book contains so much that is large with immortality and full of glory that all who read and search it earnestly receive the blessing to those "that hear the words of this prophecy, and keep those things which are written therein." One thing will certainly be understood from the study of Revelation—that the connection between God and His people is close and decided.[12]

Let us give more time to the study of the Bible. We do not understand the Word as we should. The book of Revelation opens with an injunction to us to understand the instruction that it contains. . . . When we . . . understand what this book means to us, there will be seen among us a great revival.[13]

THE CROWNING ACT OF DECEPTION

And Jesus answered and said unto them, Take heed that no man deceive you. For many shall come in my name, saying, I am Christ; and shall deceive many. Matt. 24:4, 5.

As the crowning act in the great drama of deception, Satan himself will personate Christ. The church has long professed to look to the Saviour's advent as the consummation of her hopes. Now the great deceiver will make it appear that Christ has come. In different parts of the earth, Satan will manifest himself among men as a majestic being of dazzling brightness, resembling the description of the Son of God given by John in the Revelation. . . . The shout of triumph rings out upon the air, "Christ has come! Christ has come!" The people prostrate themselves in adoration before him. . . . In gentle, compassionate tones he presents some of the same gracious, heavenly truths which the Saviour uttered; he heals the diseases of the people, and then, in his assumed character of Christ, he claims to have changed the Sabbath to Sunday, and commands all to hallow the day which he has blessed. . . .

Only those who have been diligent students of the Scriptures, and who have received the love of the truth, will be shielded from the powerful delusion that takes the world captive.[14]

The Saviour has warned His people . . . , and has clearly foretold the manner of His second coming. "There shall arise false Christs. . . . Wherefore if they shall say unto you, Behold, he is in the desert; go not forth: behold, he is in the secret chambers; believe it not. For as the lightning cometh out of the east, and shineth even unto the west; so shall also the coming of the Son of man be." Matt. 24:24-27. This coming, there is no possibility of counterfeiting. It will be universally known—witnessed by the whole world. . . .

Are the people of God now so firmly established upon His Word that they would not yield to the evidence of their senses? Would they, in such a crisis, cling to the Bible, and the Bible only?[15]

SAVED FROM VIOLENCE

Ye shall have a song, as in the night when a holy solemnity is kept, and gladness of heart, as when one goeth with a pipe to come into the mountain of the Lord, to the mighty One of Israel. Isa. 30:29.

When the protection of human laws shall be withdrawn from those who honor the law of God, there will be, in different lands, a simultaneous movement for their destruction. . . .

The people of God—some in prison cells, some hidden in solitary retreats in the forests and the mountains—still plead for divine protection, while in every quarter companies of armed men, urged on by hosts of evil angels, are preparing for the work of death. . . .

With shouts of triumph, jeering, and imprecation, throngs of evil men are about to rush upon their prey, when, lo, a dense blackness, deeper than the darkness of the night, falls upon the earth. Then a rainbow . . . spans the heavens, and seems to encircle each praying company. . . .

By the people of God a voice, clear and melodious, is heard, saying, "Look up," and lifting their eyes to the heavens, they behold the bow of promise. The black, angry clouds that covered the firmament are parted, and like Stephen they look up steadfastly into heaven, and see the glory of God, and the Son of man seated upon His throne. In His divine form they discern the marks of His humiliation; and from His lips they hear the request, presented before His Father and the holy angels, "I will that they also, whom thou hast given me, be with me where I am." John 17:24. Again a voice, musical and triumphant, is heard, saying: "They come! they come! holy, harmless, and undefiled. They have kept the word of My patience; they shall walk among the angels;" and the pale, quivering lips of those who have held fast their faith, utter a shout of victory. It is at midnight that God manifests His power for the deliverance of His people. The sun appears, shining in its strength. Signs and wonders follow in quick succession. The wicked look with terror and amazement upon the scene, while the righteous behold with solemn joy the tokens of their deliverance.[16]

"EVEN SO, COME, LORD JESUS"

Looking for that blessed hope, and the glorious appearing of the great God and our Saviour Jesus Christ. Titus 2:13.

One of the most solemn and yet most glorious truths revealed in the Bible is that of Christ's second coming, to complete the great work of redemption. . . . The doctrine of the Second Advent is the very keynote of the Sacred Scriptures. . . .

The coming of the Lord has been in all ages the hope of His true followers.[17]

The patriarch Job in the night of his affliction exclaimed with unshaken trust: "I know that my redeemer liveth, and that he shall stand at the latter day upon the earth: . . . in my flesh shall I see God: whom I shall see for myself, and mine eyes shall behold, and not another." Job 19:25-27. . . .

The Saviour's parting promise upon Olivet, that He would come again, lighted up the future for His disciples, filling their hearts with joy and hope that sorrow could not quench nor trials dim. Amid suffering and persecution, the "appearing of the great God and our Saviour Jesus Christ" was the "blessed hope." . . .

On rocky Patmos the beloved disciple hears the promise, "Surely I come quickly," and his longing response voices the prayer of the church in all her pilgrimage, "Even so, come, Lord Jesus." Rev. 22:20. . . .

"This aged world is not far from its end," said Melanchthon. Calvin bids Christians "not to hesitate, ardently desiring the day of Christ's coming as of all events most auspicious." . . . "The thoughts of the coming of the Lord," said Baxter, "are most sweet and joyful to me." "It is the work of faith and the character of His saints to love His appearing." . . .

"This is the day that all believers should long, and hope, and wait for, as being the accomplishment of all the work of their redemption, and all the desires and endeavors of their souls." "Hasten, O Lord, this blessed day!"[18]

THE KING APPEARS IN PERSON

Our God shall come, and shall not keep silence: a fire shall devour before him, and it shall be very tempestuous round about him. He shall call to the heavens from above, and to the earth, that he may judge his people. Ps. 50:3, 4.

The King of kings descends upon the cloud, wrapped in flaming fire. The heavens are rolled together as a scroll, the earth trembles before Him, and every mountain and island is moved out of its place.[19]

Jesus rides forth as a mighty conqueror. Not now a "man of sorrows," to drink the bitter cup of shame and woe, He comes, victor in heaven and earth, to judge the living and the dead. "Faithful and True," "in righteousness he doth judge and make war." And "the armies which were in heaven followed him." Rev. 19:11, 14. With anthems of celestial melody the holy angels, a vast, unnumbered throng, attend Him on His way. The firmament seems filled with radiant forms—"ten thousand times ten thousand, and thousands of thousands." No human pen can portray the scene; no mortal mind is adequate to conceive its splendor. "His glory covered the heavens, and the earth was full of his praise. And his brightness was as the light." Hab. 3:3, 4. As the living cloud comes still nearer, every eye beholds the Prince of life. No crown of thorns now mars that sacred head, but a diadem of glory rests on His holy brow. His countenance outshines the dazzling brightness of the noonday sun. "And he hath on his vesture and on his thigh a name written, King of kings, and Lord of lords." Rev. 19:16.

Before His presence, "all faces are turned into paleness;" upon the rejecters of God's mercy falls the terror of eternal despair. "The heart melteth, and the knees smite together, . . . and the faces of them all gather blackness." Jer. 30:6; Nahum 2:10. The righteous cry with trembling, "Who shall be able to stand?" The angels' song is hushed, and there is a period of awful silence. Then the voice of Jesus is heard, saying, "My grace is sufficient for you."[20]

PREPARATION FOR TRANSLATION

By faith Enoch was translated that he should not see death; and was not found, because God had translated him: for before his translation he had this testimony, that he pleased God. Heb. 11:5.

We are living in an evil age. The perils of the last days thicken around us. Because iniquity abounds, the love of many waxes cold. Enoch walked with God three hundred years. Now the shortness of time seems to be urged as a motive to seek righteousness. Should it be necessary that the terrors of the day of God be held before us in order to compel us to right action? Enoch's case is before us. Hundreds of years he walked with God. He lived in a corrupt age, when moral pollution was teeming all around him; yet he trained his mind to devotion, to love purity. His conversation was upon heavenly things. He educated his mind to run in this channel, and he bore the impress of the divine. His countenance was lighted up with the light which shineth in the face of Jesus.

Enoch had temptations as well as we. He was surrounded with society no more friendly to righteousness than is that which surrounds us. The atmosphere he breathed was tainted with sin and corruption, the same as ours; yet he lived a life of holiness. He was unsullied with the prevailing sins of the age in which he lived. So may we remain pure and uncorrupted. He was a representative of the saints who live amid the perils and corruptions of the last days. For his faithful obedience to God he was translated. So, also, the faithful, who are alive and remain, will be translated. They will be removed from a sinful and corrupt world to the pure joys of heaven. The course of God's people should be upward and onward to victory.[21]

Enoch's translation to heaven just before the destruction of the world by a flood represents the translation of all the living righteous from the earth previous to its destruction by fire. The saints will be glorified in the presence of those who have hated them for their loyal obedience to God's righteous commandments.[22]

THIS SAME JESUS SHALL RETURN

Ye men of Galilee, why stand ye gazing up into heaven? this same Jesus, which is taken up from you into heaven, shall so come in like manner as ye have seen him go into heaven. Acts 1:11.

The angels who lingered upon Olivet after Christ's ascension, repeated to the disciples the promise of His return: "This same Jesus, which is taken up from you into heaven, shall so come in like manner as ye have seen him go into heaven." [23]

Precious, indeed, was this promise to those sorrowing disciples, that they should again see Jesus, who was greatly beloved by them all. Precious also is this promise to every true follower of Christ. None who truly love Jesus will be sorry that He is coming again. . . .

Jesus is coming! But not to listen to the woes of mankind, and to hear the guilty sinner confess his sins, and to speak pardon to him; for every one's case will then be decided for life or death. Those who have lived in sin will remain sinners forever. Those who have confessed their sins to Jesus in the sanctuary, have made Him their friend and have loved His appearing, will have pardon written for all their sins. . . .

Jesus is coming as He ascended into heaven, only with additional splendor. He is coming with the glory of His Father, and all the holy angels with Him, to escort Him on His way. Instead of the cruel crown of thorns to pierce His holy temples, a crown of dazzling glory will deck His sacred brow. . . . He will not wear a plain seamless coat, but a garment whiter than snow—of dazzling brightness. Jesus is coming! But not to reign as a temporal prince. He will raise the righteous dead, change the living saints to a glorious immortality, and, with the saints, take the kingdom under the whole heaven. . . .

Dear young reader, seek a thorough preparation to meet Jesus, that when He appears you may exclaim with joy, "Lo, this is our God; we have waited for him, and he will save us." Isa. 25:9. Eternal life will then be yours, and you will be a partaker with Christ of His glory, ever to hear His glorious approving voice and behold His lovely person. [24]

A CROWN FOR EVERY SAINT

Blessed is the man that endureth temptation: for when he is tried, he shall receive the crown of life, which the Lord hath promised to them that love him. James 1:12.

I saw a very great number of angels bring from the city glorious crowns—a crown for every saint, with his name written thereon. As Jesus called for the crowns, angels presented them to Him, and with His own right hand the lovely Jesus placed the crowns on the heads of the saints. In the same manner the angels brought the harps, and Jesus presented them also to the saints. The commanding angels first struck the note, and then every voice was raised in grateful, happy praise, and every hand skillfully swept over the strings of the harp, sending forth melodious music in rich and perfect strains. . . .

Within the city there was everything to feast the eye. Rich glory they beheld everywhere. Then Jesus looked upon His redeemed saints; their countenances were radiant with glory; and as He fixed His loving eyes upon them, He said, with His rich, musical voice, "I behold the travail of My soul, and am satisfied. This rich glory is yours to enjoy eternally. Your sorrows are ended. There shall be no more death, neither sorrow nor crying, neither shall there be any more pain." . . .

I then saw Jesus leading His people to the tree of life. . . . Upon the tree of life was most beautiful fruit, of which the saints could partake freely, in the city was a most glorious throne, from which proceeded a pure river of water of life, clear as crystal. On each side of this river was the tree of life, and on the banks of the river were other beautiful trees bearing fruit. . . .

Language is altogether too feeble to attempt a description of heaven. As the scene rises before me, I am lost in amazement. Carried away with the surpassing splendor and excellent glory, I lay down the pen, and exclaim, "Oh, what love! what wondrous love!" The most exalted language fails to describe the glory of heaven or the matchless depths of a Saviour's love.[25]

THE CAPTIVITY OF SATAN

And I saw an angel come down from heaven, having the key of the bottomless pit and a great chain in his hand. And he laid hold on the dragon, that old serpent, which is the Devil, and Satan, and bound him a thousand years. Rev. 20:1, 2.

At the coming of Christ the wicked are blotted from the face of the whole earth—consumed with the spirit of His mouth, and destroyed by the brightness of His glory. Christ takes His people to the city of God, and the earth is emptied of its inhabitants. . . .

The whole earth appears like a desolate wilderness. The ruins of cities and villages destroyed by the earthquake, uprooted trees, ragged rocks thrown out by the sea or torn out of the earth itself, are scattered over its surface, while vast caverns mark the spot where the mountains have been rent from their foundations.[26]

Here is to be the home of Satan with his evil angels for a thousand years. Here he will be confined, to wander up and down over the broken surface of the earth and see the effects of his rebellion against God's law. For a thousand years he can enjoy the fruit of the curse which he has caused. Limited alone to the earth, he will not have the privilege of ranging to other planets, to tempt and annoy those who have not fallen. During this time, Satan suffers extremely. Since his fall his evil traits have been in constant exercise. But he is then to be deprived of his power, and left to reflect upon the part which he has acted since his fall, and to look forward with trembling and terror to the dreadful future, when he must suffer for all the evil that he has done and be punished for all the sins that he has caused to be committed.

I heard shouts of triumph from the angels and from the redeemed saints, which sounded like ten thousand musical instruments, because they were to be no more annoyed and tempted by Satan and because the inhabitants of other worlds were delivered from his presence and his temptations.[27]

WE SHALL JUDGE ANGELS

Know ye not that we shall judge angels? how much more things that pertain to this life? 1 Cor. 6:3.

During the thousand years between the first and the second resurrection, the judgment of the wicked takes place. . . . At this time the righteous reign as kings and priests unto God. John in the Revelation says: "I saw thrones, and they sat upon them, and judgment was given unto them." "They shall be priests of God and of Christ, and shall reign with him a thousand years." Rev. 20:4, 6. It is at this time that, as foretold by Paul, "the saints shall judge the world." 1 Cor. 6:2. In union with Christ they judge the wicked, comparing their acts with the statute book, the Bible, and deciding every case according to the deeds done in the body. Then the portion which the wicked must suffer is meted out, according to their works; and it is recorded against their names in the book of death.

Satan also and evil angels are judged by Christ and His people. Says Paul, "Know ye not that we shall judge angels?" And Jude declares that "the angels which kept not their first estate, but left their own habitation, he hath reserved in everlasting chains under darkness unto the judgment of the great day." Jude 6.

At the close of the thousand years the second resurrection will take place. Then the wicked will be raised from the dead, and appear before God for the execution of "the judgment written." Thus the revelator, after describing the resurrection of the righteous, says, "The rest of the dead lived not again until the thousand years were finished." Rev. 20:5. And Isaiah declares, concerning the wicked, "They shall be gathered together, as prisoners are gathered in the pit, and shall be shut up in the prison, and after many days shall they be visited." Isa. 24:22.[28]

The penalty for breaking the law of God is proportionate to the price paid to redeem its transgressors. What unutterable bliss is prepared for those who will be saved through Christ, and what depths of woe for those who despise and reject His great salvation![29]

DESCENT OF THE NEW JERUSALEM

And he carried me away in the spirit to a great and high mountain, and shewed me that great city, the holy Jerusalem, descending out of heaven from God. Rev. 21:10.

At the close of the thousand years, Christ again returns to the earth. He is accompanied by the host of the redeemed, and attended by a retinue of angels. As He descends in terrific majesty, He bids the wicked dead arise to receive their doom. They come forth, a mighty host, numberless as the sands of the sea. What a contrast to those who were raised at the first resurrection! The righteous were clothed with immortal youth and beauty. The wicked bear the traces of disease and death.

Every eye in that vast multitude is turned to behold the glory of the Son of God. With one voice the wicked hosts exclaim, "Blessed is He that cometh in the name of the Lord!" It is not love to Jesus that inspires this utterance. The force of truth urges the words from unwilling lips. As the wicked went into their graves, so they come forth, with the same enmity to Christ, and the same spirit of rebellion. They are to have no new probation, in which to remedy the defects of their past lives. Nothing would be gained by this. A lifetime of transgressions has not softened their hearts. A second probation, were it given them, would be occupied as was the first, in evading the requirements of God and exciting rebellion against Him.

Christ descends upon the Mount of Olives, whence, after His resurrection, He ascended, and where angels repeated the promise of His return. Says the prophet: "The Lord my God shall come, and all the saints with thee." "And his feet shall stand in that day upon the mount of Olives, which is before Jerusalem on the east, and the mount of Olives shall cleave in the midst thereof, . . . and there shall be a very great valley." Zech. 14:5, 4. . . . As the New Jerusalem, in its dazzling splendor, comes down out of heaven, it rests upon the place purified and made ready to receive it, and Christ, with His people and the angels, enters the holy city.[30]

THE SUPREMACY OF JESUS

That at the name of Jesus every knee should bow, of things in heaven, and things in earth, and things under the earth; and that every tongue should confess that Jesus Christ is Lord, to the glory of God the Father. Phil. 2:10, 11.

In the presence of the assembled inhabitants of earth and heaven the final coronation of the Son of God takes place. And now, invested with supreme majesty and power, the King of kings pronounces sentence upon the rebels against His government, and executes justice upon those who have transgressed His law and oppressed His people. . . . As . . . the eye of Jesus looks upon the wicked, they are conscious of every sin which they have ever committed. . . .

Above the throne is revealed the cross; and like a panoramic view appear the scenes of Adam's temptation and fall, and the successive steps in the great plan of redemption. . . .

The whole wicked world stand arraigned at the bar of God, on the charge of high treason against the government of heaven. They have none to plead their cause; they are without excuse; and the sentence of eternal death is pronounced against them. It is now evident to all that the wages of sin is not noble independence and eternal life, but slavery, ruin, and death. . . . Satan seems paralyzed as he beholds the glory and majesty of Christ. He who was once a covering cherub remembers whence he has fallen. A shining seraph, "son of the morning;" how changed, how degraded! . . .

Satan sees that his voluntary rebellion has unfitted him for heaven. He has trained his powers to war against God; the purity, peace, and harmony of heaven would be to him supreme torture. His accusations against the mercy and justice of God are now silenced. The reproach which he has endeavored to cast upon Jehovah rests wholly upon himself. And now Satan bows down, and confesses the justice of his sentence. . . . With all the facts of the great controversy in view, the whole universe, both loyal and rebellious, with one accord declare, "Just and true are thy ways, thou King of saints." Rev. 15:3.[31]

354

SATAN AND THE WICKED DESTROYED

Thou hast rebuked the heathen, thou hast destroyed the wicked, thou hast put out their name for ever and ever. Ps. 9:5.

Now Satan prepares for a last mighty struggle for the supremacy. As the wicked dead are raised, and he sees the vast multitudes upon his side, his hopes revive, and he determines not to yield the great controversy. . . . He represents himself to his deluded subjects as a redeemer, assuring them that his power has brought them forth from their graves. . . . At last the order to advance is given, and the countless host moves on. . . . The armies of Satan surround the city, and make ready for the onset.[32]

Fire comes down from God out of heaven. The earth is broken up. The weapons concealed in its depths are drawn forth. Devouring flames burst from every yawning chasm. The very rocks are on fire. The day has come that shall burn as an oven. The elements melt with fervent heat, the earth also, and the works that are therein are burned up. The earth's surface seems one molten mass—a vast, seething lake of fire.[33]

Satan and all who have joined him in rebellion will be cut off. Sin and sinners will perish, root and branch (Mal. 4:1)—Satan the root, and his followers the branches. . . . "They shall be as though they had not been." Obadiah 16.[34]

It will be seen that Satan's rebellion against God has resulted in ruin to himself, and to all that chose to become his subjects. He has represented that great good would result from transgression; but it will be seen that "the wages of sin is death." Rom. 6:23. . . . An end will be made of sin, with all the woe and ruin that have resulted from it. Says the psalmist, "Thou hast destroyed the wicked, thou hast put out their name for ever and ever. O thou enemy, destructions are come to a perpetual end." Ps. 9:5, 6.[35]

He [Satan] had hoped to break up the plan of salvation; but it was laid too deep. . . . He himself must finally die, and his kingdom be given to Jesus.[36]

THE JUSTICE OF GOD

He that rejecteth me, and receiveth not my words, hath one that judgeth him: the word that I have spoken, the same shall judge him in the last day. John 12:48.

The wicked receive their recompense in the earth. . . . Some are destroyed as in a moment, while others suffer many days. All are punished "according to their deeds." The sins of the righteous having been transferred to Satan, he is made to suffer not only for his own rebellion, but for all the sins which he has caused God's people to commit. His punishment is to be far greater than that of those whom he has deceived. After all have perished who fell by his deceptions, he is still to live and suffer on.[37]

In the cleansing flames the wicked are at last destroyed, root and branch—Satan the root, his followers the branches. The justice of God is satisfied, and the saints and all the angelic host say with a loud voice, Amen.[38]

While the earth is wrapped in the fire of God's vengeance, the righteous abide safely in the Holy City. Upon those that had part in the first resurrection, the second death has no power. (Rev. 20:6.) While God is to the wicked a consuming fire, He is to His people both a sun and a shield. (Ps. 84:11.)[39]

And a shout of praise and triumph ascends from the whole loyal universe. "The voice of a great multitude," "as the voice of many waters, and as the voice of mighty thunderings," is heard, saying, "Alleluia: for the Lord God omnipotent reigneth." Rev. 19:6. . . .

The fire that consumes the wicked purifies the earth. Every trace of the curse is swept away. No eternally burning hell will keep before the ransomed the fearful consequences of sin. . . .

All that was lost by sin has been restored. . . . God's original purpose in the creation of the earth is fulfilled as it is made the eternal abode of the redeemed. "The righteous shall inherit the land, and dwell therein for ever." Ps. 37:29.[40]

THE ETERNAL WEIGHT OF GLORY

For our light affliction, which is but for a moment, worketh for us a far more exceeding and eternal weight of glory. 2 Cor. 4:17.

I was pointed to the glory of heaven, to the treasure laid up for the faithful. Everything was lovely and glorious. The angels would sing a lovely song, then they would cease singing and take their crowns from their heads and cast them glittering at the feet of the lovely Jesus, and with melodious voices cry, "Glory, Alleluia!" I joined with them in their songs of praise and honor to the Lamb, and every time I opened my mouth to praise Him, I felt an unutterable sense of the glory that surrounded me. It was a far more, an exceeding and eternal weight of glory. Said the angel, "The little remnant who love God and keep His commandments and are faithful to the end will enjoy this glory and ever be in the presence of Jesus and sing with the holy angels."

Then my eyes were taken from the glory, and I was pointed to the remnant on the earth. The angel said to them, ". . . Get ready, get ready, get ready. Ye must have a greater preparation than ye now have, for the day of the Lord cometh, cruel both with wrath and fierce anger, to lay the land desolate and to destroy the sinners thereof out of it. Sacrifice all to God. Lay all upon His altar—self, property, and all, a living sacrifice. It will take all to enter glory. Lay up for yourselves treasure in heaven, where no thief can approach or rust corrupt. Ye must be partakers of Christ's sufferings here if ye would be partakers with Him of His glory hereafter."

Heaven will be cheap enough, if we obtain it through suffering. We must deny self all along the way, die to self daily, let Jesus alone appear, and keep His glory continually in view.[41]

The work of salvation is not child's play, to be taken hold of at will and let alone at pleasure. It is the steady purpose, the untiring effort, that will gain the victory at last. It is he who endureth to the end that shall be saved. It is they who patiently continue in welldoing that shall have eternal life and the immortal reward.[42]

LIVING THE LIFE OF EDEN

And I saw a new heaven and a new earth: for the first heaven and the first earth were passed away; and there was no more sea. Rev. 21:1.

Heaven is a school; its field of study, the universe; its teacher, the Infinite One. A branch of this school was established in Eden; and, the plan of redemption accomplished, education will again be taken up in the Eden school. . . .

The prophet of Patmos thus describes the location of the school of the hereafter:

"I saw a new heaven and a new earth: for the first heaven and the first earth were passed away. . . . And I John saw the holy city, new Jerusalem, coming down from God out of heaven, prepared as a bride adorned for her husband." Rev. 21:1, 2. . . .

The giving of the tree of life in Eden was conditional, and it was finally withdrawn. But the gifts of the future life are absolute and eternal. . . .

Restored to His presence, man will again, as at the beginning, be taught of God: "My people shall know my name: . . . they shall know in that day that I am he that doth speak: behold, it is I." Isa. 52:6. . . .

All the treasures of the universe will be open to the study of God's children. With unutterable delight we shall enter into the joy and the wisdom of unfallen beings. We shall share the treasures gained through ages upon ages spent in contemplation of God's handiwork. And the years of eternity, as they roll, will continue to bring more glorious revelations. "Exceeding abundantly above all that we ask or think" (Eph. 3:20) will be forever and forever, the impartation of the gifts of God. . . .

The life on earth is the beginning of the life in heaven; education on earth is an initiation into the principles of heaven; the lifework here is a training for the lifework there. What we now are, in character and holy service, is the sure foreshadowing of what we shall be.[43]

BRIGHT BEAMS OF GLORY

And his brightness was as the light; he had bright beams out of his side: and there was the hiding of his power. Hab. 3:4, margin.

Satan, by means of his success in turning man aside from the path of obedience, became "the god of this world." 2 Cor. 4:4. The dominion that once was Adam's, passed to the usurper. But the Son of God proposed to come to this earth to pay the penalty of sin, and thus not only redeem man, but recover the dominion forfeited. . . . The apostle Paul has referred to it [the restoration of the lost dominion] as "the redemption of the purchased possession." Eph. 1:14.[44]

Not only man but the earth had by sin come under the power of the wicked one, and was to be restored by the plan of redemption.[45]

The cross of Calvary, while it declares the law immutable, proclaims to the universe that the wages of sin is death. In the Saviour's expiring cry, "It is finished," the death knell of Satan was rung. The great controversy which had been so long in progress was then decided, and the final eradication of evil was made certain. The Son of God passed through the portals of the tomb, that "through death he might destroy him that had the power of death, that is, the devil." Heb. 2:14. Lucifer's desire for self-exaltation had led him to say, "I will exalt my throne above the stars of God: . . . I will be like the most High." Isa. 14:13, 14. God declares, "I will bring thee to ashes upon the earth. . . . And never shalt thou be any more." Eze. 28:18, 19.

"I saw a new heaven and a new earth. . . ." Rev. 21:1. Every trace of the curse is swept away. . . .

One reminder alone remains: our Redeemer will ever bear the marks of His crucifixion. Upon His wounded head, upon His side, His hands and feet, are the only traces of the cruel work that sin has wrought. Says the prophet, beholding Christ in His glory, "He had bright beams coming out of his side: and there was the hiding of his power."[46]

The cross of Christ will be the science and the song of the redeemed through all eternity.[47]

NO MORE DEATH—EVER!

And God shall wipe away all tears from their eyes; and there shall be no more death, neither sorrow, nor crying, neither shall there be any more pain: for the former things are passed away. Rev. 21:4.

In the home of the redeemed there will be no tears, no funeral trains, no badges of mourning. "The inhabitant shall not say, I am sick: the people that dwell therein shall be forgiven their iniquity." Isa. 33:24. One rich tide of happiness will flow and deepen as eternity rolls on. . . .

Let us consider most earnestly the blessed hereafter. Let our faith pierce through every cloud of darkness and behold Him who died for the sins of the world. He has opened the gates of Paradise to all who receive and believe on Him. . . . Let the afflictions which pain us so grievously become instructive lessons, teaching us to press forward toward the mark of the prize of our high calling in Christ. Let us be encouraged by the thought that the Lord is soon to come. Let this hope gladden our hearts. . . .

We are homeward bound. He who loved us so much as to die for us hath builded for us a city. The New Jerusalem is our place of rest. There will be no sadness in the city of God. No wail of sorrow, no dirge of crushed hopes and buried affections, will evermore be heard. Soon the garments of heaviness will be changed for the wedding garment. Soon we shall witness the coronation of our King. Those whose lives have been hidden with Christ, those who on this earth have fought the good fight of faith, will shine forth with the Redeemer's glory in the kingdom of God.

It will not be long till we shall see Him in whom our hopes of eternal life are centered. And in His presence, all the trials and sufferings of this life will be as nothingness. . . . Look up, look up, and let your faith continually increase. Let this faith guide you along the narrow path that leads through the gates of the city of God into the great beyond, the wide, unbounded future of glory that is for the redeemed.[48]

THE METROPOLIS OF THE WORLD

And the city had no need of the sun, neither of the moon, to shine in it: for the glory of God did lighten it, and the Lamb is the light thereof. Rev. 21:23.

There is the New Jerusalem, the metropolis of the glorified new earth, "a crown of glory in the hand of the Lord, and a royal diadem in the hand of thy God." Isa. 62:3. "Her light was like unto a stone most precious, even like a jasper stone, clear as crystal." Rev. 21:11.[49]

The streets of the city are paved with pure gold, and . . . the gates of the city are of gold set with pearls. The riches obtained here may be consumed. . . . There no thief shall approach; no moth or rust shall corrupt. . . . You will have an imperishable treasure which you can be in no danger of losing.[50]

In the city of God "there shall be no night." None will need or desire repose. There will be no weariness in doing the will of God and offering praise to His name. We shall ever feel the freshness of the morning, and shall ever be far from its close. "And they need no candle, neither light of the sun; for the Lord God giveth them light." Rev. 22:5. The light of the sun will be superseded by a radiance which is not painfully dazzling, yet which immeasurably surpasses the brightness of our noontide. The glory of God and the Lamb floods the Holy City with unfading light. The redeemed walk in the sunless glory of perpetual day.

"I saw no temple therein: for the Lord God Almighty and the Lamb are the temple of it." Rev. 21:22. The people of God are privileged to hold open communion with the Father and the Son. "Now we see through a glass, darkly." 1 Cor. 13:12. We behold the image of God reflected, as in a mirror, in the works of nature and in His dealings with men; but then we shall see Him face to face, without a dimming veil between. We shall stand in His presence, and behold the glory of His countenance.[51]

Let us determine that if it costs everything we will have heaven and become partakers of the divine nature.[52]

TWO WORLDS COMPARED

But as it is written, Eye hath not seen, nor ear heard, neither have entered into the heart of man, the things which God hath prepared for them that love him. 1 Cor. 2:9.

The glory of the eternal world has been opened before me. I want to tell you that heaven is worth winning. It should be the aim of your life to fit yourself for association with the redeemed, with holy angels, and with Jesus, the world's Redeemer. If we could have but one view of the celestial city, we would never wish to dwell on earth again. There are beautiful landscapes on earth, and I enjoy all these prospects of loveliness in nature. I associate them with the Creator. But I know that if I love God, and keep His commandments, there is a far more exceeding and eternal weight of glory reserved in heaven for me.[53]

There, when the veil that darkens our vision shall be removed, and our eyes shall behold that world of beauty of which we now catch glimpses through the microscope; when we look on the glories of the heavens, now scanned afar through the telescope; when, the blight of sin removed, the whole earth shall appear in "the beauty of the Lord our God," what a field will be open to our study! There the student of science may read the records of creation and discern no reminders of the law of evil. He may listen to the music of nature's voices and detect no note of wailing or undertone of sorrow. In all created things he may trace one handwriting—in the vast universe behold "God's name writ large," and not in earth or sea or sky one sign of ill remaining.[54]

Let your imagination picture the home of the saved, and remember that it will be more glorious than your brightest imagination can portray. In the varied gifts of God in nature we see but the faintest gleaming of His glory.[55]

Human language is inadequate to describe the reward of the righteous. It will be known only to those who behold it. No finite mind can comprehend the glory of the Paradise of God.[56]

THE BLESSEDNESS OF HEAVEN

He that overcometh shall inherit all things; and I will be his God, and he shall be my son. Rev. 21:7.

No man stumbles into heaven. No man goes there blindfold. If he will take time to consider, every man may know whether he is in the strait and narrow path, or in the broad road that leads to death and hell.[57]

If we do not receive the religion of Christ by feeding upon the Word of God, we shall not be entitled to an entrance into the city of God. Having lived on earthly food, having educated our tastes to love worldly things, we would not be fitted for the heavenly courts; we could not appreciate the pure, heavenly current that circulates in heaven. The voices of the angels and the music of their harps would not satisfy us. The science of heaven would be as an enigma to our minds. We need to hunger and thirst for the righteousness of Christ; we need to be molded and fashioned by the transforming influence of His grace, that we may be fitted for the society of heavenly angels.[58]

We must have a vision of the future and of the blessedness of heaven. . . . There the redeemed ones greet those who directed them to the uplifted Saviour. . . . The conflict is over. All tribulation and strife are at an end. Songs of victory fill all heaven as the redeemed stand around the throne of God.[59]

Then the nations will own no other law than the law of heaven. All will be a happy, united family, clothed with the garments of praise and thanksgiving. . . . Over the scene the morning stars will sing together, and the sons of God will shout for joy, while God and Christ will unite in proclaiming, "There shall be no more sin, neither shall there be any more death."[60]

We want to get in the habit of talking of heaven, beautiful heaven. Talk of that life which will continue as long as God shall live, and then you will forget your little trials and difficulties. Let the mind be attracted to God.[61]

SPECULATIONS ABOUT THE FUTURE LIFE

For when they shall rise from the dead, they neither marry, nor are given in marriage; but are as the angels which are in heaven. Mark 12:25.

There are men today who express their belief that there will be marriages and births in the new earth, but those who believe the Scriptures cannot accept such doctrines. The doctrine that children will be born in the new earth is not a part of the "sure word of prophecy." The words of Christ are too plain to be misunderstood. They should forever settle the question of marriages and births in the new earth. Neither those who shall be raised from the dead, nor those who shall be translated without seeing death, will marry or be given in marriage. They will be as the angels of God, members of the royal family.

I would say to those who hold views contrary to this plain declaration of Christ: Upon such matters silence is eloquence. It is presumption to indulge in suppositions and theories regarding matters that God has not made known to us in His Word. We need not enter into speculation regarding our future state. . . .

"Preach the word; be instant in season, out of season." 2 Tim. 4:2. Do not bring to the foundation wood, and hay, and stubble— your own surmisings and speculations, which can benefit no one.

Christ withheld no truths essential to our salvation. Those things that are revealed are for us and our children, but we are not to allow our imagination to frame doctrines concerning things not revealed.

The Lord has made every provision for our happiness in the future life. But He has made no revelations regarding these plans, and we are not to speculate concerning them. Neither are we to measure the conditions of the future life by the conditions of this life. . . . It is presented to me that spiritual fables are taking many captive. . . . To all who are indulging these unholy fancies, I would say, Stop; for Christ's sake, stop right where you are. You are on forbidden ground.[62]

HEAVEN BEGINS ON EARTH

Come unto me, all ye that labour and are heavy laden, and I will give you rest. Matt. 11:28.

Heaven is to begin on this earth.[63]

Those who take Christ at His word, and surrender their souls to His keeping, their lives to His ordering, will find peace and quietude. Nothing of the world can make them sad when Jesus makes them glad by His presence. In perfect acquiescence there is perfect rest. The Lord says, "Thou wilt keep him in perfect peace, whose mind is stayed on thee: because he trusteth in thee." Isa. 26:3. Our lives may seem a tangle; but as we commit ourselves to the wise Master Worker, He will bring out the pattern of life and character that will be to His own glory. And that character which expresses the glory—character—of Christ will be received into the Paradise of God. A renovated race shall walk with Him in white, for they are worthy.

As through Jesus we enter into rest, heaven begins here. We respond to His invitation, Come, learn of Me, and in thus coming we begin the life eternal. Heaven is a ceaseless approaching to God through Christ. The longer we are in the heaven of bliss, the more and still more of glory will be opened to us; and the more we know of God, the more intense will be our happiness.[64]

When the Lord's people are filled with meekness and tenderness, they will realize that His banner over them is love, and His fruit will be sweet to their taste. They will make a heaven below in which to prepare for heaven above.[65]

As we walk with Jesus in this life, we may be filled with His love, satisfied with His presence. All that human nature can bear, we may receive here. But what is this compared with the hereafter? There "are they before the throne of God, and serve him day and night in his temple: and he that sitteth on the throne shall dwell among them. . . . For the Lamb which is in the midst of the throne shall feed them, and shall lead them unto living fountains of waters." Rev. 7:15-17.[66]

HEAVEN A REAL PLACE

And my people shall dwell in a peaceable habitation, and in sure dwellings, and in quiet resting places. Isa. 32:18.

A fear of making the future inheritance seem too material has led many to spiritualize away the very truths which lead us to look upon it as our home. Christ assured His disciples that He went to prepare mansions for them in the Father's house. Those who accept the teachings of God's Word will not be wholly ignorant concerning the heavenly abode. . . .

In the Bible the inheritance of the saved is called a country. There the heavenly Shepherd leads His flock to fountains of living waters. The tree of life yields its fruit every month, and the leaves of the tree are for the service of the nations. There are ever-flowing streams, clear as crystal, and beside them waving trees cast their shadows upon the paths prepared for the ransomed of the Lord. There the widespreading plains swell into hills of beauty, and the mountains of God rear their lofty summits. On those peaceful plains, beside those living streams, God's people, so long pilgrims and wanderers, shall find a home.

"My people shall dwell in a peaceable habitation, and in sure dwellings, and in quiet resting places." Isa. 32:18. "Violence shall no more be heard in thy land, wasting nor destruction within thy borders; but thou shalt call thy walls Salvation, and thy gates Praise." Isa. 60:18. "They shall build houses, and inhabit them; and they shall plant vineyards, and eat the fruit of them. They shall not build, and another inhabit; they shall not plant, and another eat: . . . mine elect shall long enjoy the work of their hands." Isa. 65:21, 22.

There, "the wilderness and the solitary place shall be glad for them; and the desert shall rejoice, and blossom as the rose." Isa. 35:1. "Instead of the thorn shall come up the fir tree, and instead of the brier shall come up the myrtle tree." Isa. 55:13. "The wolf also shall dwell with the lamb, and the leopard shall lie down with the kid; . . . and a little child shall lead them." Isa. 11:6.[67]

THE RACE FOR ETERNAL LIFE

Wherefore seeing we also are compassed about with so great a cloud of witnesses, let us lay aside every weight, and the sin which doth so easily beset us, and let us run with patience the race that is set before us. Heb. 12:1.

In the epistle to the Hebrews is pointed out the singlehearted purpose that should characterize the Christian's race for eternal life. . . . Envy, malice, evilthinking, evilspeaking, covetousness—these are weights that the Christian must lay aside if he would run successfully the race for immortality. Every habit or practice that leads into sin and brings dishonor upon Christ, must be put away, whatever the sacrifice. The blessing of heaven cannot attend any man in violating the eternal principles of right. One sin cherished is sufficient to work degradation of character, and to mislead others.

"If thy hand cause thee to stumble," the Saviour said, cut it off: it is good for thee to enter into life maimed, rather than having thy two hands to go into hell, into the unquenchable fire. And if thy foot cause thee to stumble, cut if off: it is good for thee to enter into life halt, rather than having thy two feet to be cast into hell." Mark 9:43-45, RV. If to save the body from death, the foot or the hand should be cut off, or even the eye plucked out, how much more earnest should the Christian be to put away sin, which brings death to the soul.

The competitors in the ancient games, after they had submitted to self-denial and rigid discipline, were not even then sure of the victory. . . .

Such is not the case in the Christian warfare. Not one who complies with the conditions will be disappointed at the end of the race. Not one who is earnest and persevering will fail of success. The race is not to the swift, nor the battle to the strong. The weakest saint, as well as the strongest, may wear the crown of immortal glory. All may win who, through the power of divine grace, bring their lives into conformity to the will of Christ.[68]

REWARD FOR SOUL WINNERS

And they that be wise shall shine as the brightness of the firmament; and they that turn many to righteousness as the stars for ever and ever. Dan. 12:3.

In our life here, earthly, sin-restricted though it is, the greatest joy and the highest education are in service. And in the future state, untrammeled by the limitations of sinful humanity, it is in service that our greatest joy and our highest education will be found.[69]

"If any man's work abide . . . , he shall receive a reward." 1 Cor. 3:14. Glorious will be the reward bestowed when the faithful workers gather about the throne of God and of the Lamb. . . . They have been partakers with Christ in His sufferings, they have been workers together with Him in the plan of redemption, and they are partakers with Him in the joy of seeing souls saved in the kingdom of God, there to praise God through all eternity.[70]

A Christian once said that when he reached heaven he expected to meet with three causes of wonder. He would wonder to find some that he did not expect to see there. He would wonder not to see some that he expected to meet, and, lastly, he would wonder most to find so unworthy a sinner as himself in the Paradise of God. Many who have stood in high places as Christians upon earth will not be found with the happy throng that shall surround the throne. Those who have had knowledge and talent, and yet have delighted in controversy and unholy strife, will not have a place with the redeemed. . . . They desired to do some great work, that they might be admired and flattered by men, but their names were not written in the Lamb's book of life. "I know you not," are the sad words that Christ addresses to such. But those whose lives were made beautiful by little acts of kindness, by tender words of affection and sympathy, whose hearts recoiled from strife and contention, who never did any great work in order to be lauded of men, these are found recorded in the Lamb's book of life. Though the world counted them as insignificant, they are approved of God before the assembled universe.[71]

THE KNOWLEDGE OF GOD COVERS THE EARTH

For the earth shall be full of the knowledge of the Lord, as the waters cover the sea. Isa. 11:9.

As we enter the kingdom of God, there to spend eternity, the trials and the difficulties and the perplexities that we have had here will sink into insignificance. Our life will measure with the life of God.[72]

There, immortal minds will contemplate with never-failing delight the wonders of creative power, the mysteries of redeeming love. There will be no cruel, deceiving foe to tempt to forgetfulness of God. Every faculty will be developed, every capacity increased. The acquirement of knowledge will not weary the mind or exhaust the energies. There the grandest enterprises may be carried forward, the loftiest aspirations reached, the highest ambitions realized; and still there will arise new heights to surmount, new wonders to admire, new truths to comprehend, fresh objects to call forth the powers of mind and soul and body.

All the treasures of the universe will be open to the study of God's redeemed. Unfettered by mortality, they wing their tireless flight to worlds afar. . . . With unutterable delight the children of earth enter into the joy and the wisdom of unfallen beings. They share the treasures of knowledge and understanding gained through ages upon ages in contemplation of God's handiwork. . . . As Jesus opens before them the riches of redemption, and the amazing achievements in the great controversy with Satan, the hearts of the ransomed thrill with more fervent devotion, and with more rapturous joy they sweep the harps of gold; and ten thousand times ten thousand and thousands of thousands of voices unite to swell the mighty chorus of praise. . . .

One pulse of harmony and gladness beats through the vast creation. From Him who created all, flow life and light and gladness, throughout the realms of illimitable space. From the minutest atom to the greatest world, all things, animate and inanimate, in their unshadowed beauty and perfect joy, declare that God is love.[73]

KEY TO ABBREVIATIONS

AA	*The Acts of the Apostles*	LS	*Life Sketches of Ellen G. White*
AH	*The Adventist Home*	MB	*Thoughts From the Mount*
AUCR	*Australasian Union*		*of Blessing* (1956)
	Conference Record	MH	*The Ministry of Healing*
1BC	Ellen G. White Comments	ML	*My Life Today*
	in *The SDA Bible Com-*	MM	*Medical Ministry*
	mentary, vol. 1 (2BC, etc.,	MS	Ellen G. White manuscript
	for vols. 2-7)	MYP	*Messages to Young People*
BE	*The Bible Echo*	PK	*Prophets and Kings*
CD	*Counsels on Diet and Foods*	PP	*Patriarchs and Prophets*
CG	*Child Guidance*	RC	*The Remnant Church*
CH	*Counsels on Health*	Redemption	*Redemption: or*
COL	*Christ's Object Lessons*		*The Teachings of*
CS	*Counsels on Stewardship*		*Christ, the Anointed*
CSW	*Counsels on Sabbath*		*One*
	School Work	RH	*Review and Herald*
CT	*Counsels to Parents,*	SC	*Steps to Christ* (pocket ed.)
	Teachers, and Students	SD	*Sons and Daughters of God*
DA	*Desire of Ages, The*	1SG	*Spiritual Gifts,* vol. 1 (2SG,
Ed	*Education*		etc., for vols. 2-4)
Ev	*Evangelism*	SL	*The Sanctified Life*
EW	*Early Writings of Ellen G.*	1SM	*Selected Messages,* book I
	White		(2SM for book 2)
FE	*Fundamentals of Christian*	Sp.T	*Special Testimonies*
	Education	SR	*The Story of Redemption*
GC	*Great Controversy Between*	ST	*Signs of the Times*
	Christ and Satan, The	SW	*The Southern Watchman*
GCB	*General Conference*	1T	*Testimonies for the Church,*
	Bulletin		vol. 1 (2T, etc., for vols. 2-9)
GW	*Gospel Workers*	Te	*Temperance*
HS	*Historical Sketches of the*	TM	*Testimonies to Ministers*
	Foreign Missions of the		*and Gospel Workers*
	Seventh-day Adventists	WM	*Welfare Ministry*
Letter	Ellen G. White letter	YI	*Youth's Instructor*

SOURCE REFERENCES

JANUARY
1 5T 264
2 RH June 11, 1908
3 COL 41
4 CT 442
5 *Ibid.* 461
6 ST June 1, 1882
7 6T 160
8 ST Sept. 5, 1895
9 RH May 13, 1884
10 *Ibid.* Mar. 19, 1889
11 ST Mar. 25, 1889
12 MH 122
13 YI Mar. 23, 1893
14 6T 81
15 1SM 16
16 GC v, vi
17 1SM 22
18 GC 69
19 *Ibid.* vi, vii
20 1SM 19, 20
21 COL 126
22 CT 462
23 6BC 1095
24 COL 126-128
25 SC 88
26 GC vii
27 1SM 15-17
28 *Ibid.* 15-18
29 SC 106-109
30 *Ibid.* 106, 107
31 Ed 170
32 5BC 1124
33 8T 328
34 COL 39, 40
35 GC 288
36 Ed 183
37 MB 148
38 GC 288
39 SC 111, 112
40 YI Dec. 4, 1902
41 SC 112
42 8T 320-322
43 5T 576
44 8T 286
45 5T 576
46 FE 378
47 Ed 260

48 RH Oct. 1, 1901
49 2T 409
50 MS 109, 1897
51 SC 67
52 AA 520
53 DA 391
54 SC 51, 52
55 RH Mar. 29, 1906
56 DA 390
57 Ed 126, 127
58 MS 4, 1880
59 COL 38
60 CT 207
61 Ed 172
62 ST Sept. 5, 1895
63 RH Oct. 1, 1901
64 ST Mar. 25, 1889
65 AUCR Oct. 1, 1903
66 RH June 11, 1908
67 MH 180
68 DA 123
69 7BC 943
70 DA 123
71 MH 66
72 CT 13
73 8T 258, 259
74 *The Watchman,*
   Dec. 17, 1907
75 3BC 1154
76 Ed 134
77 COL 18
78 5BC 1087
79 YI Mar. 24, 1898
80 5BC 1087
81 SC 85
82 5BC 1087
83 4BC 1145
84 Letter 41, 1877
85 4BC 1145
86 *Ibid.* 1153
87 Ed 128, 129
88 PP 112
89 Ed 129
90 PP 113
91 Ed 130, 131
92 *Ibid.* 99
93 8T 260

94 PP 114
95 8T 263
96 PP 114
97 Ed 132
98 PP 44, 45
99 *Ibid.*
100 *Ibid.*
101 YI Apr. 16, 1907
102 Ed 15
103 YI June 21, 1894
104 Letter 164, 1900
105 YI June 21, 1894
106 *Ibid.*
107 MM 7
108 YI June 21, 1894
109 PP 47, 48
110 GC 455
111 PP 48
112 DA 281, 282
113 TM 136
114 PP 336
115 6T 349
116 8T 198
117 DA 288, 289
118 6T 351
119 *Ibid.* 353-356
120 6T 356
121 *Ibid.*
122 CG 529
123 6T 362
124 *Ibid.* 357
125 MS 34, 1897
126 MS 32a, 1894
127 2T 704, 705
128 Ed 251
129 *Ibid.* 250, 251
130 DA 207
131 Redemption 46
132 Ed 251
133 2T 583, 584
134 CG 532
135 RH July 21, 1904
136 DA 281-283
137 6T 368

FEBRUARY
1 MS 153, 1903

[2] MB 74
[3] COL 142
[4] MB 74, 75
[5] *Ibid.* 107
[6] Ev 614
[7] 5T 301, 302
[8] 6BC 1079
[9] GW 178
[10] MH 413
[11] *Ibid.* 418, 419
[12] EW 54
[13] MH 428, 429
[14] MB 106
[15] EW 122
[16] GW 176
[17] EW 122
[18] DA 613
[19] MB 106, 107
[20] MM 92
[21] MH 417
[22] Redemption 101
[23] 8T 23
[24] YI June 10, 1897
[25] FE 179,180
[26] 5T 740
[27] MYP 144, 145
[28] DA 311, 312
[29] MYP 144, 145
[30] SC 21
[31] 8T 288
[32] DA 25, 26
[33] FE 179
[34] 5BC 1126
[35] Ev 615, 616
[36] 5BC 1126
[37] Ev 615
[38] 5BC 1127
[39] 6BC 1082
[40] DA 530
[41] PP 366. 367
[42] DA 24
[43] *Ibid.* 52
[44] *Ibid.* 24, 25
[45] 6BC 1082
[46] ST July 4, 1895
[47] *Ibid.* Sept. 24, 1902
[48] 5BC 1130
[49] DA 49
[50] 7BC 929
[51] DA 117
[52] 5BC 1131
[53] 2T 202
[54] 5BC 1128

[55] *Ibid.* 1131
[56] 7BC 927
[57] *Ibid.*
[58] *Ibid.*
[59] 6BC 1084
[60] 5BC 1108
[61] *Ibid.*
[62] *Ibid.* 1114
[63] 7BC 925
[64] ST Aug. 1, 1900
[65] DA 804
[66] 5BC 1113, 1114
[67] 6T 230
[68] 9T 286
[69] Ev 616, 617
[70] ST Mar. 8, 1910
[71] AA 53
[72] DA 671
[73] CT 67
[74] DA 672
[75] RH Aug. 25, 1896
[76] *Ibid.* May 5, 1896
[77] DA 672
[78] 2BC 1038
[79] ST Aug. 22, 1892
[80] Ed 132, 133
[81] 4T 585
[82] AA 52
[83] DA 172
[84] *Ibid.* 671
[85] SC 57
[86] Ev 288
[87] RH Nov. 29, 1892
[88] DA 669-671
[89] GW 289
[90] MYP 278
[91] DA 805
[92] RH June 2, 1896
[93] DA 388
[94] 6BC 1112
[95] YI Dec. 13, 1894
[96] 6BC 1053
[97] 5T 120
[98] GW 174
[99] 5BC 1093
[100] 5T 120
[101] *Ibid.*
[102] 5BC 1093
[103] SC 32
[104] PP 33
[105] MB 75
[106] PP 33
[107] DA 57

[108] RH Jan. 3, 1907
[109] 5T 174
[110] 3T 172
[111] SC 30
[112] *Ibid.* 31, 32
[113] RH Mar. 19, 1889
[114] CT 66
[115] 3BC 1141
[116] 8T 279
[117] 3BC 1153, 1154
[118] RH Dec. 12, 1907
[119] PK 50
[120] SC 73-75
[121] 7T 71
[122] MH 85
[123] *Ibid.* 199
[124] PP 293, 294
[125] MH 471
[126] *Ibid.* 479
[127] 9T 286
[128] MB 71
[129] MH 481
[130] *Ibid.* 479
[131] *Ibid.*
[132] MB 105
[133] PK 369, 370
[134] GW 46
[135] PK 370
[136] 4T 268
[137] MB 105, 106

MARCH
[1] 4BC 1163
[2] GC 492, 493
[3] 4BC 1162, 1163
[4] Letter 43, 1895
[5] SR 13, 14
[6] CT 32, 33
[7] PK 60
[8] 5T 702
[9] DA 21, 22
[10] *Ibid.* 435, 436
[11] PK 60
[12] 4T 377
[13] WM 202
[14] 1T 132
[15] 4T 376
[16] PP 41
[17] 4BC 1143
[18] MS 82, 1900
[19] PP 309
[20] 1T 216
[21] PP 39-43

[22] 6T 66
[23] PP 78, 79
[24] GC 503, 504
[25] FE 376
[26] MS 82, 1900
[27] 3T 526
[28] GC 543
[29] *Ibid.* 672
[30] *Ibid.* 544
[31] *Ibid.* 673
[32] ST Apr. 8, 1889
[33] 1SG 18-21
[34] PP 55
[35] 1SG 21, 22
[36] TM 141
[37] MB 139, 140
[38] PP 65, 66
[39] 1BC 1085
[40] 1BC 1084
[41] *Ibid.*
[42] ST June 12, 1901
[43] YI June 14, 1900
[44] 7BC 934
[45] MS 128, 1897
[46] PP 370, 371
[47] ST Aug. 24, 1891
[48] 6BC 1077
[49] PP 371, 372
[50] ST Sept. 5, 1892
[51] PP 64, 65
[52] ST May 30, 1916
[53] RH Jan. 21, 1890
[54] YI Jan. 1, 1903
[55] 1BC 1104
[56] ST June 10, 1880
[57] *Ibid.* Jan. 9, 1912
[58] GC 434
[59] PP 69
[60] *Ibid.* 338
[61] RH Apr. 15, 1884
[62] 1SG 109-111
[63] GC 52
[64] 4BC 1171, 1172
[65] PP 331, 332
[66] 2T 294
[67] 6BC 1120
[68] MYP 29, 30
[69] RH Oct. 9, 1894
[70] PP 363-365
[71] ST June 9, 1881
[72] MS 23a, 1896
[73] 6BC 1110
[74] MS 21, 1891

[75] 1BC 1104
[76] Letter 42, 1893
[77] 5 T 388
[78] 6BC 1085
[79] YI Sept. 22, 1903
[80] SL 80
[81] DA 308, 309
[82] FE 135
[83] PP 305
[84] 1BC 1104, 1105
[85] AA 505
[86] WM 49
[87] 1BC 1105
[88] MH 84, 85
[89] SC 43
[90] MH 84, 85
[91] *Ibid.*
[92] SC 43
[93] YI Oct. 20, 1898
[94] MB 61
[95] *Ibid.* 60, 61
[96] FE 262
[97] RH July 17, 1896
[98] COL 128
[99] PP 373
[100] 6BC 1072
[101] RH Mar. 8, 1881
[102] 3BC 1153
[103] 1BC 1120
[104] 4T 294, 295
[105] MH 451, 452
[106] 3BC 1152
[107] ST Mar. 3, 1876
[108] GW 259
[109] SC 63, 64
[110] 6BC 1080
[111] YI Sept. 20, 1900
[112] PP 73
[113] 2T 161
[114] 1T 704
[115] MS 1, 1878
[116] RH Nov. 8, 1887
[117] MS 1, 1878
[118] RH Jan. 24, 1893
[119] 6BC 1073
[120] SC 59-61
[121] MH 426
[122] *Ibid.* 161
[123] CT 538
[124] 5T 48, 49
[125] *Ibid.* 17
[126] SC 68
[127] MH 161

[128] COL 301
[129] 1BC 1105
[130] *Ibid.* 1104
[131] MH 503
[132] GC 476
[133] MYP 32
[134] 3T 436
[135] MH 503
[136] 4T 16
[137] ST Jan. 11, 1877
[138] SC 18, 19

APRIL

[1] ST Dec. 30, 1889
[2] *Ibid.* Aug. 22, 1900
[3] SC 13, 14
[4] 6T 479
[5] 2T 73
[6] 5T 316, 317
[7] 3T 433
[8] ST Jan. 27, 1904
[9] MH 25, 26
[10] DA 462
[11] CH 502
[12] Letter 2, 1889
[13] DA 187
[14] *Ibid.* 195
[15] GW 262
[16] FE 348, 349
[17] DA 753
[18] ST July 22, 1913
[19] SC 13
[20] MH 502
[21] COL 326
[22] YI Mar. 8, 1900
[23] ST July 4, 1892
[24] 7BC 912, 913
[25] MS 21, 1895
[26] AA 209
[27] SC 49-51
[28] AA 209, 210
[29] SC 55
[30] 6BC 1094
[31] MS 58, 1900
[32] SR 225
[33] ST Nov. 25, 1889
[34] TM 246
[35] RH Nov. 28, 1912
[36] Letter 192, 1906
[37] ST July 4, 1892
[38] 7BC 913
[39] *Ibid.*
[40] MH 71

41 *Ibid.*
42 6BC 1094, 1095
43 *Ibid.* 1116
44 *Ibid.*
45 7BC 914
46 6BC 1071
47 DA 439, 440
48 *Ibid.* 309, 310
49 5BC 1122
50 MB 18-21
51 1SM 398
52 *Ibid.* 390, 391
53 *Ibid.* 393
54 Sp.T Ser. A, No. 9, 62
55 COL 160
56 RH Aug. 8, 1899
57 GW 103 (1893 ed.)
58 1SM 391-394
59 RH Dec. 13, 1887
60 COL 311, 312
61 MS 32a, 1894
62 GCB Apr. 23, 1901
63 MS 48, 1893
64 YI Apr. 23, 1912
65 MYP 16
66 7BC 949
67 MS 1a, 1890
68 RH May 23, 1899
69 *Ibid.* Nov. 4, 1890
70 7BC 936
71 WM 316
72 ST May 19, 1898
73 MYP 35
74 6BC 1072
75 *Ibid.* 1070
76 AA 560
77 CD 165
78 COL 100
79 SL 10
80 GC 470
81 ST Dec. 2, 1913
82 RH Jan. 22, 1895
83 2T 145
84 *Ibid.* 320, 321
85 MYP 338
86 RH May 12, 1896
87 SC 64
88 RH Sept. 19, 1899
89 SL 9, 10
90 *Ibid.* 11
91 *Ibid.* 12
92 1BC 1095
93 6T 147

94 SW Sept. 25, 1906
95 *Ibid.*
96 ST Feb. 24, 1890
97 YI May 18, 1893
98 SC 124, 125
99 2T 319, 320
100 ST May 31, 1877
101 GW 260
102 FE 341, 342
103 COL 100. 101
104 RH Mar. 12, 1889
105 SC 111
106 RH July 29, 1890
107 FE 136, 137
108 9T 287
109 SC 69, 70
110 GC 477, 478
111 GW 262, 263
112 *Ibid.* 259, 260
113 2T 319
114 GW 262

MAY
1 SC 37
2 *Ibid.* 23
3 *Ibid.* 29
4 DA 300, 301
5 SC 37, 38
6 5T 645
7 SC 38
8 AA 566
9 MB 114
10 COL 206, 207
11 7BC 951
12 YI May 18, 1893
13 MYP 73
14 MH 421
15 MB 113, 114
16 COL 251
17 MB 114, 115
18 DA 555, 556
19 MB 59
20 CS 99, 100
21 SC 30, 31
22 2T 564, 565
23 ST May 21, 1902
24 SC 52-55
25 RH Oct. 30, 1900
26 5T 46, 47
27 RH Dec. 16, 1884
28 5T 47, 48
29 MB 8
30 DA 280

31 PK 435, 436
32 DA 300
33 5T 636
34 3T 239, 240
35 EV 510
36 DA 167-171
37 YI Sept. 9, 1897
38 RH June 10, 1902
39 9T 152
40 MS 1, 1878
41 Letter 9, 1899
42 MS 1, 1878
43 2T 294, 295
44 MYP 278
45 MS 56, 1900
46 ST Feb. 26, 1885
47 AA 51
48 Letter 9, 1899
49 *Ibid.*
50 SC 51, 52
51 AA 51
52 DA 37, 38
53 TM 18
54 GC 649, 650
55 TM 18,19
56 DA 111
57 MS 57, 1900
58 CT 258
59 DA 111-113
60 *Ibid.* 172
61 Ev 306, 307
62 6T 91
63 Ev 316
64 MYP 317
65 6BC 1074
66 MS 70, 1900
67 6BC 1074
68 *Ibid.* 1075
69 Ev 308
70 4T 40, 41
71 Ev 313
72 *Ibid.* 372-375
73 GC 475, 476
74 DA 822
75 9T 20, 21
76 GW 115
77 TM 388-390
78 COL 67
79 3T 387, 388
80 2T 651
81 LS 114
82 9T 166
83 CT 23

84 5T 506
85 4T 426
86 *Ibid.* 452
87 2T 264
88 *Ibid.* 264-266
89 1T 154
90 COL 338
91 5T 520, 521
92 AA 511
93 SC 43
94 5T 513
95 SC 44-48
96 YI Oct. 17, 1895
97 MH 176
98 COL 84, 85
99 5BC 1104
100 RH Nov. 13, 1900
101 COL 85
102 3T 363
103 GW 265, 266
104 PK 164
105 DA 679
106 6BC 1114, 1115
107 7BC 944

JUNE
1 COL 342, 343
2 *Ibid.* 345
3 *Ibid.* 344
4 *Ibid.* 343, 344
5 CS 65
6 COL 351
7 CS 95-98
8 4T 480, 481
9 *Ibid.* 481
10 COL 352
11 4T 480, 481
12 COL 353-355, 360
13 DA 785
14 Ed 197, 198
15 *Ibid.* 99, 100
16 MH 414
17 CH 41
18 AA 284
19 MH 112, 113
20 CD 56
21 *Ibid.*
22 Ed 15, 16
23 *Ibid.* 297
24 MH 397, 398
25 Te 137
26 Ed 173, 178, 184
27 5T 466, 467

28 MH 472, 473
29 COL 346
30 5T 261
31 *Ibid.*
32 CS 149
33 CH 375, 376
34 MH 454
35 2SM 258, 259
36 *Ibid.* 263, 264
37 ST Feb. 13, 1912
38 5BC 1130
39 1T 344
40 GC 545, 546
41 *Ibid.* 549
42 *Ibid.* 547
43 *Ibid.* 545
44 DA 527
45 GC 535, 536
46 *Ibid.* 536
47 *Ibid.* 541-543
48 DA 107
49 GC 544
50 EW 51
51 *Ibid.* 218
52 6T 230, 231
53 *Ibid.* 230
54 1T 342
55 GC 534, 537, 541
56 PP 52, 53
57 TM 133, 134
58 COL 263
59 2T 691
60 *Ibid.* 102
61 DA 785, 786
62 6BC 1092
63 DA 787
64 ST July 9, 1902
65 6BC 1093
66 GC 549, 550
67 ML 349
68 GC 636, 637
69 EW 285
70 GC 637, 640
71 DA 786, 787
72 7BC 909
73 GC 644, 645
74 5BC 1110
75 GC 661
76 EW 292
77 *Ibid.* 52
78 GC 543
79 4BC 1143
80 YI Apr. 1858

81 6BC 1093
82 RH Nov. 22, 1906
83 GC 645
84 ML 349
85 2SM 273, 274
86 DA 530
87 *Ibid.* 787
88 *Ibid.* 530
89 *Ibid.* 388
90 *Ibid.* 454

JULY
1 PK 48, 49
2 MYP 265, 266
3 5T 491
4 PP 252
5 PK 50
6 MYP 265
7 4BC 1138, 1139
8 DA 161, 162
9 AA 50
10 PP 314
11 Ed 35, 36
12 PP 343, 344
13 6T 450
14 RH Mar. 2, 1886
15 PP 349
16 RH Mar. 2, 1886
17 PP 350-352
18 PK 684, 685
19 SC 36
20 1BC 1111
21 PP 352-354
22 *Ibid.* 354
23 *Ibid.* 353
24 *Ibid.* 354-356
25 ST Nov. 22, 1883
26 4T 120, 121, 124
27 *Ibid.* 121-123
28 PK 699
29 5BC 1109
30 DA 757
31 EW 260
32 DA 166
33 ST Apr. 16, 1902
34 GC 417
35 *Ibid.* 414, 415
36 *Ibid.* 488
37 MS 76, 1897
38 GC 488, 489
39 COL 156, 157
40 ST July 19, 1910
41 2T 591

[42] CH 374
[43] MB 9
[44] CSW 111
[45] RH May 29, 1900
[46] CSW 112
[47] GC 417, 418
[48] SR 377
[49] GC 418
[50] SR 378
[51] PP 357, 358
[52] GC 484
[53] GC 420, 421, 426
[54] *Ibid.* 422
[55] ST Mar. 12, 1902
[56] Ev 222, 223
[57] GC 410
[58] Ev 223
[59] GC 479, 480
[60] Ev 223
[61] ST Sept. 21, 1891
[62] GC 480-482
[63] 5T 331
[64] GC 486
[65] 4T 386
[66] GC 486-490
[67] *Ibid.* 483, 484
[68] ST Nov. 12, 1896
[69] GC 485
[70] ST Apr. 16, 1885
[71] GC 485, 486
[72] 2T 401, 402
[73] GC 425
[74] 4T 384-387
[75] RH Oct. 9, 1894
[76] 2T 691
[77] PP 201
[78] GC 614
[79] 8T 314
[80] 7BC 989
[81] GC 660, 661
[82] YI June 8, 1893
[83] GC 661
[84] *Ibid.* 503
[85] RH Oct. 5, 1886
[86] GC 487, 488
[87] 2T 355
[88] 1T 332, 333
[89] COL 319

AUGUST
[1] RH Apr. 26, 1906
[2] MS 31, 1911
[3] COL 149

[4] Letter 2, 1895
[5] 2T 262
[6] Letter 2, 1895
[7] ST Jan. 8, 1902
[8] Letter 2, 1895
[9] 6BC 1101
[10] *Ibid.* 1102
[11] YI Aug. 3, 1893
[12] 5BC 1143, 1144
[13] RH Jan. 2, 1900
[14] MYP 144
[15] CT 402
[16] MH 491
[17] 6BC 1100
[18] SC 99
[19] CSW 17
[20] MH 465, 466
[21] MS 4, 1880
[22] TM 80, 81
[23] 2T 283
[24] YI Oct. 1855
[25] Ed 260, 261
[26] 5T 200, 201
[27] YI Nov. 3, 1898
[28] COL 129, 250
[29] 5T 579
[30] SC 46, 47
[31] 4T 626
[32] MYP 98
[33] COL 130
[34] Ed 200, 201
[35] MH 271
[36] CH 107
[37] MH 113, 288
[38] Ed 196, 197
[39] PP 601
[40] 4T 408
[41] FE 147
[42] MH 310
[43] 1BC 1105
[44] CH 627
[45] 3BC 1146
[46] RH Mar. 30, 1886
[47] MH 241
[48] 3T 84
[49] CD 56
[50] 3T 486
[51] *Ibid.* 491
[52] CH 114, 115
[53] 9T 159
[54] CH 450
[55] CD 382
[56] MH 335

[57] *Ibid.* 325-328
[58] *Ibid.* 335
[59] CG 398
[60] CD 57
[61] YI Feb. 27, 1902
[62] PP 50
[63] FE 418
[64] MH 240, 272
[65] *Ibid.* 51
[66] DA 361, 362
[67] AH 494
[68] 4T 653
[69] RH July 25, 1871
[70] MH 127
[71] *Ibid.* 52
[72] Ed 211
[73] 4T 587, 655
[74] PP 458, 459
[75] CT 224
[76] MYP 423
[77] COL 374
[78] MH 360
[79] Letter 10, 1890
[80] 4T 580, 581
[81] Letter 2, 1895
[82] MYP 363
[83] Letter 2, 1895
[84] *Ibid.*
[85] COL 337
[86] YI Dec. 27, 1900
[87] RH Mar. 26, 1889
[88] CT 342
[89] 6BC 1085
[90] Ed 296, 297
[91] YI July 19, 1894
[92] FE 84
[93] 4T 653
[94] MYP 364
[95] Letter 10, 1890
[96] CT 336, 337
[97] AH 521
[98] Ed 210, 211
[99] AH 515, 516
[100] MB 118
[101] WM 26
[102] DA 640, 641
[103] 6T 276
[104] 3T 249
[105] SD 270
[106] DA 602
[107] AA 69
[108] 1T 361, 362
[109] AA 69

[110] 1T 360
[111] AA 518
[112] MH 444, 445
[113] MYP 272
[114] FE 93
[115] 7T 64
[116] MYP 274
[117] Ed 161
[118] 1T 497
[119] Letter 6a, 1890
[120] 9T 144
[121] 6T 367
[122] 7T 244
[123] CG 413, 420
[124] Ed 248
[125] CG 420, 421
[126] 4T 645
[127] YI Mar. 9, 1893
[128] AA 523, 524
[129] CS 65
[130] 3T 388, 389
[131] CS 81
[132] *Ibid.* 66
[133] 4T 119, 120
[134] ST Nov. 15, 1910
[135] 3T 393, 394
[136] PP 527
[137] CS 73, 74
[138] 9T 157, 158
[139] ST Mar. 9, 1876
[140] 7T 190
[141] MYP 140, 141
[142] SC 101, 102
[143] EW 114, 115
[144] TM 508
[145] 6T 273
[146] COL 301
[147] YI Jan. 1, 1903
[148] MH 160
[149] YI Feb. 13, 1902
[150] *Ibid.* Oct. 23, 1902
[151] *Ibid.* May 1, 1902
[152] RH Mar. 26, 1889
[153] 5T 200
[154] MS 36, 1891

SEPTEMBER
[1] PP 49
[2] AH 27
[3] PP 49, 50
[4] Ed 22
[5] PP 46
[6] MH 356, 357

[7] AH 102, 103
[8] MH 361
[9] 7T 46
[10] AH 120
[11] 5T 362
[12] AH 15
[13] 4T 507
[14] MB 63, 64
[15] AH 103, 120
[16] MH 360
[17] COL 290
[18] 6T 430
[19] 3T 539
[20] ST Feb. 17, 1904
[21] 4T 304
[22] MH 358
[23] AH 99
[24] 2T 133
[25] 5T 335
[26] AH 19
[27] *Ibid.* 99
[28] MH 362
[29] 1T 306
[30] MH 359
[31] AH 110, 111
[32] FE 74
[33] AH 91
[34] Ed 216
[35] MH 359
[36] 5T 362
[37] MH 359
[38] 5T 362
[39] MH 358
[40] 2BC 1000
[41] 4T 507, 508
[42] *Ibid.* 505
[43] 2BC 1031
[44] MYP 460
[45] 5T 363
[46] AH 215
[47] 1T 307
[48] MH 361
[49] AH 95, 102
[50] MH 183, 184
[51] FE 326, 327
[52] MH 365-370
[53] AH 280
[54] 2T 231
[55] *Ibid.* 647
[56] PP 84
[57] AH 160, 161
[58] *Ibid.* 279
[59] CD 218

[60] PP 561
[61] ST Feb. 26, 1902
[62] PP 561
[63] CD 219
[64] DA 74
[65] *Ibid.* 70
[66] YI Nov. 21, 1895
[67] *Ibid.* Sept. 1873
[68] AH 290
[69] DA 74
[70] FE 153
[71] MH 376
[72] AII 234
[73] RH July 8, 1902
[74] MH 388
[75] *Ibid.* 377, 378
[76] AH 231
[77] ST Nov. 10, 1881
[78] RH July 8, 1902
[79] ST Jan. 1, 1902
[80] *Ibid.* Nov. 10, 1881
[81] CG 79
[82] Ed 287
[83] AH 232
[84] CT 112
[85] AH 310
[86] 3T 532
[87] CT 158, 159
[88] AH 308
[89] *Ibid.* 421
[90] 1T 307
[91] AH 426, 427
[92] ST Nov. 14, 1892
[93] MB 82
[94] *Ibid.* 135
[95] MH 394
[96] YI Feb. 28, 1905
[97] AH 286
[98] CT 148
[99] PP 574
[100] GW 207
[101] ST Nov. 3, 1881
[102] *Ibid.* Jan. 1, 1902
[103] CG 229
[104] 2BC 1099
[105] ST Jan. 1, 1902
[106] RH Oct. 14, 1875
[107] ST Jan. 1, 1902
[108] CT 169
[109] YI Nov. 3, 1908
[110] *Ibid.*
[111] MH 375, 376
[112] CG 499

[113] 1T 400
[114] COL 195, 196
[115] Ed 185
[116] CSW 41, 42
[117] CT 207
[118] *Ibid.* 172
[119] PP 144
[120] CT 110
[121] Ed 186
[122] CT 110
[123] CG 506
[124] Ed 167, 168
[125] DA 73
[126] 5BC 1117
[127] MH 254
[128] CT 246
[129] PP 289
[130] 2T 585
[131] 6T 358
[132] Ed 250, 251
[133] 6T 358
[134] Letter 132, 1900
[135] 6T 359
[136] MH 366
[137] *Ibid.* 380
[138] YI Aug. 23, 1894
[139] CG 187
[140] Ed 249
[141] MH 354
[142] 6T 348
[143] MH 354, 355
[144] 6T 347
[145] AH 450
[146] DA 639
[147] PP 176
[148] Letter 75, 1898
[149] MH 359
[150] FE 104
[151] MH 359
[152] *Ibid.* 352
[153] PP 144
[154] AH 39
[155] MH 355
[156] Ed 307
[157] ST Nov. 14, 1892
[158] CG 481
[159] ST Nov. 14, 1892
[160] AH 545
[161] Ed 306, 307
[162] CG 13

OCTOBER
[1] 6BC 1118

[2] *Ibid.*
[3] PK 590
[4] 4T 329, 330
[5] AA 11, 12
[6] *Ibid.* 11
[7] COL 166
[8] TM 61
[9] RH Sept. 20, 1892
[10] GC 317
[11] EW 229, 230, 233
[12] GC 391
[13] EW 237
[14] GC 435, 436
[15] *Ibid.* 423
[16] *Ibid.* 409-411
[17] *Ibid.* 422, 423
[18] *Ibid.* 432
[19] *Ibid.* 389, 390
[20] EW 254
[21] GC 439, 445, 448
[22] 7BC 977
[23] GC 449
[24] *Ibid.* 594
[25] 7BC 970
[26] *Ibid.*
[27] SD 52
[28] ST June 14, 1910
[29] 7BC 968, 969
[30] 4BC 1161
[31] Letter 106, 1897
[32] 5T 216
[33] MS 20, 1899
[34] EW 58
[35] 5T 472, 473
[36] PK 605
[37] GC 623, 624
[38] 2T 105
[39] SW Mar. 21, 1905
[40] 3T 62
[41] 4BC 1184
[42] PK 716
[43] 5T 395
[44] *Ibid.* 464
[45] 9T 37
[46] 7BC 974
[47] *Ibid.* 981
[48] ST Feb. 13, 1896
[49] 7BC 975
[50] *Ibid.* 981, 982
[51] GC viii, ix
[52] COL 327
[53] 6T 291
[54] GC ix, x

[55] 8T 20
[56] COL 327, 328
[57] GC vii, viii
[58] EW 78
[59] GC xi
[60] RH June 22, 1911
[61] 1T 58 62
[62] 1SM 32
[63] 5T 67
[64] 6T 131
[65] 5T 665
[66] 2T 605
[67] 8T 298
[68] 5T 661
[69] RH July 18, 1907
[70] 5T 671
[71] Letter 12, 1890
[72] 5T 672
[73] DA 649, 650
[74] 5BC 1138, 1139
[75] DA 650
[76] 5BC 1139
[77] Ev 275
[78] DA 650
[79] Ev 275
[80] 5BC 1138
[81] DA 656
[82] YI May 1873
[83] DA 652
[84] *Ibid.* 656, 661
[85] *Ibid.* 656, 657
[86] 5BC 1102
[87] 3SG 228
[88] RH May 31, 1898
[89] DA 659, 660
[90] 5BC 1113
[91] EW 216, 217
[92] RH Jan. 21, 1890
[93] *Ibid.* July 26, 1898
[94] RC 58
[95] 1T 224
[96] RH Oct. 16, 1888
[97] TM 45, 46, 49-51
[98] 7BC 961
[99] *Ibid.* 963
[100] *Ibid.* 965
[101] *Ibid.* 965, 966
[102] *Ibid.* 965
[103] 6T 14, 15
[104] 6T 144
[105] *Ibid.*
[106] 6T 293
[107] AA 110, 111

[108] 9T 53-59
[109] DA 413, 414
[110] Ibid. 414
[111] Ibid. 413, 414

NOVEMBER
[1] GC 507
[2] PK 605, 606
[3] 5T 321
[4] ST Jan. 29, 1908
[5] ST May 24, 1877
[6] RH Apr. 15, 1880
[7] 7BC 937
[8] RH Aug. 4, 1910
[9] 2T 143-145
[10] RH July 22, 1884
[11] YI July 15, 1897
[12] RH Nov. 17, 1885
[13] 5BC 1099
[14] MH 226
[15] CH 457
[16] MH 227-231
[17] 4T 656
[18] RH Apr. 6, 1886
[19] GC 528
[20] ST Nov. 5, 1902
[21] EW 47
[22] Ibid. 46
[23] Ibid. 152, 153
[24] 5T 293, 294
[25] AA 290
[26] PP 684, 685
[27] EW 263
[28] Ibid. 262
[29] Ibid.
[30] MH 242
[31] 2SM 351, 352
[32] Ibid. 350
[33] CC 522
[34] Ibid.
[35] PP 115
[36] CT 426
[37] Ibid. 19
[38] TM 364, 365
[39] 6BC 1120
[40] MB 145
[41] AA 535
[42] GC 594
[43] YI Mar. 23, 1893
[44] 5T 470, 471
[45] 8T 42
[46] 5T 452
[47] 9T 229, 230

[48] GC 464, 465, 478
[49] Ibid. 510
[50] Ibid. 516
[51] RH Aug. 4, 1910
[52] GC 510
[53] MYP 328
[54] GC 510
[55] PP 337
[56] GC 589, 590
[57] Ibid. 517
[58] Ibid. 578, 579, 581
[59] Ibid. 601
[60] Ibid. 606-610
[61] RH Feb. 9, 1911
[62] GC 530
[63] Ibid. 529, 530
[64] ST Nov. 30, 1882
[65] 7T 64
[66] Ed 262, 271
[67] GC 611, 612
[68] RH Jan. 13, 1910
[69] AA 54, 55
[70] TM 506, 507
[71] Ibid. 506-509
[72] 6T 90
[73] EW 277
[74] GC 611
[75] EW 277, 278
[76] ST Jan. 18, 1910
[77] Ibid. 315
[78] 9T 62
[79] 8T 315
[80] GC 608
[81] 6T 332
[82] EW 71
[83] GC 425
[84] EW 71
[85] 5T 208, 209
[86] GC 627
[87] RH Aug. 5, 1884
[88] GC 613, 614, 616
[89] EW 58
[90] GC 627-629
[91] Letter 119, 1904
[92] GC 629

DECEMBER
[1] GC 337, 338
[2] DA 636
[3] Ibid. 635
[4] 5T 99-101
[5] 8T 50
[6] MYP 89, 90

[7] DA 631, 632
[8] GC 334
[9] DA 632, 633
[10] Ibid. 632
[11] PK 548
[12] TM 114
[13] Ibid. 113
[14] GC 624, 625
[15] Ibid. 625
[16] Ibid. 635, 636
[17] Ibid. 299, 302
[18] Ibid. 299, 302-304
[19] Ibid. 641, 642
[20] Ibid. 641
[21] 2T 121, 122
[22] SR 61
[23] GC 301
[24] YI Apr. 1854
[25] SR 413, 414
[26] GC 657
[27] EW 290
[28] GC 660, 661
[29] ST Oct. 24, 1906
[30] GC 662, 663
[31] Ibid. 666-671
[32] Ibid. 663, 664
[33] Ibid. 672, 673
[34] DA 763
[35] PP 341
[36] EW 178
[37] GC 673
[38] SR 429
[39] Ibid.
[40] GC 673, 674
[41] EW 66, 67
[42] 2T 101 102
[43] Ed 301, 302, 307
[44] PK 682
[45] PP 67
[46] GC 503, 504, 674
[47] Ibid. 651
[48] 9T 286-288
[49] GC 676
[50] ST Jan. 31, 1878
[51] GC 676, 677
[52] ST Jan. 27, 1888
[53] Ibid. Apr. 8, 1889
[54] Ed 303
[55] SC 86, 87
[56] SR 430, 431
[57] BE July 31, 1899
[58] RH May 4, 1897
[59] 8T 44

[60] *Ibid.* 42
[61] HS 146
[62] MM 99-101
[63] 7T 131
[64] DA 331

[65] 7T 131
[66] DA 331, 332
[67] GC 674-676
[68] AA 312, 313
[69] Ed 309

[70] 9T 285
[71] ST Feb. 24, 1890
[72] GCB Apr. 6, 1903
[73] GC 677, 678

SCRIPTURE INDEX